Global Environmental Protection through Trade

A Systematic Approach to Extraterritoriality

Barbara Cooreman

Leiden University, the Netherlands
Aerospace and Defence Industries Association of Europe, Belgium

EE Edward Elgar
PUBLISHING

Cheltenham, UK • Northampton, MA, USA

Published by
Edward Elgar Publishing Limited
The Lypiatts
15 Lansdown Road
Cheltenham
Glos GL50 2JA
UK

Edward Elgar Publishing, Inc.
William Pratt House
9 Dewey Court
Northampton
Massachusetts 01060
USA

A catalogue record for this book
is available from the British Library

Library of Congress Control Number: 2016959917

This book is available electronically in the **Elgar**online
Law subject collection
DOI 10.4337/9781786434395

MIX
Paper from responsible sources
FSC® C013604

ISBN 978 1 78643 438 8 (cased)
ISBN 978 1 78643 439 5 (eBook)

Typeset by Servis Filmsetting Ltd, Stockport, Cheshire
Printed and bound by CPI Group (UK) Ltd, Croydon, CR0 4YY

Contents

Figures

Foreword

With this book Barbara Cooreman tackles a big, controversial subject: does WTO law constitute an obstacle for countries to do something about environmental harm that occurs outside of their own borders? More specifically, does WTO law permit a country to restrict the imports of products which have been produced outside its territory in environmentally harmful ways?

The WTO treaty texts do not give a definite answer about these questions. One has to look to case law for further clarification. The *Shrimp – Turtle* rulings of the late 1990s and early 2000s remain the key precedent to date. The United States restricted imports of shrimp from third countries which were caught with nets that did not include a device that allowed turtles to escape. There was little doubt that this import restriction violated basic WTO rules. The debate focused on the question whether the United States could rely on one of the public policy exceptions included in the WTO agreements to justify its environmental concern.

The threshold issue was whether the United States was well placed to take action with respect to fishing activities outside of its territorial waters. The WTO Appellate Body dealt only summarily with this issue; because some of the turtles migrated through US waters some of the time, it found that there was a sufficient nexus between the endangered turtle species and the United States. While helping to arrive at a ruling that was ultimately turtle-friendly, this finding of the WTO Appellate Body provided only a slim basis to assess other trade measures that address environmentally bothersome production processes outside of the territory of the regulating state. It is probably fair to say that, as a result, the WTO's reputation suffered, at least in those circles that worry about the environment. Moreover, uncertainty about the WTO-legality of so-called extraterritorial trade measures may also have had a chilling effect on the adoption of otherwise worthwhile measures seeking to protect the environment.

Barbara Cooreman decided to tackle her big and sensitive subject circumspectly. Having outlined the issues as they arose under WTO and prior to that GATT law, she first looked to other areas of law to see how extraterritorial measures are dealt with. She reviewed public international law, competition law, and international human rights law, and with the perspectives she obtained there she came back to the WTO context. Here she has made significant contributions.

First, Cooreman establishes an analytical framework, a decision tree as she calls it, which provides almost step-by-step guidance to decision-makers and tribunals in reaching a more robust conclusion on the legality under WTO law of extraterritorial trade measures. Second, this framework is underpinned by a new insight. The regulating state is not only permitted to address production processes abroad when they produce substantial effects within its territory, a lesson that could be drawn notably from general public international law and competition law. In addition, when the effects on its territory are weaker, the regulating state can still draw justification to act in the WTO from environmental treaties and to some extent even soft law. This is what Barbara calls 'communicating vessels': the more international law a regulating state can point to, the fewer effects on its territory are needed before it is entitled to act. As she argues, in this respect environmental protection differs from the preserve of competition law, given that there is so little international competition law.

Accordingly, and with hindsight, the Appellate Body got it right in the *Shrimp – Turtle* case by not requiring a strong territorial link with the United States. Through a careful analysis the author adds substance to the Appellate Body's more intuitive approach. This inspires confidence for future cases. Usefully, she illustrates the viability of her research by applying her decision tree to several controversial regulations adopted by the EU concerning illegal fishing and logging, as well as aviation under the EU's emission trading system.

With these insights Barbara Cooreman achieves a breakthrough. She demonstrates that governments cannot hide any longer between the constraints allegedly found in existing treaty texts, and the difficulties and delays inherent in amending WTO law: WTO law as it stands is no excuse for environmental inaction. At the same time, the author cautions against overreach in the use of unilateral trade measures by powerful, developed nations. She also warns against the misunderstanding that her conclusion implies a preference for unilateral action over multilateral action; rather, she points out, unilateral trade measures can be a trigger for multilateral agreements on environmental protection. All this extends the interest of her work well beyond legal experts; her conclusions have societal importance. To be sure, this is no mean feat, for which she deserves high praise.

Marco Bronckers
Brussels, August 2016

Acknowledgements*

This book is based on research I conducted as Fellow at the Europa Institute (Public Law) of Leiden University. It marks the ending of a fascinating and rewarding journey and I am grateful to everyone who has accompanied me on it – for longer or shorter periods, close by or from afar. I have thoroughly enjoyed the challenging and stimulating discussions throughout – with my Leiden colleagues and with peers from all over whom I have had the privilege to meet.

Only a few people to whom I owe particular gratitude can be named here. Warm thanks to Prof. Dr. Stefaan Van den Bogaert for his trust and camaraderie. I could not have written the book without the guidance of Prof. Dr. Marco Bronckers, whose sharp mind, enthusiasm and at times healthy skepticism were major driving forces. Thanks to Dr. Freya Baetens for her support and detailed reviews. Prof. Dr. Niels Blokker, Prof. Dr. Peter Van den Bossche, Prof. Dr. Cedric Ryngaert and Prof. Joanne Scott deserve a special mention, as they have stimulated and encouraged me at different moments and in different ways to think further, both with regard to the specific content of my research and the bigger picture. Joanne, your inquisitive mind is an inspiration. Also, a sincere thanks to my editors at Edward Elgar Publishing for their great work and dedication.

Finally, this book would not have been possible without the endless cheering and love from friends and family. A thousand thanks.

* All opinions and ideas in this book are my own and do not reflect those of the Aerospace and Defence Industries Association of Europe.

Abbreviations

AB	Appellate Body
ACHPR	African Charter on Human and Peoples' Rights
ACHR	American Convention on Human Rights
ACtHPR	African Court on Human and Peoples' Rights
AG	Advocate General
ATAA	Air Transport Association of America
ATS	Alien Tort Statute (US)
CBD	Convention on Biological Diversity 1992
CBDRRC	Principle of common but differentiated responsibilities and respective capabilities
CITES	Convention on International Trade in Endangered Species of Wild Fauna and Flora
CJEU	Court of Justice of the European Union
CMS	Convention on the Conservation of Migratory Species and Wild Animals
COP	Convention of the Parties
DOJ	Department of Justice (US)
DSB	Dispute Settlement Body
DSU	Dispute Settlement Understanding
EC	European Community
ECHR	European Convention on Human Rights
ECJ	European Court of Justice
ECS	economic, social and cultural
ECtHR	European Court of Human Rights
EEA	European Economic Area
EEC	European Economic Community
EEZ	Exclusive Economic Zone
EFTA	European Free Trade Association
ESA	US Endangered Species Act 1973
EU	European Union
EU ETS	European Union Emissions Trading System
FAO	Food and Agriculture Organization of the United Nations
FLEGT	Forest Law Enforcement, Governance and Trade

FTA	free trade agreement
FTAIA	Foreign Trade Antitrust Improvements Act 1982
FTC	Federal Trade Commission (US)
GATS	General Agreement on Trade in Services
GATT	General Agreement on Tariffs and Trade
GSP	Generalized System of Preference
HRC	Human Rights Committee
IAC	Inter-American Convention for the Protection and Conservation of Sea Turtles
IACHR	Inter-American Commission on Human Rights
IACtHR	Inter-American Court on Human Rights
ICAO	International Civil Aviation Organization
ICCPR	International Covenant on Civil and Political Rights
ICESCR	International Covenant on Economic, Social and Cultural Rights
ICJ	International Court of Justice
ICN	International Competition Network
ICTSD	International Centre for Trade and Sustainable Development
ILC	International Law Commission
IPCC	Intergovernmental Panel on Climate Change
IPOA-IUU	International Plan of Action on Illegal, Unreported and Unregulated Fishing
ITO	International Trade Organization
ITTA	International Tropical Timber Agreement
IUU fishing	illegal, unreported and unregulated fishing
MDG	Millennium Development Goal
MEA	multilateral environmental agreement
MFN	most-favoured nation
NGO	non-governmental organization
NOAA	US National Oceanic and Atmospheric Administration
npr-PPM	non-product-related PPM
OECD	Organization for Economic Cooperation and Development
PCIJ	Permanent Court of International Justice
PPM	process and production method (measure)
pr-PPM	product-related PPM
REDD	reducing emissions from deforestation and forest degradation
RFMO	regional fisheries management organization

SPS Agreement	Agreement on the Application of Sanitary and Phytosanitary Measures
TBT Agreement	Agreement on Technical Barriers to Trade
TED	turtle excluder device
TEU	Treaty on the European Union
TFEU	Treaty on the Functioning of the European Union
UK	United Kingdom
UN	United Nations
UNCLOS	United Nations Convention on the Law of the Sea
UNEP	United Nations Environment Programme
UNFCCC	United Nations Framework Convention on Climate Change 1992
UNGA	United Nations General Assembly
US	United States
VCLT	Vienna Convention on the Law of Treaties 1969
VPA	voluntary partnership agreement
WTO	World Trade Organization

Table of cases

COURT OF JUSTICE OF THE EUROPEAN UNION

HUMAN RIGHTS COURTS AND TRIBUNALS

INTERNATIONAL COURT OF JUSTICE

NATIONAL CASE LAW

PERMANENT COURT OF INTERNATIONAL JUSTICE

WTO PANELS AND AB

1. Introduction

The greatest threat to our planet is the belief that someone else will save it.[1]

1.1 GLOBAL ENVIRONMENTAL CONCERNS AND TRADE: PRODUCT VS. PROCESS

The state of our environment is a global concern. Environmental degradation and climate change affect all and everyone. Some states will suffer more immediate damage and will feel the physical, social and economic consequences sooner through, for instance, rising sea levels threatening the very existence of their land, through floods and hurricanes, through desertification and extreme drought, but it is undeniable that the environmental impact will eventually affect all states in an irreversible manner.[2] It is equally undeniable that human activity has contributed to the current deplorable status, and that common action is of crucial importance to slow down future environmental deterioration.[3] Despite this increasing awareness, setting binding and ambitious commitments internationally has proven to be a very difficult process due to a multiplicity of factors, such as discords on burden-sharing between developed and developing countries, between 'historic' emitters and 'new' emitters, and disagreement on suitable protective methods, financial mechanisms or appropriate sanctioning of free-riders. International environmental negotiations can be quite frustrating 'in a world in which fisheries deplete, potable water diminishes, species vanish, the air fouls, the ozone layer thins, and the atmosphere

---

[1] Robert Swan OBE, the first man in history to walk to both the North and South Poles.

[2] See the assessment reports by the Intergovernmental Panel on Climate Change (IPCC) at www.ipcc.ch/publications_and_data/publications_and_data_reports.shtml (IPCC Reports). At the time of publication, the latest series of reports dated from 2014.

[3] See IPCC Reports; see also UNFCCC COP 21, Paris Agreement, FCCC/CP/2015/L9, 2015; UN, 2030 Agenda on Sustainable Development, UN Resolution A/RES/70/1 of 25 September 2015.

warms'.[4] In the realm of climate change, after several failed attempts throughout the last decade, a 'historic' agreement was signed in Paris in December 2015 by more than 190 states, recognizing the urgent need for international action and ambitious efforts. Nevertheless, it remains to be seen how states will convert and implement these ambitions into concrete deeds. In the absence of a stringent and coordinated international framework regulating the preservation of the environment, countries seek alternatives to promote environmental protection. Unilaterally imposed trade measures may be such an alternative, but can they be used to protect global environmental concerns or concerns located outside the territory of the regulating state?

Much has been written about the relationship between trade and environment, and I will not repeat what has been discussed extensively elsewhere.[5] In summary, trade can have both positive and negative consequences for the environment: it could contribute positively by increasing real income and standards of living, allowing countries to allocate more resources to environmental protection. Trade could also lead to higher standards when powerful states promote a regulatory 'race to the top'.[6] However, trade may also damage the environment by increasing energy consumption and pollution while accelerating the overuse of natural resources.[7] Trade could arguably lead to a 'race to the bottom' with regard

---

[4] Gregory Shaffer and Daniel Bodansky, 'Transnationalism, Unilateralism and International Law' Legal Studies Research Paper Series Research Paper No 11-34 (2011).

[5] To name a few: Daniel C Esty, *Greening the GATT: Trade, Environment and the Future* (Peterson Institute 1994); Adil Najam, Mark Halle and Ricardo Melendez-Ortiz (eds.), *Trade and Environment: A Resource Book* (International Institute for Sustainable Development, International Centre for Trade and Sustainable Development, The Regional and International Networking Group 2007); Erich Vranes, *Trade and the Environment: Fundamental Issues in International Law, WTO Law and Legal Theory* (Oxford University Press 2009); James Cameron, Paul Demaret and Damien Geradin (eds.), *Trade and the Environment: The Search for Balance* (Cameron May 1994); Thomas J Schoenbaum, 'International Trade and Protection of the Environment: The Continuing Search for Reconciliation' American Journal of International Law (1997) 91:2, 268; John H Jackson, 'World Trade Rules and Environmental Policies: Congruence or Conflict?' Washington and Lee Law Review (1992) 49:4, 1227; Eric Neumayer, 'WTO Rules and Multilateral Environmental Agreements' in *The Earthscan Reader on International Trade and Sustainable Development* (Earthscan Publications Ltd 2002); UNCTAD, *The Green Economy: Trade and Sustainable Development Implications* (2011).

[6] David Vogel, *Trading up: Consumer and Environmental Regulation in a Global Economy* (Harvard University Press 1997) 248ff.

[7] Tania Voon, 'Sizing Up the WTO: Trade-Environment Conflict and the Kyoto Protocol' Journal of Transnational Law and Policy (2000) 10:1, 71, 74.

to environmental standards and regulatory requirements, as countries would lower their standards to attract trade and foreign investment.[8] Even if the race does not literally reach the bottom, economic integration could create a regulatory dynamic in which standards are set strategically with an eye on the environmental standards in competing jurisdictions, resulting in at least suboptimal standards in some places.[9]

The traditional focus of trade law is on end products and their market impact. From the viewpoint of environmental protection and sustainable development, however, the process through which products are *made* is as important as the product, if not more important.[10] Environmental trade measures hence do not always regulate the end product, as the environmental concerns might be related more to the production process than the actual end product.[11] Targeting the production process is in line with the 'polluter pays' principle, as an established principle of environmental law. The use of trade measures linked to the production process has been a particularly knotty issue of the trade and environment debate, sharply dividing opponents and proponents. In particular, those measures targeting production methods that leave no physical trace in the end product (the so-called 'non-product-related process and production methods' or npr-PPMs) have been the subject of much (unresolved) debate.[12] Opponents claim that production is part of the comparative advantage of a state and that trade should only deal with products on the market,

---

[8] Stefan Zleptnig, *Non-Economic Objectives in WTO Law: Justification Provisions of GATT, GATS, SPS and TBT Agreements*, Vol. 1 (Mads Andenas ed., Martinus Nijhoff Publishers 2010) 37.

[9] Daniel C Esty, 'Bridging the Trade-Environment Divide' Journal of Economic Perspectives (2001) 15:3, 113, 124; Kym Anderson, 'Environmental and Labor Standards: What Role for WTO?' in Kym Anderson and Bernard Hoekman (eds.), *The Global Trading System*, Vol 4: New Issues for the WTO (IB Tauris 2002) 7.

[10] Edith Brown Weiss, 'Environment and Trade as Partners in Sustainable Development: A Commentary' American Journal of International Law (1992) 86, 728, 730.

[11] Sebastian Puth, *WTO und Umwelt: Die Produkt-Prozess-Doktrin* (Duncker and Humblot 2003) 363.

[12] Steve Charnovitz, 'The Law of Environmental "PPMs" in the WTO: Debunking the Myth of Illegality' Yale Journal of International Law (2002) 27:1, 59; Robert Howse and Donald Regan, 'The Product/Process Distinction – An Illusory Basis for Disciplining "Unilateralism" in Trade Policy' European Journal of International Law (2000) 11:2, 249; Henrik Horn and Peter C Mavroidis, 'The Permissible Reach of National Environmental Policies' Journal of World Trade (2008) 42:6, 1107; Vranes (2009); Christiane R Conrad, *Processes and Production Methods (PPMs) in WTO Law: Interfacing Trade and Social Goals* (Cambridge University Press 2011).

rather than deal with environmental conditions outside its own borders. This position was also expressed in the unadopted General Agreement on Tariffs and Trade (GATT) reports in the *US – Tuna* cases where GATT panels found that npr-PPMs could not be consistent with World Trade Organization (WTO) law.[13] A decade later the WTO Appellate Body (AB) took a different approach in *US – Shrimp*.[14] According to the AB, npr-PPMs could be accepted in principle, as long as the measure complied with the conditions of Article XX GATT, the general exceptions provision. In its report the AB touched upon important elements to consider such as the uni-or multilateral nature of the measure, the coercive effect and the requirement of a nexus between the regulating state and the concern to be protected. Despite these efforts, however, the AB did not outline a systematic approach to assess the acceptability of process and production method measures (PPMs), leaving the discussion unsettled. One particular claim that has remained unresolved relates to the alleged extraterritorial nature of PPMs: states aim at regulating processes that take place outside their jurisdiction and that leave no trace in the end product, with the objective to protect non-trade concerns that are at least partly located outside the territory of the regulating state. Due to the sensitive nature of jurisdictional claims under international law as well as the impact npr-PPMs may have on foreign producers and/or policymakers, these 'extraterritorial' measures raise questions on their legality and acceptability under WTO law.

The npr-PPM discussion has often been reduced to a normative 'good or bad' discussion, repeating the positions of the GATT panels and the AB. However, this book purports to avoid that well-trodden normative path: its starting point is to enhance legal understanding of npr-PPMs and focus on the question whether these 'extraterritorial' PPMs could be accepted under WTO law – and in particular Article XX GATT –, and if so, under which conditions. The objective is to develop a systematic approach to assess their extraterritorial reach, applicable to all types of environmental concerns targeted through trade measures. Npr-PPMs are not likely to be extinguished; if anything, they will be used even more often in the future due to globalization, increased awareness of the urgency of environmental challenges and their global impacts, as well as continuously lagging international negotiations on environmental protection in

---

[13] GATT, *United States – Restrictions on Imports of Tuna (Mexico)* GATT Panel 1991, DS21/R; GATT, *United States – Restrictions on Imports of Tuna (EEC)* GATT Panel 1994, DS29/R. For a detailed discussion, see Chapter 3.

[14] WTO, *United States – Import Prohibition of Certain Shrimp and Shrimp Products* AB Report 1998, WT/DS58/AB/R.

different fora. The question to be answered in this book is whether WTO law, as it stands, allows for 'extraterritorial' trade measures that aim at protecting transboundary environmental resources? Or does WTO law, and more particularly Article XX GATT, form a stumbling block for states seeking to address global environmental concerns through 'extraterritorial' trade measures?

1.2 EXTRATERRITORIALITY AND RELATED ISSUES

This book will focus on the extraterritorial reach of npr-PPMs. Extraterritoriality is closely related to concepts such as unilateralism and sovereignty. As these concepts will be referred to on multiple occasions throughout the book, it is useful to define and distinguish them here in order to delineate the specific scope of the research. Furthermore, the question of addressing environmental concerns through trade measures evokes other questions that will be briefly addressed here: is the WTO the appropriate forum to deal with environmental issues; how to deal with the inequity between powerful markets and minor markets with respect to npr-PPMs? Although related to the main question, these questions require a non-legal analysis that is beyond the scope of this book.

1.2.1 Unilateralism

Extraterritoriality is often equated with unilateral action and while overlapping, both notions need to be distinguished. Within the realm of this book, unilateralism is only a meaningful concept when it relates to situations that are not limited to the territory of the regulating state. In that sense the concept is closely related to extraterritoriality.[15] There is no clear definition under international law of what unilateralism entails.[16] With regard to PPMs, unilateralism can refer to two things: firstly, trade measures are imposed by the importing or exporting state, and are thus unilaterally imposed measures;[17] and secondly, the norm prescribed by

---

[15] Bernhard Jansen, 'The Limits of Unilateralism From a European Perspective' European Journal of International Law (2000) 11:2, 309, 310.

[16] See for a discussion on a possible definition of unilateral acts, International Law Commission and Victor Rodriguez Cedeno, Ninth Report on Unilateral Acts of States: Draft Guiding Principles, A/CN4/569, 2006, 54.

[17] The EU is a special case, as the Member States have agreed to a common commercial policy at EU-level. *Mutatis mutandis* EU measures are for the purpose

the measure can be of a unilateral nature, or can be based on multilateral standards. Principle 12 of the 1992 Rio Declaration, arguably referring to both meanings of unilateralism, states:

> unilateral actions to deal with environmental challenges outside the jurisdiction of the importing country should be avoided. Environmental measures addressing transboundary or global environmental problems should, as far as possible, be based on an international consensus.[18]

However, in the absence of international consensus on environmental action – let alone concrete international measures, commitments and enforcement – unilateral action might be the only way forward, as long as it is combined with a continuous effort to reach international agreement.[19] Thus, rather than a prohibition on unilateral measures, Principle 12 should be read as a good faith duty to engage in cooperation,[20] a duty that the AB has also found to be included in the *chapeau* of Article XX GATT in the landmark case *US – Shrimp*.[21] Environmental trade measures could thus be used in addition to engagements in multilateral processes and institutions, as well as transboundary networks and dialogues among states and non-state actors.[22] Unilateral action in isolation of multilateral consideration will raise more questions as to the legitimacy of those standards.[23] One could say that the legality of unilateral measures depends on the extent to which they circumvent the application or adoption of a multilateral alternative.[24]

---

of this debate seen as 'unilateral' measures as well. The fact that the EU represents the viewpoints on the Member States does not change the extraterritorial effect of an EU measure. The fact that all Member States agree on a policy (which is not guaranteed when decisions are taken based on qualified majority voting (QMV)) may only serve as an indication of broader support for a position.

[18] Rio Declaration on Environment and Development, 31 ILM 874, Principle 12 (14 June 1992).

[19] Daniel Bodansky, 'What's So Bad about Unilateral Action to Protect the Environment?' European Journal of International Law (2000) 11:2, 339, 339.

[20] Puth (2003), 369.

[21] AB Report *US – Shrimp* 1998, para. 166.

[22] Eric Dannenmaier, 'Constructing Transnational Climate Regimes' in Günther Handl, Joachim Zekoll and Peer Zumbansen (eds.), *Beyond Territoriality: Transnational Legal Authority in an Age of Globalization* (Martinus Nijhoff 2012) 521; Tim Gemkow, 'The International Law(s) of Regulatory Extraterritoriality: Causes and Consequences of Rule Variations' Paper at SGIR 7th Pan-European Conference on International Relations (2010); Bodansky (2000), 343.

[23] Laurens Ankersmit, Jessica Lawrence and Gareth Davies, 'Diverging EU and WTO Perspectives on Extraterritorial Process Regulation' Minnesota Journal of International Law (2012) 21:1, 14, 30.

[24] Michael Reisman, 'Unilateral Action and the Transformation of the World

Unilateral measures should thus be seen as a second-best option that could advance a collective agenda, where the first option of multilateral commitments is inadequate.[25] The reality is that effective, broad membership environmental treaties are difficult to achieve, so unilateralism could provide an incentive to tackle concerns collectively.[26] This has also been called 'policy-forging' unilateralism.[27] Unilateral action could form part of a dynamic process of action and reaction, of reassessment and response.[28] Eventually, the level of resistance or acceptance by other states will determine whether the advanced norm may at least partly compensate for the deficiencies in the multilateral system. Furthermore, a trade measure may also address a newly emerging concern that is not yet on the international agenda.

Unilateral action to protect the environment is arguably grounded in a combination of self-interest, superiority and altruism.[29] In order to avoid abuse of power, safeguards are required. It is, for instance, crucial that states adopting unilateral measures base the imposed norm as much as possible on existing international hard or soft law. Non-legal initiatives by civil society and scientific institutions could also be taken into account by regulating states in order to strengthen substantive support for a measure and weaken its unilateral character.

1.2.2 State Sovereignty

The concepts of extraterritoriality and unilateralism are both closely tied to the Westphalian notion of state sovereignty. They are both

---

Constitutive Process: The Special Problem of Humanitarian Intervention' European Journal of International Law (2000) 11:3; Steve Charnovitz, 'A Taxonomy of Environmental Trade Measures' Georgetown International Environmental Law Review (1993) 6:1, 1, 6.

25 Monica Hakimi, 'Unfriendly Unilateralism' Harvard International Law Journal (2014) 55:1, 105, 146.

26 Ankersmit, Lawrence and Davies (2012), 34; Hakimi (2014), 126; Joanne Scott, 'Extraterritoriality and Territorial Extension in EU Law' American Journal of Comparative Law (2014) 62, 87, 106. For some examples, see Steve Charnovitz, 'GATT and the Environment: Examining the Issues' International Environmental Affairs (1992) 4:3, 203; Bodansky (2000), 344.

27 Laurence Boisson de Chazournes, 'Unilateralism and Environmental Protection: Issues of Perception and Reality of Issues' European Journal of International Law (2000) 11:2, 315, 317.

28 Shaffer and Bodansky (2011), 8.

29 Neumayer (2002), 147; Aravind Ganesh, 'Understanding the EU Missionary Principle' 2014, Available at SSRN; Werner Meng, *Extraterritoriale Jurisdiktion im öffentlichen Wirtschaftsrecht* (Springer 1994) 550; Hakimi (2014), 111.

considered controversial because they interfere with the sovereignty of other states. States enjoy full sovereignty over their territory and any exercise of jurisdiction outside of that territory is considered extraterritorial. International law includes a number of principles permitting such extraterritorial jurisdiction, which will be discussed in Chapter 4. Npr-PPMs, targeting production processes outside the territory of the regulating state, are regarded as extraterritorial under the geographically bound Westphalian notion of sovereignty. Nevertheless, consumers may feel strongly about environmental concerns related to production of imported products and may be in favour of stricter environmental requirements conditioning market access.[30] Does it still hold in view of global challenges to require a territorial link between the regulating state and the matter to be regulated? The traditional territorial premise is increasingly challenged in today's interdependent world in a number of areas, such as jurisdiction of the port state with regard to labour standards on the high seas or pollution from ships outside territorial waters,[31] extraterritoriality in the cyber-world including data protection,[32] and privacy issues for intelligence surveillance,[33] securities regulation,[34] anti-corruption and

---

[30] Douglas A Kysar, 'Preferences for Processes: The Process/Product Distinction and the Regulation of Consumer Choice' Harvard Law Review (2004) 118:2, 526, 599.

[31] See e.g. double hull requirements for ships under the US Pollution Act; Maritime Labour Convention 2006.

[32] Christopher Kuner, 'Extraterritoriality and Regulation of International Data Transfers in EU Data Protection Law' International Data Privacy Law (2015) 5:4, 235; Christopher Kuner, 'Extraterritoriality and the Fundamental Right to Data Protection' EJIL Talk, 16 December 2013; Teresa Scassa and Robert J Currie, 'New First Principles? Assessing The Internet's Challenges To Jurisdiction' Georgetown Journal of International Law (2011) 42:4, 1017; Cedric Ryngaert, *Jurisdiction in International Law* (2nd edn., Oxford University Press 2015) 79.

[33] Anne Peters, 'Surveillance Without Borders? The Unlawfulness of the NSA-Panopticon, Part I' EJIL Talk, 1 November 2013; Carly Nyst, 'Interference-based Jurisdiction over Violations of the Right to Privacy' EJIL Talk, 21 November 2013; Dan Svantesson, 'Extraterritoriality and Targeting in EU Data Privacy Law: The Weak Spot Undermining the Regulation' International Data Privacy Law (2015) 5:4, 226.

[34] Securities regulation is a branch of financial law that governs transactions in certifications attesting the ownership of stocks. States, especially the US, have attested jurisdiction based on territorial conduct or effects related to a securities transaction. In the landmark judgment *Morrison v National Australia Bank*, 130 S.Ct. 2869, 2010, the US Supreme Court found that the Exchange Act did not apply extraterritorially, and that a stronger link to the US was required. See e.g. Ryngaert (2015); William S Dodge, '*Morrison*'s Effects Test' Southwestern Law Review (2011) 40, 687.

anti-bribery legislation,[35] and animal welfare rules.[36] This book does not purport to engage in an in-depth debate on sovereignty, but questions whether the notion of sovereignty is flexible enough to reflect the needs of this particular time.[37] The example of environmental npr-PPMs will inquire whether a looser approach to territorial sovereignty can be adopted by interpreting the law as it stands, in light of current global challenges. The analysis can be relevant to the more general question of what states can do when facing global challenges – which by their very nature are not territorial and cannot be solved by individual (state) actors – particularly when combined with the absence of multilateral consent on the best course of action.

---

[35] US anti-corruption legislation (Foreign Corrupt Practices Act) prescribes anti-bribery rules, applying to all natural and legal persons subject to US laws, as well as all 'issuers', which are companies that register securities with the US Securities and Exchange Commission and to any person acting within US territory if there is any connection with the bribery act, for instance routing payment through US bank accounts or sending an email to a US company (FCPA §78dd-1(a) in conjunction with §§78l and 78o(d)). The UK Bribery Act 2010 equally relies on the territoriality and nationality principle for an extraterritorial application. The 1997 OECD Convention on Combating Bribery of Foreign Public Officials in International Business Transactions sets legally binding standards for its 41 signatories to criminalize bribery of foreign public officials. The Convention allows for jurisdiction either when a part or the whole conduct occurs within the territory of the state (territoriality principle), or when a national of a state is bribing a foreign official (nationality principle) (Art 4 OECD Convention). A broad interpretation of the territoriality principle does not require an extensive physical connection (see Commentary 25 to the OECD Convention). In that light, it has been argued that any means of interstate commerce such as use of emails, telephone or banking system are sufficient to establish jurisdiction. (Mark Pieth, Lucinda Low and Peter Cullen, *The OECD Convention on Bribery: A Commentary* (Cambridge University Press 2007) 277.) See also Branislav Hock, 'Intimations of Global Anti-Bribery Regime and the Effectiveness of Extraterritorial Enforcement: From Free-Riders to Protectionism' 2014, 2014–009 TILEC Discussion Paper.

[36] See e.g. case *Zuchtvieh Export GmbH v Stadt Kempen* C-424/13, where the question arose whether the EU allows the restriction of an export permit if EU animal welfare standards during transport are not adhered to in third countries, even if those standards are in compliance with the laws of that third country. AG Bot argued for a territorial restriction to EU Regulation 1/2005, but the Court did not address the claims on extraterritoriality. The Court based its reasoning on an arguably faulty interpretation of Article 14 of Regulation 1/2005 and avoided the more systemic issues.

[37] Sir Robert Jennings, 'Sovereignty and International Law' in Gerard Kreijen et al. (eds.), *State, Sovereignty, and International Governance* (Oxford University Press 2002) 29.

1.2.3 WTO as the Appropriate Forum

The WTO is not an environmental organization, nor the ideal forum to achieve environmental progress. Rather, trade measures are one tool in a preferably larger toolkit for global environmental protection that includes binding environmental agreements. Where binding agreements exist, and where they include enforcement and dispute settlement mechanisms, those approaches should be preferred over trade measures, because of their multilateral, consensual nature. However, where such agreements are lacking the WTO might be an attractive alternative due to the linkages between trade and environment, but also due to the powerful nature of trade measures and the well-functioning WTO Dispute Settlement Body (DSB). As noted in the preamble to the Marrakesh Agreement, one of the objectives of the WTO is sustainable development, which includes environmental protection. Trade measures should in that light be seen as a means to an end. The question is whether adjudicators in trade dispute settlement are equipped to undertake a balancing act between trade interests and environmental interests. Can they 'objectively weigh incommensurate concerns, such as the value of commercial freedom versus the value of environmental protection, where the litigant governments will likely have different metrics for these values',[38] while not diminishing or adding to the rights and obligations in the WTO treaties?[39]

It is the task of WTO panels to determine whether a measure unduly restricts trade or is of a discriminatory nature. Is a government really intervening to protect the environment (in which case the measure could hold) or is it rather intervening to protect domestic producers (in which case the measure cannot be seen as consistent)? When a measure has been found to infringe a substantive obligation, justification can be sought under the general exception clause of Article XX GATT. As has been shown in the past, however, the conditions prescribed in Article XX do not necessarily help in deciding on issues of systemic importance, such as the extraterritorial reach of trade measures. A structural approach to balance trade and non-trade concerns has not been developed yet. The early GATT panels are perceived to have opted for a rather strict trade-over-non-trade approach. WTO panelists as well as the AB have adopted a relatively cautious approach with regard to non-trade concerns: in the few cases that have come before the AB, the AB limited its decision to the specific facts of the case, avoiding broader interpretations that could be

---

[38] Charnovitz (2002), 101.

[39] See Article 3.2 DSU.

applicable to the wider set of non-trade concerns. The model proposed in this book is an attempt to develop a systematic and structural approach to assess npr-PPMs under the law as it stands. The suggested interpretation of WTO law will draw inspiration from other fields of law where an extraterritorial application of rules is accepted, such as general international law, international human rights law and competition law. Through different steps, the model offers panelists tools to examine those elements that are essential to a trade analysis, and adopts a more deferential approach to non-trade issues, such as the most appropriate method to address a particular environmental problem.

1.2.4 Powerful Markets

A pertinent concern with regard to the use of npr-PPMs is that only a limited number of countries, namely economically powerful states, will be able to impose their laws extraterritorially in an effective manner. The usefulness of environmental trade measures lies with the power of exclusion. If access to a market is restricted or prohibited for products produced in a manner that is harmful to the environment, then those that seek access to this market will have no choice but to adapt their production process. The more powerful the import market, the stronger the *de facto* coercive effect on producers will be. Can they move export to another market? For many producers, there will be no full alternative to strong markets such as the European Union (EU) or the United States (US).[40] Complying with the rules of another jurisdiction is then the price of trading with that market.[41]

Developing countries fear that PPMs will be used by the major economic powers and will have strong trade restrictive effects on developing countries without any compensation, such as technical or financial assistance.[42] The bulk of the costs resulting from npr-PPMs will be carried by those producing under the lowest standards, as they will likely have to adapt most in order to comply with the higher standards. Developing

---

[40] See, as will be further discussed on several occasions throughout this book, but most notably in Chapter 5, Anu Bradford, 'The Brussels Effect' Northwestern University Law Review (2012) 107:1, 1; David Singh Grewal, *Network Power: The Social Dynamics of Globalization* (Yale University Press 2008); David Singh Grewal, 'Network Power and Globalization', Ethics and International Affairs (2006) 17:2, 89.

[41] Bradford (2012), 66.

[42] Gregory Shaffer, 'WTO Blue-Green Blues: The Impact of US Domestic Politics on Trade-Labor, Trade-Environment Linkages for the WTO's Future' Fordham International Law Journal (2000) 24:1, 607, 625; UNCTAD, *Trade and Environment Review* (2006).

countries fear that the imposition of environmental, technological and other qualitative standards with high thresholds set by industrialized countries may threaten their market access, and fear that their special position in the WTO, recognized in Part IV of the GATT, will not be taken into account.[43] An assessment of extraterritorial measures should include a good faith obligation on the state imposing the trade measure, which could ideally entail a duty for financial and technical assistance to developing countries where the imposed measures would require costly changes in production processes. The question is then whether this can be required under the GATT and if so, how to operationalize these responsibilities and duties. There are several international mechanisms recognizing the need for developed countries to assist developing countries;[44] however, these merely entail an obligation of conduct and can thus not be enforced.

1.3 OUTLINE OF THE BOOK

Can states, in the absence of binding international environmental agreements, impose trade measures targeting foreign production processes in order to act upon environmental problems located (at least partly) outside the territory of the regulating state? Does the WTO act as a stumbling block for alternative solutions to global environmental challenges?

This book proposes an extraterritoriality decision tree that serves as a systematic approach to assess regulatory npr-PPMs that aim at protecting an environmental problem outside the territory of the regulating state. The decision tree will be embedded within the framework of Article XX GATT as the general exceptions clause, and will guide the analysis of extraterritorial environmental concerns. It answers whether there is a jurisdictional limitation to Article XX GATT, and if so, what that limitation entails. Following the proposed steps will not lead to the infamous slippery slope consisting of an uncontainable use of unilateral and extraterritorial action: the decision model takes into consideration how the regulating country is affected by the concern at issue as well as the international support (if existing) for the imposed norms. The need to protect the concern at issue is balanced with safeguarding the fundamental

---

43 Robert Read, 'Process and Production Methods and the Regulation of International Trade' in Robert Read and Nicholas Perdikis (eds.), *The WTO and the Regulation of International Trade: Recent Trade Disputes Between the European Union and the United States* (Edward Elgar Publishing 2005) 243.

44 See e.g. the Principle of Common but Differentiated Responsibilities as recognized in the UNFCCC, 1992, Arts 3, 4; Kyoto Protocol to the UNFCCC 1997.

characteristics of the multilateral trading system through the application of several decision criteria.

The book starts with an objective assessment of the WTO legal framework for PPMs, purporting to map and describe the *lex lata* with respect to environmental concerns and npr-PPMs. The purpose of Chapter 2 is to define npr-PPMs, placing them within the broader trade-environment debate. The chapter deals with the question of how PPMs can be challenged under WTO law, and more specifically under the GATT. Chapter 3 examines the extraterritorial nature and reach of npr-PPMs. Extraterritoriality in the context of PPMs can be understood in two ways: firstly, a PPM targets the production process and thus 'regulates' activities occurring abroad; secondly, a PPM can aim at protecting a non-trade concern outside the territory of the regulating state. Are both notions problematic, and if so, why? In addition to the jurisdictional scope of the relevant WTO agreements, disputes that have dealt with jurisdiction and/or PPMs are discussed. It is concluded that the WTO agreements are silent on their jurisdictional scope, and no systematic approach to jurisdictional questions has been developed in the case law.

The analysis of WTO law is complemented with a comparative analysis of other fields of law where an extraterritorial application of laws is accepted, which will serve as a basis for the proposed extraterritoriality decision tree for trade measures (Chapter 4). The purpose of the comparative analysis is to distil the legal concept of extraterritoriality in different contexts and to analyse under which circumstances states have been willing to accept extraterritorial jurisdiction. For instance, can a parallel be drawn between economic effects on the market and environmental effects within the regulating state, and if so, can the effects doctrine as applied in competition law in an increasing number of domestic systems be applied to npr-PPMs aiming at the protection of environmental concerns outside the territory of the regulating state? Can the extraterritorial application of regional and international human rights treaties, protecting shared and fundamental values, be relevant to trade measures protecting common environmental concerns? Building upon the lessons learned from other fields of law, an extraterritoriality decision tree is proposed in Chapter 5 within the framework of Article XX GATT. The decision tree takes a normative approach as to how WTO law should be interpreted in light of global environmental challenges. The first considers the concern's location so as to determine to what extent it has an environmental impact on the regulating state, while the second step of the decision model refers to the international recognition of and support for the prescribed norm. It is not suggested that WTO law needs to be changed, as the current law can be interpreted in such a way as to accommodate extraterritorial concerns. Some critical observations are made that go beyond the legal framework.

In Chapter 6 the decision tree will be applied to four case studies, starting with the landmark case of *US – Shrimp*, in order to determine whether this approach would lead to a more satisfying analysis of the contested measure. The model is then applied to EU measures in the field of illegal, unreported and unregulated fishing (IUU fishing); the aviation measures in light of the EU Emissions Trading System (EU ETS); and the Timber Regulation as part of the EU's Forest Law Enforcement, Governance and Trade (FLEGT) Action Plan. The analysis leads to a refinement of the decision model, distinguishing between different types of measures on the basis of their norm-generating objective.

The choice of EU measures in a study on extraterritoriality under WTO law demands a short justification, even if the choice to study the EU is self-explanatory in light of the EU's trading power. Under international law the EU is a *sui generis* body of states: neither a sovereign state nor a supranational international organization. Nevertheless, in light of the EU's exclusive trade competence,[45] for the purpose of this study I consider the EU in its *sui generis* capacity more closely related to a state than to an international organization.[46] When discussing the extraterritorial application of national laws through international trade measures, this includes the extraterritorial application of EU law to activities occurring outside EU borders. Apart from its trade competence, the EU is also competent to adopt environmental policies.[47] Since the Lisbon Treaty the EU is committed to promoting environmental protection globally through Articles 3(5) and 21(2) of the Treaty on the European Union (TEU).[48]

---

[45] Article 3 TFEU.

[46] Within a WTO context, the EU as well as its Member States are Members, but are only represented by the EU. According to Article XII of the Marrakesh Agreement, the WTO's membership is not limited to a 'sovereign entity' but instead to a 'state or separate customs territory possessing full autonomy in the conduct of its external commercial relations'.

[47] Environment is a shared competence with the Member States, see Article 4 TFEU.

[48] Article 3(5) TEU reads: 'In its relations with the wider world, the Union shall uphold and promote its values and interests and contribute to the protection of its citizens. It shall contribute to peace, security, *the sustainable development of the Earth*, solidarity and mutual respect among peoples, *free and fair trade*, eradication of poverty and the protection of human rights, in particular the rights of the child, as well as to the strict observance and the development of international law, including respect for the principles of the United Nations Charter' (emphasis added). Article 21(2) TEU reads: 'The Union shall define and pursue common policies and actions, and shall work for a high degree of cooperation in all fields of

Furthermore, Article 11 of the Treaty on the Functioning of European Union (TFEU) prescribes an environmental integration requirement in other EU policies with a view to promoting sustainable development.[49] While this requirement is important with regard to internal EU policy, it is also being applied externally.[50] The EU has increasingly sought to assert itself as a prominent player in global environmental governance by gradually expanding its environmental policy from an internal policy to one with a marked external dimension. The EU has been actively engaged in the development of a number of multilateral environmental agreements (MEAs), as well as through regional and bilateral processes.[51] As will be demonstrated in Chapter 6, the EU has also undertaken unilateral action in order to promote environmental protection.

After having described what I *will* do in this book, here is what I will *not* do. With regard to the analysis under WTO law, the focus of the book is on regulatory schemes such as standards and regulations, as opposed to economic incentives such as taxes or subsidies. I will furthermore not engage in a law and economics analysis of the rationale and cost-benefits of PPMs. Neither will I embark on an effectiveness/efficiency analysis of PPMs, or go into the political theory of international relations. The scope of this book is purely legal: are there any *legal* impediments to the use of npr-PPMs under WTO law? The proposed analytical model can contribute to a more robust assessment of this question than is currently found in the case law or scholarship. With regard to the comparative analysis of how extraterritoriality is dealt with elsewhere, I do not aim to give an exhaustive overview of extraterritoriality in all fields of law but have selected those areas that I deem most relevant to the discussion on

---

international relations, in order to: . . . (d) foster the sustainable economic, social and environmental development of developing countries, with the primary aim of eradicating poverty; . . . (f) help develop international measures to preserve and improve the quality of the environment and the sustainable management of global natural resources, in order to ensure sustainable development.'

The extent of this obligation is more of a political choice. See for an interesting overview of opinions and case studies, Elisa Morgera (ed.) *The External Environmental Policy of the European Union: EU and International Law Perspectives* (Cambridge University Press 2012).

[49] Article 11 TFEU reads: 'Environmental protection requirements must be integrated into the definition and implementation of the Union policies and activities, in particular with a view to promoting sustainable development.'

[50] See for a study on this, Gracia Marin Duran and Elisa Morgera, *Environmental Integration in the EU's External Relations: Beyond Multilateral Dimensions* (Hart Publishing 2012).

[51] Ibid. 6.

PPMs. With regard to the case studies, I will not assess the effectiveness of the environmental measures, or whether a particular policy is the most appropriate one, as that would require tools and skills that go beyond any legal analysis. I will only apply the legal model to determine whether that type of measure could be accepted under WTO law. I do not deny the importance of the above questions but they are beyond the scope of this book. In order to develop proposals for feasible and effective trade policy, the outcome of the legal analysis must be complemented with findings of economic, political and environmental science analysis.

PART I

Introducing environmental trade measures

2. Product or process – outlining the scope of trade law

2.1 INTRODUCTION

Trade measures with an environmental objective often aim at the production process rather than at the product itself, as the production process can pose a heavier burden on the environment than the actual product.[1] Measures aiming at the process and production methods are called PPMs, which can either have an impact on the physical characteristics of the final product whereby the environmental effects manifest themselves during distribution/marketing/consumption,[2] the so-called product-related PPMs (pr-PPMs, such as the use of pesticides on vegetables, or production with asbestos fibres that lead to a higher health risk); or can be unrelated to the end product, the so-called non-product-related PPMs (npr-PPMs, such as production of cement in an environmental-friendly factory with lower-than-average emission levels). There has been much debate on whether PPMs can be accepted under WTO law. Traditionally, trade law is concerned with the treatment of the end product on the market, which includes pr-PPMs.[3] The question that needs to be clarified is whether a government can restrict imports of products based on their production processes that leave no trace in the final product (e.g. the use of dolphin-friendly fishing nets or the use of clean energy technologies); or whether in those cases a government is seen to impermissibly influence processes that occur beyond its territory.

This chapter answers whether WTO law can allow environmental trade measures aimed at protecting concerns related to the production process.

---

[1] Also called the rectification-at-source principle. See Sebastian Puth, *WTO und Umwelt: Die Produkt-Prozess-Doktrin* (Duncker and Humblot 2003) 363.

[2] OECD, *Processes and Production Methods (PPMs): Conceptual Framework and Considerations on Use of PPM-based Trade Measures* (1997) 10.

[3] See e.g. WTO, *European Communities – Measures Affecting Asbestos and Asbestos-containing Products* AB Report 2001, WT/DS135/AB/R; WTO, *United States – Standards for Reformulated and Conventional Gasoline* AB Report 1996, WT/DS2/AB/R. See also Chapter 3.

The 'extraterritorial' nature and reach of npr-PPMs will be examined in Chapter 3, whereas the current chapter will outline the general legal framework for npr-PPMs: how they can be challenged under WTO law, and more specifically under the GATT. First, an overview of the trade-environment debate will be given. Second, after putting the development of the WTO and the rise of environmental concerns in their historical perspective, the relevant WTO rules will be elaborated upon. Those provisions that have been invoked in disputes on PPMs will be discussed. The relationship between Article III and Article XI GATT with respect to npr-PPMs will be analysed, followed by the possible justifications under Article XX GATT.

2.2 THE TRADE AND ENVIRONMENT DEBATE

Trade and environment are indisputably linked, for instance, in the case of trade in natural resources (such as oil or valuable minerals), trade in products that contain natural resources (such as computer chips), trade in polluting end products (such as cars with high combustion engines), trade in goods with energy-intensive production (such as steel production), or lower tariffs for environmental-friendly products. States regulate the import of goods to their domestic market through bi-and multilateral trade agreements and unilateral trade measures. National environmental policies that regulate domestic production and set standards for domestic products on the market can be applicable to imports as well, possibly leading to trade restrictions.

In the beginning of the 1990s the trade-environment debate started to receive ever more attention. In 1992 the United Nations (UN) convened a landmark conference in Rio de Janeiro, the UN Conference on Environment and Development (UNCED, known as the 1992 Rio Earth Summit), to set the tone and ambitions for global policy on development and environment. Leaders in Rio recognized the substantive links between international trade and environment by agreeing to strive for mutually supportive policies in favour of sustainable development.[4] It

[4] Rio Declaration on Environment and Development 1992, A/CONF.151/26 (Vol. I). See in particular Principle 12 stating that 'States should cooperate to promote a supportive and open international economic system that would lead to economic growth and sustainable development in all countries, to better address the problems of environmental degradation. Trade policy measures for environmental purposes should not constitute a means of arbitrary or unjustifiable discrimination or a disguised restriction on international trade. Unilateral actions

was acknowledged that international trade is a key component of sustainable development, through a more efficient allocation of scarce resources and easier access for countries to, for instance, environmental goods and technologies.[5]

In the meantime, the *Tuna – Dolphin* cases under GATT 1947[6] affirmed the fear of environmentalists that the global trading system was not sufficiently open to non-trade-concerns. At issue was a US measure differentiating tuna caught in a manner that harmed dolphins from tuna caught without harming dolphins. The US measure entailed that the import of tuna was only allowed when dolphin-friendly fishing nets were used. In order to have access to the US market, other states had to prove that they protected dolphins through systems comparable to the US system. The US measure was rejected by the first and the second GATT Panel, as it was found that import bans could only protect concerns within the jurisdiction of the regulating state, that unilateral measures such as the one at issue were a threat to the multilateral trading system, and that the measure was too coercive towards other countries.[7]

The unadopted reports generated diverging reactions: on the one hand, developing countries favoured the panels' rejection, as it was feared that the imposition of such environmental standards would lead to green protectionism and would constrain development. Many non-governmental organizations (NGOs) and developed countries on the other hand, emphasized the need for a possible justification of trade restrictive measures based on legitimate and necessary environmental protection measures.[8] The fact that the Marrakesh Agreement establishing the WTO (adopted after the conclusion of the Uruguay Round in 1994) recognized the need

---

to deal with environmental challenges outside the jurisdiction of the importing country should be avoided. Environmental measures addressing transboundary or global environmental problems should, as far as possible, be based on an international consensus.'

[5] WTO, *Harnessing Trade for Sustainable Development and a Green Economy* (2011) 1.

[6] GATT, *United States – Restrictions on Imports of Tuna (Mexico)* GATT Panel 1991, DS21/R; GATT, *United States – Restrictions on Imports of Tuna (EEC)* GATT Panel 1994, DS29/R.

[7] See Section 2.4.1 for a further discussion of the legal analysis of the *US – Tuna* cases with respect to Article III and Article XI GATT, as well as Section 3.4.2 for a discussion with respect to their extraterritorial nature.

[8] Howard Mann and Yvonne Apea, 'Issues and Debates: Dispute Resolution' in Adil Najam, Mark Halle and Ricardo Melendez-Ortiz (eds.), *Trade and Environment: A Resource Book* (International Institute for Sustainable Development, International Centre for Trade and Sustainable Development, The Regional and International Networking Group 2007) 68.

for trade to be consistent with the goal of sustainable development,[9] was in large part due to the public pressure from NGOs following the *Tuna – Dolphin* cases as well as the results of the 1992 Rio Summit.[10] The Marrakesh Agreement highlighted that trade liberalization should go hand in hand with environmental and social objectives.

This debate in the early 1990s raised awareness about the link between trade and environment and public activism stimulated a continuing attempt at conciliating both interests. In a 1994 Decision on Trade and Environment, the new WTO Members acknowledged the outcomes of Rio and emphasized again the link between trade, environmental protection and sustainable development.[11] They decided to establish a WTO Committee on Trade and Environment, dedicated to dialogue between governments on the impact of trade policies on the environment and of environmental policies on trade. The WTO DSB furthermore played a pivotal role in the debate. The first case brought to the DSB after the creation of the WTO was an environmental dispute concerning the import of reformulated gasoline from Venezuela into the US.[12] The AB held that WTO law must be understood within the context of the broader body of international law, including multilateral environmental agreements (MEA),[13] and emphasized that 'in the preamble to the WTO Agreement and in the Decision on Trade and Environment, there is specific acknowledgement to be found about the importance of coordinating policies on trade and the environment'.[14]

In 1997 the *US – Shrimp* case marked a milestone in the shift towards a more innovative and integrated approach to trade and environment in the light of Article XX GATT.[15] The dispute was launched by India, Pakistan, Thailand and Malaysia against the US, and concerned a US regulation banning the import of shrimp that was not harvested in a way that was certified as complying with US standards to protect endangered sea turtles. The AB emphasized the need to balance between the rights of

---

[9] Marrakesh Agreement Establishing the World Trade Organization, 1867 UNTS 154, 33 ILM 1144, 1994, preamble.

[10] Mann and Apea, 2007, 68.

[11] Ministerial Decision on Trade and Environment, Marrakesh, 15 April 1994.

[12] WTO, *United States – Standards for Reformulated and Conventional Gasoline* Panel Report 1996, WT/DS2/R.

[13] Referring to Article 3.2 DSU.

[14] AB Report *US – Gasoline* 1996, 30.

[15] WTO, *United States – Import Prohibition of Certain Shrimp and Shrimp Products* AB Report 1998, WT/DS58/AB/R. For a closer discussion of the legal analysis, see Section 2.4.2.

WTO Members to market access and 'free' trade,[16] and the right to take measures relating to, for instance, the conservation of exhaustible natural resources under Article XX(g) of GATT.[17] It was confirmed that WTO Members have the right to adopt environmental policies, even when those have an impact on trade, whereby WTO law serves to limit the exercise of governmental discretion as agreed upon by the sovereign Members in order to guard that balance between trade and non-trade concerns.[18]

Since *US – Shrimp*, reconciling trade liberalization and environmental objectives has proven to be a challenging task. To further this end, the WTO Members launched trade and environment negotiations in the ongoing Doha Development Round.[19] Under the WTO principle of single undertaking, 'nothing has been agreed upon unless everything has been agreed upon', and as long as the Doha round is ongoing, the effect of such negotiations is limited. One of the issues on the agenda is strengthening the cooperation between the WTO and MEAs. Also on the Doha Agenda is the liberalization of environmental goods and services. The negotiations call for 'the reduction, or as appropriate, elimination of tariff and non-tariff barriers to environmental goods and services'.[20] The Committee on Trade and Environment acts as a forum within the Doha Development Round to debate environmental aspects of the negotiations.[21] While the discussion of PPMs is not on the agenda, PPMs have received a lot of scholarly attention as a possible means or alternative to address environmental concerns.[22] The central question of this book, the extraterritorial nature of PPMs, has

---

16 What is meant with free trade is not unrestricted trade, but trade consistent with the substantive obligations in the WTO agreements.

17 Mann and Apea, 2007, 69.

18 Petros C Mavroidis, 'Trade and Environment after the *Shrimps-Turtles* Litigation' Journal of World Trade (2000) 34:1, 73, 74. See for a further discussion of the case law, Chapter 3.

19 Doha Ministerial Declaration, para. 6; see also UNEP and WTO, *Trade and Climate Change: WTO-UNEP Report* (2009) xvi.

20 Doha Ministerial Declaration, para. 31(iii); see also paras. 32, 33 and 51, which set out the 'environmental mandate'.

21 For more information, see the homepage of the WTO Committee on Trade and Environment at www.wto.org/english/tratop_e/envir_e/wrk_committee_e.htm.

22 See among others Erich Vranes, *Trade and the Environment: Fundamental Issues in International Law, WTO Law and Legal Theory* (Oxford University Press 2009); Christiane R Conrad, *Processes and Production Methods (PPMs) in WTO Law: Interfacing Trade and Social Goals* (Cambridge University Press 2011); Robert Howse and Donald Regan, 'The Product/Process Distinction – An Illusory Basis for Disciplining "Unilateralism" in Trade Policy' European Journal of International Law (2000) 11:2, 249; Henrik Horn and Peter C Mavroidis, 'The Permissible Reach of National Environmental Policies' Journal of World Trade (2008) 42:6, 1107;

largely been ignored in the literature. Before examining that issue in greater detail in the following chapter, this chapter will first outline the main characteristics of npr-PPMs and review the Article XI/III debate.

2.3 PRODUCT OR PROCESS

2.3.1 PPMs Defined

An important question for environmental measures is: are we regulating the product or the process? Whereas product regulations regulate the design, characteristics, and uses of particular products, environmental PPMs regulate the production process and can 'seek to mitigate the environmental effects of private activities by specifying the conditions under which those activities must be carried out'.[23] Even though products themselves can also have an environmental impact (e.g. a polluting car), the production process will often have a greater environmental impact than the actual product. Examples are plenty: energy-intensive industries with high emissions, protection of plant life (e.g. forests, crops) or animal life (e.g. dolphins, sea turtles). PPMs can be formulated either by prescribing defined technologies, or by, for instance, specifying emissions or performance effects that need to be avoided or achieved.[24]

In general, two types of PPMs are distinguished: product-related PPMs (pr-PPMs) and non-product-related PPMs (npr-PPMs). Pr-PPMs fall within the scope of the Agreement on Technical Barriers to Trade (TBT Agreement),[25] the Agreement on the Application of Sanitary and Phytosanitary Measures (SPS Agreement)[26] as well as the GATT[27] and are

---

Steve Charnovitz, 'The Law of Environmental "PPMs" in the WTO: Debunking the Myth of Illegality' Yale Journal of International Law (2002) 27:1, 59.

[23] Sanford E Gaines, 'Processes and Production Methods: How to Produce Sound Policy for Environmental PPM-Based Trade Measures?' Columbia Journal of Environmental Law (2002) 27:2, 383, 394.

[24] OECD, 1997, 9.

[25] Annex 1.1 of the TBT Agreement does contain an explicit reference to *related* PPMs, without defining them; see below for a further discussion.

[26] Sanitary rules are addressed under the SPS Agreement, which refers to end products as well as processes and production methods. Only measures seeking to prevent risks *within* the territory of the importing country fall within the scope of the SPS, and most likely due to the nature of sanitary and phytosanitary measures most likely PPMs that do not have an impact on the physical end product would be excluded. See Annex 1 to the SPS Agreement.

[27] See for instance AB Report *EC – Asbestos* 2001.

not considered controversial. Food safety offers a good pr-PPM example of how regulators rely on process-based sanitary rules (e.g. pesticides on tomatoes).[28] Npr-PPMs on the other hand have no impact on the physical characteristics of the end product, but focus on, for example, the environmental effects during the production stage (production externalities).[29] The division between product-related and non-product-related is arguably oversimplified. Consumers may have moral and ecological concerns, which might lead to a preference for goods produced in an animal-friendly or environmental-friendly manner, even if a blindfolded consumer will not be able to distinguish the products. In that way, for the consumer, these processes *are related* to the end product. Howse has argued that the definitions of pr-PPMs and npr-PPMs are incorrect: pr-PPMs do not necessarily relate to the physical characteristics of a product, but rather include all elements that determine a product's position on the market. The market position is strongly influenced by consumer preferences, and hence even those processes that do not change the characteristics of the end product *in se* are pr-PPMs.[30]

In *EC – Seal Products*, the Panel and the AB had the opportunity to explore the issue of pr-PPMs under the first sentence of Annex 1.1 TBT. The EU imposed an import ban on all seal products due to public moral concerns with respect to the inhumane killing of seals, with exceptions for seal products from seals hunted by indigenous communities, from seals from hunts conducted for the sustainable management of marine resources, and seal products purchased by travellers. The Panel found that the EU measure laid down product characteristics, without analysing whether the measure might in the alternative also *relate* to product characteristics.[31] The AB reversed the Panel's finding that the measure laid down product characteristics, but was unable to complete the legal analysis with regard to *related* PPMs due to a lack of arguments made by the parties and an

---

28 Charnovitz, 2002, 65; Gabrielle Marceau and Joel P Trachtman, 'The Technical Barriers to Trade Agreement, the Sanitary and Phytosanitary Measures Agreement, and the General Agreement on Tariffs and Trade: A Map of the World Trade Organization Law of Domestic Regulation of Goods.' Journal of World Trade (2002) 36:5, 811, 865.

29 OECD, 1997, 10.

30 Robert Howse, 'Seals Hearing, Day I (part I)' International Economic Law Blog, 18 March 2014; See also Meredith A Crowley and Robert Howse, '*Tuna-Dolphin II*: A Legal and Economic Analysis of the Appellate Body Report' World Trade Review (2014) 13:2, 321, 327.

31 WTO, *European Communities – Measures Prohibiting the Importation and Marketing of Seal Products* Panel Report 2013, WT/DS401/R, paras.7.106, 7.112.

insufficient exploration by the Panel of the relevant issues.[32] The AB did recognize that the distinction between related and non-related PPMs raises systemic issues.[33] It found that product characteristics include objectively definable 'features', 'qualities', 'attributes' or other 'distinguishing marks' of a product;[34] and stated that it must be examined whether the prescribed PPM has 'a sufficient nexus to the characteristics of a product in order to be considered *related* to those characteristics'.[35] While it found the exceptions of the EU seals regime (the indigenous exception, the travellers exception and the marine resources exception) to not lay down product characteristics, the AB did not clarify whether the identity of the hunter, the type of hunt, or the purpose of the hunt could be seen as *related* to product characteristics.[36] Thus, without clarifying what the 'sufficient nexus' could consist of, it remains unclear whether related PPMs must thus have a physical impact on the end product. If a moral concern about the environmental impact of the production process is to be considered 'a sufficient nexus to the characteristics', the traditional distinction between pr- and npr-PPM based purely on physical characteristics should be reviewed.

However, in light of the lack of guidance by the AB on the matter, this book will use the distinction between pr-PPMs and npr-PPMs based on the physical characteristics, focusing on those PPMs that have no impact on the physical characteristics of a product (npr-PPMs), as they do not fall within the traditional trade premise that focuses on end products. For the purpose of this book even a general reference to PPMs is to be equated with npr-PPMs.

2.3.2 PPMs as Policy Tools

Governments can impose npr-PPMs for a number of reasons:[37] as a true incentive for better environmental protection,[38] as a response to consumers' desire for information, or to address economic competitiveness concerns to

[32] WTO, *European Communities – Measures Prohibiting the Importation and Marketing of Seal Products* AB Report 2014, WT/DS401/AB/R, para. 5.69.

[33] Ibid. para. 5.173.

[34] Ibid. para. 5.11.

[35] Ibid. para. 5.12.

[36] Ibid. para. 5.45.

[37] See for an overview of considerations on the motivation, feasibility, effectiveness and efficiency: OECD, 1997, 23.

[38] See for instance James Bacchus, *Global Rules for Mutually Supportive and Reinforcing Trade and Climate Regimes – E15 Expert Group on Measures to Address Climate Change and the Trade System* (ICTSD and World Economic Forum 2016).

level the playing field between domestic and imported products, where domestic production processes are subject to stringent environmental regulations.[39] If states cannot impose requirements related to the production of imports, the efficiency of (domestic) environmental policy could be undermined, as this could lead to a race to the bottom,[40] whereby countries with the least stringent environmental regimes could specialize in the most polluting or least environmental-friendly industries. PPMs can be seen as attempts 'to prevent foreign producers from reaping the benefits of lower human rights, labour, environmental, or other standards'.[41]

While not explicitly prohibited nor allowed under the WTO agreements, the use of npr-PPMs is controversial. They can restrict trade and make it harder and costlier for an exporter to supply a foreign market.[42] Differing product standards in different export markets may limit the exporter's ability to access several markets.[43] Furthermore, imposing environmental practices on other countries through npr-PPMs can create resistance in the exporting country and can be considered as interference with the exporting country's sovereignty.[44] The acceptance of environmental npr-PPM standards could also open doors to human rights or labour rights npr-PPMs, which is met with some resistance from developing countries in particular.[45] PPMs imposed by developed countries targeting developing countries may be seen as tools of eco-imperialism.[46] It is inherent to trade measures that a

---

39 Charnovitz, 2002, 62.

40 However, empirical evidence is limited and the effect seems to be overestimated – see Anu Bradford, 'The Brussels Effect' Northwestern University Law Review (2012) 107:1, 1.

41 Laurens Ankersmit, Jessica Lawrence and Gareth Davies, 'Diverging EU and WTO Perspectives on Extraterritorial Process Regulation' Minnesota Journal of International Law (2012) 21:1, 14, 31.

42 OECD, 1997, 14.

43 Johannes Norpoth, 'Mysteries of the TBT Agreement Resolved? Lessons to Learn for Climate Policies and Developing Country Exporters from Recent TBT Disputes' Journal of World Trade (2013) 47:3, 575, 578.

44 Charnovitz, 2002, 62.

45 Tom Rotherham, 'Issues and Debates: Standards and Labelling' in Adil Najam, Mark Halle and Ricardo Melendez-Ortiz (eds.), *Trade and Environment: A Resource Book* (International Institute for Sustainable Development, International Centre for Trade and Sustainable Development, The Regional and International Networking Group 2007) 184.

46 Gregory Shaffer, 'WTO Blue-Green Blues: The Impact of US Domestic Politics on Trade-Labor, Trade-Environment Linkages for the WTO's Future' Fordham International Law Journal (2000) 24, 607, 624; Tania Voon, 'Sizing Up the WTO: Trade-Environment Conflict and the Kyoto Protocol' Journal of Transnational Law and Policy (2000) 10:1, 71, 100; Charnovitz, 2002; Eric

'popular' export market is in a more powerful position to require compliance, in contrast to smaller export markets.[47] In order to prevent abuse, it is thus important to install sufficient safeguards to ensure the legitimacy of the imposed npr-PPMs.[48] However, in the current absence of binding international agreements on important environmental concerns such as climate change, npr-PPMs can also be a means to 'incentivize' all trading partners, developed and developing, to adhere to higher environmental standards. As long as non-protectionist trade requirements are coupled with other initiatives to ensure environmental protection, such as, for instance, the transfer of know-how on green technologies and financial assistance, environmental-friendly policies could lead to global benefits, both for developed and developing countries.[49] From a WTO law perspective, the challenge lies in determining the legitimacy and non-protectionist intention of npr-PPMs, thus distinguishing acceptable from unacceptable npr-PPMs.

2.4 LEGAL ANALYSIS OF NON-PRODUCT-RELATED PPMS

2.4.1 The Violation: Article XI vs. Article III GATT

The idea that npr-PPMs are always infringing a WTO rule stems from the non-adopted *Tuna – Dolphin* GATT Panel reports.[50] The first case dealt with an import ban by the US on tuna originating in Mexico: by not using special dolphin-friendly fishing nets, Mexican fishermen accidentally killed dolphins. The GATT Panel held that the US regulations did not apply to the products as such and thus could not fall within the scope of Article III GATT on national treatment. Therefore, the regulation had to be seen as an import ban, to be dealt with under Article XI GATT on

---

Neumayer, *Greening Trade and Investment: Environmental Protection Without Protectionism* (Earthscan 2001) 15.

47 See for an interesting discussion of powerful markets, David Singh Grewal, *Network Power: The Social Dynamics of Globalization* (Yale University Press 2008).

48 Gaines, 2002, 427.

49 See Chapter 5 for a further discussion of market power and safeguards under the *chapeau* of Article XX GATT.

50 GATT Panel *US – Tuna (Mexico)* 1991; GATT Panel *US – Tuna (EEC)* 1994; Mann and Apea, 2007, 74; Joost Pauwelyn, 'Recent Books on Trade and Environment: GATT Phantoms Still Haunt the WTO' European Journal of International Law (2004) 15:3, 575, 585; for a further discussion of the cases, see Chapter 3.

quantitative restrictions.[51] Under Article XI GATT the US regulations were considered illegal, and therefore prohibited, unless justified under the Article XX exceptions. The GATT Panel found that measures addressing concerns outside their jurisdiction (the safety of dolphins) could not be justified under Article XX.[52] The second GATT Panel (with this time the European Economic Community (EEC) as complainant) held that 'likeness' of products should be determined based on the physical characteristics of a product and not on the manner in which they are processed or produced. Again the US regulation was treated as an import ban rather than an internal regulation.[53] With regard to Article XX GATT, the Panel did not find a valid ground as to why policies should be limited to the conservation of resources within the territory of a Member.[54] It did find, however, that measures taken so as to coerce other countries to change their policies were not allowed.[55]

Ever since these rulings, it has been a persistent conviction among many trade observers that npr-PPMs are not allowed under WTO, a view that I believe to be incorrect. Five years after the first *Tuna – Dolphin*, the AB came back to the issue of npr-PPMs in *US – Shrimp*. The facts were similar, only this time shrimp and sea turtles were involved instead of tuna and dolphins. In this case a violation of GATT law (Article III or Article XI) was assumed and not contested by the US; hence both the Panel and the AB focused on Article XX GATT in their analysis. The AB took a different stance than the GATT panels in the first *Tuna – Dolphin* case: the AB held that the conservation measures at issue did fall within the scope of Article XX,[56] implying there is thus no principled prohibition on npr-PPMs.[57] However, as the US did not defend itself either under Article III or Article XI, the AB could not examine whether npr-PPMs could possibly be compatible with Article III.

The relationship between Article III and Article XI GATT is partly addressed in the Interpretative Note Ad Article III. The Ad Note appears to exclude a simultaneous application of both provisions.[58] According

---

[51] GATT Panel *US – Tuna (Mexico)* 1991, para. 5.14. See infra for a discussion of Article III and XI GATT.

[52] Ibid. paras. 5.26, 5.31.

[53] Ibid. para. 5.11; GATT Panel *US – Tuna (EEC)* 1994, para. 5.8.

[54] GATT Panel *US – Tuna (EEC)* 1994, para. 5.20.

[55] Ibid. para. 5.27.

[56] AB Report *US – Shrimp* 1998, para. 121.

[57] For a further discussion of these cases with a particular focus on the extraterritorial location of concerns to be protected, see Chapter 3.

[58] See also WTO, *European Communities – Measures Affecting Asbestos and Asbestos-containing Products* Panel Report 2001, WT/DS135/R, para. 8.91.

to the Ad Note, two conditions must be met for a measure to fall under Article III: firstly, the measure must apply to imported and like domestic products; and secondly, the measure must be enforced at the time or point of importation of the imported product. Domestic measures, even if applicable at the border, remain covered by Article III.[59] If a measure is applied exclusively to imported products and is solely a border measure, then the relevant provision is Article XI. Different aspects of a measure may be scrutinized under both articles, however.[60] Once a panel (or the AB) has found that a particular measure violates one GATT obligation, it does not need to investigate whether the same measure violates other GATT obligations as well.[61] Also, neither a panel nor the AB can address a provision *ex officio* when that provision has not been invoked by either complainant or defendant. For instance, in *US – Shrimp*, the US did not raise Article III in its defence, which led to the reports being focused on the justifications under Article XX GATT.

For the purpose of this chapter, the relation between Article XI and Article III is of particular interest, as measures falling under Article III can still be found to be consistent with the national treatment obligation. Under Article III a measure is only inconsistent when discriminatory, and differentiation based on production methods may not be deemed discriminatory if the products at issue are unlike or if the differentiation is not deemed to be protective of domestic products. There is no similar opportunity under Article XI, as all border measures that are capable of restricting imports will infringe this provision. Measures that are inconsistent with either provision can be justified under Article XX if they are in compliance with the conditions of both the subparagraphs and the *chapeau*.

2.4.1.1 Issues under Article XI GATT

Article XI:1 GATT reads:

> No prohibitions or restrictions other than duties, taxes or other charges, whether made effective through quotas, import or export licences or other measures, shall be instituted or maintained by any contracting party on the importation of any product on the territory of any other contracting party or

---

[59] Peter C Mavroidis, *Trade in Goods: The GATT and the Other WTO Agreements Regulating Trade in Goods* (2nd edn., Oxford University Press 2012) 66.

[60] WTO, *India – Measures Affecting the Automotive Sector* Panel Report 2001, WT/DS146/R, para. 7.224.

[61] WTO, *US – Measures Affecting Imports of Woven Wool Shirts and Blouses from India* AB Report 1997, WT/DS33/AB/R, 18.

> on the exportation or sale for export of any product destined for the territory of any other contracting party.

Article XI GATT entails a prohibition on quantitative restrictions. In principle, import and export quantitative restrictions are prohibited irrespective of their rationale. As soon as a restriction falls within the scope of Article XI, a violation can be found and no discriminatory effect needs to be established. Duties, taxes and other charges are excluded from the scope of Article XI, as they are addressed under Articles I, II and III:2 GATT. Article III:4 also covers internal measures applied at the time of importation, according to Interpretative Note Ad Article III.

The decision by the first *Tuna – Dolphin* GATT Panel to consider the US regulation under Article XI rather than under Article III, because it did not apply to the products as such,[62] supported a strictly territorial view: if the production method does not take place within the domestic market but in the exporting Member, a WTO Member cannot regulate those production methods.[63] The Panel's approach can be criticized because the regulations in question did apply to imported and domestic products and did serve a policy purpose. Once a restriction is dealt with under Article XI the violation is easily established, and the analysis will turn to Article XX GATT.

2.4.1.2 Issues under Article III GATT

While a violation under Article XI GATT is straightforward, the legal analysis of PPMs under Article III is less obvious. If a PPM measure would be dealt with under Article III there are several conditions that need to be fulfilled in order to establish a violation. Article III GATT lays down the national treatment obligation, or the obligation to treat imported products no less favourably than domestic products. National treatment prohibits discrimination against imported products once the imported product has entered the domestic market.

The relevant paragraphs of Article III GATT read:

> 1. The contracting parties recognize that internal taxes and other internal charges, and laws, regulations and requirements affecting the internal sale, offering for sale, purchase, transportation, distribution or use of products, and internal quantitative regulations requiring the mixture, processing or use of products in specified amounts or proportions, should not be applied to imported or domestic products so as to afford protection to domestic production.

---

62 GATT Panel *US – Tuna (Mexico)* 1991, para. 5.15.

63 Marceau and Trachtman, 2002, 858.

> 2. The products of the territory of any contracting party imported into the territory of any other contracting party shall not be subject, directly or indirectly, to internal taxes or other internal charges of any kind in excess of those applied, directly or indirectly, to like domestic products. Moreover, no contracting party shall otherwise apply internal taxes or other internal charges to imported or domestic products in a manner contrary to the principles set forth in paragraph 1.
>
> . . .
>
> 4. The products of the territory of any contracting party imported into the territory of any other contracting party shall be accorded treatment no less favourable than that accorded to like products of national origin in respect of all laws, regulations and requirements affecting their internal sale, offering for sale, purchase, transportation, distribution or use. The provisions of this paragraph shall not prevent the application of differential internal transportation charges which are based exclusively on the economic operation of the means of transport and not on the nationality of the product.

Article III GATT contains disciplines on domestic taxation and regulation. Article III:2 requires that imported products shall not be subject to (internal) taxes of any kind in excess of those applied to like domestic products. Article III:4 requires that imported products shall be accorded treatment no less favourable than that accorded to like domestic products in respect of laws and regulations affecting among others their sale and transportation. Article III:1 adds the general principle that none of the above shall be applied in a manner so as to afford protection to domestic production.[64] In *Korea – Alcoholic Beverages* the AB identified the objectives of Article III as 'avoiding protectionism, requiring equality of competitive conditions and protecting expectations of equal competitive relationships'.[65] The current analysis will focus on Article III:4 GATT as the centre of gravity for the legal analysis of regulatory npr-PPMs.

Article III:4 establishes a three-tier test of consistency: first, the measure at issue must be an internal regulation; second, the products concerned must be like; and third, the like imported products must not be treated less favourably than domestic products (so as to afford protection to domestic products). Article III not only covers 'in law' or *de jure* discrimination, but also covers 'in fact' or *de facto* discrimination.[66] Regulatory distinctions

---

[64] WTO, *Japan – Taxes on Alcoholic Beverages* AB Report 1996, WT/DS8/AB/R, para. 111.

[65] WTO, *Korea – Taxes on Alcoholic Beverages* AB Report 1999, WT/DS75/AB/R, para. 120.

[66] A measure discriminates *de jure* when it is clear from reading the text of the law or regulation that it is discriminatory. If on the face the measure does not seem to discriminate, a measure can still be *de facto* discriminatory if on reviewing of the facts, it becomes clear that it discriminates in practice; see James Flett, 'WTO

can be of particular relevance when dealing with *de facto* discriminatory measures.

From an environmental perspective, it would be much more beneficial to consider PPM measures under Article III than under Article XI, as this would allow WTO Members to make regulatory distinctions between two physically similar goods and consider them unlike because of their production method, based on, for instance, consumer preferences. Alternatively, regulatory purposes could be considered when examining whether distinctions relate to the foreign origin of imported goods. If the products would be considered unlike because of a different production method, or no discrimination related to the foreign origin of the goods could be detected, there would be no inconsistency with Article III and no recourse to Article XX would be needed.

Determining likeness The concept of like products is not defined in the GATT, even though likeness recurs in a number of provisions, and has thus been subject to much debate and jurisprudence. It is agreed that the concept of 'like products' has a different meaning in the different contexts where it is used. In *Japan – Alcoholic Beverages II* the AB used the image of an accordion which 'stretches and squeezes' in different provisions, depending on the context and circumstances of a given case.[67]

In general, the criteria of the GATT Working Party on Border Tax Adjustments are relied on to determine likeness. These encompass (1) physical characteristics of a product, such as the products' properties, nature and quality; (2) consumers' tastes and habits; and (3) the products' end-uses in a given market.[68] In *Spain – Unroasted Coffee*, the GATT Panel also considered the tariff classifications of the products.[69] Products do not need to be identical, but they need to be similar.[70] Like products must be in a particularly close competitive relationship in the marketplace, to be determined from the consumer's perspective. Cross-price elasticity of demand in the relevant market can be a helpful tool.[71]

Space for National Regulation: Requiem for a Diagonal Vector Test' Journal of International Economic Law (2013) 16:1, 20, 37.

[67] AB Report *Japan – Alcoholic Beverages II* 1996, para. 114.

[68] GATT, *Report of the Working Party on Border Tax Adjustments* (1970) para. 18.

[69] GATT, *Spain – Tariff Treatment of Unroasted Coffee* GATT Panel Report 1981, BISD 28S/102, para. 4.6.

[70] AB Report *Japan – Alcoholic Beverages II* 1996, para. 113.

[71] AB Report *Korea – Alcoholic Beverages* 1999, para. 121. GATT, *Italian Discrimination Against Imported Agricultural Machinery* GATT Panel Report 1958, BISD 7S/60, para. 12.

Not '*all* products which are in *some* competitive relationship are "like products" under Article III:4': the nature and extent of the competitive relationship need to be determined on a case-by-case basis, based on the known criteria of physical properties, end-use, consumer preferences and tariff classification.[72] The AB has thereby emphasized that all relevant evidence needs to be taken into account, such as, for instance, the health risk posed by asbestos, as constituting a defining aspect of the physical properties.[73]

If likeness is determined through a competitive relationship, it may well be that physically identical products may nevertheless not be 'like' when consumer preferences point to the contrary.[74] It is ultimately the consumer who determines whether a competitive relationship between products exists.[75] What if consumers have such a strong preference for green products, or for goods produced under fair and healthy labour conditions, to the extent that the less-green or unfairly manufactured shirt is no longer an alternative option? Only a very weak competitive relationship might then exist between two physically like products. To this date, no case has yet been adjudicated where products were found to be unlike because of consumer preferences, if they were otherwise found to have the same characteristics.[76]

For npr-PPMs consumer preferences could be the decisive element in a likeness determination. Nevertheless, non-likeness, or the non-existence of a competitive relationship based on consumer preferences, seems very difficult to prove.[77] Identical products are usually in a competitive relation-

---

72 AB Report *EC – Asbestos* 2001, para. 99 (emphasis in original).

73 Ibid. para. 115.

74 Reinhard Quick and Christian Lau, 'Environmentally Motivated Tax Distinctions and WTO Law: The European Commission's Green Paper on Integrated Product Policy in Light of the "Like Product-" and "PPM-" Debates' Journal of International Economic Law (2003) 6:2, 419, 431; Marco C E J Bronckers and Natalie McNelis, 'Rethinking the "Like Product" Definition in GATT 1994: Anti-Dumping and Environmental Protection' in Marco C E J Bronckers (ed.), *A Cross-Section of WTO Law* (Cameron May 2000); Donald Regan, 'Regulatory Purpose and "Like Products" in Article III:4 of the GATT (With Additional Remarks on Article III:2)' Journal of World Trade (2002) 36:3, 443, 447.

75 Pauwelyn, 2004, 586. Consumer preferences play an important role in a market-based approach; see also Conrad, 2011, 222. See also Won-Mog Choi, *'Like Products' in International Trade Law. Towards a Consistent GATT/WTO Jurisprudence* (Oxford University Press 2003), chapter II.3.

76 Note that in *EC – Asbestos* the AB considered the fibres in question as 'physically very different' because of their health risks, which would in turn influence consumers' tastes.

77 Quick and Lau, 2003, 431.

ship because they at least potentially compete with each other as substitutable products.[78] A market-based analysis requires an economic analysis of consumer preferences on a case-by-case, country-by-country basis.[79] Only if consumers are willing to pay a higher price for a product that has been produced in a different way, and where the other product is not considered a viable alternative, can the competitive relationship between identical products be ruled out.[80] Consumer preferences as a determinant factor in a likeness analysis do not guarantee an environmental-friendlier outcome, however. Notwithstanding good intentions, in most markets consumers are primarily guided by the price of products and less by, for instance, the environmental conditions of production. Even with well-informed consumers it is not clear whether a sufficiently large group of consumers would indeed change their preferences purely based on environmental grounds. That does not necessarily mean that people do not care about the environmental concerns, but studies have shown that people express different preferences as a voter/citizen than as a consumer.[81] Price awareness is even more determinant for poor consumers: wealthier consumers could more easily choose between products according to their general preferences, while poor consumers need to give more consideration to the price. Following this logic, the same measure that might be considered legal in wealthy countries, could be found illegal in poor countries.[82] A market-based approach through consumer preferences thus raises challenges with regard to environmental concerns.

Treatment no less favourable Treatment no less favourable requires effective equality of opportunities for imported products to compete with

[78] Ibid. 432.

[79] Bronckers and McNelis, 2000, 50.

[80] Conrad, 2011, 227.

[81] Cass Sunstein, 'Endogenous Preferences, Environmental Law' Journal of Legal Studies (1993) 22:2, 217, 242, explaining why some concerns may be highly valued by political participants, who are simultaneously not willing to back up that valuation as consumers on the market; Daphna Lewinsohn-Zamir, 'Consumer Preferences, Citizen Preferences, and the Provision of Public Goods' Yale Law Journal (1998) 108:2, 377, 379, arguing that consumers may perceive a sense of 'hopelessness' that is absent in political settings; Deborah Guber, *The Grassroots of a Green Revolution: Polling America on the Environment* (MIT Press, 2002), 155, noting that a critical component of an individual's willingness to engage in activity designed to support environmental causes or other public goods hinges upon the perceived efficacy of that activity.

[82] Conrad, 2011, 234.

like domestic products.[83] A distinction in treatment can be *de jure* or *de facto*,[84] but any determination of treatment no less favourable requires an assessment of the implications of the measure at issue for the group of imported products and the group of domestic products.[85] Article III:4 does not require the *identical* treatment of imported and like domestic products, but rather the *equality of competitive conditions* between these like products.[86] There is no *de minimis* standard for treatment less favourable,[87] but there must be a 'genuine relationship' between the measure at issue and the adverse impact on competitive opportunities for imported products.[88]

The AB has held that Members can draw regulatory distinctions without this necessarily leading to discrimination.[89] The tipping point seems to be where the regulatory distinctions distort the conditions of competition to the detriment of imported products.[90] However, should the assessment of treatment less favourable not go beyond a mere consideration of a detrimental effect on competitive opportunities, but rather consider whether these detrimental effects are really related to the foreign origin of the measure? The question whether to apply purportedly objective 'economic' or competition-oriented tests, on the one hand, and more subjective tests that look at the sincerity of the measure's regulatory purposes, on the other hand, has been a returning matter of debate.[91] This crucial issue will be further discussed in the following section on the inclusion of legitimate regulatory purposes in the national treatment analysis.

Aims and effects or the inclusion of regulatory purposes Differentiation between like imported and domestic products does not necessarily mean

---

[83] Panel Report *US – Gasoline* 1996, para. 6.10.

[84] Lothar Ehring, '*De Facto* Discrimination in World Trade Law: National and Most-Favoured-Nation Treatment – or Equal Treatment?' Journal of World Trade (2002) 36:5, 921.

[85] AB Report *EC – Seal Products* 2014, para. 5.101.

[86] Ibid. para. 5.108.

[87] WTO, *China – Measures Affecting Trading Rights and Distribution Services for Certain Publications and Audiovisual Entertainment* Panel Report 2009, WT/DS363/R, para. 7.1537.

[88] AB Report *EC – Seal Products* 2014, para. 5.101.

[89] AB Report *EC – Asbestos* 2001, para. 100.

[90] WTO, *Thailand – Customs and Fiscal Measures on Cigarettes from the Philippines* AB Report 2011, WT/DS371/AB/R, para. 128.

[91] Tomer Broude and Philip I Levy, 'Do You Mind If I Don't Smoke? Products, Purpose and Indeterminacy in *US – Measures Affecting The Production And Sale of Clove Cigarettes*' World Trade Review (2014) 13:2, 357, 359.

that there is also discrimination. States might have legitimate reasons to impose differential treatment on domestic and imported products. Whether these reasons and regulatory purposes should be included in a national treatment analysis (or in a likeness analysis)[92] has been much debated over the years,[93] and has revived after the 2012 TBT Agreement cases. Should legitimate regulatory purposes be excluded from the Article III GATT analysis altogether and be left to Article XX; should they be considered when determining likeness; or rather when assessing treatment less favourable?

In the traditional technical analysis of likeness as discussed above, regulatory objectives are not taken into account and the focus is limited to the conditions of competition. The text of Article III, however, is hardly unequivocal on the correct analysis of likeness.[94] It has been argued that regulatory choices should be included into the analysis of origin-neutral measures under Article III.[95] This would bring a review of national law in line with the basic objective of the GATT – banning protectionism – while leaving governments with the necessary policy space to address legitimate non-trade concerns. In the 1992 *US – Malt Beverages* case, the GATT Panel considered policy objectives in determining likeness. According to the Panel the words 'so as to afford protection to domestic production' in Article III:1 do not prevent contracting parties from differentiating between different product categories for *bona fide* policy purposes, *in casu* public health concerns.[96] The Panel's approach to look at the regula-

---

92 Regan, 2002.

93 See for instance Robert E Hudec, 'GATT/WTO Constraints on National Regulation: Requiem for an "Aim and Effects" Test' International Lawyer (1998) 32:3, 619; Michael Ming Du, 'The Rise of National Regulatory Autonomy in the GATT/WTO Regime' Journal of International Economic Law (2011) 14:3, 639; Flett, 2013.

94 For an interesting analysis of the institutional constraints of the WTO, see Ming Du, 2011. He argues that the WTO agreements are inherently vague and indeterminate due to the single undertaking-principle in the negotiations between very heterogeneous Members. The WTO tribunals interpret the texts with little democratic legitimacy, and their interpretations have differed over time. 'Not only has the line been repeatedly drawn, shifted, and erased in academic discourse, the jurisprudence also echoed this uncertainty by evolving, reaffirming the link between the horizontal trade/non-trade debate and the vertical institutional struggle between Members and the WTO adjudicate bodies' (655).

95 Conrad, 2011, 207; Regan, 2002; Donald H. Regan, 'Further Thoughts on the Role of Regulatory Purpose under Article III of the General Agreement on Tariffs and Trade' Journal of World Trade (2003) 37:4, 737.

96 *United States – Measures Affecting Alcoholic and Malt Beverages* GATT Panel 1992, DS23/R – 39S/206, para. 5.25.

tory purpose and the effect on conditions of competition would become known as the 'aims and effects' test.[97] The GATT Panel in *US – Taxes on Automobiles* further developed this test.[98] Rather than only looking at the competitive opportunities, the aim of a measure should be examined as well:

> A measure could be said to have the aim of affording protection if an analysis of the circumstances . . . demonstrated that a change in competitive opportunities in favor of domestic products was a *desired outcome* and not merely an incidental consequence of the pursuit of a legitimate policy goal.[99]

The advantages of the test were that, firstly, a violation was no longer based on a purely technical analysis of likeness but on the trade effects of a measure; and secondly, justification for legitimate regulatory purposes was no longer limited to Article XX, consisting of an exhaustive list of justification grounds and a strictly interpreted *chapeau.* This new approach was also in line with the one-stage test of violation of the new Standards Code and SPS Code (current Article 2.1–2.2 TBT and Article 2 SPS).[100]

However, the test also raised certain problems. Firstly, neither Article III:2 first sentence nor Article III:4 contain a textual reference to Article III:1, upon which the aim and effects-test was based.[101] Secondly, the burden of proof would become much heavier on the complainant, who would also have to show the aim of the measure.[102] Thirdly, Article XX could become redundant if the regulatory purpose is already taken into account under Article III.[103] The AB in *Japan – Alcoholic Beverages II* rejected the aims and effects test by stressing that the intent of legislators or regulators was irrelevant when determining likeness.[104] The AB did recognize that a measure's purpose as manifested in the design of a measure is pertinent to evaluate whether a measure is applied so as to

---

97 Hudec, 1998, 627.

98 The report remains unadopted, as the EU (complainant) blocked the adoption of the report. The EU challenged the aim and effects-test in the first WTO case dealing with the issue, *Japan –Alcoholic Beverages II.*

99 *United States – Taxes on Automobiles* GATT Panel 1994, DS31/R, para. 5.10 (emphasis added).

100 Hudec, 1998, 628.

101 WTO, *Japan – Taxes on Alcoholic Beverages II* panel report 1996, WT/DS8/R, para. 6.16.

102 Ibid.

103 Ibid. para. 6.17.

104 WTO, *Japan – Taxes on Alcoholic Beverages II* AB 1996, WT/DS8/AB/R, p. 27.

afford protection to domestic production.[105] In *EC – Asbestos* the AB noted:

> a Member may draw distinctions between products which have been found to be 'like', without, for this reason alone, according to the group of like imported products less favourable treatment than that accorded to the group of like domestic products.[106]

Even if there is less favourable treatment due to regulatory distinctions, one should consider whether the distinction is related to the origin of the products. In *Dominican Republic – Cigarettes*, the AB stated:

> the existence of a detrimental effect on a given imported product resulting from a measure does not necessarily imply that this measure accords less favorable treatment to imports *if the detrimental effect is explained by factors or circumstances unrelated to the foreign origin of the product.*[107]

Thus, even if a measure has a detrimental effect on imports as opposed to like domestic products, that effect alone may not be sufficient proof of less favourable treatment: rather, a non-protectionist objective may demonstrate that the measure is not *de facto* discriminatory based on origin.[108] In *EC – Biotech* the Panel assumed biotech and non-biotech products to be like, but found that the EC treated all biotech products alike irrespective of origin, and equally treated all non-biotech products alike irrespective of origin. As Argentina had 'not adduced argument and evidence sufficient to raise a presumption that the alleged less favourable treatment is

[105] Ibid. p. 29; WTO, *Canada – Certain Measures Affecting the Automotive Industry* AB Report 2000, WT/DS139/AB/R, para. 62.

[106] AB Report *EC – Asbestos* 2001, para. 100.

[107] WTO, *Dominican Republic – Measures Affecting the Importation and Internal Sale of Cigarettes* AB 2005, WT/DS302/AB/R, para. 96 (emphasis added). In that case, both importers and domestic producers of cigarettes had to pay a bond of 5 million pesos, which imposed a higher burden on an imported cigarette as compared to a domestic cigarette, because importers sell fewer cigarettes in the Dominican Republic than domestic producers. The AB found that the detrimental effect was thus explained by factors such as market share, but was not related to the foreign origin of the product, and thus no treatment less favourable under Article III:4 could be established.

[108] Joost Pauwelyn, 'Comment: The Unbearable Lightness of Likeness' in Marion Panizzon, Nicole Pohl and Pierre Sauvé (eds.), *GATS and the Regulation of International Trade in Services* (Cambridge University Press 2008) 365. See also for an overview of earlier WTO jurisprudence on *de facto* discrimination, Ehring, 2002.

explained by the foreign origin of the relevant biotech products', the Panel was unable to find a national treatment violation.[109]

Pauwelyn, arguing that the focal point of a national treatment analysis should lie with determining whether or not imported products are discriminated against based on their origin, supports this approach. The test for *de facto* discrimination for measures that seem origin-neutral should be seen as a weighing exercise including consideration of both the objective purpose of the regulation and its effects.[110] Pauwelyn argues that rather than focusing on likeness (criteria upon which it is permissible to distinguish), panels and the AB should focus on the one *impermissible* feature, which is national origin.[111] Thus, if a national measure distinguishes between products based on genuine features that are not origin-based (such as consumer tastes or legitimate objectives such as environmental protection), the measure should be permissible.[112]

In the 2012 TBT Agreement case law – where Articles 2.1 and 2.2 TBT were interpreted, relying extensively on the jurisprudence of Article III GATT[113] – regulatory objectives were considered for the analysis of less favourable treatment. In *US – Clove Cigarettes*,[114] *US – Tuna II*,[115] and *US – COOL*[116] the AB explicitly considered the policy objectives of the measures in determining less favourable treatment under Article 2.1 TBT (the national treatment provision). According to the AB, panels must analyse 'whether the detrimental impact on imports stems exclusively from a legitimate regulatory distinction rather than reflecting discrimination against the group of imported products' and whether the measure at issue is 'even-handed'.[117]

In the light of this reasoning, proposals have been made to include

---

109 WTO, *European Communities – Measures Affecting the Approval and Marketing of Biotech Products* Panel report 2006, WT/DS291/R, para. 7.2514.

110 Pauwelyn, 2008, 358.

111 Ibid. 363.

112 Ibid.

113 The AB's methodology has been criticized for its 'lock, stock and barrel' export of GATT solutions into the TBT; see among others Petros C Mavroidis, 'Driftin' too far from shore – Why the Test for Compliance with the TBT Agreement Developed by the WTO Appellate Body is Wrong, and What Should the AB Have Done Instead' World Trade Review (2013) 12:3, 509.

114 WTO, *United States – Measures Affecting the Production and Sale of Clove Cigarettes* AB Report 2012, WT/DS406/AB/R.

115 WTO, *United States – Measures Concerning the Importation, Marketing and Sale of Tuna and Tuna Products* AB Report 2012, WT/DS381/AB/R.

116 WTO, *United States – Certain Country of Origin Labelling (COOL) Requirements* AB Report 2012, WT/DS384/AB/R.

117 AB Report *US – Clove Cigarettes* 2012, para. 182. This was confirmed by

national regulatory autonomy in the analysis under Article III GATT as well, rather than limit it to Article XX, so as to ensure a consistent and coherent interpretation and application of both the TBT Agreement and GATT.[118] According to Flett, 'respect for regulatory autonomy should not be rendered ineffective by an excessively rigid interpretation and application of Article III:4'.[119] When permitting a modification of the conditions of competition due to a legitimate regulatory distinction under Article 2.1 TBT, the AB referred to the 'context' of Article 2.1 requiring such interpretation.[120] Such support could also be found in the context of Article III:4 GATT – specifically as supplied by Article III:1.[121] Even though in contrast to the TBT, the GATT contains a general exceptions clause, according to Crowley and Howse, there is 'no reason why a responding Member could not argue under Article III GATT that, despite features of the design and structure of its measure appearing to be non-even-handed in their impact on competing imported products, these features can in fact be fully explained by a legitimate regulatory distinction.[122]

Including regulatory distinctions in the analysis of Article III GATT would allow WTO Members to go beyond the closed list of exception grounds in Article XX GATT, without making Article XX void. Such an interpretation of Article III:4 may imply a less frequent recourse to Article XX but does not deprive the exceptions in Article XX of *effet utile*, in particular with regard to *de jure* discrimination.[123] The burden of proof under this 'new' aims and effects test would lie with the complainant to show that the differential treatment under Article III is based on the foreign origin of the products. The respondent will need to demonstrate

---

the AB in AB Report *US – COOL* 2012, para. 271. AB Report *US – Tuna II* 2012, para. 216.

[118] Flett, 2013, 27; Crowley and Howse, 2014, 322; Broude and Levy, 2014, 391. See also Weihuan Zhou, '*US – Clove Cigarettes* and *US – Tuna II (Mexico)*: Implications for the Role of Regulatory Purpose under Article III:4 of the GATT' Journal of International Economic Law (2012) 15:4, 1075; Federico Ortino, 'From "Non-Discrimination" to "Reasonableness": A Paradigm Shift in International Economic Law?' Jean Monnet Working Paper, NYU School of Law 01/05 (2004).

[119] Flett, 2013, 53.

[120] That context includes Article 2.2 TBT as well as the preamble of the TBT Agreement. AB Report *US – Tuna II* 2012, para. 213; WTO, *United States – Measures Affecting the Production and Sale of Clove Cigarettes* AB Report 2012, AB/DS406/AB/R, para. 182; AB Report *US – COOL* 2012, para. 240.

[121] William J Davey and Keith E Maskus, '*Thailand-Cigarettes (Philippines)*: A More Serious Role for the "Less Favourable Treatment" Standard of Article III:4' World Trade Review (2013) 12:2, 163, 180.

[122] Crowley and Howse, 2014, 332.

[123] AB Report *EC – Asbestos* 2001, para. 115.

the non-protectionist purpose of the measure, and show a genuine link between that purpose and the measure. When a distinction originates from a legitimate regulatory objective, a measure would not need to seek justification under Article XX, as no violation would be found in the first place.

Despite strong arguments to be made in favour of adopting a TBT-like test for consideration of legitimate regulatory purposes under Article III GATT, it seems that in *EC – Seal Products* the AB rejected such an approach, by distinguishing between the justification provisions under the TBT Agreement and the GATT.[124] The AB pointed to Article XX GATT to support its position that the balance under Article 2 TBT between the right to regulate and non-discrimination requires an examination of regulatory purpose, whereas under the GATT Article XX serves to counterweigh the non-discrimination obligations. According to the AB, 'a panel is not required to examine whether the detrimental impact of a measure on competitive opportunities for like imported products stems exclusively from a legitimate regulatory distinction'.[125] Note the AB's particular wording of 'not required to' rather than 'should not' or 'cannot'. The AB indicated that it is sufficient to establish a distinction in the competitive opportunities to the detriment of imported products, for which it does not matter whether that distinction is protectionist or whether it stems from a legitimate regulatory distinction. However, the AB did not say that *if* indeed such distinction stems from a legitimate regulatory purpose, that that would be irrelevant. In light of the previous turns the AB has taken in this matter, further confirmation of this approach is to be awaited.[126] In the 2015 *Argentina – Financial Services* General Agreement on Trade in Services (GATS) case, the Panel did rely on the TBT Agreement case law to include regulatory distinctions to determine likeness under Article II:1 GATS;[127] however, that approach was rejected by the AB.[128]

---

124 AB Report *EC – Seal Products* 2014; Michael Ming Du, '"Treatment No Less Favourable" and the Future of National Treatment Obligation in GATT Article III:4 after *EC-Seal Products*' World Trade Review (2016) 15:1, 139.

125 AB Report *EC – Seal Products* 2014, para. 5.117.

126 See also Ming Du, 2016, 155.

127 WTO, Panel Report, *Argentina – Measures Relating to Trade in Goods and Services*, 2015, WT/DS453/R, para. 7.176–179. The panel report was appealed in October 2015.

128 WTO, AB Report, *Argentina – Measures Relating to Trade in Goods and Services*, 2016, WT/DS453/AB/R, para. 6.127.

2.4.2 The Justification: Article XX GATT

WTO law provides for a set of exceptions to reconcile trade liberalization with the pursuit of other societal interests, such as environmental protection, under Article XX GATT. The provision, entitled 'General Exceptions', reads:[129]

> Subject to the requirement that such measures are not applied in a manner which would constitute a means of arbitrary or unjustifiable discrimination between countries where the same conditions prevail, or a disguised restriction on international trade, nothing in this Agreement shall be construed to prevent the adoption or enforcement by any contracting party of measures:
> (a) necessary to protect public morals;
> (b) necessary to protect human, animal or plant life or health;
> (c) . . .
> (d) necessary to secure compliance with laws or regulations which are not inconsistent with the provisions of this Agreement, including those relating to customs enforcement, the enforcement of monopolies operated under paragraph 4 of Article II and Article XVII, the protection of patents, trade marks and copyrights, and the prevention of deceptive practices;
> (e) relating to the products of prison labour;
> (f) imposed for the protection of national treasures of artistic, historic or archaeological value;
> (g) relating to the conservation of exhaustible natural resources if such measures are made effective in conjunction with restrictions on domestic production or consumption; . . .

Article XX sets out an exhaustive list of exceptions, which can be invoked by a Member when a measure has been found to be inconsistent with one of the GATT provisions. In its interpretation, a reasonable, *bona fide* balance needs to be sought between Members' rights to invoke exceptions as well as their duty to respect other Members' WTO rights and to liberalize trade.[130] According to the AB, the relationship between the commitments and the exceptions can be given meaning only 'on a case-to-case basis, by careful scrutiny of the factual and legal context in a given dispute'.[131]

---

129 Paragraphs (c), (h), (i) and (j) omitted by author. These paragraphs relate to trade in gold and silver; obligations under international commodities agreements; efforts to ensure essential quantities of materials to a domestic processing industry; and products in general or local short supply. They have been of less importance in international trade law and practice, and are furthermore of little relevance to this study.

130 AB Report *US – Shrimp* 1998, para. 128.

131 AB Report *US – Gasoline* 1996, 16; For an interesting discussion on the difficulties of this balancing act under Article XX see Christopher Doyle, 'Gimme

In order for Article XX to be successfully invoked, the conditions of said article have to be fulfilled through a two-tier test: first, the conditions of the subparagraphs must be complied with; and second, the requirements of the introductory clause, referred to as the *chapeau* must be satisfied. The design of a measure as such will be assessed under the subparagraphs, whereas the *chapeau* deals with the *application* of a measure.[132]

The focus of this book is on the extraterritorial nature of trade measures and thus also on whether and to what extent Article XX GATT precludes extraterritorial measures. Can Article XX only be invoked to protect concerns located within the territory of the imposing state? What if the measure aims at protecting 'common concerns' which are of importance to the entire international community, or concerns located abroad which create domestic moral concerns? Article XX does not contain an explicit jurisdictional limitation, but whether there is an implied jurisdiction limitation will be discussed in greater detail in Chapter 3. In this section an overview will be given of the other relevant elements of Article XX GATT with regard to environmental disputes.

2.4.2.1 Article XX(b) and (g) GATT

The paragraphs of Article XX GATT that can be used for environmental protection purposes are paragraphs (b) and (g). Article XX(b) concerns measures which are 'necessary to protect human, animal or plant life or health'. The paragraph sets out a two-tier test to determine whether a measure is provisionally justified under this provision. The policy objective pursued by the measure at issue must be the protection of life or health of humans, animals or plants; and the measure must be necessary to fulfil that policy objective.[133] It is thus not the necessity of the policy objective, but the necessity of the disputed measure to *achieve* that objective.[134] Necessary refers to 'no alternative to the measure at issue that the Member could reasonably be expected to employ'.[135] The alternative measure must

---

Shelter: The "Necessary" Element of GATT Article XX in the Context of the *China-Audiovisual Products* Case' Boston University International Law Journal (2011) 29, 143.

[132] WTO, *Brazil – Measures Affecting Import of Retreaded Tyres* Panel Report 2007, WT/DS332/R, para. 7.107.

[133] Panel Report *US – Gasoline* 1996, para. 6.20. For a more recent application of this test, see Panel report *EC – Biotech* 2006, para. 7.179; Panel Report *Brazil – Retreaded Tyres* 2007, para. 7.40.

[134] Panel Report *US – Gasoline* 1996, para. 6.22.

[135] WTO, *Thailand – Customs and Fiscal Measures on Cigarettes from the Philippines* Panel Report 2010, WT/DS371/R, paras. 73 and 75. AB Report *EC – Asbestos* 2001, para. 172.

be GATT-consistent and *as effective* in achieving the policy objective pursued as the measure at issue. In order to determine reasonableness, factors such as difficulty of implementation have to be taken into account. In later disputes it was added that the less restrictive the impact of the measure at issue is on international trade, the more easily the measure may be considered 'necessary'.[136] Levels of protection are furthermore to be determined per country, and cannot be challenged by other WTO Members.[137]

Article XX(g) concerns measures 'relating to the conservation of exhaustible natural resources if such measures are made effective in conjunction with restrictions on domestic production or consumption'. Article XX(g) sets outs a three-tier test, requiring that a measure first relates to the *conservation of exhaustible natural resources*; second *relates* to such conservation; and third must be made effective in conjunction with domestic restrictions. The first element of exhaustible natural resources has been interpreted broadly, in the sense that it encompasses both biological resources as well as non-living resources,[138] such as clean air.[139] The term 'relating to' has been held to cover a wider scope than terms used in other paragraphs such as 'necessary to' and 'essential to'. In *Canada – Herring and Salmon*, the GATT Panel found that a measure was '*relating to* the conservation of exhaustible resources' if it was '*primarily aimed at*' this policy goal.[140] In *US – Shrimp*, the AB interpreted 'relating to' as designating a 'close and genuine relationship of ends and means',[141] i.e. between the measure and the policy objective. The third element of Article XX(g) is a requirement of 'even-handedness' in the imposition of restrictions on imported and domestic products;[142] however, it does not require 'identical treatment of domestic and imported products'.[143]

In *EC – Seal Products*, the EU invoked Article XX(a) on public morals to justify its seals regime. The EU relied on public morals expressed by EU citizens on inhumane killing methods of seals to impose an import ban on

136 Panel Report *Brazil – Retreaded Tyres* 2007, para. 7.104.

137 AB Report *EC – Asbestos* 2001, para. 168.

138 AB Report *US – Shrimp* 1998, para. 131.

139 AB Report *US – Gasoline* 1996.

140 GATT, *Canada – Measures Affecting Exports of Unprocessed Herring and Salmon* GATT Panel Report 1988, BISD 35S/98, para. 4.6 (emphasis added).

141 AB Report *US – Shrimp* 1998, para. 136.

142 Peter Van den Bossche and Zdouc Werner, *The Law and Policy of the World Trade Organization: Text, Cases and Materials.* (3rd edn., Cambridge University Press 2008) 637. See also WTO, *China – Measures Related to the Exportation of Various Raw Materials* AB Report 2012, WT/DS394/AB/R, para. 357.

143 AB Report *US – Gasoline* 1996, p. 20.

seal products. The EU equally invoked Article XX(b) but did not make any substantive arguments in that respect.[144] It is clear that there can be substantive overlap between Article XX(a) and other substantive exception grounds, as the scope of moral issues can arguably be very broad.[145] It can be difficult to distinguish moral from environmental concerns: for instance, the protection of an animal species threatened with extinction can have a direct environmental impact on country A, but can be a moral concern to the not directly affected country B. The relationship between the public morals exception and the environmental exceptions will be discussed in greater detail in Chapter 5, in the context of the extraterritoriality decision tree.

2.4.2.2 The *chapeau*

Next to meeting the requirements of one of the paragraphs of Article XX, in order for a measure to be justified, the requirements of the *chapeau* of Article XX have to be met as well. The *chapeau* has been highly relevant in dispute settlement practice as for several controversial decisions the *chapeau* was the stumbling block.[146] The purpose of the *chapeau* is to protect the legal rights of the complaining party, ensuring that no abuse is made of the legal rights of the defendant to justify trade restrictive measures,[147] and thus to maintain a balance between rights and obligations of WTO Members.[148] In assessing the application of the measure, one must examine the manner in which the measure is implemented in practice and how other elements extraneous to the measure could affect the measure's ability to perform its function.[149]

The *chapeau* of Article XX prohibits 'arbitrary or unjustifiable discrimination between countries where the same conditions prevail' and 'disguised restrictions on international trade'. These concepts may be read side-by-side and impart meaning to one another.[150] WTO Members must take into account the different conditions that may occur in the territories of other Members.[151] A measure needs to be sufficiently flexible and

---

[144] WTO, Panel Report, *EC – Seal Products*, 2013, para. 7.640.

[145] Steve Charnovitz, 'The Moral Exception in Trade Policy', Virginia Journal of International Law (1998) 38, 689.

[146] In both *US – Shrimp* and *US – Gasoline* for instance the measures at issue were found by the AB to have been applied in a manner which constituted arbitrary and unjustifiable discrimination.

[147] AB Report *US – Gasoline* 1996, p. 20.

[148] AB Report *US – Shrimp* 1998, para. 156.

[149] WTO, *Brazil – Measures Affecting Import of Retreaded Tyres* AB Report 2007, WT/DS332/AB/R, para. 7.107.

[150] AB Report *US – Gasoline* 1996, p. 23.

[151] AB Report *US – Shrimp* 1998, para. 164.

should consider similar measures enacted by other Members, which can be comparable in effectiveness, to address the same policy objectives.[152] In *US – Shrimp (Article 21.5 Malaysia)*, the AB added that the *chapeau* entails a good faith obligation, whereby WTO Members must make serious efforts to negotiate concerns before resorting to trade restrictive measures.[153] With regard to 'no disguised restriction on trade', even if a measure does not discriminate, the measure shall not be protectionist in nature. It is not clear whether a measure could be justified if it combined legitimate and illegitimate purposes. Should any illegitimate purpose, even when minor compared to the legitimate purpose, suffice to fail a defence under Article XX? In the example of measures that seek to achieve environmental protection, but that at the same time aim at levelling the playing field and protecting domestic industry, this condition may yet prove to be an important aspect of the *chapeau.*[154]

2.4.3 The TBT Agreement

The TBT Agreement has also been a ground for debate with regard to PPMs. In particular, it is still unresolved whether npr-PPMs could fall within the scope of the Agreement, or whether it is limited to pr-PPMs. In GATT law, non-discriminatory policies cannot be challenged: in principle countries can do as they please as long as they do not unduly restrict imports or discriminate imports as against domestic products. Under the TBT Agreement, technical barriers to trade can be disciplined even if they do not discriminate against imports.[155] The TBT Agreement and GATT seem to be cumulatively applicable rather than mutually exclusive. In *EC – Asbestos* the AB observed that the TBT furthers the objectives of GATT 'through a specialized legal regime that applies solely to a limited class of measures. For these measures, the TBT Agreement imposes obligations on Members that seem to be *different from*, and *additional to*, the obligations imposed on Members under the GATT 1994.'[156]

The TBT covers technical regulations (mandatory compliance),

---

152 Ibid. para. 177.

153 WTO, *United States – Import Prohibition of Certain Shrimp and Shrimp Products, Recourse to Article 21.5 of the DSU by Malaysia* AB Report 2001, WT/DS58/AB/RW, para. 115.

154 Lorand Bartels, 'The Chapeau of the General Exceptions in the WTO GATT and GATS Agreements: A Reconstruction' American Journal of International Law (2015) 109:1, 95, 123.

155 See below for a discussion of Article 2.2 TBT. See also Pauwelyn, 2004, 580.

156 AB Report *EC – Asbestos* 2001, para. 80 (emphasis added).

standards (voluntary compliance) and conformity assessment procedures.[157] All technical regulations are covered by the TBT, other than sanitary or phytosanitary measures as defined in the SPS Agreement.[158] In order to determine whether the TBT is at all relevant to the discussion of environmental npr-PPMs, the scope of the agreement must be assessed first. The term 'technical regulations' has been defined in Annex 1.1, referring to:

> [A document] which lays down product characteristics or *their related processes and production methods* . . . It may also include or deal exclusively with terminology, symbols, packaging, marking or labelling requirements *as they apply to a product, process or production method.*

Annex 1.1 refers to production methods, but adds that they must be 'related' to product characteristics, when not concerning 'terminology, symbols, packaging, marking or labelling requirements'. In *EC – Seal Products*, the AB examined the meaning of 'product characteristics' and found that characteristics include objectively definable 'features', 'qualities', 'attributes' or other 'distinguishing marks' of a product.[159] The AB then found 'related' in the first sentence of Annex 1.1 to refer to these characteristics: the process or production method must thus be related to the product characteristics, or must in other words have a sufficient nexus to the characteristics of the product.[160] It is unclear what is meant by a 'sufficient nexus' in this context. If one were to argue that 'related' means that the measure must have an impact on 'objectively definable product characteristics', then npr-PPMs that do not affect the physical characteristics of a product will not be considered 'related' and thus fall outside the scope of the TBT. If a sufficient nexus could be understood as *any* link to the 'characteristics', then certain npr-PPMs could be considered related: for instance, the fact that tuna is harvested in a dolphin-friendly way, could be 'related' to the end product through its moral or ethical advantage. It remains unclear, however, what the AB could have had in mind. Any production process has an automatic 'nexus' to the product, but when is this sufficient? If assessing that nexus would imply a consideration of the

[157] Article 1.6 TBT. Mandatory technical regulations are developed and implemented by governments, whereas standards as voluntary requirements are most often developed and implemented by private bodies. See Rotherham, 2007, 179.

[158] See the definition of sanitary and phytosanitary measures in Annex A to the SPS Agreement.

[159] AB Report *EC – Seal Products* 2014, para. 5.11 (emphasis added).

[160] Ibid. para. 5.12.

objective of the PPM (e.g. an environmental objective, ethical characteristics), then how can we distinguish the test from regulatory purpose or a necessity test?

In *EC – Seal Products* the AB found that the ban on seal products imposed a characteristic on products 'by providing that they may not contain seal';[161] however, the exceptions to the EU seal regime (the indigenous communities exception, the marine resources management exception and the travellers exception) did not. According to the AB, there is no basis in the text of Annex 1.1 to 'suggest that the identity of the hunter, the type of hunt, or the purpose of the hunt could be viewed as product characteristics'.[162] As a measure must be examined as a whole, including prohibitive and permissive elements, and the main features of the EU seal regime were the exceptions rather than the criteria relating to the manner in which seal is killed, the AB considered the EU seal regime not to lay down product characteristics and thus not to constitute a technical regulation.[163] Whether these exceptions could be considered PPMs *related to* product characteristics was unfortunately left unanswered by the AB. As the Panel had not examined the issue in its report and as the parties had not submitted sufficient argumentation, the AB did not rule on this point. The AB did note that 'the line between PPMs that fall, and those that do not fall, within the scope of the TBT Agreement raises important systemic issues'.[164] The contours of npr-PPMs within the TBT Agreement have thus not yet been determined. If one were to argue that a npr-PPM were to have a sufficient nexus with the product characteristics, despite the lack of physical impact, such a measure could then fall within the scope of the TBT.

The second sentence of Annex 1.1, referring to among others labelling requirements, only refers to PPMs in general, without distinguishing between related and non-related PPMs. It can thus be accepted that for those requirements (labelling, packaging, symbols), it is irrelevant to what extent the production process impacts on the physical characteristics of the final product in order to fall within the scope of the TBT Agreement.[165]

---

161 Ibid. para. 5.39.
162 Ibid. para. 5.45.
163 Ibid. para. 5.58.
164 Ibid. para. 5.69.
165 See for instance *US – Tuna II* on dolphin-safe labels for tuna products. AB Report *US – Tuna II* 2012; Philip I Levy and Donald Regan, '*EC-Seal Products*: Seals and Sensibilities (TBT Aspects of the Panel and Appellate Body Reports)' World Trade Review (2015) 14:2, 337, 350; Norpoth, 2013, 580; Vranes, 2009, 339; Marceau and Trachtman, 2002, 861.

Labelling requirements could be seen as a special regime, exceptionally bringing npr-PPMs within the scope of the TBT. As suggested by Marceau, the regime of labelling requirements can be more flexible as such measures do not completely restrict trade but essentially provide information.[166] By informing consumers, labels can be a first tool to distinguish between products based on their production methods.[167] Whether or not the labelling measure in question is inconsistent with the agreement then needs to be determined through an analysis of the substantive TBT obligations.

Article 2 TBT, governing technical regulations, contains the most important substantive requirements in the TBT with regard to PPMs. It includes the national treatment and most-favoured-nation (MFN) obligation in Article 2.1 TBT and the additional obligation to ensure that regulations are not more trade restrictive than necessary to fulfil a legitimate objective (non-exhaustive list) in Article 2.2 TBT. Article 2.1 TBT follows a similar approach to Article III GATT with regard to the national treatment obligation. It must be determined firstly, whether the relevant products are like, i.e. in a sufficiently strong competitive relationship.[168] If not, are imported products treated less favourably compared to domestic products, and does that impact stem exclusively from a 'legitimate regulatory distinction'?[169] The context of Article 2.1 TBT, among which Article 2.2 TBT and the preamble of the TBT, supports a finding that technical regulations may pursue legitimate objectives when they are not applied in a manner that would constitute a means of arbitrary or unjustifiable discrimination.[170] When ascertaining whether a technical regulation modifies the conditions of competition to demonstrate less favourable treatment, a panel must analyse whether the detrimental impact on the imported products stems exclusively from a legitimate regulatory distinction.[171] Article 2.2 TBT establishes an additional obligation that technical regulations shall not be more trade

---

[166] Gabrielle Marceau, 'A Comment on the Appellate Body Report in *EC-Seal Products* in the Context of the Trade and Environment Debate' RECIEL (2014) 23:3, 318, 327.

[167] See Laurens Ankersmit and Jessica Lawrence, 'The Future of Environmental Labelling: *US – Tuna II* and the Scope of the TBT' Legal Issues of Economic Integration (2012) 39:1, 127, 136; Enrico Partiti, 'The Appellate Body Report in *US – Tuna II* and Its Impact on Eco-Labelling and Standardization' Legal Issues of Economic Integration (2013) 40:1, 73, 79.

[168] AB Report *US – Clove Cigarettes* 2012, para. 120.

[169] Ibid. para. 271.

[170] AB Report *US – Tuna II* 2012, para. 213; AB Report *US – Clove Cigarettes* 2012, para. 182; AB Report *US – COOL* 2012, para. 240.

[171] AB Report *US – Clove Cigarettes* 2012, para. 182.

restrictive than necessary to fulfil a legitimate objective. Article 2.2 TBT resembles the subparagraphs of Article XX GATT, with a (non-exhaustive in the case of Article 2.2) list of objectives, as well as a necessity test.[172] Technical regulations have to conform to the requirements of Article 2.2, however, irrespective of whether a measure was found to be inconsistent with Article 2.1 TBT. Article 2.2 is thus not a justification provision for inconsistencies found with other substantive obligations. This distinction between Article XX GATT and Article 2.2 TBT may have important consequences for the burden of proof: the respondent bears the burden under Article XX GATT to justify its measures, whereas the complainant likely bears the burden under Article 2.2 TBT.[173] The TBT does not contain a general exceptions clause.

Thus, in summary, a textual analysis of Annex 1.1 TBT does not seem to support the inclusion of npr-PPMs within the scope of the TBT Agreement, unless they concern requirements such as labelling or packaging that serve to inform consumers. However, the AB in *EC – Seal Products* created an opening for npr-PPMs by referring to a 'sufficient nexus' between production and end product, without clarifying whether such nexus could only consist of a physical impact. If npr-PPMs would fall within the scope of the TBT, the measure needs to be consistent with Article 2.1 and 2.2 TBT.

2.5 CONCLUSION

Throughout the years, environmental protection has received more and more attention in the WTO and is now recognized as a real and legitimate objective within international trade. The object of this book is to determine the degree of acceptance of trade measures that aim at environmental concerns located outside the territory of the regulating state through regulating the production process, and in particular npr-PPMs that have no impact on the physical characteristics of the product. Whereas Chapter 3 will focus on the extraterritorial nature of PPMs, this chapter has outlined the legal challenges for npr-PPMs under the GATT.

The case law on PPMs is scarce and has focused on Article XX GATT. By finding that npr-PPMs fall outside the scope of Article III GATT

---

172 AB Report *US – Tuna II* 2012, para. 322. As under Article XX GATT, environmental concerns are explicitly mentioned in Article 2.2 TBT.

173 Andrew Green, 'Climate Change, Regulatory Policy and the WTO: How Constraining are Trade Rules?' Journal of International Economic Law (2005) 8:1, 143, 174.

because they do not regulate products as such, the GATT panels in the *Tuna – Dolphin* cases have strongly, but arguably falsely, influenced the PPM debate. The measures were found to be import bans inconsistent with Article XI GATT, steering the analysis to Article XX GATT. The AB in the landmark *US – Shrimp* was not in the position to clarify the relation between Articles III and XI GATT as Article III was not invoked by either of the parties. The relationship between Article III and Article XI with respect to npr-PPMs thus remains unclear, but could have important consequences for npr-PPMs. A measure falling within the scope of Article XI GATT is in violation of this Article, and will thus need to be justified under the general exceptions. Under Article III, however, an inconsistency is not automatically established. Firstly, consumer preferences could influence a finding of likeness if they demonstrate a sufficiently strong preference for one product over another based on the production method. Secondly, it could be argued that treatment less favourable can only be established when the detrimental impact is due to the foreign origin of the imported products. Through a TBT-inspired, revised 'aims and effects' test, regulatory purposes might be taken into account at the stage of determining treatment less favourable, whereby states can make regulatory distinctions based on legitimate regulatory objectives. Only when the conditions of likeness and treatment less favourable are fulfilled, will the analysis turn to Article XX GATT. A measure could be justified under Article XX if the conditions of the subparagraphs and the *chapeau* are met.

3. The (extra)territorial reach of national measures under WTO law

3.1 INTRODUCTION

In the interplay between trade and global environmental concerns the issue of extraterritoriality or the 'extraterritorial effect' of trade measures cannot be ignored. Can states impose domestic policies on other states or foreign producers through trade measures? Can states regulate concerns located outside their territory?

Traditionally, trade measures protect concerns within the jurisdiction of a regulating state. For example, products that may be harmful for consumers' health can be restricted for import. As explained in Chapter 2, WTO Members can also impose npr-PPMs, addressing transnational or even global concerns. Npr-PPMs are called into question because of their extraterritorial reach. Extraterritoriality in the context of npr-PPMs can be understood in two ways: firstly, a PPM targets the production process and thus 'regulates' activities occurring abroad; secondly, a PPM may aim at protecting a non-trade concern located outside its own territory. Are both notions problematic, and if so, why?

The following chapter will seek to answer that question and identify the gaps in the existing legal analysis of extraterritorial trade measures under WTO law. Firstly, extraterritoriality in the context of international trade will be discussed; secondly, a closer look will be taken at the jurisdictional scope of different WTO agreements; and thirdly, WTO jurisprudence on jurisdiction and extraterritoriality will be analysed.

3.2 EXTRATERRITORIALITY AND INTERNATIONAL TRADE

3.2.1 Two Notions of Extraterritoriality

Under public international law, extraterritoriality refers to an exercise of jurisdiction (prescriptive, enforcement or judicial) outside a state's territory or jurisdiction.[1] In the context of international trade, it is difficult to adopt that same understanding of extraterritoriality as, by their very nature, trade measures have an impact or effect outside the borders of the country imposing such measures.[2]

A first notion of extraterritoriality relates to PPMs targeting foreign production processes. The measure will only be 'activated' when market access is sought, thus the regulating country is not actually prescribing foreign activity, but conditioning market access upon compliance with the prescribed rules. Enforcement of trade measures occurs within the territory of the imposing member, likely at the border. Producers abroad are still free to produce in their preferred or locally regulated way and their compliance with trade rules is in principle a matter of choice: they are free to choose their export markets. If they choose to export to a market, then they need to comply with that market's rules. Rather than regulating conduct abroad, 'extraterritorial' PPMs *affect* or *incentivize* conduct abroad.[3] They hence do not seem to be prima facie illegal under international law, or their illegality is at least questionable.[4] Non-compliance of a measure will lead to restricted or no market access to the imposing country, the effect of which will be more coercive the more important the market.[5] Extraterritorial trade measures might thus better be defined as measures with an extraterritorial effect or an extraterritorial reach.[6]

---

[1] See Chapter 4 on extraterritoriality under international law.

[2] WTO AB Report, *United States – Import Prohibition of Certain Shrimp and Shrimp Products* WT/DS58/AB/R (1998), para. 121.

[3] Erich Vranes, *Trade and the Environment: Fundamental Issues in International Law, WTO Law and Legal Theory* (Oxford University Press 2009) 174. This will be further discussed in Chapter 4: extraterritorial prescriptive rules might mandate conduct abroad; however, without the enforcement of such rules, their effect or legal power is seriously limited, if not non-existent. It is thus not surprising that the mere exercise of extraterritorial prescriptive jurisdiction is mostly perceived as harmless and does not meet strong opposition. It is rather where states aim to enforce their rules outside their territory that the sovereignty of other states is threatened.

[4] Stefan Zleptnig, *Non-Economic Objectives in WTO Law: Justification Provisions of GATT, GATS, SPS and TBT Agreements*, Vol. 1 (Mads Andenas ed., Martinus Nijhoff Publishers 2010) 308; See Chapter 4 for a further analysis of extraterritoriality and public international law.

[5] Laurens Ankersmit, Jessica Lawrence and Gareth Davies, 'Diverging EU and WTO Perspectives on Extraterritorial Process Regulation' Minnesota Journal of International Law (2012) 21:1, 14, 25. See also Chapter 5 for further comments on market power.

[6] Werner Meng, *Extraterritoriale Jurisdiktion im öffentlichen Wirtschaftsrecht* (Springer 1994) 76.

A second notion of extraterritoriality in a trade context refers to the location of the concern to be protected. Does the measure address environmental concerns located outside the territory of the regulating state? In order to determine whether an 'extraterritorial' npr-PPM can be accepted under WTO law, the real issue is thus not the location of the production process, but the location of the concern. For example, can a European trade measure aiming at the protection of threatened pandas or the pollution of a lake in Indonesia, concerns that are clearly located outside EU territory, be accepted? What about trade measures addressing air pollution or the protection of sea turtle species that cross territorial waters, concerns that are of a transboundary nature? This distinction is crucial to the assessment of extraterritoriality under WTO law. The question is whether WTO Members can only address concerns within their territory, or also concerns outside their territory. A useful distinction introduced by Charnovitz refers to inward-looking measures for npr-PPMs that address concerns within the regulating state, and outward-looking measures for those that address concerns outside the regulating state.[7]

3.2.2 Inward- and Outward-looking Measures

When addressing non-trade concerns, a distinction can be made between inward- and outward-looking measures.[8] Does the measure aim at protecting the environment within the territory of the Member imposing the measure or does the measure aim at a concern outside that territory? In the case of the former no problems seem to arise from a jurisdictional perspective, as those concerns fall within the territorial jurisdiction and sovereign rights of the regulating state – even though the measures might have an effect on other states' exports, such as a ban on asbestos or a ban on hormones-injected beef.

More complex is when the measure is outward-looking, or when a measure is both outward- and inward-looking. For instance, an import ban on skins of seal pups because of public outrage at the killing of baby seals,[9] or a ban on animals pelts from countries where 'internationally

---

[7] Steve Charnovitz, 'The Moral Exception in Trade Policy' Virginia Journal of International Law (1998) 38, 689.

[8] See among others Charnovitz, 1998; Ankersmit, Lawrence and Davies, 2012.

[9] Council Directive 83/129/EEC concerning the importation into Member States of skins of certain seal pups and products derived there from; see also Lüdwig Krämer, 'Environmental Protection and Trade – The Contribution of the

agreed humane trapping standards' have not been upheld,[10] a ban on products made by indentured child labour,[11] a ban on meat products unless the animals were slaughtered 'in a humane way',[12] a ban on tuna that is caught in a manner killing dolphins,[13] or a ban on shrimp harvested with nets that accidentally catch sea turtles.[14] Even though the reasons to address these concerns might be legitimate, the jurisdictional status of these trade measures is less clear, especially when a measure has both an inwardly- and outwardly-directed purpose. For instance, a US law forbidding interstate commerce of human organs has the inwardly directed purpose of preventing an immoral market for organs within the US, while having the outwardly directed purpose of protecting persons abroad from selling organs or being killed for organs.[15] Does an inward-looking link 'trump' the outward-looking purpose? When a measure is only outward-looking, a presumption of unacceptable extraterritoriality arises, as a territorial link between the state and the concern to be protected would be missing. The important questions thus relate to the location of the concern that is pursued through the measure. Is there a (physical) link still with the territory (protection of migratory turtles, protection of air) or not at all (protection of a threatened species elsewhere, protection of labour rights in the producing country)? Can a domestic moral objection suffice to establish a territorial link to protect environmental concerns located abroad? What about the global commons, whereby it is inherent that every state is affected and has an interest in their conservation?

While PPMs might have legitimate purposes, trade law also needs to respect the sovereignty of other WTO Members, as well as the multilateral nature of the trading system and of international law in general. The question thus is whether outward-looking and/or global concerns *could* and

---

European Union' in Rüdiger Wolfrum (ed.), *Enforcing Environmental Standards: Economic Mechanisms as Viable Means?* (Springer 1996).

[10] See Gillian Dale, 'The European Union's Steel Leghold Trap Ban: Animal Cruelty Legislation in Conflict with International Trade' Colorado Journal of International Environmental Law and Policy (1996) 7, 441; Charnovitz, 1998, 23; A Nollkaemper, 'The Legality of Moral Crusades Disguised in Trade Laws: An Analysis of the EC "Ban" on Furs From Animals Taken by Leghold Traps' Journal of Environmental Law (1996) 8:2, 237.

[11] Charnovitz, 1998, 25.

[12] 21 U.S.C. §620(a) (1972).

[13] See GATT Panel, *United States – Restrictions on Imports of Tuna (Mexico)* DS21/R (1991); GATT Panel, *United States – Restrictions on Imports of Tuna (EEC)* DS29/R (1994).

[14] WTO AB Report, *US – Shrimp*.

[15] Charnovitz, 1998, 4.

should be addressed through trade measures. International cooperation and agreements are the primary means to achieve common goals, such as protection of the global environment. However, it is precisely where (ambitious) international agreements are lacking,[16] a well-known problem in the environmental realm, that unilateral trade measures addressing these concerns might stand out as an effective alternative. In that light, an outright prohibition of all npr-PPMs might be throwing out the baby with the bathwater. A more sensible approach is needed to deal with inward- and outward-looking trade measures.

3.3 THE (EXTRA)TERRITORIAL SCOPE OF THE RELEVANT WTO AGREEMENTS

3.3.1 Extraterritoriality under the GATT

No territorial limitation or specification on the 'permissible jurisdictional reach'[17] is included in either the Marrakesh Agreement or the GATT. This means that the GATT does not explicitly limit the location of (environmental, social, political, etc.) concerns that WTO Members may address through trade measures. Based on the idea of reciprocal exchange of benefits,[18] WTO Members can unilaterally decide on their domestic policies and trade measures, as long as they comply with their WTO obligations. The question of which transactions can be regulated unilaterally is subordinate to that of how.[19] Under the GATT, as a first rule, trade measures have to comply with the non-discrimination obligations, that is to say, the principles of MFN and national treatment. If a measure complies with these obligations, a possible extraterritorial effect is ignored. If a measure is inconsistent with substantive obligations, because of, for instance, less favourable treatment of imported like products, a justification needs to

16 Such agreement can be lacking for a number of reasons: because it is not a priority to all states, because the resources or institutions are lacking to reach and administer such agreement, because international negotiations can take a long time etc. See Chapter 4 for a discussion of extraterritoriality in the field of human rights and the matter of universal concerns. It is in the interest of trading partners to not impose absurd requirements, because without any reasonable ground the rule will most likely be considered inconsistent with WTO law, and trading partners might limit trade with the imposing country.

17 See Henrik Horn and Peter C Mavroidis, 'The Permissible Reach of National Environmental Policies' Journal of World Trade (2008) 42:6, 1107, 1108.

18 Preamble Marrakesh Agreement.

19 Horn and Mavroidis, 2008, 1108.

be sought under the exception provisions, such as Article XX GATT.[20] Under this exhaustive list of general exceptions, WTO Members can impose trade restrictive measures on public policy grounds, as long as they meet the standard of necessity,[21] do not constitute 'a means of arbitrary or unjustifiable discrimination' or 'a disguised restriction on trade'.[22] WTO Members hence retain sovereignty over their national policy, as long as that policy is not extended through trade measures for protectionist purposes. The GATT only sets out what is not allowed, rather than establishing common policies that all Members should follow.[23]

A few of the disputes that have come before GATT panels and the WTO DSB contained jurisdictional elements, but the jurisdictional (or territorial) limitation of the WTO agreements has not yet been adequately addressed. This is partly due to the fact that the parties did not make a jurisdictional claim. Panels are limited to an objective assessment of what is before them,[24] and cannot add to the complainant's claims, based on the legal maxim *non ultra petita*.[25] Panels can, however, review the content of their own competence to adjudicate a dispute.[26] This means they can thus verify, on their own initiative, whether they have the competence required to decide the dispute (*Kompetenz-Kompetenz*).[27] In *Mexico – Corn Syrup (Article 21.5 US)*, the AB stated that

> panels have to address and dispose of certain issues of a fundamental nature, even if the parties to the dispute remain silent on those issues. In this regard, we have previously observed that '[t]he vesting of jurisdiction in a panel is a fundamental prerequisite for lawful panel proceedings'. For this reason, panels cannot simply ignore issues, which go to the root of their jurisdiction – that is, to their authority to deal with and dispose of matters. Rather, panels must deal with such issues – if necessary, on their own motion – in order to satisfy themselves that they have authority to proceed.[28]

---

[20] See Chapter 2.

[21] See the different subparagraphs of Article XX GATT for the required degree of necessity.

[22] *Chapeau* Article XX GATT.

[23] Horn and Mavroidis, 2008, 1109.

[24] Article 11 DSU.

[25] Horn and Mavroidis, 2008, 1122; WTO AB Report, *Mexico – Anti-Dumping Investigation of High-Fructose Corn Syrup (HFCS) from the United States* WT/DS132/AB/RW (2001), para. 36.

[26] Horn and Mavroidis, 2008, 1122.

[27] Isabelle Van Damme, 'Inherent Powers of and for the WTO Appellate Body' Graduate Institute Geneve CTEI Working Paper 102 (2008), 17.

[28] WTO AB Report, *Mexico – Anti-Dumping Investigation of High-Fructose Corn Syrup (HFCS) from the United States*, para. 36.

In order to determine whether a panel should, for instance, address an issue of extraterritoriality which has not been raised by the complainant, the question is whether the issues are 'of such a nature that they could have deprived the panel of its authority to deal with a matter'.[29] It is unlikely that the extraterritorial nature of a concern would indeed be considered such a fundamental issue as to put into doubt a panel's jurisdiction. Rather, extraterritorial concerns would form part of an examination of the merits. The Dispute Settlement Understanding (DSU) states that DSB rulings and recommendations 'shall not nullify nor impair benefits accruing to any Member under those agreements, nor impede the attainment of any objective of those agreements'.[30] This implies that, in the absence of explicit claims on jurisdiction, it is still the panel's duty to ensure that the objectives of the WTO agreements are attained, which can involve (and has involved in previous case law) the question whether addressing concerns outside a Member's territory would preclude such attainment.

So far, the extraterritoriality discussion in GATT cases has taken place under Article XX GATT. This does not exclude the possibility of this issue arising under other provisions, for instance, in light of an 'aims and effects'-test or a regulatory purpose-test under a *de facto* discrimination examination under Article III GATT.[31]

3.3.2 Extraterritoriality under the TBT Agreement

During the Tokyo Round (1979) a first attempt to deal with technical barriers to trade was made with the adoption of the GATT Standards Code. The aim of this code was twofold: on the one hand, the GATT parties wanted to achieve greater harmonization through international standards; while at the same time restricting the negative trade effects of national regulations and standards adopted by states pursuing non-trade concerns.[32] The current TBT Agreement was adopted in the Uruguay Round (1994), thereby further developing the original Standards Code. Like GATT and GATS, the TBT Agreement is silent on its jurisdictional scope. As discussed in Chapter 2, it is not clear whether npr-PPMs fall within the scope of the TBT Agreement. Apart from labelling and packaging requirements, there is no textual support in the agreement to conclude that npr-PPMs could fall within its scope. If they would, there is nothing

29 Ibid. para. 53.
30 Article 3.5 DSU.
31 See Chapter 2.
32 Zleptnig, 2010, 367.

to be found in the text or jurisprudence regarding a possible jurisdictional limitation. With regard to labelling, in the *US – Tuna II* case,[33] there was no discussion whether the US could apply dolphin-safe labels to imported tuna. The US differentiated between tuna products on the basis of the area where the tuna was harvested and based on the technique used for fishing. As the US measure mainly served to inform domestic consumers, the fact that the label also had as its objective the protection of dolphins outside US waters did not seem to matter.[34]

Article 2.4 TBT encourages the use of relevant international standards as a basis for Members' technical regulations, unless the international standards do not achieve the legitimate objective pursued. The question is when a standard can be considered relevant to the subject matter of the regulation at issue.[35] For purposes of the TBT Agreement, standards must be approved by an international body, membership of which must be open to the relevant bodies of at least all WTO Members.[36] This interpretation of relevant standards demonstrates that while the TBT Agreement does not impose a hard norm that Members must use the same standards, the use of common standards, adopted by consensus,[37] is highly encouraged. Thus, those PPMs falling within the scope of the TBT Agreement should be based on international standards, unless the regulating state can prove that these standards do not effectively achieve the legitimate objective pursued by the measure.[38]

---

[33] WTO, AB Report, *United States – Measures Concerning the Importation, Marketing and Sale of Tuna and Tuna Products*, WT/DS381/AB/R, 2012.

[34] WTO Panel Report, *United States – Measures Concerning the Importation, Marketing and Sale of Tuna and Tuna Products* WT/DS381/R (2011); WTO AB Report, *United States – Measures Concerning the Importation, Marketing and Sale of Tuna and Tuna Products* WT/DS381/AB/R (2012).

[35] Decision of the TBT Committee on Principles for the Development of International Standards, Guides and Recommendations with Relation to Articles 2, 5 and Annex 3 of the Agreement, G/TBT/1/Rev.9, 2000.

[36] Annex 1.2 to the TBT Agreement; WTO AB Report, *United States – Measures Concerning the Importation, Marketing and Sale of Tuna and Tuna Products*, para. 359.

[37] Explanatory Note to Annex 1.2 TBT Agreement.

[38] Article 2.4 TBT reads as follows: 'Where technical regulations are required and relevant international standards exist or their completion is imminent, Members shall use them, or the relevant parts of them, as a basis for their technical regulations except when such international standards or relevant parts would be an ineffective or inappropriate means for the fulfilment of the legitimate objectives pursued, for instance because of fundamental climatic or geographical factors or fundamental technological problems.'

3.3.3 Extraterritoriality under the SPS Agreement

The SPS Agreement provides a multilateral framework for the use of sanitary (human and animal life and health) and phytosanitary (plant life and health) measures. The SPS Agreement was adopted to address non-tariff barriers resulting from the use of sanitary and phytosanitary measures at national level, and is a further development of Article XX(b) GATT.[39] SPS measures differ considerably throughout countries as each country decides on its own policies regarding the regulation of life, health and safety matters. Perception of risk and the regulatory response to that risk may vary greatly from country to country.[40] Article 1 SPS states that the Agreement applies to 'all sanitary and phytosanitary measures which may, directly or indirectly, affect international trade'. The scope of the SPS Agreement is further clarified in para.1 of Annex A, listing the possible SPS measures. In that list, there is a clear territorial reference in contrast to the other described agreements: every measure aims at the protection of health 'within the territory of the Member'. Outward-looking measures seem thus not to be covered under the SPS Agreement.

3.4 CASE LAW

While there is no official *stare decisis* doctrine in the WTO legal system, in practice, panels and the AB do refer to and rely on precedent.[41] Litigants will thus also rely on previous case law to persuade a panel or the AB. The DSB has interpreted the jurisdictional scope of the GATT in different ways. In the following section, these disputes will be discussed, whereby a distinction will be made between the inward and outward direction of the trade measure at issue. It is generally accepted that the protection of concerns within a Member's territory falls within the scope of Article XX GATT. Disputes dealing with inwardly directed measures will only be briefly mentioned, as it is clear from the panel and AB reports that jurisdiction did not play any significant role in these disputes: jurisdiction is barely, if at all, addressed by parties to the dispute or the adjudicating body. For that reason, this section will mainly focus on the cases

---

[39] Zleptnig, 2010, 117.

[40] Ibid. 332.

[41] WTO, AB Report, *United States – Final Anti-Dumping Measures on Stainless Steel from Mexico*, WT/DS344/AB/R, 2008, paras. 158–162.

dealing with outwardly directed npr-PPMs, as they remain the object of controversy.

3.4.1 Inward-looking

Many, if not all, of the trade measures seeking justification under Article XX GATT have an extraterritorial effect, as in that producers in exporting countries will need to adapt their production and processing methods in order to have access to the market of the imposing Member. As has been explained above, this can be the side-effect of a lawfully applied measure under WTO rules,[42] and it has been generally accepted in the case law that such effect does not lead to violations of the trading rules. Where the inward-looking measures in the following examples of disputes were found inconsistent with a Member's WTO obligations, they failed on grounds other than jurisdiction.

In the first WTO case, *US – Gasoline*, Venezuela and Brazil challenged the US rules discriminating against gasoline imports.[43] The US Clean Air Act was adopted to improve air quality in the most polluted areas of the country by controlling toxic and other pollution caused by the combustion of gasoline manufactured in or imported into the US, whereby baseline levels on chemical characteristics of 1990 could not be exceeded. The rules to determine baseline levels were stricter for imported gasoline than for domestically refined gasoline. The US argued that the Act was aimed at the protection of clean air within the US. Whereas the Panel found that the measures could not be justified under Article XX(g) as the measures did not 'relate to the conservation of exhaustible natural resources', the AB found that they did, but that the conditions of the *chapeau* were not fulfilled. The AB held that with regard to the baseline establishment rules for importers, alternative courses of action were available to the US, which had no discriminatory effect,[44] leading to a finding of unjustifiable discrimination. By protecting clean air *within* the US threatened by the combustion of gasoline, the measure was inward-looking.

In *Brazil – Retreaded Tyres*, Brazil imposed an import embargo on retreaded, but not on new tyres.[45] The measure was based on environmental and health concerns within Brazil, as retreaded tyres have a shorter

---

42 WTO AB Report, *US – Shrimp*, para. 121.

43 WTO AB Report, *United States – Standards for Reformulated and Conventional Gasoline* WT/DS2/AB/R (1996).

44 Ibid. p. 25.

45 WTO AB Report, *Brazil – Measures Affecting Import of Retreaded Tyres* WT/DS332/AB/R (2007).

lifespan than new tyres, and would hence lead to a faster accumulation of waste tyres, thereby providing breeding grounds for mosquito-borne diseases and causing difficult-to-control fires. Disposing of waste tyres furthermore had negative environmental consequences. Both the Panel and the AB accepted the environmental arguments by Brazil, but as the measure discriminated between MERCOSUR and other countries, found the measures to be an arbitrary and unjustifiable discrimination.[46]

In *EC – Asbestos*, Canada challenged French legislation banning the sale of asbestos-containing construction material into its market because of public health reasons.[47] Canada argued that asbestos-containing and asbestos-free materials were like products and should thus receive the same regulatory treatment. The Panel found the measure to be justified under Article XX(b) after finding a violation of Article III:4 GATT, whereas the AB overturned the Panel report and found that the products were unlike due to the health risks as a particular characteristic of asbestos.[48] The measure hence did not violate Article III:4 GATT.

3.4.2 Outward-looking

In contrast to inward-looking disputes, the number of outward-looking adjudicated disputes remains very small. The first dispute dealing with an extraterritorial measure was the GATT case *Belgian Family Allowances*, in which the GATT Panel did not address jurisdiction. The only other outward-looking disputes so far adjudicated by the DSB are the well-known GATT *US – Tuna* disputes, its WTO follow-up *US – Shrimp*, *EC – Tariff Preferences* and *EC – Seal Products*. A couple of cases have furthermore been settled outside the DSB. Members announced they were considering restoring to WTO litigation, but did not follow through,[49] or a request for the establishment of a panel was received (e.g. the EU's request with regard to a Massachusetts law prohibiting government procurement of goods and services from any person doing business with Burma[50] or the

---

46 Ibid. para. 233.

47 WTO AB Report, *European Communities – Measures Affecting Asbestos and Asbestos-containing Products* WT/DS135/AB/R (2001).

48 Ibid. para. 116.

49 See for instance on the EU ban on fur from animals caught with leg hold traps, Dale, 1996; Charnovitz, 1998, 23; Nollkaemper, 1996. States also threatened to bring a claim to the WTO for the EU Aviation Directive, see Chapter 6 on the EU ETS and Aviation.

50 *United States – Measure Affecting Government Procurement*, WT/DS88, panel proceedings suspended.

EU's request with regard to the US Cuba Act regarding trade sanctions against Cuba),[51] but a mutually agreed solution was found in these cases leading to the withdrawal of these requests. Given the political sensitivity of these measures with an extraterritorial effect, one can assume that states prefer to settle these conflicts in diplomatic negotiations, rather than having a technical trade panel decide on it.

Through Article 3.2 DSU, the WTO agreements are generally interpreted following the general international rules of treaty interpretation laid down in the Vienna Convention on the Law of Treaties (VCLT).[52] While not all WTO Members are parties to the VCLT, the AB has recognized the status of VCLT rules on treaty interpretation (Articles 31 and 32) as customary international law.[53] Under Article 31(1) VCLT, a treaty is to be interpreted in good faith. Any interpretation must begin with an examination of the ordinary meaning of the words, read in their context, and in the light of the object and purpose of the treaty involved. The AB has stated that the object and purpose of the treaty as a whole will only be taken into account where the meaning of the text itself and in its context is equivocal or inconclusive, or where further confirmation of the correctness of the reading of the text is desired.[54] When the means of Article 31 VCLT do not resolve a problem of interpretation, Article 32 VCLT provides for supplementary tools of interpretation, including the *travaux préparatoires* and the circumstances of the treaty's conclusion. In the following discussion of case law, one will notice that interpretations of the territorial limitation of Article XX GATT have differed over disputes and time, and no generally accepted position on (extra)territoriality has been articulated so far.

3.4.2.1 *Belgian Family Allowances*

The first dispute under GATT dealing with an outward-looking measure was the *Belgian Family Allowances* case in 1952.[55] Under this dispute dealing with a MFN violation, the jurisdictional issue was not addressed,

---

[51] *United States – The Cuban Liberty and Democratic Solidarity Act*, WT/DS38.

[52] Vienna Convention on the Law of Treaties, 1969, entry into force 27 January 1980, 8 ILM 679. WTO, AB Report, *United States – Standards for Reformulated and Conventional Gasoline*, WT/DS2/AB/R, 1996, p. 16.

[53] WTO AB Report, *Japan – Taxes on Alcoholic Beverages* WT/DS8/AB/R (1996), p. 10.

[54] WTO AB Report, *US – Shrimp*, para. 114.

[55] GATT Panel Report, *Belgium – Family Allowances* G/32 – BISD 1S/59 (1952).

nor did Belgium argue that its measure was justified under Article XX. The case, a very short 1952 GATT Panel report, was the first case addressing the PPM issue in the context of Article I GATT (or GATT in general). Norway and Denmark alleged a violation by Belgium of the MFN principle in Article I GATT, as a tax exemption was given to Sweden and not to them, while the same conditions in all three Scandinavian countries prevailed. At issue was a Belgian law that charged a levy on foreign goods purchased by Belgian government bodies, which was used to broaden the revenue base for Belgium's family allowance programme, which had until then been funded primarily through a payroll tax on Belgian employers.[56] Countries that applied a system of family allowances similar to the Belgian system were exempted from this tax. Sweden received the exemption, while having a similar family allowances programme as Norway and Denmark, who did not get the exemption.

The GATT Panel found a violation of Article I GATT on the mere ground that Belgium treated goods differently based on country of origin, and stated that an exemption had to be granted unconditionally to all GATT contracting parties.[57] The Panel did not look into the Norwegian or Danish policies. No justification through Article XX was argued.[58] Apart from finding an inconsistency with Article I, the Panel added that the Belgian law 'was based on a concept which was difficult to reconcile with the spirit of the General Agreement',[59] without, however, qualifying what exactly was meant with that concept: PPMs, the lack of a link between the product and the purpose of the measure, extraterritorial application or a coercive effect on other governments?

This early GATT dispute is a clear example of an outward-looking measure, whereby Belgium attempted to influence other Members' family allowances system. The purpose of the Belgian measure was not related at all to the end product. It is unknown whether, if the measure had been related to the product, Belgium would have invoked Article XX GATT or whether the Panel would have accepted product-related PPMs under Article I.[60] Remarkable is that Norway and Denmark did not contend that

---

56 Steve Charnovitz, '*Belgian Family Allowances* and the Challenge of Origin-based Discrimination' World Trade Review (2005) 4:1, 7, 8.

57 GATT Panel Report, *Belgium – Family Allowances*, para. 3.

58 According to Charnovitz, even if Belgium would have invoked Article XX as a defence – even under current WTO jurisprudence – Belgium would still have lost the case; See Charnovitz, 2005, 7.

59 GATT Panel Report, *Belgium – Family Allowances*, para. 8.

60 This was later clarified by the Panel in *Indonesia – Autos* (WT/DS54/R, 1998, para. 14.143) finding that an advantage under Article I GATT could not 'be made

the system of exemptions was an Article I violation, but they argued that they deserved the exemption as much as Sweden did.[61] They thus seemed to accept the existence (and GATT-consistency) of 'extraterritorial' conditions as such. It seems as if all parties to the dispute believed that the practice of linking a tax to the government policy in the exporting country would be GATT-consistent, as long as the conditions upon which the tax would be levied were applied even-handedly to all GATT parties. While the case could have been important in determining the jurisdictional scope of trade measures and npr-PPMs, it is now mainly remembered for its very rigorous interpretation of Article I GATT while leaving important issues unresolved.

3.4.2.2 GATT *US – Tuna (Mexico)*

In 1991 the trade-environment debate was brought into the spotlights by the (unadopted) GATT *Tuna – Dolphin* reports. It was the first time that the lawfulness of trade measures with an extraterritorial focus or effect was addressed by a panel. The US prohibited the import of tuna that was caught in a way that resulted in the incidental killing of dolphins. In order to have access to the US market, the measure required that other states prove that they protected dolphins through systems comparable to the US system. In the first case Mexico challenged the provision on the grounds that its tuna exporters were negatively affected. The GATT Panel found that the measures violated Article XI GATT and thus needed to be justified under Article XX. The important question was whether Article XX could be applied for non-economic objectives outside the territory of the imposing Member. The Panel observed that previous panels had interpreted Article XX narrowly, as a limited and conditional exception from obligations under other provisions of the GATT.[62]

The Panel looked at the drafting history of Article XX(b) and came to the conclusion that the concerns of the drafters focused on objectives within the jurisdiction of the importing country.[63] The grounds upon which the Panel came to that conclusion are rather questionable, however. When the GATT 1947 was drafted, there was very little discussion about

---

conditional on any criteria that is not related to the imported product itself'. The Panel in *Canada – Autos* (WT/DS139/R, 2000, para. 10.23) explained unconditionally as 'the extension of [an advantage under Article I:1] may not be made subject to conditions with respect to the situation or conduct' of the exporting country.

[61] Charnovitz, 2005, 12.

[62] GATT Panel, *United States – Restrictions on Imports of Tuna (Mexico)*, para. 5.22.

[63] Ibid. para. 5.26.

its scope, probably because the exceptions were very similar to what could be found in a number of bilateral treaties, as well as in the International Trade Organization (ITO) Charter.[64] The Panel noted that the proposal for Article XX(b) originated from the Draft Charter of the ITO. The exception in the New York draft read: 'For the purpose of protecting human, animal or plant life or health, if corresponding domestic safeguards under similar conditions exist in the importing country.'[65] The latter part of the proviso was later dropped as unnecessary. According to the Panel, this proviso indicates that the drafters focused on life or health of humans, animals or plants within the jurisdiction of the importing country,[66] even though it seems more logical that the reference to the importing country applies to the corresponding domestic safeguards. Furthermore, the Panel might have erred by only looking at the New York draft of the ITO Charter, as the legislative history goes back to the negotiations of the International Convention for the Abolition of Import and Export Prohibitions and Restrictions 1927,[67] which may not support the Panel's interpretation. The general exceptions were negotiated for the 1927 Convention first and were later copied by the ITO Charter.[68] Article 4 of the 1927 Convention contained an exception for trade restrictions imposed for the protection of public health, animals and plants, without any reference to a territorial limitation. Much of the wording of Article 4 is to be found in Article XX GATT today. There is no apparent evidence that Article 4 was limited to a strictly territorial interpretation. The US, for instance, had 'extraterritorial' import prohibitions in effect at the time, such as an import ban on certain whale species, and one can thus assume that they perceived the text of Article XX as including such trade measures.[69]

With regard to Article XX(g), creating an exception for measures relating to the conservation of exhaustible natural resources when made effective in conjunction with restrictions on domestic production, the

---

64 Rainer Grote, 'Article XXIII GATS' in Rüdiger Wolfrum, Peter-Tobias Stoll and Clemens Feinäugle (eds.), *WTO-Trade in Services* (Martinus Nijhoff Publishers 2008) 502.

65 Article 37 1947 New York Draft Charter of the International Trade Organization.

66 GATT Panel, *United States – Restrictions on Imports of Tuna (Mexico)*, para. 5.26.

67 Not entered into force.

68 Salman Bal, 'International Free Trade Agreements and Human Rights: Reinterpreting Article XX of the GATT' 10:1, Minnesota Journal of International Law 62 (2001), 104.

69 Steve Charnovitz, 'GATT and the Environment: Examining the Issues' International Environmental Affairs (1992) 4:3, 203, 209.

Panel referred to a previous GATT Panel interpretation of 'in conjunction with' domestic production restrictions as 'primarily aimed at rendering effective these restrictions'.[70] It then noted that 'a country can effectively control the production or consumption of an exhaustible natural resource only to the extent that the production or consumption is under its jurisdiction' and suggested that Article XX(g) was intended to permit Members to adopt trade measures primarily aimed at rendering effective restrictions on production or consumption within their jurisdiction.[71] While it is logical to conclude that domestic restrictions will take place within a Member's jurisdiction, this reading of the second part of Article XX(g) in no way implies that the exhaustible natural resources as the object of conservation policies also need to be located within that jurisdiction.

The Panel furthermore expressed its concern about an 'extra-jurisdictional interpretation'[72] of Article XX, as such interpretation would allow for unilateral measures that would jeopardize the multilateral framework of the GATT.[73] The US failed to demonstrate that it had exhausted all other reasonable options, such as the negotiation of an international agreement.[74] As has been discussed earlier, unilateralism is related but not identical to extraterritoriality.[75] The Panel's concern seems to have been focused more on the unilateral nature of the measure, rather than the extraterritorial nature of it.

3.4.2.3 GATT *US – Tuna (EEC)*

In the second *Tuna* case, the same US measures were challenged by the EEC and the Netherlands. The GATT Panel followed the first Panel's reference to the term 'extra-jurisdictional' and developed that

---

70 GATT Panel Report, *Canada – Measures Affecting Exports of Unprocessed Herring and Salmon* L/6268 – 35S/98 (1988), para. 4.6. This interpretation has been rejected by the AB in *China – Raw materials*, whereby the AB stated that Article XX(g) permits trade measures relating to the conservation of exhaustible natural resources if such trade measures *work together with* restrictions on domestic production (WTO AB Report, *China – Measures Related to the Exportation of Various Raw Materials* WT/DS394/AB/R (2012), para. 360).

71 GATT Panel, *United States – Restrictions on Imports of Tuna (Mexico)*, para. 5.31.

72 The Panel did not use the term 'extraterritorial' but referred only to 'extra-jurisdictional' application of Article XX, without explaining the relevant distinction (if any distinction) between the two.

73 GATT Panel, *United States – Restrictions on Imports of Tuna (Mexico)*, paras. 5.27, 5.31.

74 Ibid. para. 5.28.

75 See Chapter 1.

argument more explicitly. Since it did not find any interpretative aid in the wording of the relevant provisions, the Panel looked at the context of the other paragraphs of Article XX, such as Article XX(e) relating to products of prison labour (abroad) and observed that it 'could not be said that the GATT proscribed in an absolute manner measures that related to things located, or actions occurring, outside the territorial jurisdiction of the party taking the measure'.[76] The Panel agreed with the US that Article XX(g) could in principle apply to measures aiming at the protection of exhaustible natural resources outside the territory of a state, insofar as international law permits governments to exercise jurisdiction over their nationals and vessels outside their territory.[77] According to the Panel, the drafting history does not support any other conclusion.[78] Measures could apparently be extraterritorial but not extra-jurisdictional.[79]

It then investigated whether trade measures could be allowed to have a coercive effect on other states to change their policy in respect of the exhaustible natural resource in question.[80] It concluded that in the light of the object and purpose of the GATT, allowing such measures would seriously impair the multilateral framework of the GATT.[81] Measures taken so as to force other countries to change their policies cannot be seen as to be 'primarily aimed at' the protection of natural resources, because they were too indirect, and hence the measures could not be justified under Article XX(g).[82] The Panel followed a similar reasoning regarding Article XX(b) and found that measures aiming at the protection of human or animal life outside the jurisdiction of the imposing member did fall within the scope of the provision,[83] in contrast to the findings of the first *Tuna* GATT Panel. In its consideration of 'necessary', it stated that measures that force other states to change their policies cannot be considered necessary. The Panel accepted an earlier definition of 'necessary' to the effect that there must be no less trade

---

[76] GATT Panel, *United States – Restrictions on Imports of Tuna (EEC)*, para. 5.16.
[77] Ibid. para. 5.20.
[78] Ibid.
[79] Ilona Cheyne, 'Environmental Unilateralism and the WTO/GATT System' Georgia Journal of International and Comparative Law (1995) 24:3, 433, 453.
[80] GATT Panel, *United States – Restrictions on Imports of Tuna (EEC)*, para. 5.24.
[81] Ibid. para. 5.26.
[82] Ibid. para. 5.27.
[83] Ibid. para. 5.33.

restrictive alternative measure consistent with the GATT available,[84] but did not exactly follow that definition, as again its argument was based entirely on the directness of the measures. It found the import restrictions to be too indirect as they could not, by themselves, achieve the objective sought since that was dependent upon a change in policies and practices of other countries.[85] Since the US measures were coercive and insufficiently direct, they could not be justified under Article XX(b).[86] The Panel hereby implied that all 'coercive' measures or all PPM measures, as they relate to a process or production beyond the territory of a state, could hence never be necessary or relate to their objective: by their nature they would be too indirect as the achievement of their objective depends upon the change of practices in exporting countries. Bartels has correctly pointed out that the Panel 'mistook an effect of an excess of jurisdiction (coercion) for the rules governing the proper exercise of jurisdiction in the first place'.[87] While it indicated the importance of rules of legislative jurisdiction, it (as well as the first *Tuna* Panel) failed to correctly apply them to the case at hand.

The Panel also shortly referred to the interpretative rules of Article 31(3) VCLT, according to which (a) subsequent agreements and (b) subsequent practice between the parties can be taken into account.[88] The Panel observed that the treaties cited by the parties to the dispute[89] were bilateral or plurilateral and could hence not apply to the interpretation of the GATT. There are no agreements ratified by all Members that establish clear practice of extraterritorial trade restrictive measures. Even though the Panel did not address Article 31(3)(c) VCLT, referring to the 'relevant rules of international law applicable between the parties', it might be useful to complete the reasoning. Article 31(3)(c) does not make other norms of international law directly *applicable* to the dispute, but allows other norms to be used to give proper meaning to the provision. It has been argued that only those treaties that have identical membership as the WTO agreements

---

84 Ibid. para. 5.35.
85 Ibid. para. 5.23.
86 Ibid. para. 5.39.
87 Lorand Bartels, 'Article XX of GATT and the Problem of Extraterritorial Jurisdiction: The Case of Trade Measures for the Protection of Human Rights' Journal of World Trade (2002) 36:2, 353, 390.
88 GATT Panel, *United States – Restrictions on Imports of Tuna (EEC)*, para. 5.19.
89 E.g. GATT Panel, *United States – Restrictions on Imports of Tuna (EEC)*, para. 3.21, referring to the Convention Relative to the Preservation of Fauna and Flora in their Natural State 1993; or Convention on Nature Protection and Wild Life Preservation in the Western Hemisphere 1940.

can be taken into account.[90] This approach has also been adopted by the Panel in *EC – Biotech*, stating:

> it makes sense to interpret Article 31(3)(c) as requiring consideration of those rules of international law which are applicable in the relations between all parties to the treaty which is being interpreted. Requiring that a treaty be interpreted in the light of other rules of international law which bind the States parties to the treaty ensures or enhances the consistency of the rules of international law applicable to these States and thus contributes to avoiding conflicts between the relevant rules.[91]

This approach, while logical, creates significant difficulty, as there are hardly any treaties with identical membership to the WTO. By contrast, the argument has been made that the term 'parties' in Article 31(3)(c) refers to the parties to the dispute.[92] If that were to be the case, then any treaty concluded between the parties to a dispute could be invoked for the interpretation of WTO law. The problem, however, is that such interpretation would only be valid for those parties, and could not count as a legitimate interpretation for all other WTO Members who would, through the interpretation of WTO law, be indirectly bound to a treaty they have never agreed to. Pauwelyn has suggested a middle approach, focusing on the common intentions of all parties. Rather than being formally and legally bound, these common intentions refer to the at least implicit acceptance or tolerance of norms by all WTO parties.[93] Nevertheless, how can one deduce such common intentions of all parties? Would it suffice if a large number of Members support a certain view? What if a large number of small countries are party to an agreement, but a large country is not? Should that make a difference?

For instance, an MEA calling for the imposition of certain trade restrictions, ratified by approximately half of the WTO membership, may constitute significant support that a trade restrictive measure in accordance with that agreement could indeed be necessary for the

---

[90] Zleptnig, 2010, 71.

[91] WTO Panel Report, *European Communities – Measures Affecting the Approval and Marketing of Biotech Products* WT/DS291/R (2006), para. 7.70.

[92] Zleptnig, 2010, 73; Gabrielle Marceau, 'A Call for Coherence in International Law: Praises for the Prohibition Against "Clinical Isolation" in WTO Dispute Settlement' Journal of World Trade (1999) 33:5, 87, 124; Campbell McLachlan, 'The Principle of Systemic Integration and Article 31(3)(c) of the Vienna Convention' International and Comparative Law Quarterly (2005) 54:2, 279.

[93] Joost Pauwelyn, 'The Role of Public International Law in the WTO: How Far Can We Go?' American Journal of International Law (2001) 95:3, 535, 576.

protection of human health under Article XX(b) GATT.[94] There are a number of conventions, which are widely ratified, where an extraterritorial application of trade measures is employed for the protection of global environmental interests, such as the 1989 Basel Convention on the Control of Transboundary Movements of Hazardous Wastes and Their Disposal,[95] prohibiting exports and imports of hazardous and other wastes by parties to the Convention to and from non-party states; or CITES,[96] regulating imports and exports of certain species of animals and plants. If it could be established that the trade-related aspects of these treaties are tolerated by a sizeable number of WTO Members (e.g. half of the WTO Members), these treaties could support an extraterritorial interpretation of Article XX GATT. However, the size of the membership cannot be the decisive factor, as the agreements' relevance to the subject of the dispute as well as the content of the rules need to be taken into consideration when determining whether non-WTO rules can help to interpret WTO provisions.[97]

3.4.2.4 *US – Shrimp*

US – Shrimp is a case very similar in facts to the GATT *US – Tuna* disputes. Instead of tuna and dolphins, in the dispute at hand the US banned the import of shrimp not harvested in a way that was certified as complying with US standards to protect endangered sea turtle. Certifications were issued to countries that had essentially the same protective policy in place, and little leeway was left for alternative programmes. The Panel report was appealed before the AB in the main proceedings, with a follow-up of both Panel and AB proceedings under Article 21.5 DSU.

The Panel emphasized the multilateral nature of the WTO when examining the *chapeau* of Article XX GATT.[98] Unilateral measures would lead to an abuse of the exceptions contained in Article XX and would undermine the WTO trading system.[99] With regard to the 'extra-jurisdictional application of US law' the Panel did not consider the effect outside the juris-

---

94 Ibid. 572.

95 Basel Convention on the Control of Transboundary Movements of Hazardous Wastes and Their Disposal, March 22, 1989, 28 ILM 649.

96 Convention on International Trade in Endangered Species of Wild Fauna and Flora (1973).

97 Marceau, 1999, 124.

98 WTO Panel Report, *United States – Import Prohibitions of Certain Shrimp and Shrimp Products* WT/DS58/R (1998), para. 7.43.

99 Ibid. para. 7.44.

diction of the US as problematic, only when a measure 'operates so as to affect other governments' policies in a way that threatens the multilateral trading system'.[100] The Panel and later the AB emphasized that negotiations of international agreements and standards are desirable. The Panel did not, however, address the difficulty with negotiating such agreements, nor that in the absence of multilateral agreement or binding international standards, unilateral measures might be a more result-oriented solution. International environmental law tends to articulate broad principles rather than concrete compliance measures and that very weakness might necessitate the unilateral adoption of specific implementation measures.[101] The Panel started its analysis of Article XX with the *chapeau* and because of the unilateral and coercive nature of the US measure did not examine the paragraphs.

The AB did not agree with the Panel's finding on unilateralism under the *chapeau* and stated:

> conditioning market access to a Member's domestic market on whether exporting Members comply with, or adopt, a policy or policies unilaterally described by the importing Member may, to some degree, be a common aspect of measures falling within the scope of one or another of the exceptions (a) to (j) of Article XX.[102]

Requiring compliance from exporting countries does not render a measure a priori incapable of justification under Article XX, as this would render the specific exceptions of Article XX inutile.[103] After stating that the Panel incorrectly reversed the order of the two-tier test of Article XX, the AB continued the analysis under Article XX(g). When considering the location of the turtles, the AB refrained from taking any stand on the jurisdictional limitation of Article XX(g), stating:

> We do not pass upon the question of whether there is an implied jurisdictional limitation in Article XX(g), and if so, the nature or extent of that limitation. We note only that in the specific circumstances of the case before us, there is a sufficient nexus between the migratory and endangered population involved and the United States for purposes of Article XX(g).[104]

---

[100] Ibid. para. 7.51.

[101] Chantal Thomas, 'Should the World Trade Organization Incorporate Labor and Environmental Standards?' Washington and Lee Law Review (2004) 61, 347, 365.

[102] WTO AB Report, *US – Shrimp*, para. 121.

[103] Ibid.

[104] Ibid. para. 133.

Even though the AB did not say it in that many words, this sufficient nexus with sea turtles allowed the US to impose these largely outward-looking measures. Some of the turtles migrating through US waters some of the time, sufficed to establish a nexus. Did the AB refer to a territorial link? As the AB did not specify which criteria need to be fulfilled in order to establish a sufficient nexus, this rather broad concept is open for interpretation.[105]

The AB then referred to the possible coercive effect of the US measure when dealing with the *chapeau*, after having found that the conditions of Article XX(g) had been complied with:

> Perhaps the most conspicuous flaw in this measure's application relates to its *intended and actual coercive effect* on the specific policy decisions made by foreign governments (emphasis added). [The measure] in its application, is, in effect, an economic embargo, which requires *all other exporting Members*, if they wish to exercise their GATT rights, to adopt *essentially the same policy* . . . as that applied to . . . US domestic shrimp trawlers (original emphasis).[106]

The AB's interpretation of coercive effect differs from the GATT Panel's interpretation in *US – Tuna.* The AB in *US – Shrimp* could not accept that exporting countries *had to adopt the exact same policy*, rather than adopting a policy of a comparable effect, with a degree of discretion or flexibility; whereas according to the GATT Panel's reasoning in *US – Tuna*, *any measure with extraterritorial effect* was seen as coercive and sufficient to fall outside the scope of Article XX. The AB eventually found the US measure to entail arbitrary and unjustifiable discrimination because of the rigidity and lack of policy discretion for the exporting countries, but did, in principle, accept the fact that WTO Members can impose unilateral measures aiming at concerns outside their territory. The fact that the AB emphasized what it did not decide confirms this point:

> And we have not decided that sovereign states should not act together bilaterally, plurilaterally or multilaterally, either within the WTO or in other international fora, to protect endangered species or to otherwise protect the environment.[107]

The preference for multilateral action over unilateral action was reiterated in both the Panel and the AB report in the Article 21.5 DSU follow-up of the case. However, the AB was also clear on the point that the conclusion

---

[105] See also Chapter 4 on the territoriality principle under international law.
[106] WTO AB Report, *US – Shrimp*, para. 161.
[107] Ibid. para. 185.

of an international agreement cannot in and of itself be a requirement for justification under Article XX GATT.[108]

> WTO Members do have an obligation to seek in good faith multilateral solutions, but if the failure to conclude such agreement would impede justification under Article XX, this would imply that every other WTO Member has, in effect, a veto over that Member's fulfillment of its WTO obligations.[109]

The protection of sea turtles was accepted as a legitimate environmental aim. The AB stated that the words of Article XX must be read by a treaty interpreter 'in the light of contemporary concerns of the community of nations about the protection and conservation of the environment'.[110] The AB hence recognized that the notion of exhaustible resources under Article XX(g) must not be interpreted in light of the original intent of the GATT parties, but in light of present realities and of the emerging necessity to cooperate in the enforcement of conservation of endangered species.[111] This evolutionary interpretation of a changed context is particularly important in the discussions about the environment, as environmental concerns are by their nature not limited to territorial borders; not only endangered species, but also biodiversity and climate change have impact beyond borders.

3.4.2.5 *US – Tuna II (Mexico)*

The most recent *US – Tuna II (Mexico)* dispute dealt with non-discrimination under the TBT Agreement. The measure at issue established conditions for use of a 'dolphin-safe' label on tuna products and conditions for access to that official label. The US differentiated between tuna products on the basis of the area where tuna were harvested and based on the technique used for fishing. While the most important part of the judgment relates to the inclusion of regulatory purpose under the 'less favourable treatment' test of Article 2.1 TBT,[112] the case does raise some questions with regard to the extraterritorial scope. The terms extraterritoriality or extra-jurisdictionality have not been used by the Panel or the AB, but

---

108 WTO AB Report, *United States – Import Prohibition of Certain Shrimp and Shrimp Products, Recourse to Article 21.5 of the DSU by Malaysia* WT/DS58/AB/RW (2001), para. 124.

109 Ibid. para. 123.

110 WTO AB Report, *US – Shrimp*, para. 129.

111 Ibid. para. 130; see also Francesco Francioni, 'Environment, Human Rights and the Limits of Free Trade' in Francesco Francioni (ed.), *Evironment, Human Rights and International Trade* (Hart Publishing 2001).

112 See Chapter 2.

Mexico referred in its claim to the 'coercive objective' of the US measure.[113] The AB accepted the US regulatory objective of its measures as legitimate: 'contributing to the protection of dolphins, by ensuring that the US market is not used to encourage fishing fleets to catch tuna in a manner that adversely affects dolphins'[114] and did not react to the claim of coerciveness.

What does this non-reaction by the AB (and Panel) mean? Pauwelyn wondered whether this meant that WTO Members can be legitimately concerned about the welfare of animals outside their own territory, 'to the extent that the action is limited to avoiding that their own domestic market is used to encourage adversely affecting those animals'.[115] Does this mean that 'extraterritorial' trade measures would now be legitimate and 'territorial' because the imposing Member argues that it does not want its own domestic market to be used to encourage activities it cannot support because of its public policy grounds? Restricting or prohibiting access to a domestic market is exactly the leverage states have through trade measures, and if states use that leverage, is there not always a coercive intention or effect? If the above stated reasoning is indeed what the AB meant, then the discussion on many cases with an extraterritorial element would seem to be closed, as all measures conditioning access to a domestic market through regulatory purposes would be accepted. It could also be, however, that as the measure dealt with a labelling requirement that served to inform domestic consumers, that 'domestic' objective sufficed to no longer consider the 'extraterritorial effects'. Furthermore, labelling requirements can be subject to a more flexible interpretation as their trade restrictive effect is smaller compared to other trade restrictions.[116] If non-related process requirements can be considered to fall within the scope of the TBT Agreement,[117] a restrictive interpretation of the reach of the labelling measure would make no sense. Npr-PPMs will, by their very nature, have an effect on processes occurring outside the territory of the importing state. Nevertheless, in light of the sensitive nature of the topic, further case law clarifying the jurisdictional reach of the TBT Agreement and the coerciveness of measures is to be awaited.

---

113 WTO AB Report, *United States – Measures Concerning the Importation, Marketing and Sale of Tuna and Tuna Products*, para. 335.

114 Ibid. para. 337.

115 Joost Pauwelyn, International Economic Law and Policy blog, 22 May 2015, at http://worldtradelaw.typepad.com/ielpblog/2012/05/index.html.

116 Gabrielle Marceau, 'A Comment on the Appellate Body Report in *EC-Seal Products* in the Context of the Trade and Environment Debate' RECIEL (2014) 23:3, 318, 327.

117 See Chapter 2.

3.4.2.6 *EC – Seal Products*

In the *EC – Seal Products* dispute, Norway and Canada claimed that the EU's ban on seal products was in violation with the GATT and the TBT Agreement. Three exceptions limit the scope of the ban: the import and sale of seal products resulting from traditional hunts by Inuit or other indigenous communities that contribute to their subsistence (the indigenous exception);[118] the importation of goods purchased abroad by travellers for casual or non-commercial use (the travellers' exception);[119] and products resulting from hunting conducted for the sustainable management of marine resources (MRM) to be placed on the market on a not-for-profit-basis (the MRM exception).[120] Seal products originate both from within and outside the EU, and the EU ban was phrased in a neutral way, giving the measure both an inward- and outward-looking element. The arguments of the parties did not focus on the possible extraterritorial aspect and the Panel did not address the issue.[121] Neither did the AB, even though it made the following statement, recognizing the importance of clarity on the (extra)territorial scope of Article XX:

> As set out in the preamble of the Basic Regulation, the EU Seal Regime is designed to address seal hunting activities occurring 'within and outside the community' and the seal welfare concerns of 'citizens and consumers' in EU member states. The Participants did not address this issue in their submissions on appeal. Accordingly, while *recognizing the systemic importance of the question of whether there is an implied jurisdictional limitation* in Article XX(a), and, if so, the *nature and extent of that limitation*, we have decided in this case not to examine this question further.(emphasis added)[122]

The EU had invoked the public morals exception of Article XX(a) GATT to justify its import ban, because of the moral concerns of EU citizens about seals' welfare. As with the labelling issue in *US – Tuna II*, it could be argued that the territorial link of moral concerns *within* the territory of the EU (the morals of EU citizens) 'trumps' the extraterritorial element

---

[118] European Commission Regulation 737/2010 (2010 OJ L216), Article 2.1.
[119] Ibid. Article 2.2.
[120] Ibid.
[121] WTO, Panel Report, *European Communities – Measures Prohibiting the Importation and Marketing of Seal Products*, WT/DS401/R, 2013. For a discussion of possible legal arguments, see Robert Howse and Joanna Langille, 'Permitting Pluralism: The *Seal Products* Dispute and Why the WTO Should Accept Trade Restrictions Justified by Noninstrumental Moral Values' Yale Journal of International Law (2012) 37:2, 367.
[122] WTO AB Report, *European Communities – Measures Prohibiting the Importation and Marketing of Seal Products* WT/DS401/AB/R (2014), para. 5.173.

of seals outside Europe. The question is then whether the public morals exception could then be used to circumvent possible territorial limitations of the environmental exceptions?[123] The *Seal Products* case has not clarified the debate on jurisdiction and extraterritoriality, so further case law on this issue, as well as on the relationship between the public morals exception and the environmental exceptions, is to be awaited.

3.4.2.7 *EC – Tariff Preferences*

In addition to Article XX GATT, WTO Members may justify differential treatment of developing Members based on their Generalized System of Preferences (GSP)[124] through the Enabling Clause.[125] This clause permits developed country Members to grant preferential tariff treatment to products originating in developing countries on a non-reciprocal and voluntary basis under a GSP scheme.[126] GSP schemes are exceptions to Article I GATT, as 'like products' from other industrialized members do not receive the same treatment.[127] Paragraph 3c of the Enabling Clause provides that more favourable treatment for developing countries 'be designed and, if necessary, modified, to respond positively to the development, financial and trade needs of developing countries'. According to the AB, any such needs must be assessed according to an objective standard.[128] It is not required that benefits under the GSP schemes have a territorial link with or an effect on the donor country. GSP schemes shall be non-discriminatory,[129] but differentiation is allowed when based on objective criteria, as has been held by the AB.[130]

---

[123] See Chapter 5 for a discussion of public morals and environmental concerns. See also Barbara Cooreman, 'Testing the Limits of Article XX(a) GATT after *Seals*' Journal of International Trade and Arbitration Law (2016) 5, 519.

[124] As described in the Decision of the Contracting Parties of 25 June 1971, relating to the establishment of 'generalized, non-reciprocal and non-discriminatory preferences beneficial to the developing countries' (BISD 18S/24).

[125] Decision of the Contracting Parties on Differential and More Favourable Treatment, Reciprocity and Fuller Participation of Developing Countries, 28 November 1979, L/4903.

[126] Gracia Marin Duran and Elisa Morgera, 'Case Note: WTO India-EC GSP Dispute: The Future of Unilateral Trade Incentives Linked to Multilateral Environmental Agreements' Review of European Community and International Environmental Law (2005) 14:2, 173, 173.

[127] WTO AB Report, *European Communities – Conditions for the Granting of Tariff Preferences to Developing Countries* WT/DS246/AB/R (2004), para. 99.

[128] Ibid. para. 163.

[129] Footnote 3 to paragraph 2a of the Enabling Clause.

[130] WTO AB Report, *European Communities – Conditions for the Granting of Tariff Preferences to Developing Countries*, para. 162.

The only (adjudicated) case on GSP so far, *EC – Tariff Preferences*, dealt with the EC's GSP scheme, based on Council Regulation 2501/2001/EC applying a GSP scheme for the years 2002–2004.[131] The regulation provided for five preferential tariff arrangements, among which special incentive arrangements for the protection of labour rights, for the protection of the environment (outward-looking), and to combat drug production and trafficking. India requested a panel to consider the consistency with WTO law of all three arrangements, but opted later to limit its legal complaint to the GSP Drugs, which was the only arrangement dealt with by the Panel and the AB. The Panel and the AB found the EC's Drug Arrangements to be inconsistent with the Enabling Clause, as no objective criteria were provided to differentiate between the beneficiaries of the Drug Arrangements and other developing countries that did not receive said treatment. The EC's measure could thus not be justified.

The Panel also considered a justification under Article XX(b) GATT, as the EC argued that narcotic drugs pose a risk to human life and health in the EC (inward-looking) and that the tariff preferences contribute to the fight against illicit production and drug trafficking, thereby reducing the supply to the EC. It held that the policy reflected in the Drug Arrangements was not designed for the purpose of protecting human life or health in the EC and therefore cannot fall under Article XX(b) GATT. This could be understood in two ways: firstly, the measure is not related to health; and secondly, the measure is not related to health *within* the EU. With regard to the first element, according to the Panel, the EC measure aimed at eradication of poverty and promotion of sustainable development in the developing countries.[132] With regard to the second element, if that is what the Panel aimed at, it did not clarify why Article XX(b) would require a territorial link with the imposing Member, and whether a measure aiming at the protection of health in general (including in the exporting countries) could possibly be justified if considered necessary.[133] The Panel continued its analysis of Article XX but found that the measure was neither necessary, nor complied with the conditions of the *chapeau*. The issue was not appealed, and so the AB only addressed the Enabling Clause (under which the legal issue was not territory-related).

---

131 Council Regulation (EC) No 2501/2001 of 10 December 2001 applying a scheme of generalised tariff preferences for the period from 1 January 2002 to 31 December 2004.

132 WTO Panel Report, *European Communities – Conditions for the Granting of Tariff Preferences to Developing Countries* WT/DS246/R (2003), para. 7.201.

133 Ibid. para. 7.210.

3.5 CONCLUSION

The jurisdictional scope of the WTO agreements in general, and more specifically Article XX GATT, is still subject to debate. There is no explicit jurisdictional limitation and neither the *travaux préparatoires* nor any relevant instruments or subsequent agreements reveal the intent of the parties in that regard. In a trade context, extraterritoriality can be understood in two ways: firstly, PPMs can be said to be extraterritorial in that they target production processes abroad (all PPMs are extraterritorial in this sense); and, secondly, they can aim at protecting concerns outside their territory (not all PPMs are extraterritorial in this sense). The first interpretation of extraterritoriality has not been subject to legal scrutiny in the case law. Chapter 4 will elaborate on the extraterritorial reach of PPMs from a public international law perspective.

More is to be said with regard to the second interpretation of extraterritoriality and the question whether npr-PPMs can protect concerns (partly) located outside the territory of the regulating Member. A useful distinction has been made in literature to distinguish between inward- and outward-looking measures: measures that aim at the protection of a non-trade concern within the territory (e.g. air pollution through gasoline combustion), as opposed to measures that aim at the protection of a concern outside the territory of the regulating state (e.g. the protection of a foreign threatened species). From the case law analysis, the following can be noted: firstly, inward-looking measures do not seem to raise jurisdictional issues. Outward-looking measures, protecting concerns outside the territory of a WTO Member, can be accepted when a 'sufficient nexus' to the regulating state exists. It is yet unclear when a nexus could be considered 'sufficient'. Secondly, while a certain coercive effect is inherent to trade measures, measures should allow for sufficient leeway in reaching a required objective. Thirdly, multilateral solutions are preferred over unilateral solutions. However, the question remains to what extent the degree of uni- or multilateralism can determine the acceptability of extraterritorial PPMs.

PART II

Theoretical framework for an extraterritoriality decision tree

4. A broader perspective on extraterritoriality

4.1 INTRODUCTION

The second part of this book engages in a closer study of the concept of extraterritoriality through the analysis of extraterritorial jurisdiction under general public international law as well as two particular fields where extraterritoriality is regularly applied (international human rights law and competition law).[1] The purpose of the comparative analysis is to distil the legal concept of extraterritoriality in different contexts and to analyse under which circumstances states are willing to accept extraterritorial jurisdiction in order to shed light on extraterritoriality in a WTO context. Two notions of extraterritoriality with regard to npr-PPMs have been identified in the previous chapter: firstly, a PPM targets the production process and thus prescribes activities occurring abroad; secondly, a PPM can aim at protecting a non-trade concern abroad. Whereas the former does not seem to be considered problematic in the jurisprudence, the latter element has raised more controversy. Can these extraterritorial aspects of npr-PPMs be justified under WTO law? As has been discussed in the previous chapters, the WTO agreements are silent on their jurisdictional scope, and no systematic approach to jurisdictional questions has yet been developed in the case law. The WTO is not and cannot be a closed system, impervious to other sources of international law[2] and the WTO agreements cannot be interpreted 'in clinical isolation of international law'.[3] Article 31.3(c) of the VCLT, referring to the 'relevant rules of

---

[1] For the elaborate analysis of extraterritoriality in these fields of law, see Barbara Cooreman, *Addressing Global Environmental Concerns through Trade: Extraterritoriality Under WTO Law From a Comparative Perspective* (Leiden: Meijers Research Institute and Graduate School of the Leiden Law School of Leiden University 2016).

[2] Article 3.2 DSU; Stefan Zleptnig, *Non-Economic Objectives in WTO Law: Justification Provisions of GATT, GATS, SPS and TBT Agreements*, Vol. 1 (Mads Andenas ed., Martinus Nijhoff Publishers 2010) 57.

[3] WTO AB Report, *United States – Standards for Reformulated and Conventional Gasoline* WT/DS2/AB/R (1996).

international law', allows panels and the AB to look at non-WTO rules to inform the interpretation of the WTO agreements.[4]

This chapter will first give a theoretical overview of types of jurisdiction and extraterritoriality from a general international law perspective. The section will among others elaborate on the difference between extraterritorial measures *stricto sensu* and measures with an extraterritorial effect in order to determine the legal status of PPMs, not only under WTO law, but also under international law. The general jurisdictional principles will be discussed, identifying which principle(s) could be of relevance to assess the extraterritorial effect of npr-PPMs. The second part of the chapter will give an insight into the rationale of the effects doctrine as applied in (national) competition laws, seeking to determine whether the effects doctrine can be of relevance where the environment of states is affected by activities occurring abroad. Lastly, the analysis will turn to the extraterritorial application of international and regional human rights treaties. What is the legal ground for such extraterritorial application and how far do these extraterritorial obligations extend? The lessons learned will be applied to an environmental context to see whether a more flexible understanding of the boundaries of traditional territorial jurisdiction and sovereignty can be justifiable when transboundary or global concerns are at issue.

4.2 JURISDICTION AND EXTRATERRITORIALITY: A THEORETICAL FRAMEWORK

Sovereign states are the main actors under international law. Under the law of nations, states are equal in legal terms by having uniform legal personality and sovereignty.[5] States have exclusive jurisdiction over their

4 Geraldo Vidigal, 'From Bilateral to Multilateral Law-Making: Legislation, Practice, Evolution and the Future of Inter Se Agreements in the WTO' European Journal of International Law (2013) 24:4, 1027, 1030; Joost Pauwelyn, 'The Role of Public International Law in the WTO: How Far Can We Go?' American Journal of International Law (2001) 95:3, 535, 576.

5 This chapter will focus on the jurisdictional aspect of sovereignty and does not allow an in-depth discussion of what sovereignty as a concept entails today. For interesting contributions on sovereignty see among others Gerard Kreijen et al. (eds.), *State, Sovereignty, and International Governance* (Oxford University Press 2002); Michael Ross Fowler and Julie Marie Bunck, *Law, Power and the Sovereign State: The Evolution and Application of the Concept of Sovereignty* (Pennsylvania State University Press 1995); L Ali Khan, *The Extinction of Nation-States: A World Without Borders* (Kluwer Law International 1996); John

territory and population, while being under a duty of non-intervention with the exclusive jurisdiction of other states.[6] Jurisdiction is a quintessential aspect of sovereignty and refers to a state's competence under international law to regulate the behaviour of its nationals (natural and legal persons) and persons present in its own territory. Only with the consent of another state, can a state intervene on the territory of that other state, outside its own jurisdiction. There can be overlap in jurisdiction, however, when for instance a national of state A breaks the law in country B. In an increasing number of areas, jurisdiction is being exercised extraterritorially because it is required by the subject matter.[7] The fact that jurisdiction is so closely associated with sovereign authority infuses it with conflict-generative potential.[8] States have the highest power within their territory, but where their actions affect other states international law comes into play. Wherever its international implications are concerned, jurisdiction is limited by rules of international law.[9] Public international law provides the principles under which states can exercise jurisdiction,[10] whereas private international law will fill in the limits of jurisdiction and determine through conflict rules which forum is most appropriate and which law will apply.[11]

The general international law permissive principles for jurisdiction depend on the type of jurisdiction being exercised. Different types of jurisdiction can be identified. Firstly, the power to make laws or rules or *prescriptive* jurisdiction (also termed legislative jurisdiction or *compétence normative)*; secondly, the power to enforce those rules or *enforcement* jurisdiction (executive jurisdiction or *compétence d'exécution*); and thirdly, *judicial* jurisdiction (adjudicatory jurisdiction): the power to hear and decide on matters that have occurred in the territory and abroad. This latter form of jurisdiction is often designated as part of one or both of the

---

H Jackson, 'Sovereignty-Modern: A New Approach to an Outdated Concept' American Journal of International Law (2003) 97:4, 782.

6 James Crawford, *Brownlie's Principles of Public International Law* (8th edn., Oxford University Press 2012) 447.

7 For instance, criminal law, data protection, internet law, anti-fraud rules, competition law, international human rights law. See Cedric Ryngaert, *Jurisdiction in International Law* (2nd edn., Oxford University Press 2015).

8 Dan E Stigall, 'International Law and Limitations on the Exercise of Extraterritorial Jurisdiction in US Domestic Law' Hastings International and Comparative Law Review (2012) 35:2, 323, 328.

9 Frederick A P Mann, 'The Doctrine of Jurisdiction in International Law' Recueil des Cours of The Hague Academy of International Law (1964) 111, 1, 17.

10 See Section 4.3.

11 Mann, 1964, 19.

former categories.[12] Judicial jurisdiction can be categorized as prescriptive when courts interpret the jurisdictional scope of legal acts, or as part of enforcement jurisdiction, when laws are given effect through courts.[13] Where a court convicts, sentences and punishes, it is also exercising enforcement jurisdiction.[14] The fact that a court can deal with a matter that has occurred abroad does not necessarily mean that domestic law will be applied to that matter. Private international law regulates the appropriate forum as well as the law to be applied in civil and commercial matters.[15]

The different types of jurisdiction lead to different degrees of intrusiveness when exercised extraterritorially.[16] The exercise of enforcement jurisdiction outside a state's territory is the most problematic: absent consent of the territorial state, enforcement abroad is clearly intruding on the sovereign domain of other states. Enforcement abroad can take different forms, including physical force by state organs or investigations in another country in light of, for instance, criminal, administrative or fiscal procedures.[17] Prescriptive jurisdiction strictly speaking is a less obvious intrusion. States may prescribe norms governing persons, property or conduct outside its territory. The mere act of prescribing rules to subjects outside a state's territory does not necessarily need to have an impact on other states, if there is no attempt to enforce these rules outside that

[12] International Bar Association – Legal Practice Division, *Report of the Task Force on Extraterritorial Jurisdiction* (2009), 8. Authorities differ over whether judicial jurisdiction represents a separate form of jurisdiction. Brownlie for instance distinguishes prescriptive and enforcement jurisdiction (Crawford, 2012) whereas Shaw distinguishes legislative, executive and judicial jurisdiction (Malcolm N Shaw, *International Law* (6th edn., Cambridge University Press 2008)). The Third Restatement on Foreign Relations Law also distinguishes jurisdiction to prescribe, adjudicate and enforce.

[13] In criminal law legislative jurisdiction and judicial jurisdiction are one and the same: if a court has jurisdiction, it applies its own law; if the *lex fori* applies, then the court has jurisdiction. In civil law, these two do not necessarily coincide: a court may have jurisdiction and yet apply foreign law, while a state may legislate for cases which fall beyond the jurisdiction of its courts. (Michael Akehurst, 'Jurisdiction in International Law' British Yearbook of International Law (1972–1973) 46, 145, 179.)

[14] International Bar Association – Legal Practice Division, *Report of the Task Force on Extraterritorial Jurisdiction*, 10.

[15] For instance, under Council Regulation (EC) No 44/2001 of 22 December 2000 on jurisdiction and the recognition and enforcement of judgments in civil and commercial matters (Brussels I – Regulation).

[16] Andrea Bianchi, 'Comment on Harold G. Maier – Jurisdictional Rules in Customary International Law' in Karl M. Meessen (ed.), *Extraterritorial Jurisdiction in Theory and Practice* (Kluwer Law International 1996) 78.

[17] Mann, 1964, 138.

territory. Nevertheless, it is legitimate to expect that a state wants to give effect to its rules prescribed. Such enforcement of rules can very well happen *within* the territory of a state, and would thus be territorial. PPMs illustrate this well: even though a PPM might prescribe standards for a production process abroad, the rules will only be enforced within the territory (or at the border by denying access to the territory). Without market access, the prescribed standards will remain without effect for foreign producers. They will become effective only once a territorial link has been established (in other words where the application of rules has been 'activated' through a territorial connection, for instance entering the market). It has been argued that because of that 'market trigger' npr-PPMs are not extraterritorial as 'nothing that has happened outside the border attracts, by itself, any criminal or civil sanction. Foreign producers may use whatever processes they want, and use them with impunity. The only thing they cannot do is bring products produced through certain processes into the country.'[18]

An implicit reference to 'market activation' can also be found in the Court of Justice of the European Union's (CJEU) reasoning in the ATAA-case on the EU ETS[19] whereby non-EU flight operators would be included in the EU ETS for their emissions of entire flights (both within and outside EU airspace) when landing or departing from EU airports. The Court referred to the physical presence of such operators in the EU at the moment of landing or departing, and did not see any extraterritorial application of rules because of this territorial trigger. However, to entirely deny an extraterritorial aspect here would stretch the concept of territoriality too much. The controversy and proposed countermeasures by other states in reaction to the EU's aviation measures, for instance, demonstrate the sensitive nature of these 'territorial measures'.[20] It is

---

[18] Robert Howse and Donald Regan, 'The Product/Process Distinction – An Illusory Basis for Disciplining "Unilateralism" in Trade Policy' European Journal of International Law (2000) 11:2, 249, 274.

[19] CJEU Grand Chamber, *Air Transport Association of America et al. v Secretary of State for Energy and Climate Change* C-366/10 (21 December 2011), para. 125.

[20] A coalition of 26 countries opposing the EU ETS signed the New Delhi Agreement, including India, the US, China, the Russian Federation, Japan, Brazil and Saudi Arabia. ('coalition of the unwilling'). The US adopted the 'European Union Emissions Trading Scheme Prohibition Act' in 2011, making it illegal for US airlines to comply with the EU ETS requirements. China has also forbidden its airlines to comply with EU ETS obligations, after blocking a billion-dollar order of Airbus aircrafts by Hong Kong Airlines, citing that as a retaliatory measure against the EU ETS. See also Lorenzo Schiano di Pepe, 'European Union Climate

thus clear that different forms or 'degrees' of extraterritoriality can be discerned.

In order to classify a measure as extraterritorial, Bartels proposes to consider whether a measure is *defined* by something located or occurring abroad.[21] A mere impact on activities or persons abroad cannot suffice, as practically all economic legislation will have some impact abroad.[22] Whether a measure is defined by something abroad can be hard to determine, however. For instance, if a domestic regulation prescribes certain standards on emissions for production of cement, and these standards are applied to imported cement as well, that measure has the extraterritorial effect of prescribing production standards abroad, but applies equally in law and in fact to domestic and imported goods, and is thus not *per se* defined by something occurring abroad. In my view, whether there is any discriminatory or protectionist nature needs to be determined in an evaluation of the application of the rule in *law* and in *fact*, but the extraterritorial character of the rule does not change.

Meng suggests that a measure is extraterritorial if its effects abroad are substantial, foreseeable and not reasonable. He distinguishes between extraterritorial measures and legislation with extraterritorial links.[23] Both may influence what is occurring abroad, but the first category is characterized by *its intended coercive* effect on the addressee abroad, while mere factual foreign effects are not necessarily characterized by such an intention (but can be).[24] Npr-PPMs would fall within the latter category. According to Meng, npr-PPMs are not extraterritorial, not even when the regulatory objective of a certain measure – for instance protection of the environment – is focused on production processes, both domestic and abroad.[25] The extraterritorial effects of trade measures follow naturally from a cross-border economic order and must thus be considered factual

---

Law and Practice at the End of the Kyoto Era: Unilateralism, Extraterritoriality and the Future of Global Climate Law Governance' in Robert Percival, Jolene Lin and William Piermattei (eds.), *Global Environmental Law at a Crossroads* (Edward Elgar Publishing 2014) 292. See also Chapter 7 on the EU ETS Aviation measure.

[21] Lorand Bartels, 'Article XX of GATT and the Problem of Extraterritorial Jurisdiction: The Case of Trade Measures for the Protection of Human Rights' Journal of World Trade (2002) 36:2, 353, 381.

[22] Bartels, 2002, 379. See also WTO AB Report, *United States – Import Prohibition of Certain Shrimp and Shrimp Products* WT/DS58/AB/R (1998), para. 121.

[23] Werner Meng, *Extraterritoriale Jurisdiktion im öffentlichen Wirtschaftsrecht* (Springer 1994) 75, 742.

[24] Ibid. 86.

[25] Ibid. 77.

extraterritorial effects. He argues that lawful extraterritorial regulation is an 'indispensable factor of economic self-determination of States, i.e. of their freedom to reconcile economic needs with other political aims'.[26]

Scott makes a conceptual distinction between 'extraterritorial measures' and 'measures giving rise to territorial extension'.[27] Extraterritorial measures are defined as measures that 'impose obligations on persons who do not enjoy a relevant territorial connection with the regulating state',[28] whereas measures of territorial extension are 'triggered by a territorial connection but in applying the measure the regulator is required, as a matter of law, to take into account conduct or circumstances abroad'.[29] The circumstances that are to be taken into account can variably be defined by individual transactions (conduct exclusively related to that transaction, such as PPMs linked to the production process of a particular import product, irrespective of their origin) or can be countrywide (for instance, whether a certain country adopted its own measures aiming at the same objective).[30]

All three approaches imply that 'real' extraterritorial measures are more intrusive to the jurisdiction and sovereignty of other states than measures with an extraterritorial effect or of territorial extension. Under the latter two approaches it can be argued that trade measures, and in particular npr-PPMs, are not to be considered strictly extraterritorial. However, just as not all extraterritorial measures are by their nature unacceptable, perhaps not all measures with territorial extension should be considered acceptable. It is here that the public international law rules on jurisdiction (permissive principles) can be of help. Can these principles be relied upon to determine whether an environmental concern abroad is a sufficiently strong nexus to 'justify' the extraterritorial *effect* of the measure? The extraterritorial effect of npr-PPMs is then not as much a pure jurisdictional question, but rather part of the substantive analysis of the measure. Nonetheless, for lack of rules governing substantive exterritorial effects, it is submitted that the general jurisdictional principles are relevant guidance for this question.

---

[26] Ibid. 752.

[27] Joanne Scott, 'Extraterritoriality and Territorial Extension in EU Law' American Journal of Comparative Law (2014) 62, 87, 90.

[28] For instance, US sanctions against Iran.

[29] For examples of measures with territorial extension in different policy domains, see Joanne Scott, 'Extraterritoriality and Territorial Extension in EU Law' The American Journal of Comparative Law (2014) 62, 87, 96.

[30] Ibid. 106.

4.3 PERMISSIVE PRINCIPLES OF JURISDICTION

Under public international law, two main approaches can be discerned with regard to jurisdiction. Either states are allowed to exercise jurisdiction as they see fit, unless there is a prohibitive rule to the contrary; or states are prohibited from exercising jurisdiction, unless there is a permissive rule to the contrary.[31] State practice and customs incline towards a territoriality approach, whereby states can only exercise jurisdiction outside their territory through a *permissive* rule of international law.[32] These permissive rules of customary international law with regard to prescriptive jurisdiction are based on the broad principle that there needs to be a sufficiently close connection between the state and the matter to be regulated.[33] These principles were outlined in the Harvard Research on International Law, which was carried out in the 1920s and 1930s in an effort to codify the international rules of jurisdiction.[34] The later American Law Institute's Restatements (Second and Third) on Foreign Relations Law can be seen as its follow-up.[35] The fact that a permissive principle allows a state to exercise prescriptive jurisdiction outside its territory does by no means entail that that state is also entitled to enforce its laws extraterritorially. For instance, a state may ask all its nationals (including

---

[31] Ryngaert, 2015, 29. The Permanent Court of Justice in the 1927 Lotus case, the only case in which an international body expressed a general position on extraterritorial jurisdiction adhered to the approach that states are allowed to exercise jurisdiction, unless a prohibitive rule would preclude that (Permanent Court of International Justice *S.S. Lotus* Series A, No 10 (7 September 1927)). It is questionable whether *Lotus* is still good law today though, as extraterritorial jurisdiction seems to be much more restricted than *Lotus* would imply.

[32] Restatement of the Law (Third) on Foreign Relations Law of the United States (1986); International Law Commission, *Report on the Work of the Fifty-eighth Session – Annex V: Extraterritorial Jurisdiction* (2006), 231; International Bar Association, *Report of the Task Force on Extraterritorial Jurisdiction* (2009), 9; Mann, 1964, 36.

[33] Crawford, 2012, 457.

[34] 'Harvard Research on International Law: Jurisdiction with Respect to Crime' 29: supplement 1, American Journal of International Law (1935), 435, 445.

[35] Restatement volumes are codifications of case law with highly persuasive authority as they are built on input from academics, attorneys and judges. They seek to inform about general principles of common law. The Restatements are extensively cited by courts throughout the US. To date there have been three series of Restatements, all published by the American Law Institute. The Third Restatement dates from 1986 and the ALI is currently working on a Fourth Restatement. Both the Harvard principles and the Restatement aim to depict the global status of jurisdictional principles, rather than only the US position on the matter.

those living abroad) to complete military service, but cannot send officers to neighbouring states to bring its nationals within the state's boundaries to comply with that duty.[36]

4.3.1 Subjective Territoriality Principle

The starting point for jurisdiction is that all states have competence over events occurring and persons present (either nationals, residents or otherwise) within their territory.[37] This is the most common and least controversial basis for jurisdiction and entails that states may prescribe laws within their territory. One can discern *subjective* territoriality, which creates jurisdiction over crimes or acts commenced within the state even if completed or consummated abroad, and *objective* territoriality, according to which jurisdiction is founded when any essential constituent element of a crime or act is consummated on the forum state's territory.[38] The objective territoriality principle is also called the effects doctrine and will be further discussed at Section 4.3.2.

When the AB in *US – Shrimp* referred to a sufficient nexus requirement in relation to the migratory sea turtles in and outside US waters,[39] it seemed to justify its position by relying on the territoriality principle. The GATT does not limit its territorial scope in any way and the AB did not clarify why it found it needed to establish a territorial link.[40] The AB did not elaborate on the concept of 'sufficient nexus', but the notion bears resemblance to what has been proposed by Mann: rather than a strict territorial link, he proposed instead to rely on a 'meaningful connection' or 'genuine link' between the regulating state and the matter being regulated. He referred to a connection, 'so close, so substantial, so direct, so weighty, that legislation in respect of [the given set of facts] is in harmony with international law', adding that a 'merely political, economic, commercial or social interest does not in itself constitute a specific connection'.[41] It is unclear whether the protection of environmental global commons could

---

36 Mann, 1964, 13.

37 International Bar Association – Legal Practice Division, *Report of the Task Force on Extraterritorial Jurisdiction* 11. For a historical overview of the developments of the territoriality principle, see Ryngaert, 2015, 50.

38 Crawford, 2012; Harold G Maier, 'Jurisdictional Rules in Customary International Law' in Karl M Meessen (ed.), *Extraterritorial Jurisdiction in Theory and Practice* (Kluwer Law International 1996) 67.

39 See Chapter 3 for a discussion of the case, as well as Chapter 6 for the case revisited.

40 WTO AB Report, *US – Shrimp*, para. 133.

41 Mann, 1964, 49.

be seen as a sufficiently close connection for all states. The objective territoriality principle or the effects doctrine could be more relevant to strengthen jurisdictional claims for environmental matters.

4.3.2 Objective Territoriality Principle or Effects Doctrine

The objective territoriality principle or effects doctrine permits a state to exercise jurisdiction with regard to activities that originate abroad but which have a substantial, direct and foreseeable effect upon or in its national territory.[42] The effects doctrine is only recognized as a separate legal basis (rather than an interpretation of the territoriality principle) by a few countries, such as the US, Brazil and Singapore. The Third Restatement of Foreign Relations Law refers explicitly to the effects doctrine, referring to foreign conduct that has or is intended to have substantial effects.[43] The effects doctrine is best known from its application under competition law, which will be discussed in greater detail below at Section 4.4. The existence of direct and substantial effects[44] on the state's territory, whether on its economy, or, for instance, on its air, water or soil, would support a finding of a connection, link, or legitimate interest. The effects doctrine or objective territoriality principle could be relevant for assessing the extraterritorial character of npr-PPMs when states can demonstrate that their environment is affected by what is the foreign production process and the environmental threat.[45]

4.3.3 Active Personality Principle

Under the nationality or active personality principle states are entitled to exercise jurisdiction over its nationals, even when they are outside the territory of that state.[46] The nationality principle might easily create overlap in jurisdiction in cases of double nationality or cross-border movement, and states can place limitations on the nationality principle by confining

---

[42] See also amongst others Jason Coppel, 'A Hard Look at the Effects Doctrine of Jurisdiction in Public International Law' Leiden Journal of International Law (1993) 6:1, 73.

[43] Restatement of the Law (Third) on Foreign Relations Law of the United States §402(1)(c).

[44] Ibid.

[45] See Section 4.4.2.

[46] In private international law, national law often follows the national outside the territory as far as his personal status is concerned. Courts may thus apply foreign law provided it does not violate domestic law. See Ryngaert, 2015, 104.

it to serious offences, for instance.[47] Such restrictions are not required by international law; states have the unlimited right to base jurisdiction on the nationality of the accused.[48] Variations to the nationality principle could be an active personality application to residents of the prosecuting state, or the flag state for crew of merchant vessels.[49] An exercise of prescriptive jurisdiction does not mean that the prescribed rules can be enforced extraterritorially: enforcement always requires the consent of the territorial state. As long as the national is abroad, the effect of the prescribed rule may be limited without enforcement, but nationals can be bound by their home country laws and face enforcement when they return to that home country.

The nationality principle is of little help to the discussion on npr-PPMs, based on the premise that the producers of the imported goods are not nationals of the market of entry.

4.3.4 Passive Personality Principle

According to the passive personality principle, a state may exercise jurisdiction over aliens for acts committed abroad that are harmful to nationals of the forum state, even where these aliens are not within the forum's state territory.[50] This principle has stirred more controversy than the territoriality or active personality principles as it is perceived as quite aggressive. According to Mann, the passive personality principle 'should be treated as an excess of jurisdiction'.[51] It would imply that people living in an international city could within the hour be subject to a multiplicity of foreign criminal codes.[52] Nevertheless, the passive personality principle is today recognized as legitimate with regard to certain crimes, such as international terrorism.[53] The principle also finds recognition in criminal law treaties, where *aut dedere aut iudicare* provisions authorize (not compel) protection of nationals.[54] State practice remains limited, however, as only

---

[47] Ibid. 105.

[48] Akehurst, 1972–1973, 156.

[49] Ibid.

[50] Crawford, 2012, 461.

[51] Mann, 1964, 92.

[52] Dissenting Opinion Mr. Moore to the *Lotus* case, Permanent Court of International Justice *S.S. Lotus*, p. 92.

[53] Shaw, 2008, 666. See for instance the US Anti-Terrorism Act 1986.

[54] E.g. Article 4(b) of the Convention of Offences Committed on Board Aircraft, Tokyo, 14 September 1963, 220 UNTS 10106; Article 6(2)(b) of the Convention for the Suppression of Unlawful Acts Against the Safety of Maritime

a few states have actually applied their laws in this way.[55] Outside the realm of criminal law, the passive personality principle has little relevance.

4.3.5 Protective Principle

Under the protective principle, states can assert jurisdiction over acts committed abroad which (might) harm security interests, the territorial integrity, political independence or other key interests of the state.[56] The principle is well established, but in addition to a required sense of gravity, it remains unclear which interests could fall under the protective principle. The principle has been abused in the past: during the Cold War the protective principle was used to harm other states rather than safeguard a state's own political independence, and at that point, lost its validity.[57] Nevertheless, the protective principle exists mainly because there can easily be a gap in the domestic law of one state when it comes to offences against the security and integrity of foreign states, such as, for instance, the act of treason.[58] Through an extraterritorial application of laws, each state can thus determine their own vital interests and act accordingly. In practice states make only limited use of the protective principle, and when they do, the circumstances prove uncontroversial for the assertion of jurisdiction, such as forgery, counterfeiting of foreign currency or false visa claims.[59] The protective principle can also be discerned in the practice of trade restrictions or boycotts. Article XXI GATT authorizes trade restrictions in order to protect national security. Secondary boycotts, whereby states boycott foreign actors who have commercial relations with a boycotted state and which are thus extraterritorial in nature, may be premised on the protective principle.[60]

Navigation, Rome, 10 March 1988, 222 UNTS 29004; Article 5(1)(c) of the UN Torture Convention, New York, 10 December 1984, 1465 UNTS 85.

55 The International Criminal Court may not exercise jurisdiction based on the passive personality principle, but only based on the territoriality or active personality principle (Article 12 Rome Statute).

56 Akehurst, 1972–1973, 158.

57 Ibid.

58 Shaw, 2008, 667.

59 Cedric Ryngaert, *Jurisdiction in International Law* (edition by Vaughan Lowe, Oxford University Press 2008) 99.

60 Ibid. For instance in 1996 the US enacted the Cuban Liberty and Democratic Solidarity Act (Helms-Burton), (Public Law 104th-114, 12 March 1996, 110 Stat 785, 22 USC §6021) after two US planes were downed in Cuba. Apart from a comprehensive economic boycott of Cuba, the Act prohibited any person (of whatever nationality) from dealing in confiscated property in Cuba belonging

Even though the exact limitations of the protective principle are unclear (i.e. which interests could be seen as key interests of a state), it is questionable whether the protection of the environment could be seen as such an interest, although for some countries, current environmental challenges do form an actual and realistic threat to the very existence of their country and territory.[61] In that way, the protective principle could offer an additional basis supporting the urgency of certain acts with extraterritorial effects.[62] However, as with the territoriality principle, rather than serving as a free-pass, reliance on the protective principle would need to be supported by more concrete arguments based on the context and effect of the act in question.

4.3.6 Universality Principle

Universal jurisdiction amounts to the assertion of (criminal) jurisdiction for individual crimes in breach of international law, without necessarily requiring a specific link with the forum state: the character of the crime concerned is more relevant. The principle can be invoked in respect of particularly heinous crimes that are a threat to the international order, namely war crimes, genocide, crimes against humanity, slavery and

---

to American citizens and visas would be refused to any person that trafficked or owned such confiscated property, as well as to his or her family. The US seemed to justify the extraterritorial scope of the Act under the protective principle where it considered that Cuba formed a national security threat to the US (Section 2(28); Section 3(3)). The US Act was met with strong opposition: the EU challenged the Act before a WTO panel (suspended) and blocking legislation was adopted. (Council Regulation (EC) 2271/96 of 22 November 1996 Protecting Against the Effects of the Extraterritorial Application of Legislation Adopted by a Third Country, and Actions Based Thereon or Resulting Therefrom).

[61] See for instance Walter Kälin, 'Displacement and Climate Change: Towards Defining Categories of Affected Persons' Working Paper submitted by the Representative of the UN Secretary-General on the Human Rights of Internally Displaced Persons, 25 August 2008; Walter Kälin and Nina Schrepfer, 'Protecting People Crossing Borders in the Context of Climate Change Normative Gaps and Possible Approaches' UNHCR, PPLA/2012/01, 2012. Several scenarios are identified that could cause environmentally induced movements: sudden onset disasters (e.g. hurricanes, floods), environmental degradation (e.g. sea-level rise, desertification), slow onset events for low lying small island states (resulting in loss of territory), resource stress triggering disturbances, violence and armed conflict. See also Pierre-Marie Dupuy and Jorge E Vinuales, *International Environmental Law* (Cambridge University Press 2015) 369.

[62] See e.g. Felicity Deane, 'The WTO, the National Security Exception and Climate Change' Carbon and Climate Law Review (2012) 2, 149, in which she explores the options to rely on Article XXI for climate change purposes.

piracy.[63] There has been much debate whether a link with the state is required, or whether states can rely on the principle without any link at all.[64] If a defendant can be tried based on another basis of jurisdiction (such as the territorial principle, so that the defendant will be tried in the state where the acts were committed), that approach should be preferred.[65] Only a few states have exercised universal jurisdiction,[66] but few states oppose it.[67] A number of treaties explicitly authorize or even require the exercise of (quasi-)universal criminal jurisdiction, such as the UN Torture Convention[68] or the Geneva Conventions,[69] the latter being ratified by virtually all states.[70] Such treaties are frequently characterized by the

---

63 Crawford, 2012, 468.

64 See for instance, International Court of Justice *Arrest Warrant of 11 April 2000 (Democratic Republic of Congo v Belgium)* ICR Rep. (2002), p. 3.

65 International Law Association, *Final Report on the Exercise of Universal Jurisdiction in Respect of Gross Human Rights Offences* (2000), 20; The Princeton Principles on Universal Jurisdiction (2001), Princeton University, Principle 8.

66 For instance, Belgium, Spain, the US. A comprehensive study from 2011 by Langer has found that only thirty-two such cases have gone to trial since World War II. See Maximo Langer, 'The Diplomacy of Universal Jurisdiction: The Political Branches and the Transnational Prosecution of International Crimes' American Journal of International Law (2011) 105:1, 1, 7. See also Eugene Kontorovich, 'Kiobel Surprise: Unexpected by Scholars but Consistent with International Trend' Notre Dame Law Review (2014) 89, 1671, 1684.

67 The UK for instance has long been opposed to the principle as it adhered to a true territoriality principle, but arrested Pinochet in 1998 based on an international arrest warrant issued by a Spanish judge. (*R v Bow Street Metropolitan Stipendiary Magistrate, Ex Parte Pinochet Ugarte,* [1998] UKHL 41; 3 WLR 1456 (HL 1998)); Menno T Kamminga, 'Universal Civil Jurisdiction: Is It Legal? Is It Desirable?' American Society of International Law Proceedings (2005) 99, 123, 124; Ryngaert, 2008, chapter 4.5; UN Secretary-General, *The Scope and Application of the Principle of Universal Jurisdiction: Report of the Secretary-General* (United Nations 2011)

68 Convention Against Torture and Other Cruel, Inhuman or Degrading Treatment or Punishment, UN Doc. A/39/51 (1984), 1465 UNTS 85.

69 International Committee of the Red Cross, Geneva Convention for the Amelioration of the Condition of the Wounded and Sick in Armed Forces in the Field (I), 1949, 75 UNTS 31; Geneva Convention for the Amelioration of the Condition of Wounded, Sick and Shipwrecked Members of Armed Forces at Sea (II), 1949, 75 UNTS 85; Geneva Convention Relative to the Treatment of Prisoners of War (III), 1949, 75 UNTS 135; Geneva Convention Relative to the Protection of Civilian Persons in Time of War (IV), 1949, 75 UNTS 287.

70 Cedric Ryngaert, 'Universal Tort Jurisdiction over Gross Human Rights Violations' Netherlands Yearbook of International Law (2007) 38:3, 3, 16; Article 5.2 of the UN Torture convention; articles 49/50/129/146 of the 1949 Geneva Conventions; see also Article 5.2 of the Montreal Convention for the Suppression of Unlawful Acts Against the Safety of Civil Aviation; Article 3.2 of the Convention on the Prevention and Punishment of Crimes Against Internationally

obligation of *aut dedere aut iudicare*: a state should either try the accused when present in its territory or extradite him/her to a state party that is willing to do so.[71]

Universal jurisdiction is often equated with criminal jurisdiction. However, states may also be willing to establish universal *civil* jurisdiction, thereby allowing their courts to hear complaints for damages by victims of serious infringements of international law, such as serious human rights violations.[72] The argument is that civil remedies should be available to the victims of criminal acts of universal concern,[73] as is already a possibility for breaches of domestic criminal law in virtually all domestic legal systems.[74] Only a few states so far have asserted universal civil jurisdiction,[75] with a well-known example being the US through its 1789 Alien Tort Claims

---

Protected Persons; Art 5.2 International Convention Against the Taking of Hostages. For a comprehensive overview of treaties authorizing universal or quasi-universal jurisdiction, see Shaw, 2008, 673 and Secretary-General of the UN, *The Scope and Application of the Principle of Universal Jurisdiction: Report of the Secretary-General* (United Nations 2011) 43.

[71] Crawford, 2012, 470. See also International Court of Justice *Questions Concerning the Obligation to Prosecute or Extradite (Belgium v Senegal)* (2012). For a discussion, see www.asil.org/insights/volume/16/issue/29/belgium-v-senegal-international-court-justice-affirms-obligation.

[72] Ryngaert, 2007, 4. European Commission, Brief of the European Commission on Behalf of the EU as Amicus Curiae in Support of Neither Party in *Kiobel v Royal Dutch Petroleum Co.* (2012) 4.

[73] European Commission, Brief of the European Commission on Behalf of the EU as Amicus Curiae in Support of Neither Party in *Kiobel v Royal Dutch Petroleum Co.* (2012) 18.

[74] Donald Francis Donovan and Anthea Roberts, 'The Emerging Recognition of Universal Civil Jurisdiction' American Journal of International Law (2006) 100:1, 142, 142; In 2015, within the EU such proceedings were available in Austria, Belgium, Denmark, Finland, France, Germany, Greece, Italy, Luxembourg, the Netherlands, Poland, Portugal, Romania and Sweden. See European Commission, Brief of the European Commission on Behalf of the EU as Amicus Curiae in Support of Neither Party in *Kiobel v Royal Dutch Petroleum Co.* (2012) 18; For countries beyond Europe see Amnesty International, *Universal Jurisdiction: A Preliminary Survey of Legislation Around the World* (2011). Work has also been undertaken for a treaty on universal tort jurisdiction (Convention of Jurisdiction and Foreign Judgments in Civil and Commercial Matters) by The Hague Conference on Private International Law, but negotiations have stalled (see www.cptech.org/ecom/jurisdiction/hague.html). Article 18(3) of the 1999 Preliminary Draft Convention (Preliminary Document No 11) stated that courts should not be prevented from exercising universal jurisdiction in cases between private actors in respect of serious crimes under international law or gross human rights violations.

[75] For other examples, see International Law Association, *Final Report on the Exercise of Universal Jurisdiction in Respect of Gross Human Rights Offences* 22.

Act, known as the Alien Tort Statute (ATS).[76] The ATS has been invoked for acts outside US territory, leading US courts to exercise extraterritorial jurisdiction.[77] In the 2013 *Kiobel* case, the US Supreme Court found no reference to an extraterritorial scope of the ATS in a textual and historical interpretation thereof,[78] and found 'no indication that the ATS was passed to make the United States a uniquely hospitable forum for the enforcement of international norms'.[79] Rather, the Court continued, the ATS was enacted to provide judicial relief to foreign officials injured *in* the US. It noted that 'claims [must] touch and concern the territory of the United States with sufficient force'.[80]

In sum, while the universality principle might appeal at first sight with regard to the global environmental concerns, there is no state practice that would support the application of the principle for environmental protection through npr-PPMs.

---

[76] For a more comprehensive overview of ATS litigation, see among others Debora L Spar, 'Developments in the law: Extraterritoriality' Harvard Law Review (2011) 124:5, 1226; Anja Seibert-Fohr, 'United States Alien Tort Statute' Max Planck Encyclopedia of Public International Law (2012); Jochen von Bernstorff, Marc Jacob and John Dingfelder Stone, 'The Alien Tort Statute before the US Supreme Court in the *Kiobel* Case: Does International Law Prohibit US Courts to Exercise Extraterritorial Civil Jurisdiction over Human Rights Abuses Committed Outside of the US?' Zeitschrift für Ausländisches Öffentliches Recht und Völkerrecht (2012) 72:3, 579; L Austen Parrish, '*Kiobel*, Unilateralism, and the Retreat from Extraterritoriality' Maryland Journal of International Law (2013) 28:1, 208.

[77] Apart from extraterritorial judicial jurisdiction, there is no exercise of extraterritorial prescriptive jurisdiction (the applicable law is 'the law of nations' however, within the frame of US procedural rules), nor is there any extraterritorial enforcement jurisdiction. Cases are brought before the US civil courts by private parties. For a discussion on whether the ATS constitutes an exercise of prescriptive or adjudicative jurisdiction, see Anthony J Colangelo, '*Kiobel*: Muddling the Distinction Between Prescriptive and Adjudicative Jurisdiction' Maryland Journal of International Law (2013) 28:1, 65.

[78] US Supreme Court, *Kiobel v. Royal Dutch Petroleum Co.* 133 S.Ct. 1659 (2013), 7.

[79] Ibid. 12.

[80] Ibid. 14; The Court came to a unanimous conclusion (that in this case the ATS cannot be applied extraterritorially); however, four justices followed a different reasoning in a concurring opinion in judgment, with two other concurring opinions added.

4.3.7 Comity, Reasonableness and Effective Connection

The different permissive principles could lead to an overlap of jurisdictional claims, which can be moderated through principles such as international comity,[81] a rule of reason,[82] or a balancing of legitimate claims.[83]

Comity has multiple meanings and it is difficult to identify a unified standard for the application of comity.[84] In French comity is referred to as *courtoisie internationale*, in German as *Völkercourtoisie*, terms not pointing to any legal obligation, but rather a matter of respect and good manners. In English, however, the term is more ambiguous. Comity can be used as a synonym for private international law and conflict rules,[85] but can also serve as a limiting principle for extraterritorial jurisdiction under public international law. In the latter sense it may, for instance, serve as a means to avoid 'true conflict' between different laws where, for instance, the foreign law required a party to act contrary to domestic law.[86]

The Restatement (Third) on Foreign Relations Law lists a number of criteria according to which legislators and courts are to consider the connections and degree of interests of all the affected states, such as the importance of the regulation to the international political, legal or economic system, the extent to which the regulation is consistent with the traditions of the international system or the likelihood of conflict with

---

[81] Bernhard Jansen and Mauritz Lugard, 'Some Considerations on Trade Barriers Erected for Non-Economic Reasons and WTO Obligations' Journal of International Economic Law 1999) 2:3, 530, 535; Maier, 'Jurisdictional Rules in Customary International Law' 1996, 69.

[82] Ryngaert, 2008, 134 ff.

[83] Bianchi, 'Comment on Harold G. Maier – Jurisdictional Rules in Customary International Law' 1996, 84.

[84] For a comprehensive overview of the developments of the comity doctrine, see T M de Boer, 'Living Apart Together: The Relationship Between Public and Private International Law' Netherlands International Law Review (2010) 57:2, 183; Joel R Paul, 'The Transformation of International Comity' Law and Contemporary Problems (2008) 71:3, 19; Ryngaert, 2008, 138.

[85] In the US the principle of comity as a conflict rule is used to determine which law will be applied in a situation where laws of different states may apply. See e.g. Paul, 2008, 19. Comity in this sense is almost unknown in the EU, as these matters are regulated under the Rome regulations (Regulation 593/2008/EC of the European Parliament and of the Council of 17 June 2008 on the Law Applicable to Contractual Obligations (Rome I); Regulation 864/2007/EC of the European Parliament and of the Council of 11 July 2007 on the Law Applicable to Non-Contractual Obligations (Rome II).) See Ryngaert, 2008, 167.

[86] *Hartford Fire Ins. Co. v California*, 509 US 764 (1993) at 769.

regulation by another state.[87] Under this comity or reasonableness test, interests are balanced in order to answer the question of which state has a stronger interest in regulating a certain matter.[88] Even actions that would be deemed legally permissible could still be unreasonable in a certain context. There is thus a two-step test: first, one must determine whether the dispute has a sufficient nexus to justify the assertion of jurisdiction (through one of the jurisdictional bases); and second, one must determine whether such an assertion would be reasonable in the light of international fairness and competing national interests.[89] Thus, even when extraterritorial jurisdiction is exercised on an internationally recognized legal basis, that exercise may nevertheless be limited through an additional analysis of reasonableness. This is a reflection of comity in the sense of goodwill and courtesy: if a state recognizes that the interests of another state are greater in a certain case, in a future case where the interests might be reversed, the same reasonableness can be expected from that other state.[90] There is little evidence, however, that courts outside the US believe this is a required approach under international law.[91] European states tend to focus on the sufficiently close legal connection and disregard 'mere political, economic, commercial or social interests'.[92] However, the different approaches are not that different. The requirement of a 'weighty' and 'significant' connection cannot but include a trace of a reasonableness test as known in the US.[93] While a pure connection approach sounds more objective than the connection-plus-interest approach, the distinction between 'greater interest' and 'significant connection' seems to be a subtle one.[94] Scott has argued that the guidance on reasonableness might be too broad, as the focus is 'virtually exclusive on the question of whether it is reasonable for a state to act – as opposed to the question of whether

---

[87] Restatement of the Law (Third) on Foreign Relations Law of the United States §403(2).

[88] Hannah L Buxbaum, 'Territory, Territoriality, and the Resolution of Jurisdictional Conflict' American Journal of Comparative Law (2009) 57, 631, 649.

[89] 'Notes: Constructing the State Extraterritorially: Jurisdictional Discourse, the National Interest and Transnational Norms' Harvard Law Review (1990), 103:6, 1273–1305, 1274.

[90] Maier, 1996, 73.

[91] Stigall, 2012, 338; Maier, 1996, 73.

[92] Frederick A P Mann, 'The Doctrine of International Jurisdiction Revisited After Twenty Years' Recueil des Cours of The Hague Academy of International Law (1984) 186, 9, 29.

[93] Bianchi, 1996, 90.

[94] Ryngaert, 2008, 171.

it is reasonable for a state to act in the manner it has, having regard to the design features of the measure at hand'.[95] Thus even if different states have different interests, these interests can be taken into account when designing a measure, which can be seen as a more practical and realistic approach to reasonableness. Such consideration of other state's interests can be crucial for the acceptance by other states of (trade) measures with an extraterritorial effect.

4.4 EXTRATERRITORIALITY IN COMPETITION LAW

Extraterritoriality in a competition law context refers to the extraterritorial application of national competition laws. The rationale behind such application is to safeguard the objectives of competition rules, which would be impaired if competition could be applied exclusively to conduct of nationals (including legal persons). As Wagner-von Papp stated, 'a cartel is no less harmful just because the cartelists travelled to an exotic location for their meetings; and consumers are hardly interested in the nationality of those who exploit them'.[96] Theoretically, one could rely on a system of home jurisdiction, where states rely exclusively on antitrust enforcement by the jurisdiction in which the anti-competitive conduct takes place. However, there is no guarantee that the home state has antitrust legislation in place or sufficient resources to enforce existing legislation effectively.[97] The home state may also be unwilling to enforce its competition law in respect of export cartels that do not affect its own market.[98] Under the effects doctrine a state can legislate activities that originate abroad but that have a substantial, direct and foreseeable effect upon or in its national territory. In other words, a state can exercise jurisdiction over acts taking place outside its territory because its market is affected by those actions. The recognition of this doctrine under general international law remains

[95] Joanne Scott, 'The New EU "Extraterritoriality"' Common Market Law Review (2014) 51, 1, 34.

[96] Florian Wagner-von Papp, 'Competition Law and Extraterritoriality' in Ariel Ezrachi (ed.), *Research Handbook on International Competition Law* (Edward Elgar Publishing 2012) 22.

[97] Ibid. 23.

[98] See for example the US Webb-Pomerene Export Trade Act, 15 USC §§ 61–66 (2000), adopted first in 1918. See also Margaret Levenstein and Valerie Suslow, 'The Changing International Status of Export Cartel Exemptions' American University International Law Review (2005) 20:4, 785.

uncertain,[99] but does not generate major controversy anymore.[100] The Third Restatement of Foreign Relations Law accepts prescriptive jurisdiction over foreign conduct that has or is intended to have substantial economic effects,[101] but only a few countries, such as the US, actually recognize the effects doctrine as a separate legal basis. When not considered a separate legal basis, effects jurisdiction can be seen as a degree of territorial connection under the territoriality principle.[102]

The US have taken a lead in the extraterritorial development of competition law,[103] but other jurisdictions such as the EU,[104]

---

[99] The effects doctrine was approved by the International Law Association as a principle of international law at its 55th Conference in 1972 where the effect is a constituent element of the act. L'Institut de Droit International stated during its session in 1977 that the effects doctrine could be applied extraterritorially to anti-competitive behaviour of multinationals where effects where intentional or foreseeable, substantial, direct and immediate. These approvals bear no hard law value; however, their recognition has been important for growing support for the theory.

[100] Yves Botteman and Agapi Patsa, 'The Jurisdictional Reach of EU Anti-Cartel Rules: Unmuddling the Limits' European Competition Journal (2012) 8:2, 365, 365.

[101] Restatement of the Law (Third) on Foreign Relations Law of the United States §402(1)(c), §415. See also Section 4.3.2.

[102] See for instance Alan C Swan, 'The Hartford Insurance Company Case: Antitrust in the Global Economy – Welfare Effects and Sovereignty' in Jagdeep S Bhandari and Alan O Sykes (eds.), *Economic Dimensions in International Law: Comparative and Empirical Perspectives* (Cambridge University Press 1997) 551.

[103] For a full overview of the relevant legislation see US Department of Justice and the Federal Trade Commission, *Antitrust Enforcement Guidelines for International Operations*, 1995, at www.justice.gov/atr/public/guidelines/internat.htm. The 1890 Sherman Act (15 U.S.C. §§ 1–7) sets forth the basic antitrust prohibition against cartels and monopolies and has been amended by the 1982 FTAIA delineating the rules for conduct involving trade or commerce other than imports, and the 1914 Clayton Act on mergers 1914 ((15 U.S.C. § 12–27), Section 7 Clayton Act). Its scope has been interpreted among others in the landmark judgments *American Banana Co v United Fruit Co* 213 US 347 (1909) 2d Cir; *US v Aluminium Co of America (Alcoa)* 148 F.2d 416 (1945); 9th Cir. *Timberlane Lumber Co. v Bank of America* 549 F.2d 597, 613 (1977); US Supreme Court *Hartford Fire Insurance v California* 509 US 764, 796; 113 S.Ct. 2891 (1993).

[104] The EU competition rules are constituted by Articles 101 (cartels and concerted practices) and 102 TFEU (abuse of dominant position), as well as by various guidelines and regulations governing mergers and other relevant matters. The EU courts have adopted several approaches throughout the years to justify an extraterritorial application of EU rules, such as the economic entity theory in Court of Justice of the European Union, *Imperial Chemical Industries Ltd. v Commission (Dyestuffs)* case 48/69 ECLI:EU:C:1972:70 (1972); the implementation theory in Court of Justice of the European Union, *Ahlström Osakeyhtiö et al. v Commission (Wood Pulp I)* Joined cases 89, 104, 114, 116, 117, 125-129/85

Japan,[105] Brazil[106] or India[107] have applied their competition rules to conduct taking place abroad. While there is an increasing number of bi- and multilateral cooperation agreements,[108] in practice, the unilateral extraterritorial application of national competition laws is still the most effective tool to address foreign anti-competitive behaviour that affects domestic markets. Nonetheless, cooperation agreements (as well as informal understandings between countries) are playing an important

---

ECLI:EU:C:1988:447 (1998); and the effects doctrine in General Court of the EU *Gencor v Commission* T-102/96 ECLI:EU:T:1999:65 (1999). See for an overview: Botteman and Patsa, 2012; Wagner-von Papp, 2012; Damien Geradin, Marc Reysen and David Henry, 'Extraterritoriality, Comity and Cooperation in EU Competition Law' in Andrew T Guzman (ed.), *Cooperation, Comity and Competition Policy* (Oxford University Press 2011); James J Friedberg, 'The Convergence of Law in an Era of Political Integration: The Wood Pulp Case and the Alcoa Effects Doctrine' University of Pittsburgh Law Review (1991) 52:2, 289, 291. National courts have been reluctant to accept the effects doctrine, except for Germany. In *Phillip Morris, Inc v Bundeskartellamt* (1984 ECC 393) (Case Kart 16/82), the German Federal Cartel Authority embraced the effects doctrine.

[105] See e.g. Charles A Brill and Brian A Carlson, 'US and Japanese Antimonopoly Policy and the Extraterritorial Enforcement of Competition Laws' The International Lawyer (1999) 33:1, 82; Kameoka Etsuko, *Competition Law and Policy in Japan and the EU* (Edward Elgar Publishing 2014); Chie Sato, 'Extraterritorial Application of EU Competition Law: Is It Possible for Japanese Companies to Steer Clear of EU Competition Laws?' Journal of Political Science and Sociology (2010) 11, 23, 40; Naoki Uhkubo and Zenichi Shishido, 'Cooperation, Comity and Competition Policy: Japan' in Andrew T. Guzman (ed.), *Cooperation, Comity and Competition Policy* (Oxford University Press 2011) 89.

[106] Federal Antitrust Law, Federal Law 8884 of 1994, Section 2. Brendan Sweeney, 'International Governance of Competition and the Problem of Extraterritorial Jurisdiction' in John Duns, Arlen Duke and Brendan Sweeney (eds.), *Comparative Competition Law* (Edward Elgar Publishing 2015) 378; Javier Tapia and Alexandre Ditzel Faraco, 'Latin American Antitrust Law and Policy: An Overview of Three Jurisdictions – Brazil, Chile and Colombia' in John Duns, Arlen Duke and Brendan Sweeney (eds.), *Comparative Competition Law* (Edward Elgar Publishing 2015).

[107] Indian Competition Act 2002, No 12 of 2003, section 32. Kartik Maheshwari and Simone Reis, 'Extraterritorial Application of the Competition Act and Its Impact' Competition Law Reports January 2012, 144, 147; Nishith Desai, *Competition Law in India: A Report on Jurisprudential Trends* (June 2015), at www.nishithdesai.com.

[108] The need for bi- and plurilateral approaches has increased tremendously. At the end of the 1970s only nine jurisdictions had competition rules in place, whereas at the end of 2013, about 127 jurisdictions had competition rules in place, of which 120 had a functioning competition authority (OECD, *Challenges of International Cooperation in Competition Law Enforcement* (2014), 26).

role with regard to investigations, collecting of evidence and exchange of information.[109] At the multilateral level, there are a few non-binding initiatives, such as the Organization for Economic Cooperation and Development (OECD) recommendations and best practices,[110] initiatives under the WTO,[111] and the Restrictive Business Practices Code (RBP Code)[112] under the auspices of the United Nations Conference on Trade and Development (UNCTAD). A number of regional organizations such as the European Competition Network (ECN) or the Association of Southeast Asian Nations (ASEAN) provide opportunities for national competition authorities to cooperate and continue a process of convergence of substantive competition standards.[113] Outside these networks, bilateral agreements are the most important instruments to resolve some of the problems that have occurred due to the internationalization of business practices. They are mostly cooperation agreements or Memoranda of Understanding, but free trade agreements (FTAs) can also contain clauses on competition cooperation and

---

109 Wagner-von Papp, 2012, 24. See also Eleanor M Fox, 'Antitrust Without Borders: From Roots to Codes to Networks' in Andrew T Guzman (ed.), *Cooperation, Comity and Competition policy* (Oxford University Press 2011) 274. For an overview of the costs of under- and over-regulation, see OECD, *Challenges of International Cooperation in Competition Law Enforcement*, 2014.

110 Recommendation of the Council concerning Cooperation between Member Countries on Restrictive Business Practices Affecting International Trade of 5 October 1967, C(567)33(final) – amended in 1973, 1979, 1986 and 1995; Recommendation of the Council concerning Cooperation between Member-Countries on Anti-competitive Practices Affecting International Trade of 21 September 1995, C(95)130(final); Recommendation of the Council concerning Effective Action Against Hard-Core Cartels, C(98)35(final); OECD, Best Practices for the Formal Exchange of Information Between Competition Agencies in Hardcore Cartel Investigations, October 2005, at www.oecd.org/competition/cartels/35590548.pdf.

111 For information on and documents by the Working Group on the Interaction between Trade and Competition Policy (WGTCP) see www.wto.org/english/tratop_e/comp_e/comp_e.htm. The working group is currently closed down. See also the sector-specific competition law agreement on Telecommunications (1997 Agreement on Telecommunications Services, designated as the Fourth Protocol to the GATS).

112 The Set of Multilaterally Agreed Equitable Principles and Rules for the Control of Restrictive Business Practices, UN Doc TD/RBP/CONF 10/Rev.1 (1980), endorsed by GA Res. 63, UN Doc A/RES/35/63 (1980), 19 ILM 813 (1980).

113 OECD, *Challenges of International Cooperation in Competition Law Enforcement* (2014) 17; Daniel Sokol, 'International Antitrust Institutions' in Andrew T Guzman (ed.), *Cooperation, Comity and Competition Policy* (Oxford University Press 2011); OECD, *International Enforcement Cooperation: Secretariat Report on the OECD/ICN Survey on International Enforcement Cooperation* (2013), 89.

harmonization.[114] Despite the increase in cooperation over the last 20 years,[115] more cooperation is needed. Business is ever more globalized and integrated, and more jurisdictions have adopted or are adopting competition rules. The OECD has measured the complexity of cooperation, measured by the number of pairs of competition authorities needing to cooperate, and found that by 2014 the complexity in cartel cases had increased by 53 times since 1990.[116]

4.4.1 Direct, Substantial and Foreseeable Effects

Under the effects doctrine states can legislate activities that originate abroad but that have effects upon or in their national territory. Section §403(2)(a) of the Third Restatement of Foreign Relations Law requires effects to be substantial, direct and foreseeable. The test is difficult to apply as it lacks doctrinal clarity and can be criticized for being overly broad in scope: in theory almost everything can affect almost anything. When are the effects considered sufficient to trigger the application of domestic rules to foreign conduct?[117] Courts and legislature have continuously tried to qualify the effects that are necessary to trigger an extraterritorial reach.[118] It is not always very clear what each element entails and how they relate to each other. Firstly, when can an effect be said to be *direct*? The US Department of Justice (DOJ)/Federal Trade Commission (FTC) Guidelines consider, for instance, that the domestic effect is

---

[114] The US has cooperation agreements with Australia, Brazil, Canada, Chile, EU, Germany, Israel, Japan and Mexico, while the EU has cooperation agreements with US, Canada, Japan, Republic of Korea and Switzerland. Both the EU and the US have Memoranda of Understanding with other competition authorities, such as China and India. For an example of competition clauses in FTAs, see chapter 11 of the EU–South Korea FTA. See for a more comprehensive discussion Maher Dabbah, 'Future Directions in Bilateral Cooperation: A Policy Perspective' in Andrew T Guzman (ed.), *Cooperation, Comity and Competition Policy* (Oxford University Press 2011) 287.

[115] The International Chamber of Commerce called upon increased international cooperation between antitrust authorities in a Policy Statement of 28 March 1996 (ICC Statement on International Cooperation Between Antitrust Authorities, Doc No 225/450).

[116] OECD, *Challenges of International Cooperation in Competition Law Enforcement* (2014) 6.

[117] Robert Y Jennings, 'Extraterritorial Jurisdiction and the United States Antitrust Laws' British Yearbook of International Law (1957) 33, 146, 159; see also L Austen Parrish, 'The Effects Test: Extraterritoriality's Fifth Business' Vanderbilt Law Review (2008) 61:5, 1455, 1480.

[118] Parrish, 2008, 1481.

sufficiently direct where a foreign cartel sells the affected products to an unrelated intermediary, who will foreseeably sell them on to buyers in the US.[119] In this interpretation, the distinction between direct and reasonably foreseeable becomes blurred however, making the requirement of directness arguably redundant. Nevertheless, the emerging view seems to be that competition authorities must be able to *show* the direct effect on the market, as *assuming* that, for example, price-fixing will harm competition on the market is not good enough.[120] The Ninth Circuit has interpreted 'direct' as an 'immediate consequence' of the defendant's conduct,[121] whereas the Seventh and Second Circuits rejected that approach and read a 'reasonably proximate causal nexus' in directness.[122] In a similar vein was the suggestion by Advocate General Darmon in the EU *Wood Pulp* case to adopt criteria of direct and immediate effects.[123]

Secondly, the requirement of *substantial* effects also raises questions. In *Alcoa* the potential effects were sufficient, as long as the absence of actual effect was not shown. The DOJ/FTC Guidelines also consider that potential harm can qualify as substantial under the 1982 Foreign Trade Antitrust Improvements Act (FTAIA).[124] The third requirement of foreseeability seems to be the operative one. If it is foreseeable that conduct will have anti-competitive effects in the US, the rules can be applied to that conduct. If, however, somehow US markets are implicated in conduct in a way that the actors did not and could not foresee, then it is a matter of legal certainty not to apply foreign laws to these actors.[125] The US FTAIA requires in that regard 'reasonably foreseeable' effects.[126]

In the 1945 US *Alcoa* case, the US Supreme Court required intent in addition to the effects alone. Judge Learned Hand rejected jurisdiction over unintended effects, as 'almost any limitation on the supply of goods in Europe, for example, or in Latin America, may have repercussions in

---

[119] DOJ/FTC Antitrust Enforcement Guidelines for International Operations (April 1995), Section 3.121.

[120] See e.g. CJEU *InnoLux Corp., formerly Chimei InnoLux Corp. v European Commission* ECLI:EU:C:2015:451 (9 July 2015); US Court of Appeals, 7th Cir. *Motorola Mobility LLC v AU Optronics Corp.* 775 F.3d 816 (26 November 2014).

[121] 9th Cir. *United States vs LSL Biotechnologies* 379 F.3d 672, 680 (2004).

[122] 2d. Cir. *Lotes Co. v Hon Hai Precision Indus.* 753 F.3d 395, 410 (2014); 7th Cir. *Minn-Chem Inc. v Agrium Inc.* 683 F.3d 845, 856–57 (2012).

[123] Opinion of Advocate General Darmon, ECLI:EU:C:1988:258, 36–42, 53.

[124] DOJ/FTC Antitrust Enforcement Guidelines for International Operations (April 1995), Section 3.121.

[125] Wagner-von Papp, 2012, 35.

[126] See 15 U.S. Code § 6a – Conduct involving trade or commerce with foreign nations.

the United States, if there is trade between the two. Yet (. . .) Congress did not intend the Sherman Act to cover them.'[127] Intent was thus indispensable to avoiding 'international complications'.[128] Subsequent courts have not always been very clear on the precise requirements and the relationship between intent and effects. The Supreme Court in *Hartford Fire* seems to reaffirm *Alcoa*'s proposition that intent and effects are required cumulatively by stating that 'it is well established by now that the Sherman Act applies to foreign conduct that was *meant to* produce and did in fact produce some substantial effect in the United States'.[129] The intent required is not a specific, but a general intention, which can also be retraced in requirements of foreseeability and directness of effects.[130] Foreseeability and intent might not differ that much, as it has never been made entirely clear whether the 'intent' requirement refers to a subjective or objective intent. If objective intent would suffice, then that would arguably be fulfilled when domestic effects were reasonably foreseeable.[131]

4.4.2 Environmental Effects

One of the main reasons for an extraterritorial application of competition law is the fact that the marketplace is increasingly globalized and economic transactions can have a transnational impact. A similar reasoning can be applied with respect to global environmental challenges and thus it is suggested that the effects doctrine can be relevant to environmental protection measures.[132] However, how should the effects theory be applied in an environmental context and how can the magnitude of the required effects be determined?

Effects under competition law must be direct, substantial and foreseeable, generally without requiring intent. Any exercise of extraterritorial jurisdiction should respect the legitimate interests of other sovereign

---

127 2d Cir. *US v Aluminium Co of America (Alcoa)*, 443.

128 Ibid.

129 US Supreme Court, *Hartford Fire Insurance v California* 1993, 509 US 764, 796; 113 S.Ct. 2891.

130 Coppel, 1993, 85.

131 Wagner-von Papp, 2012, 30.

132 Eckard Rehbinder, 'Extra-Territoriality of Pollution Control Laws From a European Perspective' in G Handl, J Zekoll and P Zumbansen (eds.), *Beyond Territoriality: Transnational Legal Authority in an Age of Globalization* (Martinus Nijhoff 2012) 128; Henrik Horn and Peter C Mavroidis, 'The Permissible Reach of National Environmental Policies' Journal of World Trade (2008) 42:6, 1107, 1133; Geert Van Calster, *International and EU Trade Law: The Environmental Challenge* (Cameron May 2000) 214.

states, and should avoid conflict where possible through comity or the rule of reason. The principles of comity, rule of reason or proportionality all lead to the result that the country with the most important or primary interests will have jurisdiction. In a comity analysis two questions need to be considered: firstly, are the effects felt in one state more direct than those felt in other states; and secondly, are the effects felt in one state more substantial than what is felt in other states?[133]

Applied to the protection of environmental concerns outside the territory of the regulating state,[134] a number of challenges arise with regard to these standards. It makes sense that jurisdiction based upon effects where such effects were an unintended consequence or a mere side-effect, seems to create more resistance than where the effects were clearly intended. Considering foreseeability seems more accurate: could the damaging effects have been foreseen by the party causing the damage? Also, are the effects a direct result of the actions taken? Are the actions taken the sole cause of the environmental effects, and if not, to what extent have they contributed to the damage? Can effects be foreseen if other factors contributing to environmental damage are uncertain, and if the aggregate effects of all factors combined are also uncertain? Foreseeability of effects raises the question of future effects: environmental damage can take much longer to realize than the speed of a bullet hitting its victim, or the reactions of financial markets. Can states, in the absence of sufficient scientific evidence, rely upon the precautionary principle when determining effects? Closely related to foreseeability is the matter of directness of effects. When is an environmental effect direct? Can severe droughts on the African continent be considered direct effects of pollution caused by steel producers in China? Must there necessarily be damaging effects to the environment in the territory of the imposing state itself, or could moral concerns about environmental damage occurring fully outside a state's territory (for instance, a severely polluted lake located in another state) also be taken into account? This option of moral concerns would seem too indirect to qualify as an environmental

133 Akehurst, 1972–1973, 198.

134 See for support in literature that the effects doctrine can be applied to environmental law, Rehbinder, 'Extra-Territoriality of Pollution Control Laws From a European Perspective' 2012, 128; Jeremy Remy Nash, 'The Curious Legal Landscape of the Extra-Territoriality of US Environmental Laws' in G Handl, J Zekoll and P Zumbansen (eds.), *Beyond Territoriality: Transnational Legal Authority in an Age of Globalization* (Martinus Nijhoff 2012) 163; see also Philippe Sands, *Principles of International Environmental Law* (Cambridge University Press 2003) 238; Patricia Bernie, Alan Boyle and Catherine Redgwell, *International Law and the Environment* (3rd edn., Oxford University Press 2009) 712.

effect. Next to foreseeable and direct, the effects doctrine also requires effects to be substantial. But what is the standard for substantial effects? Must the effects be appreciable? The notions of direct, substantial and foreseeable effects are closely linked, but as in competition law, their precise interpretation may depend on the circumstances, as there is no exact definition. The body of international environmental law can, for instance, be of relevance when assessing environmental effects: widespread international support for an environmental concern could justify a more lenient approach to the criteria, allowing the justification of weaker or more uncertain effects. Furthermore, determining effects in an environmental context requires a scientific analysis, the details, requirements and limitations of which will depend on the specific environmental concern, on the knowledge available on a specific topic, as well as the data and information available within a certain time frame. That analysis will inform the criteria of direct, substantial and foreseeable. When proposing the extraterritoriality tree in Chapter 5, the questions put forward here will be elaborated upon.

While raising challenging questions with regard to its application to environmental concerns, the effects doctrine allows for a more feasible and widely applicable assessment of environmental npr-PPMs. In the landmark WTO decision in which jurisdiction was shortly touched upon, *US – Shrimp*, the AB relied on a 'sufficient nexus' as a jurisdictional link between the US and the sea turtle species that the US aimed to protect through its measures. The AB seemed to imply a territorial link, as it referred to 'some of the turtles' crossing US waters 'some of the time'.[135] It failed, however, to define or further qualify what such nexus could consist of. Looking beyond the specific circumstances of migrating sea turtle species, a 'sufficient nexus' test creates considerable vagueness and uncertainty about what a nexus could consist of. Can such a nexus be imagined in a context of climate change, air pollution, or global commons? The effects doctrine offers a better-suited tool to determine whether states can impose trade measures that aim at protecting environmental concerns located outside the territory of the regulating state, and whether they are affected by activities abroad that have an impact on the environment. Can the extraterritorial effect of environmental npr-PPMs be permitted? The existence of direct, substantial and foreseeable effects could establish a link with the regulating state permitting the extraterritorial reach of inward-looking or partly outward-looking npr-PPMs. Those concerns that do not affect the regulating state in any way would not be justifiable through the effects doctrine.

---

[135] WTO AB Report, *US – Shrimp*, para. 133.

4.5 EXTRATERRITORIALITY IN INTERNATIONAL HUMAN RIGHTS LAW

Extraterritoriality under international human rights law refers to an extension of states' obligations to respect and protect human rights not only within their own territory, but also when acting outside their territory. International human rights obligations stem from regional and international human rights treaties, which have been interpreted by regional and international human rights bodies to also apply outside the territory of the state party to the human rights treaty. Also, when acting outside their home state territory, state actors remain bound by their duty to respect human rights. Even though such a concept of extraterritoriality (extension of a state's own obligations to its own actions abroad) differs from the concept of extraterritorial effect of npr-PPMs (extending a national measure to apply outside the regulating state's territory with the objective to address concerns outside its territory), the analysis of human rights law is relevant as it raises a number of questions that may be useful to assessing environmental npr-PPMs. Why did the regional and international human rights bodies opt for a broad scope of application of the treaties? What is the legal ground for such extraterritorial application? How far do these extraterritorial obligations extend? Are states willing to stretch the boundaries of traditional territorial jurisdiction and sovereignty when transboundary or global concerns are at issue?

When referring to international human rights treaties the basic reference is the Universal Declaration of Human Rights, adopted by the United Nations General Assembly (UNGA) on 10 December 1948, marking the beginning of contemporary international human rights protection.[136] The Universal Declaration contains a wide range of rights to be protected, including basic rights such as the right to life, civil liberties such as freedom of opinion, and a series of economic, social and cultural rights such as the right to education. For the first time in history, states agreed at a global level on a list of core guarantees that serve to protect the dignity of human beings, regardless of their nationality, race or gender.[137] The Declaration itself is a non-binding instrument, but its content is now firmly established in a number of legally binding conventions, such as the international UN

[136] UN General Assembly, Universal Declaration of Human Rights, 10 December 1948, 217 A (III).

[137] Walter Kälin and Jörg Künzli, *The Law of International Human Rights Protection* (Oxford University Press 2009) 3.

human rights treaties;[138] in regional instruments, such as the European Convention on Human Rights (ECHR); and in domestic law, often via Bills of Rights in constitutions. The international and regional instruments impose obligations on states, meaning they can be invoked only against states.[139] As they cannot be directly invoked against private actors, international human rights in this sense differ from the fundamental rights that can be guaranteed in national constitutions.[140] In principle, depending on the jurisdictional scope of the treaty in question,[141] all individuals within a state's jurisdiction can rely upon the state's obligation to protect human rights. In certain circumstances individuals beyond a state's jurisdiction – in the general public international law sense referring to sovereign territory – can also invoke human rights obligations against a state:

---

138 International Covenant of Economic, Social and Cultural Rights, 16 December 1966, 993 UNTS 3; International Covenant on Civil and Political Rights, 19 December 1966, 999 UNTS 171; Convention on the Prevention and Punishment of the Crime of Genocide, 9 December 1948, 78 UNTS 277; International Convention on the Elimination of All Forms of Racial Discrimination, 21 December 1965, 660 UNTS 195; Convention Against Torture and Other Cruel, Inhuman or Degrading Treatment or Punishment, 10 December 1984, 1465 UNTS 85; Convention for the Protection of All Persons from Enforced Disappearance, 20 December 2006, 2715 UNTS; Convention relating to the Status of Refugees, 28 July 1951, 189 UNTS 137; Convention on the Elimination of All Forms of Discrimination against Women, 18 December 1979, 1249 UNTS 13; Convention on the Rights of the Child, 20 November 1989, 1577 UNTS 3; Convention on the Protection of the Rights of All Migrant Workers and Members of Their Families, 18 December 1990, A/RES/45/158; Convention on the Rights of Persons with Disabilities, 24 January 2007, A/RES/61/106.

139 Kälin and Künzli, 2009, 31. See the International Law Commission, Articles on Responsibility of States for Internationally Wrongful Acts (Articles on State Responsibility) (Report of the ILC on its fifty-third session, 2001, UN Doc A/56/10, Supplement No 10) for guidance on the determination of state organs or agents whose conduct can be attributed to the state.

140 If national law does not ensure sufficient protection of its obligations it has signed onto, then that failure could lead to a claim against the state before the regional or international human rights bodies. For an interesting overview of the status of human rights violations by private persons and entities, see Ineta Ziemele, 'Human Rights Violations by Private Persons and Entities: The Case Law of International Human Rights Courts and Monitoring Bodies' EUI Working Papers 2009/8, 2009.

141 While most treaties explicitly refer to the 'jurisdiction' or 'territory' of states, the European Charter of Fundamental Rights for instance, as a *sui generis* human rights treaty, is only applicable to acts of EU institutions and Member States when implementing EU law. Because of the special character of the European Charter of Fundamental Rights that is characteristic for the EU context, the Charter will not be discussed further within this chapter.

this is in cases where the human rights obligations of states are applied to state actions outside their territory, i.e. extraterritorially. The instances in which this has been accepted will be discussed in Section 4.5.1.

International human rights obligations entail both positive and negative obligations. States must refrain from interfering with the enjoyment of rights (negative obligations) as well as take action to ensure protection of human rights (positive obligations). In other terms, the obligations of states can be classified as the duty to respect (no interference), the duty to protect (through both preventive and remedial action) and the duty to fulfil (ensure the fulfilment of rights).[142] For instance, a state is respecting the freedom of the press when not interfering with the press. A state complies with its duty to protect by ensuring police protection where necessary, or by taking the required safety measures in order to limit possible damage that can occur through natural disasters. The duty to fulfil adds an additional layer to the duty to protect as it requires the adoption of wide-ranging legislative or administrative measures to ensure human rights protection.[143] For instance, in order to ensure a fair trial, the state has to provide for operative investigative authorities and an independent judiciary; in order to realize the right to education, the state has to provide schools; with regard to the right to health, the state has to provide adequate health services. The availability of resources can then determine the actual scope of the right, which can be different for each state.

The internationalization of human rights protection has created individual rights under international law that can be invoked against states. However, protection remains deficient in a number of ways.[144] Firstly, these mechanisms are principally only available to individuals in those states who have ratified a relevant treaty. Secondly, the invocation of the internationally recognized rights before domestic bodies depends on the domestically regulated relationship between international and national law (monism vs. dualism).[145] Thirdly, not all decisions of treaty bodies have binding value. Even though the decisions of the UN human rights bodies are often seen as authoritative,[146] there are no enforcement options

---

142 For a comprehensive overview of the different obligations, see among others Kälin and Künzli, 2009, 96.

143 Ibid. 112.

144 Ibid. 15.

145 Ibid. None of the human rights treaties contains a clause that it is directly applicable in the national legal orders.

146 Rosanne van Alebeek and André Nollkaemper, 'The Legal Status of Decisions by Human Rights Treaty Bodies in National Law' in Helen Keller and

in respect of non-complying states. The European Court of Human Rights (ECtHR),[147] the Inter-American Court on Human Rights (IACtHR)[148] and the American Court of Human and Peoples' Rights (ACtHPR)[149] can issue binding decisions and impose penalties, but these courts have little leeway to 'force' persistent states to change their behaviour, apart from political pressure – a 'pitfall' common under international law. The most important international bodies with regard to human rights protection are the International Court of Justice (ICJ),[150] the Human Rights Committee (HRC) (monitoring the ICCPR) and the Committee on Economic, Social and Cultural Rights (CESCR) (monitoring the ICESCR).[151] The most active regional human rights bodies are the ECtHR (monitoring the ECHR) and the IACtHR (monitoring the ACHR).[152] More recently, the ACtHPR was established[153] and the League of Arab States is, at the time

---

Geir Ulfstein (eds.), *Human Rights Treaty Bodies: Law and Legitimacy* (Cambridge University Press 2011).

147 European Convention on Human Rights, Article 46.

148 American Convention on Human Rights, Article 68. Individuals cannot bring a complaint directly to the Court, but only to the Inter-American Commission on Human Rights (who can herself lodge complaints to the Court after the prescribed procedures). See ACHR, Articles 41, 44, 61.

149 Protocol to the African Charter on Human and Peoples' Rights on the Establishment of an African Court on Human and Peoples' Rights, Article 30. Individuals have no direct right to submit complaints to the Court, but the Court may entitle them to institute cases directly before it (Article 5(3) of the Protocol). Individuals cannot petition the African Commission, but the Commission's mandate includes ensuring the protection of human rights as laid down by the Charter (Article 45 of the African Charter on Human and Peoples' Rights).

150 The ICJ is not a human rights court, but in the state-to-state contentious cases before it and in its advisory opinions, it has dealt with and interpreted the scope of human rights obligations. Article 36 of the Statute of the International Court of Justice grants the ICJ jurisdiction in disputes on the interpretation of treaties and any question of international law. Article 38 refers to the sources of law the Court shall apply in resolving disputes, including international conventions.

151 Both Covenants foresee in an individual petition system and inter-State complaints through optional Protocols (Optional Protocol of 2008 foresees in the complaint procedure for the ICESCR, whereas Optional Protocol of 1966 provides for a right to individual petition under the ICCPR).

152 Individuals cannot bring complaints before the IACtHR, in contrast to the individual complaint procedure under the ECHR. Only the Inter-American Commission on Human Rights or state parties can refer cases.

153 Protocol to the African Charter on Human and Peoples' Rights on the Establishment of an African Court on Human and Peoples' Rights, 10 June 1998, Article 6(3).

of writing, in the process of strengthening its human rights system by establishing an Arab Court of Human Rights.[154]

4.5.1 The Concept of Jurisdiction in a Human Rights Context

The extraterritorial application of human rights treaties depends on the jurisdictional scope of those treaties. Most treaties have jurisdictional clauses limiting their reach. Article 1 ECHR and Article 1 ACHR refer to persons 'within their jurisdiction', whereas Article 2(1) ICCPR refers to 'individuals within its territory and subject to its jurisdiction'. It is up to the treaty bodies to interpret the scope of that 'jurisdiction'.[155] The HRC for example stated in its General Comment 31 that '[a] State Party must respect and ensure the rights laid down in the Covenant to anyone within the power or effective control of the State Party, even if not situated within the territory of the State Party'.[156] The international human rights jurisprudence builds on a concept of jurisdiction distinct from the general international law understanding of jurisdiction.[157] Whereas the latter refers to the lawful or unlawful exercise of jurisdiction (prescriptive, enforcement, judicial) by a state within or outside its territory (*de jure* jurisdiction), the human rights courts and monitoring bodies use jurisdiction as a *factual* concept, in which the factual authority or control over a territory and persons forms the basis for a state's obligations, both within and outside its sovereign territory. *De jure* jurisdiction refers to the *right* and the power to regulate

---

[154] The Statute for the Human Rights Court is criticized for not including individual complaint procedures; see International Commission of Jurists, *The Arab Court of Human Rights: A Flawed Statute for an Ineffective Court* (2015).

[155] For a full analysis of the different treaties and the relevant case law, see Barbara Cooreman, *Addressing Global Environmental Concerns through Trade: Extraterritoriality Under WTO Law From a Comparative Perspective* (Leiden: Meijers Research Institute and Graduate School of the Leiden Law School of Leiden University 2016).

[156] HRC General Comment 31: Nature of the General Legal Obligation Imposed on States Parties to the Covenant, 26 May 2004, CCPR/C/21/Rev.1/Add.13; 11 IHHR 905 (2004) at para. 10.

[157] For a thorough analysis of the different notions of jurisdiction, see Marko Milanovic, *Extraterritorial Application of Human Rights Treaties: Law, Principles and Policy* (Oxford University Press 2011) chapter II. See also Michael Duttwiler, 'Authority, Control and Jurisdiction in the Extraterritorial Application of the European Convention on Human Rights' Netherlands Quarterly of Human Rights (2012) 30:2, 137, 157. Samantha Besson, 'The Extraterritoriality of the European Convention on Human Rights: Why Human Rights Depend on Jurisdiction and What Jurisdiction Amounts to' Leiden Journal of International Law (2012) 25, 857, 873.

and enforce regulation, whereas jurisdiction as factual control refers to the *duty* to respect human rights, even when such control is illegitimate.[158] If states would only have human rights obligations when lawfully exercising their jurisdiction abroad, this would create an unacceptable legal vacuum, whereby states would have no human rights obligations when they are not acting lawfully. The ICJ has held that the ICCPR 'is applicable in respect of acts done by a State in the exercise of its jurisdiction outside its own territory',[159] both with regard to Israel and the Palestinian territories[160] and with regard to armed activities perpetrated by Uganda on Congolese territory.[161] It would be wrong if states could do abroad what they have undertaken not to do at home. As the ECtHR noted in *Cyprus v Turkey*, 'any other finding would result in a regrettable vacuum in the system of human rights protection'.[162] *De jure* and *de facto* jurisdiction can, of course, fully overlap: where states have sovereignty over a territory, it is obvious that their human rights obligations apply. The substantive content of the rights that need to be respected would then be proportional to the extent of control that is being exercised. Positive obligations require a degree of governmental power, in contrast to negative obligations.[163] Obligations could in that regard be 'divided and tailored'.[164]

---

[158] ECHR Grand Chamber, *Loizidou v Turkey* 15318/89 (23 March 1995), para. 62.

[159] ICJ Advisory Opinion, *Legal consequences of the construction of a wall in the occupied Palestinian territory* ICJ Reports 2004, 136 (2004), para. 111.

[160] Ibid. paras. 109, 113.

[161] ICJ *Armed Activities on the Territory of the Congo (Democratic Republic of the Congo v Uganda)* (19 December 2005), paras.179, 216.

[162] ECHR Grand Chamber, *Cyprus v Turkey* 25781/94 (10 May 2001), para. 78. The Court challenged its own understanding in *Bankovic*, introducing the concept of *'espace juridique'* or 'legal space', meaning that ECHR obligations could only apply extraterritorially within the legal space of the ECHR (i.e. within the territories of the Parties) due to the 'essentially regional context' of the ECHR. (ECHR Grand Chamber (Adm. Dec.) *Bankovic et al. v Belgium et al.* 55207/99 (12 December 2001), para. 59.) This concept makes little sense, because either protection is purely territorial and thus regional, or protection extends extraterritorially and extends to the locations of acts by ECHR party states. This distinction has not been reiterated in any of the later ECtHR jurisprudence.

[163] Olivier De Schutter, 'Globalization and Jurisdiction: Lessons from the European Convention on Human Rights' Baltic Yearbook on International Law (2006) 6, 185, 245; Hugh King, 'The Extraterritorial Human Rights Obligations of States' Human Rights Law Review (2009) 9:4, 521, 538. See also the ECtHR, stating that 'the scope of the positive obligations must be interpreted in a way that does not impose an impossible or disproportionate burden on the authorities' in ECHR *Osman v United Kingdom* 23452/94 (28 October 1998), para. 116.

[164] ECHR Grand Chamber, *Ilascu and others v Moldova and Russia* 48787/99

The grounds upon which the international and regional human rights bodies have based their extraterritorial application of the treaties can be classified under two main headings. The first ground is founded upon a link with the territory, such as control over territory, and can be classified as spatial jurisdiction.[165] The second refers to a relationship of control over an individual, and can be classified as personal jurisdiction.[166]

Spatial jurisdiction can be established when one state has 'effective control' over the territory of another state. For example, the ECtHR noted with regard to Turkish occupation in northern Cyprus:

> Having effective overall control over northern Cyprus, its responsibility cannot be confined to the acts of its own soldiers or officials in northern Cyprus, but must also be engaged by virtue of the acts of the local administration, which survives by virtue of Turkish military and other support.[167]

Control can also be established when one state is 'under the decisive influence' of another state through, for instance, military, economic, financial and political support, as was the case in *Ilascu and others v Moldova and Russia*, where the ECtHR found that citizens arrested in the Moldovian Republic of Transdniestria fell within the jurisdiction of Russia as well.[168] A consequence of the effective control doctrine is that states that have lost control can no longer hold the same duties regarding human rights protection. States must in such cases take all the appropriate measures which are still within its power to comply with their obligations.[169]

Personal jurisdiction can be established in cases of actual authority over persons, for instance with regard to extraterritorial obligations in detention cases. The ECtHR held on several occasions that as soon as prisoners were detained by a state, they fell under the control, and therefore the jurisdic-

---

(8 July 2004), paras. 441ff; ECHR Grand Chamber, *Al-Skeini v UK* 55721/07 (7 July 2011), para. 139.

165 ECHR Grand Chamber, *Al-Skeini v UK*, paras. 138ff.

166 Ibid. paras. 133ff.

167 ECHR Grand Chamber, *Cyprus v Turkey*, para. 77. See also the positions of the Inter-American Commission in IACHR Petition, *Victor Saldano v Argentina* IACHR Report No 38/99 (11 March 1999), para. 19, and the African Commission in Communication 227/1999, *Democratic Republic of the Congo (DRC) v Burundi, Rwanda and Uganda*, 20th Annual Activity Report (2006), para. 93.

168 ECHR Grand Chamber, *Ilascu and others v Moldova and Russia* para. 392.

169 Ibid. paras. 313, 331. Serbia for instance was found to lack effective control over Kosovo after its withdrawal in 1999, see ECHR *Azemi v Serbia* 11209/09 (5 November 2013).

tion, of the detaining state.[170] There has been discussion whether control over detention facilities abroad should be seen as control over an area or over persons. Both the ECtHR with regard to UK-run Iraqi prisons and the Inter-American Commission with regard to Guantanamo accepted control over the facility (that is an 'area') as a sufficient ground.[171] In *Al-Skeini v UK*, the ECtHR combined personal jurisdiction with spatial jurisdiction by emphasizing the exercise of public powers, which would make the exercise of personal jurisdiction more exceptional.[172] The Inter-American Commission relied on personal jurisdiction when victims that were shot by Cuban state agents outside Cuba's territory were found to be within the control, and thus jurisdiction, of the Cuban agents.[173] It is difficult to determine the exact scope of personal jurisdiction. Does the capacity to hurt another person suffice?[174] Or is a more legal relationship required?[175] Lawson suggests a direct and immediate link between the extraterritorial conduct of a state and the alleged violation of an individual's right to trigger jurisdiction. The decision to cut development aid,

---

[170] ECHR Grand Chamber, *Medvedyev and others v France* 3394/03 (29 March 2010), para. 67; ECHR *Öcalan v Turkey* 46221/99 (12 March 2003), para. 93; ECHR Grand Chamber, *Hassan v UK* 29750/09 (16 September 2014), para. 76. See also Dutch troops in command of a checkpoint, ECHR Grand Chamber, *Jaloud v Netherlands* 47708/08 (20 November 2014), paras. 143, 149.

[171] ECHR AdmDec, *Al-Saadoon and Mufhdi v United Kingdom* 61498/08 (30 June 2009), para. 88. A similar position was adopted by the UK House of Lords in House of Lords, Great Britain (UK) *Al-Skeini et al. v Secretary of State for Defence* [2007] UKHL 26 (13 June 2007); IACHR *Request for Precautionary Measures Concerning the Detainees at Guantanamo Bay, Cuba* 41 ILM (2002) 532 (12 March 2002). See also Christina M Cerna, 'Extraterritorial Application of the Human Rights Instruments of the Inter-American System' in Fons Coomans and Menno T Kamminga (eds.), *Extraterritorial Application of Human Rights Treaties* (Intersentia 2004), 264.

[172] ECHR Grand Chamber, *Al-Skeini v UK*, para. 150. At this point, the Court combined a concept of spatial jurisdiction through exercising public powers in the area with a concept of personal jurisdiction (physical control over a person), as will be further discussed below.

[173] IACHR *Armando Alejandro Jr. et al. v Cuba (Brothers to the rescue)* IACHR Report No 86/99, Case No 11.589 (29 September 1999).

[174] Would an attack by drones lead to sufficient control to establish jurisdiction? See Jordan J Paust, 'The Bush-Cheney Legacy: Serial Torture and Forced Disappearance in Manifest Violation of Global Human Rights Law' Barry Law Review (2012) 18:1, 61.

[175] Rick Lawson, 'Life After Bankovic: On the Extraterritorial Application of the European Convention on Human Rights' in Fons Coomans and Menno T Kamminga (eds.), *Extraterritorial Application of Human Rights Treaties* (Intersentia 2004) 95.

for instance, should not be sufficient ground to fall within the scope of the Convention. On the other hand, it would be too restrictive to require a formal legal or structural relationship, as this would unjustifiably exclude jurisdiction in situations of factual control.[176]

In addition to effective control, a broader scope of extraterritorial obligations for economic, social and cultural rights has been suggested in the non-binding Maastricht Principles on Extraterritorial Obligations of States in the Area of Economic, Social and Cultural Rights.[177] Principle 9 suggests establishing jurisdiction based, firstly, on effective control; secondly, where state acts or omissions bring about foreseeable *effects* on the enjoyment of rights within or outside its territory; and thirdly, and very notably, 'situations in which the State, acting separately or jointly, whether through its executive, legislative or judicial branches, is *in a position* to exercise *decisive influence* or to take measures to realize economic, social and cultural rights extraterritorially, in accordance with international law'.[178]

It is not clear what the drafters meant exactly with 'in a position to exercise decisive influence' and the Commentary to the Maastricht Principles does not elaborate on this point. Can powerful markets that are in a position to address global environmental concerns through trade measures be seen as being 'in a position to exercise decisive influence' and hence have the duty to use that influence? Principle 25 sets out 'the relevant bases to

[176] Rick Lawson, 'The Concept of Jurisdiction and Extraterritorial Acts of State' in Gerard Kreijen et al. (eds.), *State, Sovereignty, and International Governance* (Oxford University Press 2002) 294.

[177] Maastricht Principles on Extraterritorial Obligations of States in the Area of Economic, Social and Cultural Rights (2012). The Maastricht Principles were developed over a two-year period between 2009 and 2011 and subsequently adopted by human rights experts at a meeting in 2011 convened by Maastricht University and the International Commission of Jurists. Signatories include current and former members of UN human rights treaty bodies, former and current Special Rapporteurs of the Human Rights Council, along with academics and legal advisers of leading non-governmental organizations. The Extraterritorial Obligations Consortium created in 2007 and composed to date of leading academics and NGOs played a pivotal role throughout the process. (Olivier De Schutter et al., 'Commentary to the Maastricht Principles on Extraterritorial Obligations of States in the Area of Economic, Social and Cultural Rights' Human Rights Quarterly (2012) 34, 1084.) They are the opinion of an international group of experts suggesting extraterritorial obligations needed to fill a legal vacuum in the sphere of economic, social and cultural rights.

[178] Maastricht Principles on Extraterritorial Obligations of States in the Area of Economic, Social and Cultural Rights, Principle 9 (emphasis added).

exercise extraterritorial (prescriptive) jurisdiction by a state'.[179] It reads that 'States must adopt and enforce measures to protect economic, social and cultural rights through legal and other means' when among others 'the harm or threat of harm originates or occurs on its territory'. The commentary to Principle 25 advances that when states seek to contribute to concerns of interest to all (such as the Millennium Development Goals (MDGs)), 'a more flexible understanding of the limits on prescriptive extraterritorial jurisdiction may be justified'.[180] Principle 26 suggests that states 'that are in a position to influence the conduct of non-State actors even if they are not in a position to regulate such conduct', should exercise their influence. Protecting common concerns through trade measures – for instance, restricting market access unless exporters respect certain environmental standards – seems to fall within the scope of this Principle: a state is not actually regulating conduct, but exercising its influence if certain values are not respected.

4.5.2 Shared and Fundamental Environmental Concerns

The concept and use of extraterritoriality in a human rights context differs from that in a trade context. Whereas the extraterritorial application of international human rights treaties relates to an extension of the *own* human rights obligations of a state when acting abroad – obligations that a state has committed to within its own sovereign territory – extraterritoriality through npr-PPMs imposes obligations *on others*. In a human rights context, a state's own obligations are 'activated extraterritorially' to apply to its own actions abroad in cases of factual control over persons or territory, whereas in a trade context, a state's rules are extended to apply to the actions of others (foreign producers), through the trigger of market access. While clearly different, there is a common element: concerns about human rights and concerns about the environment can arguably be seen as shared, global or even universal concerns. The purpose of protecting human rights as well as the environment in an extraterritorial manner envisages the protection of those who are not immediately linked to the sovereign territory of the acting state in the traditional sense, but are undeniably linked through a common 'concern'. A lack of human rights protection can lead to abuse of state power, insecurity and instability, which can have an impact beyond state borders – either factually, through spill-over effects, or morally. Likewise, a lack of environmental protection

179 De Schutter et al., 2012, 1139.
180 Ibid.

does not only affect one state, and environmental harm does not stop at the border. Depending on the environmental concerns at issue, their impact will spread more or less quickly and will cause more or less harm, but it is without doubt that we have to share our planet, and are thus all affected by a lack of environmental protection. The common element in the human rights case law, and in what this chapter seeks to demonstrate, is the need for an extension of jurisdictional boundaries in case of common, transboundary or global concerns.

The analysis of jurisdictional clauses in human rights treaties will be of little help to the interpretation of the scope of the WTO agreements, as these do not contain a jurisdictional clause. Similarly, the interpretation of jurisdiction by the human rights bodies as *factual* jurisdiction (linked to control over either territory or individuals) makes little sense in a trade context: the question in the latter is whether it is lawful to 'regulate' over actions occurring abroad through npr-PPMs with the objective of addressing non-trade concerns located outside the territory of the regulating state, without any factual control over the territory in which production is occurring or over the producers: the only control is exercised through conditioning market access. The human rights law analysis is nevertheless relevant, because human rights courts and tribunals have shown willingness to think creatively in order to address transboundary concerns so as to avoid a legal vacuum in human rights protection. That willingness and creativity could be applied in a trade and environment context as well, because of the current legal vacuum in (certain areas of) environmental protection. In the absence of binding international agreement, environmental npr-PPMs aim to fill a legal vacuum that exists because common environmental concerns cannot be dealt with by one state alone. Human rights courts and tribunals protect the values as enshrined in regional and international human rights treaties. While there might be few binding environmental agreements, there is a large body of soft law, recognizing the urgency of global protection, such as the 2015 Paris Agreement, CITES or Food and Agriculture Organization (FAO) guidelines on deforestation. Could this body of soft law be considered as a strengthening factor for the justification of the extraterritorial effects of npr-PPMs addressing those environmental concerns?

The suggestions with respect to extraterritorial obligations for economic, social and cultural rights as laid down in the Maastricht Principles can furthermore be relevant to npr-PPMs. Firstly, the Principles point to a possible duty for states that are in a position to influence to help realize ECS rights extraterritorially, which could be translated into a duty for states with a powerful market to use their market power to help realize transboundary or global environmental protection. Secondly, they refer to a duty to prevent harm from activities abroad, whereby the specific nature of common goals should be taken into account in order to allow for a more flexible understanding of jurisdictional limits. MDG 7, the goal to ensure environmental sustainability, emphasizes the common nature of environmental threats. Thirdly, according to the Principles, states should also aim at influencing the conduct of non-state-actors to help realize ECS rights. By targeting producers and their production processes, npr-PPMs are a pre-eminent example of such influence on non-state-actors.

Surely, the exercise of these powers requires a sound system of checks and balances to avoid abuse. In a trading context, these checks can be found in the non-discrimination principles, both in the substantive obligations and under the general exceptions (e.g. the *chapeau* to Article XX). It is key that the common nature of the objective pursued by a PPM is emphasized and that a unilateral trade measure is based to the extent possible upon multilaterally agreed norms, standards or concerns, relying to the extent possible on international hard or soft law.[181]

4.6 CONCLUSION

This chapter has given an overview of the theoretical framework of jurisdiction and extraterritoriality. Whereas enforcement jurisdiction is always prohibited, absent consent of the territorial state, extraterritorial prescriptive jurisdiction is not *per se* unlawful: when a state can rely on a connecting factor through one of the permissive principles, an extraterritorial exercise of jurisdiction can be permitted. Imposing environmental requirements on foreign production processes through npr-PPMs is an exercise of extraterritorial prescriptive jurisdiction, as all enforcement remains territorial.

Different degrees of extraterritoriality have been discerned with regard to prescriptive measures. In Chapter 3, two notions of extraterritoriality related to npr-PPMs were identified: firstly, regarding the foreign production process targeted by a PPM; secondly, regarding the non-trade concern that is located (partly) outside the territory of the regulating state. The first notion refers to a question of definition. Are PPMs in general

---

[181] See among others Ian Manners, 'The Normative Ethics of the European Union' International Affairs (2008) 84:1, 45 (arguing that the EU promotes a series of normative principles that are generally acknowledged to be universally applicable). Questioning the real normative model of the EU, see Kalypso Nicolaidis and Robert Howse, ''This Is My EUtopia . . .': Narrative as Power' Journal of Common Market Studies (2002) 40:4, 767.

'extraterritorial measures', and if so, do states have jurisdiction to impose such measures? As discussed in this chapter, npr-PPMs are not fully extraterritorial, as they need to be activated through a territorial connection, being market access. Rather, they can be designated as measures with an extraterritorial effect or territorial extension. Through an analysis of extraterritoriality in the fields of competition law and international human rights law, different grounds have been identified that could strengthen a justification of the extraterritorial effect of npr-PPMs addressing global environmental concerns, in addition to a requirement of reasonableness when different interests must be balanced.

The effects doctrine, as known in competition law, could be applied to environmental npr-PPMs by assessing environmental effects on the territory of the regulating state. Those concerns that are inward-looking, or partly outward-looking and that affect the regulating state could be permitted through reliance on the effects doctrine. The practical application of direct, substantial and foreseeable effects in an environmental context raises a number of questions that must be considered on a case-by-case basis. Chapter 5, proposing the extraterritoriality decision tree, as well as Chapter 6, applying the tree to case studies of npr-PPMs, will elaborate on these. In light of the existing body of international environmental law – consisting of a wide array of soft law in addition to a few binding instruments – it also could be argued that weaker or uncertain effects could lead to justification of the extraterritorial effects of npr-PPMs, when the norm imposed by the PPM is supported by such an international instrument.

Reference to substantive norms can be found in the analysis of the extraterritorial application of international and regional human rights treaties. Despite the obvious differences between the extraterritorial application of international human rights and the extraterritorial effect of npr-PPMs, the analysis of human rights practice can still be of guidance. The human rights perspective offers valuable insight on the general willingness to protect common values and concerns. Through the creative interpretation of the human rights treaty bodies of jurisdiction as factual control, these bodies have shown that, where necessary, the notions of jurisdiction and sovereignty can be elastic. The extraterritorial application enshrines the 'normative basis for the protection of fundamental rights as rights of human beings rather than as rights of citizens',[182] a statement that could be

[182] Stephen Gardbaum, 'Human Rights and International Constitutionalism' in Jeffrey L Dunoff and Joel P Trachtman (eds.), *Ruling The World? Constitutionalism, International Law, and Global Governance* (Cambridge University Press 2009) 233.

equally applied to the right to a cleaner environment. Where the common nature of human rights is evidenced by the almost universal membership of the UN human rights treaties, as well as by the extensive membership of regional human rights treaties, the common nature of environmental concerns can be evidenced by the large body of largely soft environmental law, but also, in lack thereof, by civil society and science.[183] A more lenient approach in this regard is justified with respect to environmental standards prescribed by a npr-PPM, as npr-PPMs do not impose any legal duty on states – in contrast to the human rights context, where an extraterritorial application of human rights obligations does impose a legal duty on the state that is bound by those obligations.

[183] See e.g. common concern of mankind (UN General Assembly Resolution 43/53 para. 1 (climate change)); IPCC Fifth Assessment Report 2013–2014.

5. The proposal of a WTO extraterritoriality decision tree

5.1 INTRODUCTION

Protecting environmental concerns through npr-PPMs raises two distinct but related extraterritoriality questions. Firstly, extraterritoriality related to the location of the activity that has detrimental effects on the environment, i.e. the location of the 'production' abroad, for example, the fishing of tuna in foreign waters: can states 'regulate' foreign production activities, by conditioning market access on whether foreign producers comply with prescribed rules? Secondly, extraterritoriality related to the location of the concern that a measure aims to protect, e.g. dolphins or migratory sea turtles, clean air or biodiversity: can states use trade measures to protect transboundary environmental concerns or concerns located outside the territory of the regulating state? The previous chapters have analysed the application of extraterritoriality in different fields of international law, such as public international law, competition law and international human rights law. Due to the lack of guidance on jurisdictional issues and extraterritoriality in the WTO agreements and in case law, and because the WTO agreements should not be interpreted in clinical isolation of public international law,[1] the lessons learned from the analysis of those other fields will now be applied to a WTO context.

Public international law is relevant to the first question. As has been demonstrated, npr-PPMs should not be seen as extraterritorial measures *stricto sensu.* 'Extraterritorial' trade measures *affect* or *incentivize* conduct abroad, rather than *regulate* that conduct. The measure is only activated once access to the market is sought. Npr-PPMs should instead be qualified as measures with an extraterritorial effect or measures of territorial extension.[2] Enforcement of trade measures is territorial as it occurs within

[1] WTO, *United States – Standards for Reformulated and Conventional Gasoline* AB Report 1996, WT/DS2/AB/R, 17.

[2] Joanne Scott, 'Extraterritoriality and Territorial Extension in EU Law' American Journal of Comparative Law (2014) 62, 87, 90. See also Stefan Zleptnig, *Non-Economic Objectives in WTO Law: Justification Provisions of GATT,*

the territory of the imposing member, likely at the border. Even when not unlawful from a general international law perspective, npr-PPMs still raise questions concerning their legality and acceptability under WTO law, due to their potential impact on foreign producers and/or policymakers.

This leads to the second question: whether WTO law, and in particular the GATT, allows states to use trade measures to address environmental concerns that may be located outside the territory of the regulating state or whether it acts as a stumbling block. As has been discussed in Chapter 2, there has been much debate on whether npr-PPMs should be addressed under Article III GATT or Article XI GATT. While that choice is of importance for the determination of infringements, neither provision *de lege lata* takes into account the objective of a measure, nor do they contain any reference to a jurisdictional limitation. Even if npr-PPMs have the objective to protect 'extraterritorial' environmental concerns, as long as a npr-PPM is not inconsistent with substantive GATT or other WTO obligations, the extraterritorial element is not relevant for the WTO analysis.

However, a npr-PPM in violation with substantive obligations can be justified under Article XX GATT, at which point the objective of the measure will be assessed. Article XX has so far been the principal battle-field for PPM regulations, and will most likely remain so. Similar to the rest of the GATT, Article XX does not contain any reference to jurisdiction. In *US – Shrimp*, in answer to the question whether the US could only act to protect a concern within its jurisdiction, the AB referred to a 'sufficient nexus' between the migratory sea turtles and the US, without defining the required nexus. In *EC – Seal Products*, the AB emphasized the systemic importance of determining the jurisdictional limitations of Article XX GATT, but did not explore the issue further due to a lack of arguments made by the parties.[3] The question thus remains whether trade measures that aim to protect an environmental concern located outside the territory of the regulating state can be accepted.

This chapter proposes an extraterritoriality decision tree within the framework of Article XX GATT, offering a systematic approach to assess the 'extraterritorial' objectives of npr-PPMs. The model finds its legal basis in the paragraphs of Article XX GATT and functions as an

---

GATS, SPS and TBT Agreements, Vol. 1 (Mads Andenas ed., Martinus Nijhoff Publishers 2010) 308; Erich Vranes, *Trade and the Environment: Fundamental Issues in International Law, WTO Law and Legal Theory* (Oxford University Press 2009) 174.

[3] WTO, *European Communities – Measures Prohibiting the Importation and Marketing of Seal Products* AB Report 2014, WT/DS401/AB/R, para. 5.173.

extraterritoriality threshold question before the measure can further be examined under the subparagraphs and *chapeau* of Article XX GATT. Some critical observations will be made with regard to certain challenges and dilemmas, some of which go beyond the legal framework but are nonetheless worth noting.

5.2 ASSESSING THE EXTRATERRITORIAL EFFECT OF ENVIRONMENTAL NPR-PPMS UNDER ARTICLE XX GATT: A DECISION TREE

5.2.1 The Environmental Exception Grounds and Necessity

5.2.1.1 Environmental concerns

As has been discussed in Chapter 2, if a violation of a substantive GATT obligation has been established, justification can be sought under Article XX GATT. The analysis of the paragraphs of Article XX GATT consists of a two-tier test: firstly, the objective must be covered by one of the listed areas; and secondly, with regard to the relationship between the measure at issue and the societal value pursued, a degree of necessity – depending on the wording of the particular paragraph – must be shown.

Paragraphs (b) and (g) of Article XX GATT allow WTO Members to rely on environmental objectives to justify measures that are inconsistent with the substantive obligations of GATT. Article XX(b) refers to the protection of human, animal or plant life and health, while Article XX(g) refers to the conservation of exhaustible natural resources. Generally, the concerns at issue relate either to pollution or to resources.[4] Competitiveness concerns and economic motivations related to environmental concerns, such as measures to 'level the playing field' by insisting that foreign producers use the same production practices as domestic producers in order to offset regulatory costs differences, cannot be justified by virtue of Article XX.[5] Commercial externalities due to environmental policy differences cannot be accepted as a possible justification ground for PPMs with an extraterritorial effect. Lax environmental policies could, however, lead to environmental harm, either within the territory of the importing state or transboundary harm, or lead to damage to the global commons. These

---

[4] OECD, *Processes and Production Methods (PPMs): Conceptual Framework and Considerations on Use of PPM-based Trade Measures* (1997) 27.

[5] Petros C Mavroidis, 'Reaching Out For Green Policies: National Environmental Policies in the WTO Legal Order' EUI Working Papers RSCAS 2014/21, 2014, 9.

physical environmental externalities are likely to fall within the scope of paragraphs (b) and (g) of Article XX and the economic concerns can very well be intertwined with the environmental concerns. The primary motivation must be environmental, though.[6]

The question at issue is whether there is an implied jurisdictional limitation to Article XX: are paragraphs (b) and (g) limited to concerns within the territory or jurisdiction of the imposing member, or can members also rely on the exceptions to address environmental concerns outside their territory? Under Article 31(1) VCLT, a treaty is to be interpreted in good faith, starting with an examination of the ordinary meaning of the words, read in their context, and in the light of the object and purpose of the treaty involved. When the tools offered by Article 31 VCLT do not resolve a problem of interpretation, Article 32 VCLT allows for supplementary means of interpretation, including the *travaux préparatoires*.[7] Neither paragraph (b) nor (g) of Article XX GATT contain a reference to territory or jurisdiction. There are no subsequent agreements between the parties on the jurisdictional scope of Article XX, nor do the *travaux* reveal the intent of the parties with respect to the appropriate limitation of Article XX.[8] What is known is that WTO Members' trade relations should allow for 'the optimal use of the world's resources in accordance with the objective of sustainable development, seeking both to protect and preserve the environment'.[9] Given this lack of direction on a territorial or jurisdictional scope, there is no ground to assume that Members can only protect concerns that are strictly within their territory. Especially in light of the non-territorial nature of environmental challenges, a broader

---

[6] Robert Howse and Donald Regan, 'The Product/Process Distinction – An Illusory Basis for Disciplining "Unilateralism" in Trade Policy' European Journal of International Law (2000) 11:2, 249, 280.

[7] While not all WTO Members are parties to the VCLT, the AB has recognized the VCLT's rules on treaty interpretation (Articles 31 and 32) as customary international law and its relevance for the interpretation of the WTO Agreements, thereby making them binding on all States. See WTO, *Japan – Taxes on Alcoholic Beverages II* AB 1996, WT/DS8/AB/R, p. 10.

[8] The GATT was drafted by governments at the UN Conference on Trade and Development between 1946–1948. The Conference negotiated a Charter for the International Trade Organization, and the GATT was viewed as an interim agreement pending the implementation of the ITO Charter. The preparatory work of the ITO Charter is thus considered the preparatory work of the GATT. No references are made to a territorial limitation. See also Steve Charnovitz, 'The Moral Exception in Trade Policy' Virginia Journal of International Law (1998) 38, 689, 700.

[9] Marrakesh Agreement Establishing the World Trade Organization, 1867 UNTS 154, 33 ILM 1144, 1994, preamble.

interpretation of the listed environmental objectives, including concerns located outside the territory of the regulating state, seems appropriate. The increasing awareness of the global nature of environmental concerns such as climate change justifies a broad interpretation of Article XX, considering the AB's finding that the WTO agreements should be interpreted in light of contemporary concerns.[10]

Nonetheless, acceptance of environmental objectives without any jurisdictional limitation would distort the appropriate balance between regulatory space and free trade. In *US – Shrimp*, the AB relied on a 'sufficient nexus' between the concern (sea turtles) and the regulating state (the US), implicitly requiring a territorial link by referring to the turtles swimming through US waters. The AB failed to give further guidance on the requirements of a nexus. In order to approach more systematically the assessment of concerns, the proposed extraterritoriality decision tree relies on environmental effects within the territory of the regulating state and distinguishes as a first step between internal or inward-, external or outward-, and inward/outward-looking measures, based on the location of the concern.[11] This distinction will be elaborated on below when discussing the first step of the decision tree.

5.2.1.2 Necessity

In addition to having a legitimate environmental objective, a trade measure seeking justification must also comply with a necessity test, taking different forms in the different paragraphs of Article XX GATT. Overall, the necessity test involves a process of weighing and balancing a series of factors, which results in an ad hoc, contextual assessment of each measure, such as the contribution of the measure to the end pursued, the restrictive effect of the measure, and whether a WTO-consistent alternative measure is reasonably available.[12] Article XX(b) demands that measures are *necessary* to protect the environment, whereas Article XX(g) does not refer to *necessary* but instead requires a measure to be *related to* the protection of an exhaustible resource. Being *related to* is a more lenient standard than *necessity*, where only a reasonably available least-restrictive measure will pass the test, and not merely a measure that indeed relates to the stated objective.

---

[10] WTO, *United States – Import Prohibition of Certain Shrimp and Shrimp Products* AB Report 1998, WT/DS58/AB/R, para. 129.

[11] Charnovitz introduced this distinction in Charnovitz, 1998, 695.

[12] See AB Report *Korea – Various Measures on Beef*, WT/DS161/AB/R, 2000, paras. 161–164; AB Report *EC – Asbestos* 2001, para. 170–172; AB Report *Brazil – Retreaded Tyres* 2007, paras. 141–144.

In *Korea – Various Measures on Beef* the AB found that with regard to 'necessary' in Article XX(d), one should 'take into account the relative importance of the common interests or values that the law or regulation to be enforced is intended to protect. The more vital or important those common interests or values are, the easier it would be to accept as "necessary" a measure designed as an enforcement instrument.'[13] In this light, the seriousness of the concern could be considered: measures taken in light of fairly grave and imminent environmental threats may be more necessary than measures taken in the light of less imminent, less serious types of environmental threats.[14] Necessity furthermore requires taking into account the level of contribution of the measure to the realization of the end pursued.[15] In *Brazil – Tyres*, the AB noted that the fact that the contribution of a law to the protection of an environmental concern is not immediately obvious, because it is part of a broader programme of which the impact can only be evaluated over time, should not prevent a finding of necessity.[16] The 'extent to which the compliance measure produces restrictive effects on international commerce' is another element that can determine the required level of necessity. The broader the impact, the higher the necessity threshold will be[17] so it must be examined whether less trade restrictive measures could secure the same objective and level of protection.[18]

Article XX(g) does not refer to 'necessary' but requires that measures are 'related to' the conservation of exhaustible natural resources. In *US – Gasoline*, the AB looked at whether 'the means are, in principle, reasonably related to the ends'.[19] In *US – Shrimp*, the AB examined 'the relationship between the general structure and design of the measure here at stake, and the policy goal it purports to serve'.[20] The AB furthermore emphasized the wide support for the concern at issue when discussing whether the measure at stake was related to the legitimate policy concern.[21]

---

[13] WTO, *Korea – Measures Affecting Imports of Fresh, Chilled and Frozen Beef* AB Report 2000, WT/DS161/AB/R, para. 162.

[14] Richard B. Bilder, 'The Role of Unilateral State Action in Preventing International Environmental Injury' Vanderbilt Journal of Transnational Law (1981) 14:1, 51, 61.

[15] AB Report *Korea – Various Measures on Beef* 2000, para. 163.

[16] WTO, *Brazil – Measures Affecting Import of Retreaded Tyres* AB Report 2007, WT/DS332/AB/R, para. 151.

[17] AB Report *Korea – Various Measures on Beef* 2000, para. 163.

[18] AB Report *Brazil – Retreaded Tyres* 2007, para. 178.

[19] AB Report *US – Gasoline* 1996, 20.

[20] AB Report *US – Shrimp* 1998, para. 156.

[21] Ibid. para. 135.

In view of a possible jurisdictional limitation of Article XX and the required balance between the WTO Members' rights, the necessity test allows to further qualify which concerns could be reasonably accepted. The more common and important the interest, the more easily a measure will be deemed necessary. Whereas it is important to take into account how the regulating state values the concern at issue, an analysis should equally consider how a concern is of importance to the broader WTO membership, especially where the environmental concern is (partly) located outside the jurisdiction of the regulating state. The threatened harm must be important enough to justify a violation of the substantive obligations of GATT.[22] Determining the degree of necessity then forms the basis for the second step of the extraterritoriality decision model, to be further elaborated below: assessing the international recognition and support for a norm. According to the AB, a treaty should be interpreted in light of contemporary concerns, which can be evidenced by international instruments of environmental law.[23] Taking into consideration international environmental law in order to assess necessity is also supported by the AB's finding that the WTO agreements are not to be read 'in clinical isolation' from public international law.[24] The more international support for an environmental concern, the easier a measure will be considered 'necessary' to that policy objective.[25] Where less international support exists for an objective or method to reach that objective, the threshold for proving there are no less trade restrictive alternatives (with fewer extraterritorial effects) will become higher. Equally, if a PPM is enforcing a treaty obligation, then that measure will most likely be considered appropriate

---

[22] Robert E Hudec, 'GATT Legal Restraints on the Use of Trade Measures Against Foreign Environmental Practices' in Jagdish Bhagwati and Robert E Hudec (eds.), *Fair Trade and Harmonization: Prerequisites for Free Trade?*, Vol. 2 (The MIT Press 1996) 127. However, international recognition of a norm and the importance of a norm does not necessarily equal the seriousness of possible environmental harm. I do not propose to include graduations of seriousness in the determination of an acceptable extraterritorial effect, as was suggested by Esty: major harm *v* narrower harm; rapid harm *v* less *v* least rapid harm; certain harm *v* less certain harm; irreversible harm *v* reversible harm (see Daniel C Esty, *Greening the GATT: Trade, Environment and the Future* (Peterson Institute 1994) 283). It is likely that more serious harm will be a stronger incentive for states to cooperate internationally and seek agreement; however, lacking both textual support as well as support in practice of international law, the seriousness of harm is not an explicit factor to be taken into account in addition to the proposed elements of location and nature of the concern.

[23] AB Report *US – Shrimp* 1998, para. 129.

[24] AB Report *US – Gasoline* 1996, p. 17.

[25] AB Report *US – Shrimp* 1998, para. 135.

and not more trade restrictive than necessary. Broader acceptance of a norm also reduces potential trade barriers for producers: having to comply with a multilaterally supported norm or standard is less of a burden than having to comply with an infinite number of different norms or standards.

The structure and design of the measure will determine whether a npr-PPM based upon a unilateral concern is considered to be too trade restrictive: for instance, a full ban will be more difficult to justify than other less trade restrictive measures such as a tax or a label. The second step of the decision tree, as outlined below, will be of help to the weighing and balancing process of necessity.

5.2.2 Step 1 of the Decision Tree: Location of the Concern

The first step of the proposed extraterritoriality analysis refers to the location of the concern. Environmental PPMs can be imposed to protect an internal or *inward-looking* concern (e.g. the chemical composition of gasoline can influence pollution levels within the regulating country, often in the form of a product-related PPM), to protect an external or *outward-*

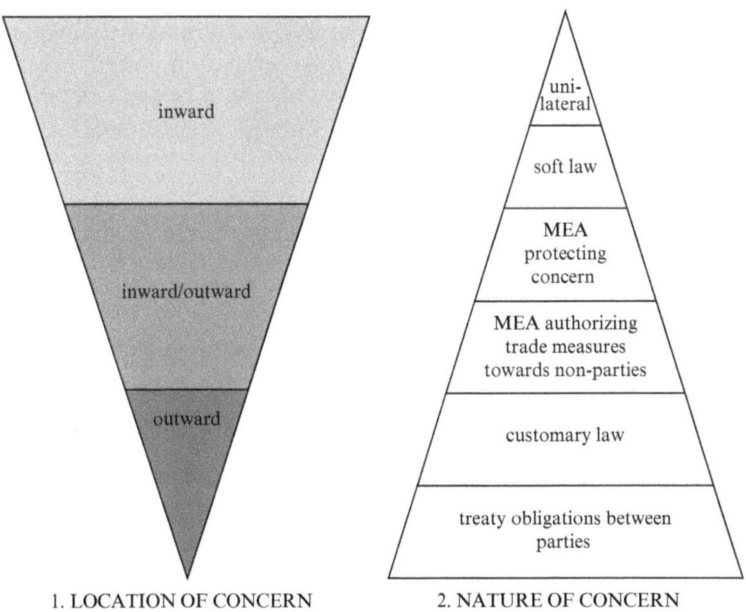

Figure 5.1 Step 1 of the decision tree: location of the concern

looking concern (e.g. dolphin-friendly fishing techniques can lead to fewer dolphins being caught in fishing nets outside the regulating country, typical npr-PPMs), or both inward and outward (e.g. protection of the global commons, the global effects of a preserved rainforest, or sea turtles swimming within and outside territorial waters).[26] Is there a (physical) link still with the territory? Often environmental concerns abroad might be linked to domestic moral concerns (e.g. consumers in country A are morally concerned about the pollution of a lake in country B, which could affect the local supply of drinking water), which could lead to the invocation of the public moral justification under Article XX(a) GATT.[27] The relation between the environmental exceptions and the public morals exception will be discussed in more detail below.[28]

Neither the AB nor any panel have made this explicit distinction, but distinguishing between measures with an inward- or outward-looking purpose allows for a better assessment of the acceptability of PPMs that address activities occurring outside the territory of the regulating country. Purely inward-looking measures, even when non-product-related, will have a much stronger (territorial) connection or nexus than purely outward-looking measures. However, an outward-looking concern could still be an acceptable justification ground if the regulating state is substantially affected by the environmental impact. Without environmental effects on the territory, it is submitted that fully outward-looking concerns will not pass the extraterritoriality threshold and cannot be justified under Article XX GATT.

5.2.2.1 Inward

Inward-looking measures are measures that aim at protecting legitimate concerns within the domestic territory of the importing Member by regulating production activities abroad that have either an impact on the physical characteristics of the imported end product (pr-PPMs) such as a ban on products containing asbestos, a ban on hormones-injected beef or prescriptions for the chemical composition of gasoline;[29] or where the production activities have direct environmental effects on the

---

26 Inspired by the distinction of inward- and outward-looking introduced by Charnovitz, 1998. Robert Hudec refers to the term 'externally-directed' in Hudec, 1996, 116.

27 See AB Report *EC – Seal Products* 2014.

28 See Section 5.3. Environmental Concerns and Public Morals.

29 WTO, *European Communities – Measures Affecting Asbestos and Asbestos-containing Products* AB Report 2001, WT/DS135/AB/R; WTO, *European Communities – Measures Concerning Meat and Meat Products (Hormones)* AB

territory, such as industry in a neighbouring country polluting a transboundary river. States can impose PPMs when the foreign production activity can or will lead to environmental harm within the territory of the importing state. This position finds support under the jurisdictional principles of international law, as harm within the territory allows the state in question to exercise prescriptive jurisdiction over the matter.[30] Jurisprudence has emphasized that states are free and sovereign to determine their own level of environmental protection within their territory.[31]

5.2.2.2 Inward/outward and effects

Most environmental npr-PPMs have both an inward- and outward-directed purpose. The objective they are aiming to protect is of a transboundary nature, such as air pollution, protection of biodiversity or animal species, like the migratory sea turtles in *US – Shrimp*. Transboundary concerns can even take the form of global concerns, where every state is affected by it, such as climate change. The classification of inward- and outward-looking concerns only refers to 'physical' environmental concerns, rather than moral concerns. A measure can address an outward-looking physical environmental concern, combined with an inward-looking moral concern; for instance, concerns by consumers in country A about a polluted lake in country B that local villagers depend on for drinking water, or moral concerns by European consumers about the threatened extinction of pandas. Environmental concerns should first be addressed under the environmental exceptions, before turning to Article XX(a), if environmental protection is the main objective. This relation between the environmental exceptions and moral exception will be discussed in more detail in Section 5.3 of this chapter.

With regard to physical environmental inward-and-outward-looking concerns, the question is how the ratio of inward and outward effects can be determined. In *US – Shrimp*, the AB required a 'sufficient nexus' between the regulating country and the concern to be protected, without

---

Report 1998, WT/DS26/AB/R; AB Report *US – Gasoline* 1996; AB Report *Brazil – Retreaded Tyres* 2007.

30 See *International Bar Association – Legal Practice Division: Report of the Task Force on Extraterritorial Jurisdiction* (2009) 11; Crawford, 2012, 458; Albert Lin, 'The Unifying Role of Harm in Environmental Law' Wisconsin Law Review (2006) 3.

31 AB Report *EC – Asbestos* 2001, para. 168; AB Report *EC – Hormones* 1998, para. 77. See also John H Knox, 'The Judicial Resolution of Conflicts Between Trade and the Environment' Harvard Environmental Law Review (2004) 28, 1, 54.

clarifying what that nexus could consist of: it sufficed for *some of the turtles* to traverse US waters *some of the time*.[32] A territorial connection was implied by the AB, but the question is how such connection must be established in light of the nature of environmental concerns where there is no immediate tangible territorial nexus, or where that nexus seems rather random, as with migratory sea turtles. In particular, global concerns such as air pollution, climate change or biodiversity disruption challenge the traditional understanding of a territorial connection: a clear causal link cannot easily be established, harm is likely to be caused by multiple actors, the harm is not immediately observable and can have different cross-border impacts. It is clear, however, that these environmental concerns can have widespread effects. For example, unsafe use of chemicals in an industrial plant in country A may cause groundwater pollution, leading to river pollution in country B, which could lead to toxic fish in country C.

In this context, the effects doctrine as relied on to justify the extraterritorial application of competition law can be of help.[33] For lack of relevant international competition law rules, national competition law is being applied extraterritorially by a growing number of states, addressing foreign anti-competitive behaviour that affects domestic economic interests.[34] The marketplace no longer has a territorial base and a global economy increases the level of international economic transactions; transnational firms operate in different countries. This line of reasoning can be transposed to environmental challenges and npr-PPMs.[35] Competition law focuses on the effects that anti-competitive behaviour can have on the domestic market; environmental npr-PPMs focus on the effects that production processes can have on the (domestic) environment of the regulating state.

The competition law effects doctrine requires effects to be direct,

---

32 AB Report *US – Shrimp* 1998, para. 133.

33 See Chapter 4 on the effects doctrine and competition law.

34 See Chapter 4.

35 Henrik Horn and Peter C Mavroidis, 'The Permissible Reach of National Environmental Policies' Journal of World Trade (2008) 42:6, 1107, 1133. See also Geert Van Calster, *International and EU Trade Law: The Environmental Challenge* (Cameron May 2000) 214. See also in this regard a report by the OECD countries, agreeing in 1995 already that they should not use trade measures to pressure other countries to change their policies and practices with respect to environmental problems whose effects are limited to the jurisdiction of those countries (OECD, *Report on Trade and Environment to the OECD Council at Ministerial level* (1995) 6).

substantial and foreseeable.[36] With regard to the criteria of direct and substantial effect, it is likely that they will be considered together in an environmental context, as it is not always clear to distinguish between direct and indirect effects, especially with regard to pollution concerns. A substantial effect is clearer and easier to measure, once a threshold is determined.[37] Nevertheless, a requirement of substantial effects raises challenging questions related to the choice of scientific standards and measurement methods. By whom and how will such threshold be determined? Is a substantial effect an *appreciable* effect? Can *potential* effects be sufficient?[38] What about effects that are not yet observable, but likely to manifest themselves in the future? Environmental risks can be very difficult to predict and can often not be specified by a few precisely determined variables, but may instead be driven by the interaction of changes taking place at very different temporal and/or spatial scales.[39] Slow changes that have been taking place over decades or centuries can accumulate with human influences and lead to abrupt changes, for instance. Determining the existence of environmental effects will thus very much depend on the scientific knowledge and available data with regard to a particular concern. It may very well be the case that certain risks are still uncertain. Would it be possible in these cases to adopt a precautionary approach in light of uncertainty?

The precautionary approach refers to action that can be taken with respect to threats of serious or irreversible environmental damage, where there is no full scientific certainty.[40] GATT does not make any explicit

---

[36] See Restatement of the Law (Third) on Foreign Relations Law of the United States, 1986. See §402 on general principles for extraterritorial jurisdiction and §415 on antitrust law.

[37] Whereas antitrust law often relies on clear *de minimis* thresholds before domestic law will be applied to foreign anticompetitive conduct, it is more difficult to establish similar environmental thresholds, as it is almost impossible to estimate the effect of e.g. one ton of CO_2 emissions by a certain activity in a certain location on EU air quality.

[38] In *Alcoa* (*US v Aluminium Co of America*, 148 F.2d 416 (2d Cir. 1945) ('Alcoa')) the potential effects were sufficient, as long as the absence of actual effect was not shown. The US Department of Justice/Federal Trade Commission Guidelines also considers that potential harm can qualify as substantial effects in an antitrust context (Antitrust Enforcement Guidelines for International Operations, April 1995, section 3.121).

[39] Rosie Cooney and Andrew T F Lang, 'Taking Uncertainty Seriously: Adaptive Governance and International Trade' European Journal of International Law (2007) 18:3, 523.

[40] Rio Declaration on Environment and Development, 31 ILM 874, Principle 15 (June 14, 1992).

reference to precaution. A limited recognition of the precautionary principle can be found in Article 5.7 of the SPS Agreement, where Members may act on the basis of available information and where they need to seek additional information for a more objective assessment of risk within a reasonable period of time. The AB in *EC – Hormones* and the Panel in *EC – Biotech* referred to the unclear status of the precautionary principle in international law (and the different positions taken in literature) and left the question whether the principle had crystallized to become a general principle of law unsettled.[41] In addition to Article 5.7 SPS, the AB found the precautionary principle reflected in Article 3.3 SPS, which explicitly recognizes the right of Members to establish their own level of protection, which may be more stringent than that required by existing international standards.[42] Furthermore, Members may also 'rely, in good faith, on scientific sources which, at that time, may represent a divergent, but qualified and respected, opinion' and are thus not obliged to follow the majority scientific opinion.[43] Based on international state practice, one could argue that the precautionary principle has become a principle of environmental law.[44] In light thereof, it could be taken into account for the interpretation of relevant WTO provisions, such as Article XX GATT, even without explicit reference, pursuant to Article 31(3)(c) VCLT.[45]

In cases of inward-looking concerns, states may indeed rely upon the

---

[41] AB Report *EC – Hormones* 1998, para. 123; WTO, *European Communities – Measures Affecting the Approval and Marketing of Biotech Products* Panel report 2006, WT/DS291/R, para. 7.87.

[42] AB Report *EC – Hormones* 1998, para. 123.

[43] Ibid. para. 178.

[44] Principle 15 of the Rio Declaration (1992) provides that 'in order to protect the environment, the precautionary principle shall be widely applied by States according to their capabilities. Where there are threats of serious or irreversible damage, lack of full scientific certainty shall not be used as a reason for postponing cost-effective measures to prevent environmental degradation.' See also among others Tim O'Riordan, James Cameron and Andrew Jordan (eds.), *Reinterpreting The Precautionary Principle* (Cameron May 2001); Ilona Cheyne, 'The Use of the Precautionary Principle in WTO Law and EC Law' (European Union Studies Association Biennial Conference 2005); Mary Stevens, 'The Precautionary Principle in the International Arena' Sustainable Development Law and Policy (2002) 2:2, 13; Alan O Sykes, 'Domestic Regulation, Sovereignty and Scientific Evidence Requirements: A Pessimistic View' Chicago Journal of International Law (2002) 3:2, 353.

[45] Gabrielle Marceau and Joel P Trachtman, 'The Technical Barriers to Trade Agreement, the Sanitary and Phytosanitary Measures Agreement, and the General Agreement on Tariffs and Trade: A Map of the World Trade Organization Law of Domestic Regulation of Goods' Journal of World Trade (2002) 36:5, 811, 849.

precautionary principle as only a state itself can consider its appropriate level of protection.[46] However, when a concern is partly outward-looking a stricter balance must be struck between the domestic interests and the sovereignty of other states affected. As the territorial link (effects) becomes weaker, the interests of the exporting states will carry more weight.[47] Where the protection of the global commons is at issue, the strength of the territorial link cannot apply as such: by its very nature, every state has an equal interest in protecting the global commons. The fact that some states experience less physical harm today than others (or vice versa) should not be the sole ground to determine which state has an 'overriding interest'. Additional weighing factors could then include international consensus on how to protect the concern at issue (i.e. following steps of the decision tree) as well as good faith requirements (in general and as read in the *chapeau*), such as flexibility in the application of the measure, dialogue and international responsiveness.[48]

5.2.2.3 Outward

A third category of measures relates to environmental concerns which are located entirely within the territory of a foreign state, such as a polluted lake in a foreign country, a foreign plant species or foreign animal threatened with extinction.[49] The distinction between foreign harm and transboundary harm depends on the determination of directness of harm: environmental concerns such as polluted or dried out lakes could indirectly lead to other transboundary harm; however, those effects can no longer be considered 'direct' and 'substantial'. Where the environmental effects caused by an activity are too indirect, or too insignificant, a npr-PPM regulating that activity should be considered outward-looking.

Trade barriers solely based on outward-looking concerns, without any territorial link, nexus or effects, cannot be accepted under Article XX GATT, as there is no support for such practice under international law. It is then up to the affected states or the international community as a whole to act. It would be possible to adopt less trade restrictive measures, such as labelling requirements that provide information on the production process

---

46 AB Report *EC – Hormones* 1998, para. 186.

47 See by analogy a reasonableness or comity test as applied in international law and competition law to avoid conflict between the interests of two or more sovereign states in the exercise of extraterritorial jurisdiction. This requires a careful balancing act, whereby the interests of other countries need to be taken into account as much as possible.

48 See Section 5.4.

49 Horn and Mavroidis, 2008, 1166.

(market incentives rather than market bans) that could be accepted under the TBT Agreement.[50] Alternatively, a Member may seek justification under the moral exception of Article XX(a).[51] In the absence of moral concerns or environmental effects on the territory, it is very unlikely that a PPM addressing a fully demarcated foreign environmental harm with no or only an indirect environmental impact on the regulating state would be accepted under Article XX GATT.

5.2.3 Step 2 of the Decision Tree: Nature of the Concern and Norm Recognition

The analysis above has shown that npr-PPMs can be more easily accepted when they are inward-looking; or have a connection or nexus through effects and thus inward/outward-looking. The weaker this territorial connection, however, the more additional support a state will need in order to justify imposing npr-PPMs. In those cases, the level of international recognition and support of a particular norm or concern to be protected is important to determine whether the 'end can justify the means'.[52] As argued above, the necessity test of the paragraphs of Article XX can be interpreted to give added value to international support. In *US – Shrimp*, the AB emphasized the wide support for the concern at issue when discussing whether the measure at stake was related to the legitimate policy concern.[53] Furthermore, the analysis of extraterritoriality in the context of international human rights law has shown that jurisdictional boundaries can be more elastic when common norms are concerned.[54] If

---

[50] The second sentence of Annex 1.1 TBT, referring to among others labelling requirements, only refers to PPMs in general, without distinguishing between related and non-related PPMs. It can thus be accepted that it is then irrelevant to what extent the production process impacts on the final product in order to fall within the scope of the TBT Agreement. See e.g. WTO, *United States – Measures Concerning the Importation, Marketing and Sale of Tuna and Tuna Products* AB Report 2012, WT/DS381/AB/R. See also Gabrielle Marceau, 'A Comment on the Appellate Body Report in *EC-Seal Products* in the Context of the Trade and Environment Debate' RECIEL (2014) 23:3, 318, 327.

[51] See Section 5.3. Environmental Concerns and Public Morals.

[52] According to the AB, Article 3.2 DSU supports that WTO law must be understood within the context of the broader body of international law, including multilateral environmental agreements. AB Report *US – Gasoline* 1996, p. 30.

[53] AB Report *US – Shrimp* 1998, para. 135.

[54] See Chapter 4. A distinction between the human rights context and the trade-environment is that international human rights obligations will apply when states exercise 'effective control' over territory outside their borders. The actual territorial state is at that point unable to ensure sufficient human rights protection

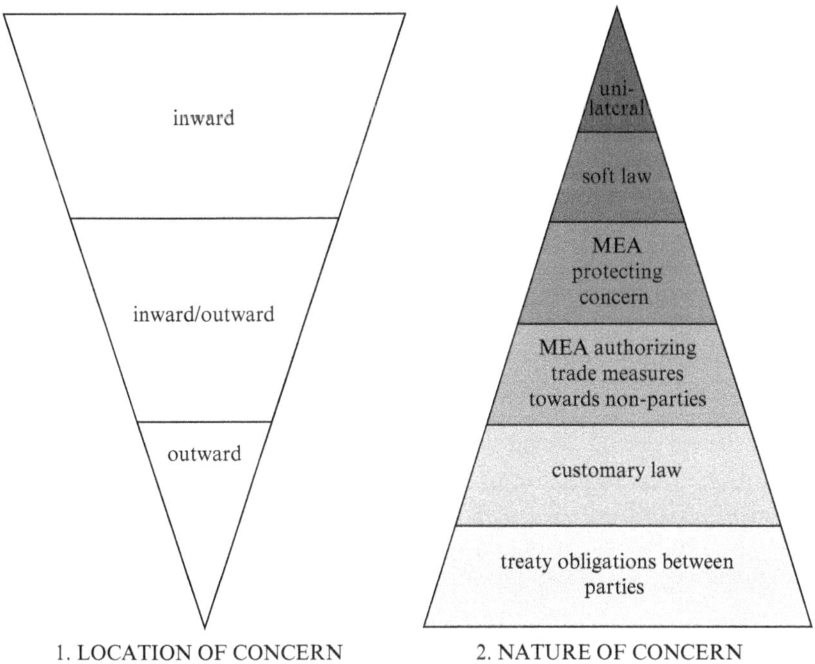

Figure 5.2 Step 2 of the decision tree: nature of the concern and norm recognition

this observation is applied to a trade and environment context, it seems that the more a certain environmental norm is recognized and supported internationally, the more acceptable a npr-PPM protecting that norm through regulating an activity outside its borders will be,[55] and the likelihood of the PPM having a protectionist objective will decrease. Scott

in its territory due to lack of control. In an environmental context, a PPM would apply to all imported goods, without distinguishing between states that are unable to ensure a sufficiently high level of environmental protection, and states that are unwilling to ensure that level of protection.

[55] Under international human rights law, the obligations at issue are laid down in regional and universal human rights treaties, which leads to strong international recognition of these norms by a high number of states (almost universal membership of the UN treaties). As a large number of states have expressed support for the same norms, extraterritorial jurisdiction is definitely easier to accept and the risk of conflicting regulation is dramatically diminished. The main difference in this regard between human rights law and current environmental law is that the former

refers in this regard to the 'international characterization' of norms.[56] The importance of international support is also recognized in Principle 12 of the Rio Declaration on Environment and Development, stating that 'environmental measures addressing transboundary and global environmental problems should, as far as possible, be based on international consensus'. The identical phrase is found in paragraph 2.22(i) of Agenda 21. In combination with the previous step of the decision tree, assessing the location of the concern, a compelling and widely supported international norm could give additional support to npr-PPMs addressing inward/outward-looking concerns, even when the effects would be weaker. Vice versa, in case of little 'back-up' for the norm, the stronger must be the evidence of effects in order to pass the extraterritoriality threshold.

The biggest challenge here is how to determine the international characterization of norms: the formal codification of environmental norms and objectives by the international community has shown to be a slow and difficult process, because of multiple reasons, such as uncertainty or disagreement about the extent of environmental harm, about the appropriate scope and methods of action, about burden-sharing, about historical responsibilities etc. Furthermore, should the assessment of international support only be measured by state action, or could one also take into account positions advocated by NGOs? The suggested categorization of international support below takes into account legal reality,[57] assuming that governments act upon their task to take into account the public interest and to involve civil society,[58] while also allowing for a contextual analysis.

Even though panels and the AB cannot make findings on violations of other (non-WTO) agreements, that does not exclude external rules to be applied in WTO proceedings.[59] Whether the applicable law to WTO

---

consists mainly of binding treaties and declarations, whereas the latter includes many non-binding declarations and other soft law instruments.

56 Scott, 2014, 89.

57 Respecting legal certainty and legal expectations where possible.

58 The political structures of WTO Members vary radically, from full democracies to authoritarian, non-democratic systems. Despite the political structure, it can still be expected that functioning governments represent the interests of their country. If there would be a public outcry, supported by civil society, without the government acting upon this, I submit that that could be an element to take into account in the contextual analysis, e.g. for failure to conclude an agreement. If international agreements cannot be concluded, but there is wide support by civil society, that support (claim, magnitude, etc.) should be considered.

59 WTO, *Mexico-Tax Measures on Soft Drinks and Other Beverages* AB Report 2006, WT/DS308/AB/R, para. 56; Articles 7 and 11 DSU. Zleptnig,

disputes is limited to WTO law or whether and to what extent 'external' international law can be invoked in WTO law is a topic of wide scholarly debate, absent a clear statement on the matter by panels or the AB.[60] Arguably, external rules could be relied upon to interpret a WTO obligation when the external treaty would have the same membership as the WTO.[61] Article 31(3) VCLT, referring to 'subsequent agreement between the parties', 'subsequent practice in the application of a treaty', or 'relevant rules of international law', could allow panels and the AB to look at non-trade agreements to inform the interpretation of the WTO agreements.[62] It is unclear whether Article 31(3)(c) VCLT, referring to the 'relevant rules of international law applicable in the relations between the parties', should be interpreted in a WTO context as the parties to a dispute, or rather as the parties to the WTO as a whole.[63] In *EC – Biotech*, the Panel adopted the latter interpretation, stating that only those rules 'applicable

---

2010, 59; Emily Reid, *Balancing Human Rights, Environmental Protection and International Trade* (Hart Publishing 2015) 207.

[60] For a discussion of the different views held, see Joost Pauwelyn, *Conflict of Norms in Public International Law: How WTO Law Relates to Other Rules of International Law* (Cambridge University Press 2009); Ronnie R F Yearwood, *The Interaction Between World Trade Organisation (WTO) Law and External International Law: The Constrained Openness of WTO Law (A Prologue to a Theory)* (Routledge 2012); Gabrielle Marceau, 'A Call for Coherence in International Law: Praises for the Prohibition Against "Clinical Isolation" in WTO Dispute Settlement' Journal of World Trade (1999) 33:5, 87.

[61] Article 31 VCLT. Article 2(1)(g) VCLT defines 'party' as a 'State which has consented to be bound by the treaty and for which the treaty is in force'. When interpreting obligations under a treaty in light of subsequent agreements or subsequent practice, it only makes sense if the entire Membership has agreed to those. See Joost Pauwelyn, 'The Role of Public International Law in the WTO: How Far Can We Go?' American Journal of International Law (2001) 95:3, 535, 575; WTO, *European Communities – Customs Classification of Certain Computer Equipment* AB Report 1998, WTO/DS62/AB/R, para. 84. The requirement of all parties has a broad scope though, for instance in *US – Cloves* a Doha Ministerial Decision was accepted as representing the 'common understanding' of the membership and in *US – Tuna II* the AB accepted a TBT Committee Decision as a subsequent agreement. It thus seems that all decisions made by consensus by organs and bodies comprising 'all WTO Members' can take decisions that qualify as subsequent agreements. Geraldo Vidigal, 'From Bilateral to Multilateral Law-Making: Legislation, Practice, Evolution and the Future of Inter Se Agreements in the WTO' European Journal of International Law (2013) 24:4, 1027, 1034.

[62] Knox, 2004, 65.

[63] See Reid, 2015, 204. See also for a discussion on Article 31(3)(c) VCLT, Campbell McLachlan, 'The Principle of Systemic Integration and Article 31(3)(c) of the Vienna Convention' International and Comparative Law Quarterly (2005) 54:2, 279; Marceau, 1999, 124; Philippe Sands, 'Treaty, Custom and the

in the relations between all parties to the treaty which is being interpreted' can be taken into account.[64] The Panel then observed, however, that 'the mere fact that one or more disputing parties are not parties to a convention does not necessarily mean that a convention cannot shed light on the meaning and scope of a treaty term to be interpreted'.[65] The AB has adopted a subtle middle way: rules must establish the 'common intention of the parties':[66] under Article 31(3)(c) VCLT the intentions of the broader WTO membership must be taken into account, and a rule must be 'at least implicitly accepted or tolerated by all WTO Members'.[67] It is submitted that when assessing a generally applicable trade measure, a panel must indeed assess the broader interests of the WTO Membership and not only those of the parties to a dispute. The decision tree as proposed here does not suggest any interpretation of WTO provisions by relying on external treaties, however. Rather, what is proposed is that external rules are considered when assessing a norm imposed by a PPM, in order to determine whether that PPM can be considered necessary in light of the common interests of the WTO Members.

5.2.3.1 Treaty obligations between parties

The first category in the second pyramid of the decision model relates to measures that are mandated or authorized by a treaty to which all affected states (i.e. all states with an interest in production and/or export of the good subject to the PPM in question) are a party, and include both mandated PPMs as well as trade sanctions in response to non-observance of the treaty in question.[68] The DSB cannot make findings on violations

---

Cross-Fertilization of International Law' Yale Human Rights and Development Law Journal (1998) 1:1, 85.

64 Panel report *EC – Biotech* 2006, para. 7.71. See also Reid, 2015, 204.

65 Panel report *EC – Biotech* 2006, para. 7.94.

66 WTO, *European Communities – Measures Affecting Trade in Large Civil Aircraft* AB Report 2011, WTO/DS316/AB/R, para. 845.

67 Vidigal, 2013, 1030; Pauwelyn, 2001, 576.

68 Steve Charnovitz, 'The Law of Environmental "PPMs" in the WTO: Debunking the Myth of Illegality' Yale Journal of International Law (2002) 27:1, 59, 105; Lorand Bartels, 'Article XX of GATT and the Problem of Extraterritorial Jurisdiction: The Case of Trade Measures for the Protection of Human Rights' Journal of World Trade (2002) 36:2, 353, 391. For an overview of multilateral environmental treaties prescribing trade measures see Duncan Brack and Kevin Gray, *Multilateral Environmental Agreements and the WTO* (2003); Peter Van den Bossche, Nico Schrijver and Gerrit Faber, *Unilateral Measures Addressing Non-Trade Concerns: A Study on WTO Consistency, Relevance of Other International Agreements, Economic Effectiveness and Impact on Developing*

of other agreements, and thus any panel's findings must be limited to WTO rules.[69] The treaty between the affected parties could, however, be considered when determining the necessity of a npr-PPM.[70] Thus, within the scope of WTO disputes, regulating WTO Members could refer to bi- or plurilateral treaties to substantiate the requirement of necessity of a disputed trade measure, and measures executing obligations under or complying with such treaty will easily pass the extraterritoriality test.[71] However, this reasoning is only valid where the npr-PPM in question only affects those states that are a party to the modifying treaty.

Examples include sustainability clauses in FTAs[72] (the EU, for instance, has an extensive network of bilateral preferential agreements, in which market access is often used as a bargaining chip to obtain changes in environmental policy of the EU's trading partner);[73] international resource conservation agreements that authorize trade measures to enforce the agreements among the parties;[74] or agreements that foresee trade sanctions when their standards are not respected.

Countries of Measures concerning Non-Product-Related Processes and Production Methods (2007) 165.

[69] AB Report *Mexico – Soft Drinks* 2006, para. 56; WTO, *European Communities – Measures Affecting Importation of Certain Poultry Products* AB Report 1998, WT/DS69/AB/R, whereby the bilateral oilseeds agreement was not applicable law and could not be enforced by the WTO DSB. If there is a conflict between the GATT/WTO and the other treaty in question, as a general rule the later treaty will prevail according to Article 30 VCLT.

[70] Article 31 VCLT.

[71] Note that the measure will still need to comply with the conditions of the *chapeau* of Article XX, as any other trade measure seeking justification under Article XX GATT.

[72] See for instance EU–South Korea FTA Article 1.1(g), Article 13(6); Ludo Cuyvers, 'The Sustainable Development Clauses in Free Trade Agreements: An EU Perspective for ASEAN?' UNU-CRIS Working Papers W-2013/10, 2013.

[73] Sophie Meunier and Kalypso Nicolaidis, 'The European Union as a Conflicted Trade Power' Journal of European Public Policy (2006) 13:6, 906, 913. For some examples of such agreements, see Article 20 Cotonou Convention, signed 23 June 2000; Article 52 EU–Ukraine Partnership and Cooperation Agreement [1998] OJ L51/3; Article 9 1988 Cooperation Agreement with the Gulf Cooperation Council [1989] OJ L54/3.

[74] E.g. Convention on International Trade in Endangered Species 1973. The International Commission for the Conservation of Atlantic Tunas recommended that parties take non-discriminatory trade restrictive measures on specified fishery products from listed countries that are adjudged to be violating the Convention. See Resolution by ICCAT Concerning an Action Plan to Ensure Effectiveness of the Conservation Program for Atlantic Bluefin Tuna, Jan 23, 1995, www.iccat.org.

5.2.3.2 Customary international law

A second category with broad international support, but more debated than treaty obligations between affected parties, is customary international law. In order to determine whether a rule has the status of customary international law, there must be consistent and uniform state practice, and a belief that such practice is required by law (*opinio juris*).[75] Once a rule is recognized as custom, it is binding on all states, except for persistent objector-states who have expressly shown that their practice has always differed.[76] In the area of environmental law, very few rules have gained the status of customary law.[77] While there might be consensus on the broader need to protect the environment, or at least a clear prohibition on causing transboundary pollution, there are no rules of customary international law that determine how to address certain concerns or how environmental harm can be punished. References to common concerns of humankind or the global commons should not be considered under the category of customary law as long as there is no consistent practice and *opinio juris* on the matter.

5.2.3.3 Multilateral treaty authorizing trade measures towards non-parties

A third layer of the decision tree refers to environmental trade measures authorized and supported by MEAs towards states that are not a party to that treaty. The regulating Member (party to the MEA) cannot legally rely on its treaty obligations towards the Member that is not a party to the MEA. However, that MEA can still offer support for npr-PPMs in the contextual analysis of determining the common nature of the concern to the international community as a whole. If the treaty has a substantial membership (including a large number of WTO Members, for instance) establishing wide international support for the norm to be protected but the exporting country has not signed the agreement, a balance of the interests at stake might tip to the advantage of the state imposing the

---

[75] Malcolm N Shaw, *International Law* (6th edn., Cambridge University Press 2008) 72.

[76] See e.g. Jonathan Charney, 'The Persistent Objector Rule and the Development of Customary International Law' British Yearbook of International Law (1985) 56:1, 1; Joel P Trachtman, 'Persistent Objectors, Cooperation, and the Utility of Customary International Law' Duke Journal of Comparative and International Law (2010) 21, 221.

[77] One example could be the 1982 United Nations Convention on the Law of the Sea (UNCLOS), which in part already codified existing customary law, and of which many norms now have the status of customary law as well, as non-parties to the treaty also follow many of the UNCLOS norms.

measure.[78] From an environmental perspective, this approach makes most sense, as this does not allow states to escape their (moral/ethical) responsibilities and to free-ride on the environmental efforts of other states.[79]

If the MEA has a more limited membership, relying on the MEA becomes more complicated and sensitive, as one needs to balance individual interests of states, which might all find support in international practice. This balancing of interests will need to be determined on a case-by-case basis, as there is no conclusive general answer. Elements that can be taken into account are the composition of the membership and the affected states (e.g. can an MEA consisting only of developed countries be relied on as support for a measure that mostly affects developing countries?). It could also be considered whether the non-signatory party has clearly opted for not being involved in negotiations or not signing the treaty (e.g. fundamental disagreement), or whether there is another reason why it has not become a party to the MEA yet (e.g. closed membership, delay in negotiations, or other priorities).

Examples of treaties authorizing trade measures towards non-parties include the Basel Convention on the Control of Transboundary Movements of Hazardous Wastes and Their Disposal, which requires parties to prohibit imports of hazardous waste from non-parties;[80] CITES,which does not permit trade of threatened species with non-parties unless with documentation equivalent to CITES permits;[81] the Wellington Convention on Driftnets, which states that a party may take measures *consistent with international law* to prohibit the importation of fish caught using a driftnet;[82] the Anadromous Stocks Convention, which directs

---

[78] Hudec, 1996, 124. See by analogy the reasoning of the AB with regard to recognized international standards under the TBT Agreement. The obligations and privileges associated with international standards pursuant to the TBT Agreement apply with respect to *all* WTO Members, not merely those who participated in the development of the respective standard. Still, the AB found that the larger the number of countries that participate in the development of a standard, the more likely it can be said that the respective body's activities in standardization are recognized. See AB Report *US – Tuna II* 2012, para. 390.

[79] Hudec, 1996, 131.

[80] Basel Convention on the Control of Transboundary Movements of Hazardous Wastes and Their Disposal, March 22, 1989, 28 ILM 649), Article 4.5.

[81] Convention on International Trade in Endangered Species of Wild Fauna and Flora, 993 UNTS 243, 1973.

[82] Convention for the Prohibition of Fishing with Long Driftnets in the South Pacific, Nov 24, 1989, 29 ILM 1454, Article 3(2). Note that it is not clear what is meant with 'consistent with international law' as no reference is made to jurisdictional rules or extraterritoriality.

parties to prevent trafficking in illegally caught anadromous fish;[83] and the Montreal Protocol on Substances that Deplete the Ozone Layer, which bans the import of controlled substances from any non-party.[84]

5.2.3.4 Multilateral treaty aiming at protecting concern at issue

This category of the decision tree refers to trade measures that are protecting an environmental cause that is supported by a treaty, whereby the treaty does not refer to the use of PPMs or any other trade measures.[85] If the agreement at issue is an MEA to which the importing and the exporting state are parties, there should be little disagreement on the environmental objective in case of a dispute. Any discussion will most likely focus on the measure's design and application (including the preferred method to reach an environmental objective). If only the importing member is a party to the MEA, the size of the MEA's membership should be considered in order to assess the degree of international recognition for the environmental objective, as discussed in the previous section.[86] Whether the npr-PPM is aiming to protect a regional concern, or a global concern (protection of the global commons or common concerns of humankind) should be taken into account in the assessment of the MEA's membership. In case of a regional concern, a sizeable membership from the affected region could suffice.

The Kyoto Protocol is an example of an agreement aiming at protecting an environmental concern, without imposing binding commitments on all treaty parties: if a measure is taken with the objective of tackling climate change, the Kyoto Protocol can be relied upon to demonstrate the wide recognition of the need for emission reduction. The targets are binding, even though the Protocol does not prescribe how states should facilitate the necessary reductions.[87] This reference to the Kyoto Protocol raises the

---

83 Convention for the Conservation of Anadromous Stocks in the North Pacific Ocean, Feb 11, 1992, US Senate Treaty Doc 102–30, Article III:3 (www.npafc.org).

84 Montreal Protocol on Substances that Deplete the Ozone Layer, 1987, Articles 4.1, 4.9. The parties also examined the feasibility of banning or restricting from countries not party to the protocol the import of products *produced with* but not containing controlled substances; however, found that it was not feasible to impose such a ban or restriction on imports. See OECD, 1997, 20.

85 The majority of MEAs do not contain trade measures. Eric Neumayer, 'WTO Rules and Multilateral Environmental Agreements' in *The Earthscan Reader on International Trade and Sustainable Development* (Earthscan Publications Ltd 2002) 141.

86 See Section 2.4.3.

87 Kyoto Protocol to the UNFCCC, 1997.

question how specific the international agreement should be. Is it sufficient to share the concern (e.g. global warming) or should the prescribed standards (e.g. emission limits, specific technologies, measurements techniques) also be agreed on internationally? A binding international agreement that regulates the appropriate methods to reach an objective definitely increases the likelihood that a measure will be considered necessary or related to the objective. If the MEA only recognizes the need for protecting the particular concern, panels would need to scrutinize the available (scientific) evidence in order to determine whether the specific measure is not more trade restrictive than necessary. The question is thus whether the measure at issue seeks to enforce internationally recognized standards, or whether the npr-PPMs is aiming at protection levels considerably stricter than the corresponding international standards. In the latter case, the stricter part of the npr-PPM could possibly be considered a unilaterally recognized concern,[88] making it more difficult for WTO Members to justify its extraterritorial effect.[89]

5.2.3.5 Soft law

This layer of the decision tree relates to trade measures protecting an environmental concern that is only addressed in non-binding or soft law, such as UN Declarations.[90] A widely recognized soft law norm could also strengthen a claim for justification of partly outward-looking measures. The recognition of the norm of non-binding agreement must be considered: have a large number of states expressed support to the norm? In other words, can the norm be considered as largely consensual within the international community of states, rather than solely between certain states or within a specific regime?[91] The smaller the support, the stronger the environmental effects on the regulating state must be in order to justify a measure with extraterritorial effects. While the lack of binding agreements could imply a lack of international consensus or sense of urgency at the international level, the choice for a soft law instrument could also be a conscious choice in order to avoid concerns about legal compliance and resulting shallow commitments – in particular in areas of high uncertainty.[92] Despite the weaker incentives for compliance, soft

---

[88] See Section 5.2.3.6.

[89] Joanne Scott, 'The New EU "Extraterritoriality"' Common Market Law Review (2014) 51, 1, 62.

[90] E.g. Rio Declaration on Environment and Development, 1992.

[91] Vidigal, 2013, 1038.

[92] Kal Raustiala, 'Form and Substance in International Agreements' American Journal of International Law (2005) 99:3, 581, 611. Raustiala provides a very

law agreements do demonstrate states' policy concerns and can even entail more clearly drafted and ambitious commitments.[93]

An example of where trade measures are based on soft law is the EU Timber Regulation,[94] which prohibits placing illegally harvested timber on the market to combat illegal logging, a cause supported in several soft law norms, such as the Rio Forest Principles or the 2001 Bali Declaration.[95]

5.2.3.6 Unilateral norms

Concerns that find no support under international law, not even under soft law, are classified in this decision tree as unilateral norms.[96] The absence of international (soft or hard) law does not necessarily mean that there is no state practice by states other than the imposing state, but that there is no concerted formal instrument yet, which increases the level of scrutiny. An element that should be considered here is whether states have started bi- or multilateral negotiations. In *US – Shrimp*, the AB addressed this point under the *chapeau* of Article XX GATT as an aspect of the good faith test implied in the prohibition on arbitrary and unjustifiable discrimination.[97] However, it is submitted that it is more appropriate to consider at this stage of the decision tree whether states have started negotiations, and why they might have failed. In the words of Nollkaemper, 'the preference for multilateralism does not affect the legality of unilateralism when agreements are only hypothetically

---

interesting discussion on why and how states opt for soft or hard law (pledges or contracts).

93 Ibid. 612.

94 Regulation EU/995/2010. For a discussion of the EU Timber Regulation, see Chapter 6.

95 Report of the United Nations on Environment and Development, Non-legally Binding Authoritative Statement of Principles for a Global Consensus on the Management, Conservation and Sustainable Development of all Types of Forests, A/CONF.151/26 (Vol. III), Annex III, 14 August 1992; Ministerial Declaration, Forest Law Enforcement and Governance East Asia Ministerial Conference, Bali September 2001, p. 2. The EU Timber Regulation is particular in that it is not only based on international soft law norms, but also relies explicitly on the national law of the producing country to determine the legality of timber. As the producing country is not necessarily the exporting country to the target market, the soft law support is still relevant.

96 I do not refer to *unilaterally described* policies, as that might be a common aspect of all measures seeking justification under Article XX (AB Report *US – Shrimp* 1998, para. 121.) Unilaterally described policies can still find broader support in international law as the previously discussed categories demonstrate.

97 Ibid. para. 166.

available'.[98] In case of failed negotiations, it is important to take a closer look at the reason for failure: is there a lack of consensus on the concern to be protected, or on how to protect it?[99] As the AB has noted, 'it is one to thing to *prefer* a multilateral approach . . . it is another to require the *conclusion* of a multilateral agreement'.[100] Environmental concerns that are deemed in need of protection by a large group of states, although no agreement has so far been reached in terms of specific commitments or compliance mechanisms, differ from concerns that find very little approval internationally. If there is wide(r) consensus on the urgency and need to protect an environmental threat, which could, for instance, be evidenced by scientific reports or environmental NGO activities, all actors involved should aim at formal cooperation with respect to the particular threat.[101] Such formal cooperation, either through hard or soft law, could then legitimize further unilateral action through, for example, npr-PPMs.

In the absence of multilateral solutions or international recognition of a need due to uncertainty about harm, its seriousness, or its causes, could states rely upon the precautionary principle to protect an environmental concern?[102] Npr-PPMs relating to a unilateral concern run the risk of being

---

98 A Nollkaemper, 'The Legality of Moral Crusades Disguised in Trade Laws: An Analysis of the EC "Ban" on Furs From Animals Taken by Leghold Traps' Journal of Environmental Law (1996) 8:2, 237, 251.

99 In *US – Shrimp* the measure was originally regarded as discriminatory because a multilateral approach was not pursued in the implementation of the measures. After the first AB report the US reached agreements with a number of countries, including three out of the four complainants (not Malaysia). The AB had not found the measure discriminatory because of the lack of consent, but because of the lack of pursuing a multilateral approach. In the compliance case, the AB concluded that this time the US had provided shrimp-exporting countries with 'similar opportunities to negotiate' an international agreement. As a number of countries consented to the US proposal, it is likely that the US proposal could be considered a serious negotiating offer. It is then interesting to examine why other countries did not enter into negotiations or accepted the offer. (WTO, *United States – Import Prohibition of Certain Shrimp and Shrimp Products, Recourse to Article 21.5 of the DSU by Malaysia* AB Report 2001, WT/DS58/AB/RW, para. 131.)

100 Ibid. para. 124.

101 NGOs can be very active participants in treatymaking, in particular in the field of environmental law. After conclusion, they may also monitor implementation, chastise the non-compliant, and encourage reform and renegotiation. See Kal Raustiala, 'NGOs in International Treatymaking' in Duncan B Hollis (ed.), *The Oxford Guide to Treaties* (Oxford University Press 2012).

102 Laurence Boisson de Chazournes, 'Unilateralism and Environmental Protection: Issues of Perception and Reality of Issues' European Journal of International Law (2000) 11:2, 315, 325.

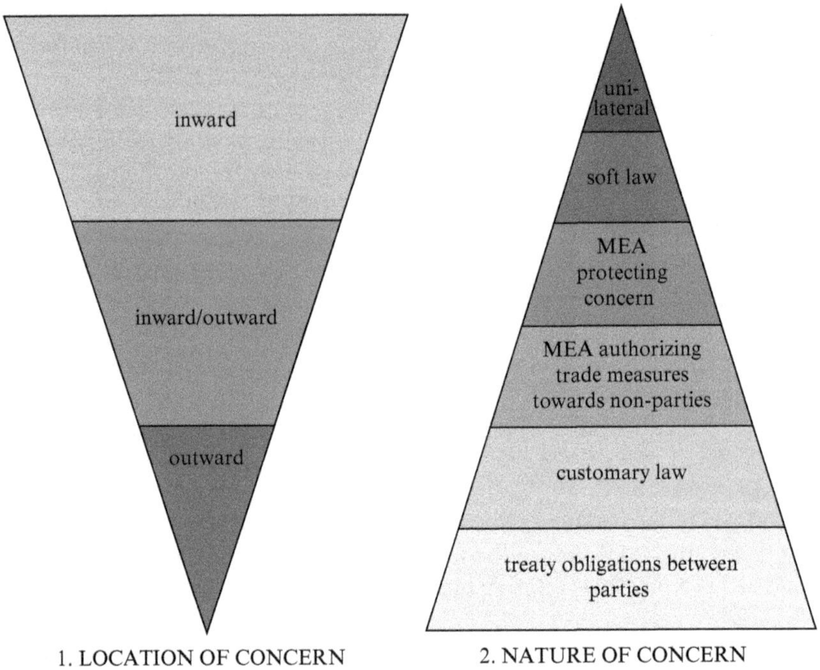

Figure 5.3 Extraterritoriality decision tree

seen as protectionist and will be subject to very strict scrutiny. Within an international organization such as the WTO, it is important to balance the different interests of the Member States and respect for multilateralism, while at the same time realizing the need to protect (yet uncertain) important values in the absence of international action.

Where state interests (unilateral, or more widely supported) conflict with interests of other states, a comity or reasonableness test can be applied.[103] The legitimate interests of the importing country must be balanced against the legitimate interests of the exporting country. For

[103] See Section 5.2.3.2. In the context of competition law, 'true conflict' has been used when conduct complying with one state's regulation is in violation with another state's regulation. When one can comply with both without necessarily violating one set of regulations, there would be no true conflict (*Hartford Fire Ins. Co. v California*, 509 US 764 (1993) (Scalia J., dissenting)). According to Regan and Howse, such true conflict is not very likely, as 'not many countries require that shrimpers use turtle-unfriendly nets, or that cosmetics be tested on animals'. See Howse and Regan, 2000, 286.

example, environmental requirements for imported biofuels could clash with foreign interests such as food security or land grabbing. This requires a difficult balancing act, in which the context and impact of the measure need to be carefully assessed.

Unless the npr-PPM is inward-looking, it is submitted that states cannot impose npr-PPMs that find no support in any formal instrument of law, whether soft or hard law. States should in such a situation raise international awareness and focus on international negotiations and other means of action; or where states and/or their consumers are genuinely concerned, bring an argument under Article XX(a) GATT.

5.3 ENVIRONMENTAL CONCERNS AND PUBLIC MORALS

Seal pups being inhumanly clubbed to death, pandas threatened with extinction, pollution by industry of a lake that is the local supply of drinking water: these examples raise concerns related to human and animal welfare and environmental protection. Even though the environmental concern is located entirely within the territory of another state, and there may be no transboundary environmental externality (no effects), domestic consumers can have strong moral objections or concerns about the foreign activity and the resulting environmental harm.[104] As Howse and Regan argue:

> even if the physical effects of the disfavoured processing method occur entirely outside the importing country, the importing country may be concerned to avoid the moral discredit . . . of . . . encouraging harm or wickedness – and the moral discredit occurs within the importing country, regardless of where the physical harm occurs.[105]

It can be difficult to distinguish moral from environmental concerns: for instance, the fact that an animal species is threatened with extinction can have a direct environmental impact on country A, but can be a moral concern to the not directly affected country B. In the recent *EC – Seal Products* case, the public morals exception under Article XX(a) GATT

---

[104] Note that if consumer preferences are very strong that this could already influence the finding of likeness of products under Article III GATT (if npr-PPMs would be taken into account under said article). If products would be deemed unlike based on consumer preferences, there would be no inconsistency with Article III and no need for any further analysis of the extraterritorial effect.

[105] Howse and Regan, 2000, 279.

was invoked by the EU to justify an import ban on seal products, while Article XX(b) was invoked as a back-up argument.[106] The Panel and the AB accepted the reliance on Article XX(a) without questioning the relationship with the environmental exception grounds of Article XX(b).

Thus, when could states invoke the public morals exception to address environmental concerns? Two questions must be answered: firstly, is there a jurisdictional limitation to the public morals exception, or in other words, to what extent can states invoke the public morals exception to address concerns outside the regulating state? Secondly, can the public morals exception be relied on to address environmental concerns? This is of particular relevance if there is no jurisdictional limitation to Article XX(a). As it is argued that there is no territorial limitation to the public morals exception, criteria will be proposed to determine the acceptability of a public morals defence.

5.3.1 Territorial Scope of Article XX(a) GATT

In *EC – Seal Products*, the EU invoked the public morals exception to justify its seals regime. Unfortunately, neither the Panel nor the AB addressed the question of jurisdictional limitation. The AB did mention the systemic importance of determining the jurisdictional scope of Article XX(a); however, it could not examine the issue further as no arguments were made by the parties in this regard.[107] The jurisdictional limitation of public morals refers to the question of whose morals can be protected. Can Article XX(a) only be relied on in order to protect the public morals of people within the regulating state's territory (e.g. an import ban on alcohol or pornography), or could it also serve to protect public morals of people outside that territory (e.g. an import ban aiming at the protection of children subject to child labour or an export ban on pornography to protect the morals of foreign citizens)?[108] It seems to be most likely that the

---

[106] WTO, Panel Report, *European Communities – Measures Prohibiting the Importation and Marketing of Seal Products*, WT/DS401/R, 2013; WTO, AB Report, *EC – Seal Products*, 2014.

[107] AB Report *EC – Seal Products* 2014, para. 5.173.

[108] Charnovitz used the distinction between inward- and outward-looking measures, whereby inward-directed measures are used to protect the morals of persons in one's own country, and outward-directed measures are used to protect the morals of foreigners residing outside one's own country. He indicates himself that the terms are somewhat arbitrary, because a ban on goods made by children might be 'haracterized as inwardly-directed to prevent domestic consumers from suffering a moral taint from serving as a market for such products' (Charnovitz, 1998, 695). As I would submit that most, if not all, moral concerns could be

protection of public morals must be interpreted as referring to the morals of the people within the territory of the regulating state, who can be concerned about actions occurring both within and/or outside that territory, which could relate to the environment, human rights, religion or even politics both within and outside the territory. This protection of public morals within the territory can also lead to protection of public morals outside the territory, but the exception cannot be used if it is solely aimed at protecting the latter. For example, if country A is morally concerned about child labour, both in country A and B, an import ban aiming at goods produced by child labour would be considered a domestic moral concern, even if the concerns related to an activity occurring abroad. An export ban on pornography would not be considered an issue of domestic moral concern, if pornographic materials are allowed within the domestic market. It is then not up to country A to determine what is morally accepted for country B. Domestic consumers and their concerns are thus the jurisdictional link to activities occurring abroad.[109]

A WTO Member invoking the public morals exception will then need to demonstrate that, firstly, its citizens and consumers are indeed concerned about the activity to be regulated[110] (show the existence of a moral concern), and secondly, that the measure is necessary to attain the objective, which includes a process of weighing and balancing factors such as the importance of the objective and the trade-restrictiveness of the measure.[111] Lastly, the good faith conditions of the *chapeau* must have been complied with, as for any measure seeking justification under Article XX.

---

rephrased as inward-looking concerns, I will not refer to this distinction (used elsewhere in this book) when it comes to moral concerns. One could think of a test where one would need to look at the primary aim of the measure (for instance is the measure more aimed at protecting the children abroad, or is the measure more aimed at protecting the domestic consumers?). However, evidencing such claims would be difficult and remain subjective, and thus would be of little help in distinguishing between genuine inward-looking or outward-looking concerns. As Wu puts it, all types of restrictions arise out of the importing state's moral concern, the difference is that the 'outwardly-directed' concerns may also be seeking to protect certain individuals beyond the restricting state's own borders. (Mark Wu, 'Free Trade and the Protection of Public Morals: An Analysis of the Newly Emerging Public Morals Clause Doctrine' Yale Journal of International Law (2008) 33, 215, 236.)

[109] Robert Howse, Joanna Langille and Katie Sykes, 'Pluralism in Practice: Moral Legislation and the Law of the WTO after *Seal Products*' New York University Public Law and Legal Theory Working Papers, 2015, 46.

[110] AB Report *EC – Seal Products* 2014, para. 5.136.

[111] Ibid. para. 5.169.

5.3.2 Validity of Public Morals

What can be considered as a public moral? Could any type of concern be considered a public moral? The scope of the public morals exception is not revealed by looking at the text of Article XX(a), nor do the *travaux préparatoires* offer much help.[112] After having examined moral exceptions in other trade treaties, Charnovitz found that these exceptions were initially a response to a broadly felt need to be able to impose trade restrictions relating to narcotics, alcohol, slaves, pornography as well as animal cruelty, among others.[113] However, these historic examples cannot be considered exhaustive. As the AB noted in *US – Shrimp*, generic terms are by definition evolutionary rather than static, and should thus be interpreted in light of current concerns.[114] The Panel in *US – Gambling* held that the term public morals 'denotes standards of right and wrong conduct maintained by or on behalf of a community or nation'.[115] The Panel recognized that the content of public morals can 'vary in time and space, depending upon a range of factors, including prevailing social, cultural, ethical and religious values'.[116] For those reasons, WTO adjudicators in determining the validity of public morals should adopt a deferential approach and should not exercise a normative power that they do not hold.[117]

Nevertheless, it has been suggested that additional 'checks' should be taken into account when determining the scope of valid 'public morals'. For instance, in *EC – Seal Products*, Canada argued that WTO Members must be consistent in their protection of public morals, and that the lack

---

112 Charnovitz, 1998, 704.

113 Ibid. 713.

114 AB Report *US – Shrimp* 1998, para. 130.

115 WTO, *United States – Measures Affecting the Cross-Border Supply of Gambling and Betting Services* Panel Report 2004, WT/DS285/R, para. 6.465.

116 Ibid. para. 6.461. This reading of the public morals exception under GATS was reiterated by the panel in *China – Audiovisuals* when dealing with the public morals exception under GATT. WTO, *China – Measures Affecting Trading Rights and Distribution Services for Certain Publications and Audiovisual Entertainment* Panel Report 2009, WT/DS363/R, para. 7.759.

117 This does not mean that public morals in the WTO should not be read in conjunction with other sources of international law. Howse et al. give the example of an import ban based on racist hatred towards individuals of third countries, based on the countries 'moral' values. Such a ban would likely violate the *jus cogens* norm against racial discrimination. See Howse, Langille and Sykes, 2015, 23; International Court of Justice, *Barcelona Traction, Light and Power Company Lth (Belgium v Spain)* 1970, Rep3, 105. See also Salman Bal, 'International Free Trade Agreements and Human Rights: Reinterpreting Article XX of the GATT' Minnesota Journal of International Law (2001) 10:1, 62, 93.

of (philosophical) consistency could lead to a finding that a concern is not a genuine moral belief. Canada claimed that the EU invoked public morals on animal welfare with regard to seals, but was inconsistent in its approach with regard to, for instance, slaughterhouses within the EU.[118] The argument was rejected by the AB, stating that states 'may set different levels of protection even when responding to similar interests of moral concern'.[119] Members should be able to distinguish, as long as this distinction can be explained by legitimate reasons.[120]

Another proposed check is that public morals must be shared widely or even universally. So, must a Member's definition of public morals find support in an international interpretation?[121] On the one hand, international consensus on values can support the argument that a measure can indeed relate to a shared value or public moral;[122] however, imposing an internationally uniform definition of morals would take away the whole point that Members are free in determining their own level of protection.[123] Moreover, practically speaking, when a norm is widely shared, states will have less need to impose import or export restrictions to protect those morals.[124] Wu adds an additional element with regard to shared values. He argues that the country at which the restriction is directed, must also have embraced the norm and a restriction could not be imposed against

---

[118] Canada's appellant's submission, para. 395. Canada argued that the EU claimed its main objective was animal welfare and to prevent suffering for animals, but in the meantime included a tolerance for other types of suffering, for instance for slaughterhouses and wildlife hunts.

[119] AB Report *EC – Seal Products* 2014, para. 5.200. See also on the argument that a measure should be coherent and consistent with other domestic regulation, Tamara Perisin, 'Is the EU Seal Products Regulation a Sealed Deal? EU and WTO Challenges' International and Comparative Law Quarterly (2013) 62:2, 373, 373.

[120] See in that regard also Article 5.5 SPS, stating that Members shall avoid arbitrary and unjustifiable distinctions in the levels they consider to be appropriate in different situations.

[121] Wu, 2008, 231.

[122] The Panel in *EC – Seal Products* took into account the growing global tendency towards taking animal welfare seriously in concluding that it could be a component of the public morals exception. See WTO, *European Communities – Measures Prohibiting the Importation and Marketing of Seal Products* Panel Report 2013, WT/DS401/R, para. 7.420.

[123] Nicolas Diebold, 'The Morals and Order Exceptions in WTO Law: Balancing the Toothless Tiger and the Undermining Mole' Journal of International Economic Law (2008) 11:1, 43. He gives the example of Israel who would be unable to prohibit the importation of non-kosher meat products unless the kosher requirement was considered as part of the internationally uniform public morals.

[124] Wu, 2008, 232.

a country for violating a norm that it has never endorsed.[125] However, domestic concerns should not (and cannot) be conditional on the moral policy of another state. Furthermore, in order to be consistent with the *chapeau* of Article XX, a measure cannot discriminate arbitrarily or unjustifiably and a Member thus cannot distinguish between countries in imposing trade restrictive measures. The argument that states would abuse the public morals exception if public morals can be determined unilaterally needs to be rebutted by a stringent assessment of the evidentiary proof of the existence of actual public morals, as well as the necessity test.[126]

5.3.3 Evidence of Public Morals

In light of the proposed deferential approach to accepting public morals as valid, it is important to constrain the scope of the public morals exception by focusing on a factual evidence analysis. A clear distinction must be made between the principled validity of moral concerns and the actual existence of such a concern. The Panel in *EC – Seal Products* can be criticized for not making such a distinction, and for accepting too easily that the EU's concerns could be considered as a matter of Article XX(a).[127]

The burden of proof is on the respondent to prove that the policy objective pursued by the challenged measure really does relate to matters of domestic public morals[128] and that, if the state were not to act, it would be 'harming' public morals.[129] The fundamental question is whose moral concerns are at issue: can the government determine the content of morals, or must there be a clearly expressed concern by the public, and if so, in their capacity as citizens (voters) or as consumers? Must the concerns be shared by a significant number of people, a majority of the people, or would a sizeable minority suffice as well? Diebold argues that based on the principles of a democratic society, the majority of a Member's population should endorse the moral value in order for it to qualify under Article XX(a) GATT.[130] However, requiring a majority preference does not seem to be the right threshold to measure moral concerns, as it raises questions related to the reliability of measuring methods as well as the feasibility in federal or quasi-federal systems such as the UK or Belgium. Lamy referred

---

[125] Ibid. 246.
[126] See Sections 5.3.3 and 5.3.4.
[127] Panel Report *EC – Seal Products* 2013, para. 7.631.
[128] AB Report *EC – Seal Products* 2014, para. 5.136.
[129] If the objective of the measure was not to harm animals (rather than public morals), the relevant exception ground would be Article XX(b) GATT.
[130] Diebold, 2008, 19.

in this regard to 'collective preferences', whereby 'collective choices are binding on a society as a whole and transcend individual preferences'.[131]

What would be legitimate evidence that the public is indeed morally concerned?[132] Would this be an opinion poll, a referendum or regulation?[133] Legislative acts could support the existence of a public moral concern: public morals could be assessed in light of their legislative history, the hierarchy of law (e.g. constitutional law) and the nature of legislative acts (e.g. criminal law, administrative law).[134] If one were to focus on legislative acts, would the WTO implicitly be endorsing a theory of democratic legitimacy? As political structures of WTO Members vary radically, what should be the proper standard to determine whether a belief really is an expression of the morality of a particular society?[135] A requirement of 'democratic legitimacy' cannot be read in Article XX(a). Governments can decide what is 'good' or 'bad' for their citizens, and while legislative support may be acceptable evidence to a public morals claim, such support cannot be *required*.[136]

Next to 'publicly' determined morals by citizens and governments, it is worth taking a closer look at the role of consumers, especially where 'ethical' moral concerns are at issue.[137] If consumers value highly certain

---

131 Speech by Pascal Lamy as European Commissioner, 'The Emergence of Collective Preferences in International Trade: Implications for Regulating Globalisation' 15 September 2004, at http://ec.europa.eu/archives/commission_1999_2004/lamy/speeches_articles/spla242_en.htm.

132 Wu, 2008, 233.

133 In *EC – Seal Products* the EU submitted a series of opinion polls to evidence that seal welfare was indeed a moral concern by the EU population. (First written submission by the European Union (21 December 2012), para. 194.) See for a critical analysis of the EU opinion polls, Paola Conconi and Tania Voon, '*EC-Seal Products*: The Tension Between Public Morals and International Trade Agreements' World Trade Review (2016) 15:2, 211, 231.

134 Diebold, 2008, 23.

135 Howse, Langille and Sykes, 2015, 6.

136 See in that regard also the position of Panel and AB in *China – Audiovisuals,* condoning in principle China's appeal to the right of censorship. Panel Report *China – Publications and Audiovisual Products* 2009, para. 7.752; WTO, *China – Measures Affecting Trading Rights and Distribution Services for Certain Publications and Audiovisual Entertainment* AB Report 2009, WT/DS363/AB/R, para. 233.

137 It might be relevant to distinguish between 'order-disturbing' public morals and 'ethical' public morals. In the former category, a stronger role should be given to governments, rather than consumer preferences (consumers might for instance be very much interested in the 'immoral' goods such as pornography). As to the latter category, more weight could be given to consumer preferences and behaviour to determine the existence of a genuine moral concern.

morals, in principle the market principle of demand should already lead to decreased imports. Why then still rely on trade restrictive measures? People hold and express different preferences in their consumer role and in their citizen role. Some morals may be highly valued by political participants, but as consumers on the market they are not willing to back up that valuation, due to, for example, a perceived sense of hopelessness for consumers;[138] or free-rider problems revealed in voting patterns. People may also be aware of their own selfishness and might commit themselves in democratic processes to a course of action that they consider to be in the general interest.[139] If citizens/voters express strong values, beliefs and preferences which they do not implement as individual consumers, which action is then the more realistic reflection of those preferences?[140] Can the alleged moral concerns of citizens/voters then be considered genuine? If citizens are willing to take a strong moral stand in theory but not in practice (when it comes to the choice of 'good' products over 'bad' products), how fair is it then to pass on the bill to foreign producers who might need to adjust production processes or suffer the economic consequences as a result of trade restrictions based on ambiguous public morals?[141]

The crucial question seems to be: should trade measures address public morals as reflected by consumer preferences, voters' opinions, or both?[142] It is submitted that both must be taken into account when examining the evidence of a genuine public moral, especially in light of information asymmetries and information manipulation. The available information

---

[138] Daphna Lewinsohn-Zamir, 'Consumer Preferences, Citizen Preferences, and the Provision of Public Goods' Yale Law Journal (1998) 108:2, 377, 379. As Deborah Lynn Guber has also argued, 'a critical component of an individual's willingness to engage in activity designed to support environmental causes or other public goods hinges upon the perceived efficacy of that activity'. See Deborah Guber, *The Grassroots of a Green Revolution: Polling America on the Environment* (MIT Press 2002) 155.

[139] Cass Sunstein, 'Endogenous Preferences, Environmental Law' Journal of Legal Studies (1993) 22:2, 217, 242.

[140] Note in that regard the interesting wording in *EC – Seal Products* re the objective of the measure: 'addressing public moral concerns relating to the EU public's participation as consumers in the market for products derived from inhumanely killed seals'. AB Report *EC – Seal Products* 2014, para. 5.223.

[141] Note that citizens in the regulating country might pay a price for imposing trade-restrictive measures. If the market is more limited, prices are likely to increase. In other words, the bill is not merely passed on the foreign producers' part of the bill but will also be on domestic consumers.

[142] Lewinsohn-Zamir, 1998, 378. See also Gregory Shaffer and Joel P Trachtman, 'Interpretation and Institutional Choice at the WTO' Virginia Journal of International Law (2011) 52:1, 103, 146.

for consumers must be taken into account, such as, for instance, the comprehensiveness and clarity of labels: labels could be misleading, and patterns of consumer preferences could be influenced by governments through prescribing the amount of information that must or may be disclosed to consumers.[143] Public opinion can be manipulated both by governments but also by the corporate sector that has its own specific interests.[144] Furthermore, consumers might be primarily led by the price of products, and might decide to buy the cheaper product and 'free ride'. In addition, those consumers who do not plan on consuming a particular product might also be morally concerned (e.g. vegetarians can still be concerned about sustainable production of meat).[145] If market behaviour were to be the only indicator of genuine moral concerns, more socially protective regulation might no longer pass the evidence threshold. This is also relevant in relation to new issues or new risks on which the public has not yet had the time to form an opinion, or about which insufficient information is available.

Assessing these concerns and this type of evidence is a complex task to undertake for panels and it could be argued that the exception might be easily abused. However, assessing the credibility of evidence and complex fact-finding is not new to WTO panels.[146] Panels have the authority to seek information from any relevant source,[147] which could include civil society organizations, public opinion firms, local government officials and citizens.[148]

5.3.4 Necessity

Once the validity of public morals has been accepted and its factual existence has been established, the respondent must demonstrate that the measure is necessary to attain the objective. As noted in Section 5.2.1.2, the necessity test involves a process of weighing and balancing a series of factors, such as the interests at stake, the importance of the objective, the

---

143 Douglas A. Kysar, 'Preferences for Processes: The Process/Product Distinction and the Regulation of Consumer Choice' Harvard Law Review (2004) 118:2, 526, 579.

144 This is made all too clear in Naomi Oreskes and Erik M Conway, *Merchants of Doubt* (Bloomsbury Press 2010).

145 Shaffer and Trachtman, 2011, 146.

146 Jeremy Marwell, 'Trade and Morality: The WTO Public Morals Exception after *Gambling*' 2006, New York University Law Review (2006) 81, 802, 825.

147 Article 13 DSU.

148 Marwell, 2006, 825.

contribution of the measure to that objective, the negative trade impact, and possible less trade restrictive alternatives that could secure the same objective and level of protection.[149] This balancing act results in an ad hoc, contextual assessment of each measure.[150] A measure seeking justification based on public morals does not necessarily need to make a material contribution[151] or seek to further concrete effects, but can also be issued merely to express moral convictions.[152]

5.3.5 Morals in Relation to the Environmental Exceptions

Without any territorial limitation Article XX(a) GATT might invite attempts to circumvent territorial limitations in other exceptions, where states need to comply with a higher threshold to demonstrate a sufficient nexus and/or international support for the environmental concern they aim to protect. A too lenient assessment of Article XX(a) could in that regard deprive the other exceptions of their *effet utile*. Public morals should not be read in a way to deny the other paragraphs of Article XX independent meaning.[153] Whereas there might be some overlap in different clauses, justification for a measure should be sought on the most applicable ground or in other words the main objective of the measure. If a state relies on the public morals exception, a panel must check whether the rule in question is genuinely concerned with standards of right and wrong within a society[154] and is thus actually aimed at the protection of public morals. The emphasis on evidence and necessity as discussed above must serve to avoid abuse of the exception.

---

149 Panel Report *US – Gambling* 2004, para. 6.492; AB Report *Brazil – Retreaded Tyres* 2007, para. 178; AB Report *EC – Seal Products* 2014, para. 5.169. The burden of proof to propose alternative measures is on the complaining party.

150 See WTO, AB Report, *Korea – Measures Affecting Imports of Fresh, Chilled and Frozen Beef*, WT/DS161/AB/R, 2000; WTO, AB Report, *European Communities – Measures Affecting Asbestos and Asbestos-containing Products*, WT/DS135/AB/R, 2001; AB Report *Brazil – Retreaded Tyres* 2007.

151 AB Report *EC – Seal Products* 2014, para. 5.216.

152 Howse, Langille and Sykes, 2015, 2. According to the authors, the EU ban on seal products for instance was introduced to make a statement about the problematic nature of cruelty to animals and the impermissibility of consumptive behaviours that tolerate and encourage such cruelty. An important aspect of the ban's meaning and purpose was the expression of a deontological belief that seals ought not to be treated in the manner permitted by the hunts in Canada and other sealing nations. The ban was a statement of fundamental European moral and ethical beliefs about the proper treatment of non-human animals.

153 Marwell, 2006, 823.

154 Howse, Langille and Sykes, 2015, 25.

The proposed extraterritoriality decision tree has little relevance in a context of public morals: if we indeed consider the existence of a moral concern within the territory of the regulating state sufficient nexus, public morals fall by definition within the inward-looking concerns, which establishes a jurisdictional nexus, and there would be no need to go further to the second step of the tree. Even if one were to consider the second step (international support), it would be of no value as it is intrinsic to the concept of public morals that these can be local, and cannot be determined based on the existence or lack of international support. Hence it is submitted that the risk to an 'uncontainable' Article XX(a) or the slippery slope is not its extraterritorial reach but an overly broad acceptance of public morals.[155]

5.4 THE *CHAPEAU* OF ARTICLE XX GATT

Once a measure falls under one of the exceptions of Article XX GATT, and has thus passed the 'extraterritoriality threshold', the analysis turns to the *chapeau* of Article XX. In assessing the application of the measure, the *chapeau*'s purpose is to prevent abuse or misuse of the specific exemptions provided for in Article XX.[156] The analysis of the *chapeau* is not specific to npr-PPMs with an extraterritorial objective, but can offer additional safeguards against a possible overreach. According to the AB, the *chapeau* is an expression of the principle of good faith as a general principle of law.[157] Good faith in this context can be reflected in a duty to cooperate, and to show systematic respect for multilateralism and the international community's interests.[158] Basically, the integrity of the measure should be key.[159] The *chapeau* analysis does not form part of the decision tree, but this section will

---

[155] For a more extensive analysis of public morals in this context, see Barbara Cooreman, 'Extraterritorial Environmental Concerns and Public Morals: Testing the Limits of Article XX(a) GATT after *Seals*' Journal of International Trade and Arbitration Law (2016) 5, 519.

[156] AB Report *US – Shrimp* 1998, para. 119, 156; AB Report *US – Gasoline* 1996, 25.

[157] AB Report *US – Shrimp* 1998, para. 158.

[158] Elisa Morgera, 'The EU and Environmental Multilateralism: The Case of Access and Benefit-Sharing and the Need for a Good-Faith Test' Cambridge Yearbook of European Legal Studies (2013) 16, 109, 119.

[159] Sanford E Gaines, 'Processes and Production Methods: How to Produce Sound Policy for Environmental PPM-Based Trade Measures?' Columbia Journal of Environmental Law (2002) 27:2, 383, 431.

highlight some key elements that can be of particular relevance to environmental npr-PPMs.

5.4.1 Countries Where the Same Conditions Prevail

A measure imposed by a WTO Member may not arbitrarily or unjustifiably discriminate between countries where the same conditions prevail. This latter condition is sometimes under-emphasized. Any discrimination must relate to the objective of the measure, as found under the respective paragraph of Article XX GATT. In the case of environmental PPMs, this means that any discrimination must be rationally related to the environmental objective. The explicit wording of 'countries where the same conditions prevail' leads to the interpretation that the environmental conditions must be the same (those conditions that are relevant to the main objective), or in other words that a PPM cannot discriminate between countries where the same environmental conditions prevail, such as, for instance, all countries with tropical woods in relation to PPMs on the logging of timber. A PPM that imposes different requirements to countries with similar environmental contexts would then constitute unjustifiable discrimination.[160]

Purely economic conditions should not play a role under the *chapeau* when seeking justification for environmental npr-PPMs. However, economic conditions can be related to the environmental context of a country, and can in particular lead to a distinction between resourceful, developed countries and less developed countries without the necessary resources or technologies to attain high environmental standards. A PPM that targets all producers in a neutral way is likely to have a greater impact on producers in developing countries that might have fewer economic resources and technical knowledge. Thus, even though similar natural resources may be available in developed and developing countries, or equally polluting activities might take place in developed and developing countries, the technical know-how, capacity and economic means to protect environmental concerns differ. Arguably, to the extent that economic conditions of a country relate to its environmental conditions, these could or even should be taken into account for finding that countries are not similar, if the PPM in question were to distinguish between developed and developing countries.[161] In *US – Shrimp*, the AB found that discrimination also

---

[160] Ibid. 429.

[161] This would most likely be a violation of the MFN obligation under Article I GATT, which would then need to be justified under Article XX GATT. See also

results 'when the application of the measure at issue does not allow for any inquiry into the appropriateness of the regulatory program for the conditions prevailing in exporting countries'.[162] Considering development factors in order to determine whether 'the same conditions prevail' could find support in the GATT Enabling Clause that allows for differential and more favourable treatment for developing countries.[163] Different contextual factors related to the 'development, financial and trade needs' allow Members to differentiate between developing countries as well, as long as the distinguishing criteria are objective and generally applicable.[164] This distinction is also reflected in the principle of common but differentiated responsibility, a principle justifying the design of different international obligations on the basis of differences in the current socio-economic situations of countries and their historical contribution to a specific environmental problem.[165]

---

by analogy WTO, *European Communities – Conditions for the Granting of Tariff Preferences to Developing Countries* AB Report 2004, WT/DS246/AB/R, in which the AB contended that different developing countries were not 'similarly situated' when they had 'different needs' and thus could be subject to 'performance requirements' as long as these were objective, transparent and indeed non-discriminatory in the broad sense. For a hypothetical analysis of differential treatment for Kyoto-signatories and non-signatories with reference to *EC – Tariff Preferences*, see Jagdish Bhagwati and Petros C Mavroidis, 'Is Action against US Exports for Failure to Sign Kyoto Protocol WTO-legal?' World Trade Review (2007) 6:2, 299.

[162] AB Report *US – Shrimp* 1998, para. 165.

[163] GATT Contracting Parties, Decision of 28 November 1979 (L/4903) on differential and more favourable treatment reciprocity and fuller participation of developing countries. The Enabling Clause has been applied with regard to tariff preferences, but also allows for special and differential treatment with regard to non-tariff measures (paragraph 2(b)). See also Alexander Keck and Patrick Low, 'Special and Differential Treatment in the WTO: Why, When and How?' WTO Staff Working Paper, ERSD-2004–03, 2004.

[164] GATT Contracting Parties, Differential and More Favourable Treatment Reciprocity and Fuller Participation of Developing Countries (Enabling Clause), L/4903, 28 November of 1979, para. 3(c); WTO, *European Communities – Conditions for the Granting of Tariff Preferences to Developing Countries* AB Report 2004, WTO/DS246/AB/R, para. 156.

[165] UNFCCC, 1992, preamble, Article 4; Martin Khor, 'The Climate and Trade Relation: Some Issues' South Centre Research Paper, 2009, 22; Morgera, 2013, 117; Pieter Pauw et al., 'Different Perspectives on Differentiated Responsibilities: A State-of-the-Art Review of the Notion of Common but Differentiated Responsibilities in International Negotiations' Deutsches Institut für Entwicklungspolitik Discussion Paper, 6/2014 (2014), 36. For a discussion of CBDRRC in the context of climate change, see Chapter 6.

5.4.2 Coercive Effect

In *US – Shrimp*, the AB noted in its analysis of unjustifiable discrimination that 'the most conspicuous flaw in the measure's application related to its intended and actual coercive effect on the specific policy decisions made by foreign governments. [The measure at issue . . .] requires *all other exporting Members* . . . to adopt *essentially the same* policy . . .'[166]

Shrimp harvesting methods comparable in effectiveness to those required by the US were not accepted. This was proof to the AB that the measure in its application was more concerned with effectively influencing other WTO Members to adopt the same policy, rather than inquiring into the appropriateness of different comparable programmes to protect the concern at issue. The AB considered this 'rigidity and inflexibility' to also constitute arbitrary discrimination within the meaning of the *chapeau*.[167] Flexibility in the application of the measure is thus important, as a measure must allow for comparable programmes to reach the objective. A WTO Member imposing environmental npr-PPMs should focus on the end result and the required standards, rather than prescribe exactly how those results should be achieved. The ease with which a standard allows translation from other standards, or adoption of parallel standards, and facilitates access to the market without requiring the adoption of a specifically prescribed norm is an important consideration.[168]

One way of attaining the required flexibility, and recognizing measures comparable in effectiveness, is through mutual recognition.[169] This can either be in a negotiated and reciprocal context, whereby several parties pledge to mutually recognize each other's practices if common minimum

---

166 AB Report *US – Shrimp* 1998, para. 161.

167 Ibid. para. 177.

168 David Singh Grewal, 'Network Power and Globalization' Ethics and International Affairs (2006) 17:2, 89, 97.

169 Marceau and Trachtman, 2002, 844. Mutual recognition provisions can be found in the SPS Agreement Articles 3 and 4, as well as in Article 6 and Annex 3(D) of the TBT Agreement. Next to the mutual recognition rules within the internal market (implemented in secondary law), the EU has concluded a number of (sectoral) mutual recognition agreements with Australia, Canada, Israel, Japan, New Zealand, Switzerland and the US. For an overview see http://ec.europa.eu/growth/single-market/goods/international-aspects/mutual-recognition-agreements/index_en.htm. Mutual recognition agreements are often sectoral. For an interesting assessment of mutual recognition in EU–US relations and the current TTIP negotiations, see Jacques Pelkmans and Anabela Correia de Brito, *Transatlantic MRAs: Lessons for TTIP?* (CEPS Special Report, 2015).

standards are respected,[170] but recognition can also be a unilateral inclusion, whereby the regulating state affirms that practices abroad that reach the required standards will be accepted and recognized.[171]

Coerciveness can furthermore relate to the 'target' of the measure. A distinction can be made between process-based measures and country-based measures, whereby the former are to be preferred as they target the individual producer and the odious production practice, rather than force a government to adopt a certain policy.[172] A measure should thus focus on the origin-neutral production process that can have an environmental impact, rather than focus on whether the government has adopted a specific policy regulating the concern at issue. Country-based discrimination is too trade restrictive: a producer within a country who could comply with the prescribed production requirements would still not be able to trade freely. While process-based measures may be less effective and unsatisfactory for environmentalists, as Charnovitz rightly observed, it is one thing for country A to specify a PPM for the fish that it imports from country B; it is quite another for country A to say that it will not import *any* fish from country B unless *all* of B's fish catch are caught in the prescribed way.[173] Furthermore, as noted by the Panel in *US – Shrimp*, 'it would be impossible for exporting Members to comply at the same

---

[170] Kalypso Nicolaidis and Gregory Shaffer, 'Transnational Mutual Recognition Regimes: Governance Without Global Government' Law and Contemporary Problems (2005) 68, 263, 275. States could choose effectively to recognize the other state's standard as equivalent, but they could for instance also agree that each regulatory system will recognize only its own standards, but agree that a conformity assessment of the importing state's standards will be carried out in the exporting state.

[171] Joel P Trachtman, 'Regulatory Jurisdiction and the WTO' Journal of International Economic Law (2007) 10:3, 631, 639. Recognition by the importing Member of the exporting Member's regulation could also be an element in a necessity analysis under the subparagraphs of Article XX GATT. Sometimes, the least trade restrictive alternative will be simple recognition of the effectiveness of the home country regulation.

[172] See Howse and Regan, 2000, 269. Charnovitz uses a similar distinction between 'government-policy' and 'how-produced' restrictions. Charnovitz, 2002, 107; Steve Charnovitz, 'A Taxonomy of Environmental Trade Measures' Georgetown International Environmental Law Review (1993) 6:1, 1, 40. Government-policy-standards or country-based measures may be more efficient in inducing the participation of other countries in multilateral environmental agreements though. For an interesting discussing on the efficiency of these measures, see Howard Chang, 'An Economic Analysis of Trade Measures to Protect the Global Environment' Georgetown Law Journal (1995) 83:6, 2131.

[173] Charnovitz, 2002, 69.

time with multiple conflicting policy requirements'.[174] The difficulty of process-based measures, on the other hand, relates to the development and enforcement of an effective system to keep those products produced in a 'good' way, separate from those produced in a 'bad' way.[175]

5.4.3 Good Faith and International Contingency

Good faith in the context of the *chapeau* of Article XX GATT can be seen as a general principle reflected in a duty to cooperate and to negotiate, or in a broader sense showing respect to the international legal order.[176] Good faith serves to balance domestic interests and values against jurisdictional overreach and international tensions,[177] necessitating systematic respect for multilateral norms and institutions.[178] Where no international agreements yet exist, respect for multilateralism can manifest itself through engaging in negotiations for bi- or plurilateral cooperation with respect to the respective concerns.[179]

The legitimacy of environmental trade restrictions will be strengthened if the measure is 'contingent'[180] upon or 'responsive'[181] to international developments, and sufficiently flexible in light of those, for instance by including review clauses that can be triggered expressly by developments at the multilateral level and inputs from third countries at the bilateral level.[182] The 2009 EU Climate and Energy Package, for instance, contains review clauses linked to the outcome of ongoing international negotiations.[183] Responsiveness to international action is thus related to multilateral negotiations. Legitimate unilateral action does not oppose multilateral action: unilateral acts would be imposed because of the

---

174 WTO, *United States – Import Prohibitions of Certain Shrimp and Shrimp Products* Panel report 1998, WT/DS58/R, para. 7.45.

175 Nollkaemper, 1996, 254.

176 Morgera, 2013, 119.

177 Robert Howse, 'From Politics to Technocracy – and Back Again: The Fate of the Multilateral Trading Regime' American Journal of International Law (2002) 96, 94, 106; Scott, 2014, 4.

178 Morgera, 2013, 119.

179 AB Report *US – Shrimp* 1998, 166.

180 Joanne Scott and Lavanya Rajamani, 'EU Climate Change Unilateralism' The European Journal of International Law (2012) 23:2, 469.

181 Morgera, 2013, 121.

182 Ibid. 121.

183 See for instance Directive 2009/29/EC amending Directive 2003/87/EC so as to improve and extend the greenhouse gas emission allowance trading scheme of the Community, Articles 10b(1) and 11a.

absence of effective multilateral alternatives, especially in light of grave and urgent environmental threats.[184] Unilateral PPMs should then be seen as a sort of interim measure, pending further international action. That also implies willingness to consider 'disapplying' legislation when the foreign conduct in question has been satisfactorily regulated by another state or by an international body.[185] If a state refuses to join in a multilateral arrangement, and instead continues to act unilaterally, the credibility of its case for unilateral action will erode.[186] It is thus important that a PPM is drafted in such a way that there is room for adaptation and flexibility, which should also be monitored strictly and revised where necessary.

Responsiveness does not only relate to developments at a multilateral level, but also includes genuine dialogue and the exchange of views with third countries and stakeholders. This does not necessarily have to relate to law-making initiatives, but can relate to capacity building, research, monitoring efforts, joint activities etc.[187] Such dialogue may involve relevant bodies under MEAs or relevant international organizations. In the absence of binding international agreement, these efforts can then be taken into account in a contextual analysis to demonstrate genuine attempts for multilateral solutions and respect for both the sovereignty of other countries and the multilateral system.

5.5 THE DILEMMAS OF TRADE LEVERAGE FOR ENVIRONMENTAL PROTECTION

This chapter has proposed an extraterritoriality decision tree, building upon positive law from other fields of law, with the purpose of coming to a

---

184 Bilder, 1981, 91.

185 Scott, 2014, 24. Scott gives the EU's Derivatives Regulation (EMIR; Reg. 648/2012) as an example of 'contingency' whereby the EU is taking into account regulation by other countries. As she states, 'the Commission is empowered to adopt decisions declaring that the legal, supervisory and enforcement arrangements of a third country are equivalent to those laid down in EMIR and that these third country arrangements are being effectively applied and enforced in an equitable and non-distortive manner so as to ensure effective supervision and enforcement in that third country. Where at least one counterparty to a derivatives contract is established in a third country that benefits from an equivalence decision of this kind, all of the counterparties to the contract will be deemed to have fulfilled the specified obligations under EU law' (Article 13(3)).

186 Bilder, 1981, 92.

187 Morgera, 2013, 123.

more systematic assessment of extraterritoriality claims under Article XX GATT. However, the use of npr-PPMs to further environmental protection raises certain dilemmas. For instance, there is an inherent inequity to trade leverage as large, powerful markets will be more able to make use of PPMs than smaller markets. Also, little-known or newly emerging environmental concerns could not be addressed through npr-PPMs under the current legal framework, even though these threats might be in most need of alternative solutions for lack of multilateral recognition. The following section will expound these dilemmas and make suggestions where relevant.

5.5.1 Market Power and the Unfairness of PPMs

Is the proposed legal framework of the decision tree able to guarantee fair and equal opportunities for WTO Members to indeed make use of npr-PPMs to attain environmental objectives? In principle, every WTO Member can make use of PPMs that will be subjected to the same legal assessment in order to test their WTO-consistency. The impact of PPMs, however, will depend on a number of factors, such as market power of the imposing country relative to that of the exporting country, trade dependence of the specific industry, the volume and direction of trade in the affected product, supply and demand, the type and combination of instruments used, and the appropriateness and feasibility of the requirement imposed.[188] The most crucial factor seems to be market power: can the exporter divert exports to another market? Foreign producers that are forced to comply with higher standards in order to gain market access can either choose voluntarily to converge to the required standard; try to compel the market power to change its rules through, for instance, diplomacy, WTO complaints or sanctions; seek a cooperative solution; or choose not to export to that market.[189] If exporters have no alternative strategy that is economically viable, they will need to adapt to the PPM-prescribed standards, which may instigate a positive change with regard to the allegedly harmful activity. The size and attractiveness of the market will thus be important factors for a PPMs' success.[190]

Grewal has argued in his theory on network power that in order to enjoy the benefits of globalization one sometimes has no choice but to accept a

188 OECD, 1997, 32.

189 Anu Bradford, 'The Brussels Effect' Northwestern University Law Review (2012) 107:1, 1, 50.

190 This question differs from the question whether the environmental policy prescribed by a PPM is effective from an environmental perspective, as that will depend on the substance of the measure.

specific set of dominant standards. These standards are not in the traditional way determined by one actor, nor are they 'forced' upon others, but they become more valuable when more actors use them. In a way, the free choice over alternatives decreases if one wants to take part in the network (the 'unfreedom of globalization'). While participation is a choice, and acceptance of standards is driven by consent, some form of 'informal power' or unequal dependence can be discerned.[191] Large trading blocks, such as the EU, have a valuable asset for which actors would be 'willing' to adopt standards, namely access to the EU market (also named the Brussels effect).[192] This reveals the inherent economic inequity of PPMs: only those states with substantial market power will reasonably be able to take advantage of PPMs.[193] In light of this equity concern one can understand the opposition by developing countries to PPM-based measures and other analogous 'product' requirements such as environmental packaging and eco-labelling.[194] While the power of markets is an unavoidable reality, the decision tree's emphasis on international support and multilateral solutions with regard to the concern to be protected is one contributing element to strengthen a rules-based approach to trade relations.[195]

However, being a powerful market could also entail a responsibility, or even a duty,[196] for the larger states: protection of the commons, of a public good, might require leadership. States who *can* might have a moral duty to act when others cannot.[197] Caney identifies two types of responsibilities with regard to climate justice: first-order responsibilities, the obligation for an agent to do its fair share; and second-order responsibilities, responsibilities that seek to induce agents that fail to comply with their first-order responsibilities to step into line.[198] Second-order responsibilities would

---

[191] See David Singh Grewal, *Network Power: The Social Dynamics of Globalization* (Yale University Press 2008); Grewal, 2006.

[192] Bradford, 2012; Meunier and Nicolaidis, 2006, 907.

[193] Gaines, 2002, 427.

[194] Ibid. 623; Gregory Shaffer, 'WTO Blue-Green Blues: The Impact of US Domestic Politics on Trade-Labor, Trade-Environment Linkages for the WTO's future' Fordham International Law Journal (2000) 24:1, 607.

[195] Jonathan Skinner, 'A Green Road to Development: Environmental Regulations and Developing Countries in the WTO' Duke Environmental Law and Policy Forum (2010) 20:1, 245, 265.

[196] Francesco Francioni, 'Extraterritorial Application of Environmental Law' in Karl M Meessen (ed.), *Extraterritorial Jurisdiction in Theory and Practice* (Kluwer 1996) 132.

[197] Anne Schwenkenbecher, 'Bridging the Emissions Gap: A Plea for Taking Up the Slack' Philisophy and Public Issues (2013) 3:2, 271.

[198] Simon Caney, 'Two Kinds of Climate Justice: Avoiding Harm and Sharing Burdens' Journal of Political Philosophy (2014) 22:2, 125, 134. See also Joanne

operate on the principle that 'with power comes responsibility', whereby power can be defined as 'A has power over B to the extent that he can get B to do something that B would not otherwise do'.[199] A strong market can thus become a powerful tool to incentivize conduct through market access, because of a moral responsibility to exploit that power. However, the concept of second-order responsibilities should not be abused by free-riders who want to evade their own first-order responsibilities.

The responsibility of the regulating states to 'use' their market for better environmental protection would need to be closely linked with an obligation to ensure that the imposed regime provides the necessary management elements for success for producers that are not able to comply with higher standards, such as technical and possibly financial assistance.[200] Such assistance of developed countries helping developing countries implement environmental policy could be seen as an implementation of the common but differentiated responsibilities principle, recognizing the different responsibilities of developed and developing states in light of common responsibilities.[201] The current Article XX GATT does not include such a duty for positive obligations, even though positive action in combination with negative action (trade restrictions) can be taken into account in a good faith assessment.[202] Any legally enforceable duty (as opposed to a mere moral duty) would need to be agreed upon by the international community of states.

5.5.2 The Necessity of Environmental Trade Leverage

An important question in addition to the legal assessment of extraterritorial npr-PPMs is whether the environment can indeed be adequately

---

Scott, 'The Geographical Scope of the EU's First-Order and Second-Order Climate Responsibilities: An Exploration' Cambridge Yearbook of European Legal Studies (2015) 17, 92.

199 Caney, 2014, 141.

200 Thomas Cottier, *Renewable Energy and Process and Production Methods* (The E15 Initiative: Strengthening the Global Trade and Investment System for Sustainable Development 2015) 5; Richard W Parker, 'The Use and Abuse of Trade Leverage to Protect the Global Commons: What We Can Learn From the Tuna-Dolphin Conflict' Georgetown International Environmental Law Review (1999) 12:1, 1, 119; Charnovitz, 2002, 74.

201 Elisa Morgera, 'Ambition, Complexity and Legitimacy of Pursuing Mutual Supportiveness through the EU's External Environmental Action' Edinburgh School of Law Research Papers, 2012/02, 2012, 7. See also for a further discussion of the principle, Chapter 7.

202 Shaffer, 2000, 626.

protected through the use of unilateral trade leverage. Whether PPMs will be effective in addressing environmental concerns, i.e. whether they will indeed lead to better/more protection of the environment, depends on, firstly, whether trade leverage is an appropriate tool for environmental protection; and secondly, the specific design, content and feasibility of the measure.[203] As the latter element requires a substantive analysis and scientific expertise that would go beyond my capabilities, the former element deserves closer attention.

In a study on the use and abuse of trade leverage, Parker identifies situations in which outside enforcement is more, or less, needed. He argues that when natural resources are used by a limited group, which are equally dependent on the resource, these users are often able to manage the shared resources themselves, as can be seen, for instance, in regional agreements for managing regional seas. For the (relatively small group of) states involved, there is reciprocity of advantage in seeing that conservation works, and no pressing need for use or threat of leverage.[204] On the other hand, in case of truly global challenges, such as high seas, distant-water fisheries, there is a risk of free-riding: if others make conservation efforts, free-riders can reap the gains without enduring the costs. This applies equally to other global challenges, such as climate change and ozone depletion.[205] In these examples trade leverage (especially by powerful trading partners) can then offer a useful incentive to comply with environmental norms (see e.g. the trade measures foreseen in the Montreal Protocol or CITES). However, trade leverage without management regimes does not work. Rather the effectiveness of trade leverage is the degree to which it supports, and is supported by, effective management approaches.[206] Equally, global commons management regimes without trade leverage have been less successful, as illustrated by the ineffectiveness of most high seas fisheries management regimes,[207] or climate treaties.[208] Parker lists a number of global commons management options such as capacity building through technical and financial assistance[209] or monitoring, reporting and verification of compliance by an international secretariat.[210]

---

203 OECD, 1997, 30; Gaines, 2002, 405.
204 Parker, 1999, 100.
205 Ibid. 101.
206 Ibid. 107.
207 According to the FAO, approximately 70 % of the world's fish stocks are overfished.
208 Parker, 1999, 104.
209 See also Cottier, 2015, 5.
210 Parker, 1999, 104.

This book has started from the premise that in certain areas international agreement is lacking or has insufficient tools to ensure better environmental protection. Can npr-PPMs be a tool to stimulate better global management, serving as an incentive to enhance international cooperation? Can PPMs serve as regime generators or norm creators? According to Hakimi, trade leverage can help to 'develop new norms, prevent existing norms from eroding, reconcile competing objectives, and strengthen or recalibrate regimes'.[211] The practice and experience of trade leverage measures can furnish experience upon which other states (and the international community) can usefully draw,[212] and can help to clarify 'grey areas' in international law.[213] Unilateral trade measures as alternatives to an ineffective or non-existent global regime can incentivize states to get involved in the development of an international environmental regime. Such involvement would allow states a say in the decision-making (rather than being subject to unilateral measures), and economic disadvantages for producers and exporters can be avoided if the country of export has legislation similar to the country of import. Where legislation between countries of import and export differs, an incentive can be created to discuss and share practices, and increase cooperation. Hakimi has termed this behaviour 'unfriendly unilateralism',[214] which can help to overcome inaction and give a boost to collective decision-making. Depending on the existing international legal framework, trade leverage could be adopted with the objective of enforcing an existing international norm, of furthering and strengthening an existing norm, or could serve to create a norm.

However, even if PPMs can be a tool to develop new norms, the current tree might not allow the promotion of little-known or newly emerging environmental needs (if there is not yet international support). Even though arguably PPMs are most needed in cases of these 'new' yet unsupported concerns, states should commit to multilateralism and involve other states before imposing trade measures that will affect other countries and their producers. Notwithstanding its benefits, unilateral action in the form of PPMs can only be a second-best alternative. Unilateral environmental

---

[211] Monica Hakimi, 'Unfriendly Unilateralism' Harvard International Law Journal (2014) 55:1, 105, 107.

[212] Bilder, 1981, 80.

[213] Thomas J Schoenbaum, 'International Trade and Protection of the Environment: The Continuing Search for Reconciliation' American Journal of International Law (1997) 91:2, 268, 299.

[214] Hakimi, 2014, 107.

action is inherently limited in its efficiency and effectiveness: concerted action is required to achieve a more effective solution.[215]

5.6 CONCLUSION

Can states make use of npr-PPMs to address transboundary environmental challenges, or does WTO law form a stumbling block for this type of measure with an extraterritorial effect? This chapter has proposed an extraterritoriality decision tree building on lessons learned from other fields of law that can serve as a systematic step-by-step plan to assess extraterritoriality claims within the scope of Article XX GATT.

The following points are worth noting. First, as the basic economic rationale of the WTO is free trade, accepting that countries can have a competitive advantage over others is 'part of the deal'. If states want to address environmental concerns through trade measures, they need to ensure that the measures are based upon legitimate environmental objectives as laid down in the general exceptions. Second, in addition to a territorial link through market access, in order to justify extraterritorial effects of npr-PPMs, states must demonstrate that their environment is affected by the activities abroad (inward or inward/outward-looking). Effects must be direct, substantial and foreseeable. In contrast to competition law, where there is no relevant body of international rules, determining effects in an environmental context can be more lenient: international (soft and hard) environmental law can be taken into account to strengthen state action, where the effects are weaker or uncertain in light of environmental complexity. When a measure is fully outward-looking, the extraterritorial effect cannot be permitted, irrespective of the international support for the norm at issue. Third, when a measure is partly outward-looking but addressing a concern that finds no support yet in any international instrument (soft or hard law), the extraterritorial effect cannot be permitted either, so as to respect the multilateral character of the WTO. Fourth, the *chapeau* plays an important role even if the *chapeau* analysis does not form part of the extraterritoriality assessment and is common to all trade measures seeking justification: it is under the *chapeau* that the legitimacy of the measure will be determined, taking into account the flexibility of the measure, responsiveness to international actions and good faith. Measures accompanying the PPM such as management tools and technical assistance can be crucial for the success of a PPM. Lastly, despite the

---

215 Bilder, 1981, 85; Skinner, 2010, 265.

structured legal framework, there is no one-size-fits-all model. Due to the nature of environmental concerns, as well as the particularities of the international legal framework, a contextual case-by-case analysis, with respect for the interests of importing and exporting countries, as well as producers and the public, is key when assessing the different criteria. Such contextual analysis can be seen as a continuing duty of reasoned justification on the regulating state in order to demonstrate that the imposed npr-PPMs do meet the set standards.[216]

In conclusion, the current WTO rules allow for sufficient regulatory space for states to address their environmental concerns, even when these are located outside the territory of the regulating state, where these concerns lead to environmental effects in the regulating country and where multilateral efforts support the unilateral action.

216 Scott, 2014, 26.

PART III

Case studies

6. The application of the extraterritoriality decision tree: case studies

6.1 INTRODUCTION

Chapter 5 has proposed an extraterritoriality decision tree, developing a systematic approach to assess environmental npr-PPMs with an extraterritorial effect under Article XX GATT.[1] The tree raises a number of challenges and dilemmas, both on a practical and on a more conceptual level. Practically, the functioning of the tree is dependent on choices made with regard to scientific measurement methods and benchmarks, to determine the existence of environmental effects and of international support. Conceptually, one is faced with certain questions, such as: what to do with little-known concerns? Could npr-PPMs play a role in regime formation and norm creation? How to operationalize the principle of common but differentiated responsibilities? How to incorporate the precautionary principle?

This chapter will illustrate the application of the proposed decision tree in concrete cases. The tree will first be applied to the *US – Shrimp* case, discussed at multiple stages throughout this book and to date still the landmark judgment with regard to npr-PPMs and extraterritoriality. This case study will test whether the decision tree can systematize and substantiate the AB's nexus test to assess measures protecting environmental concerns (partly) outside the territory of the regulating state. The tree will furthermore be applied to three examples of EU environmental law: first, the IUU Fishing Regulation; second, the aviation measures in the framework of the EU ETS; and third, the Timber Regulation as part of the EU's FLEGT Action Plan.[2] Pursuant to Article 11 TFEU, 'environmental

[1] See Figure 5.3 for the extraterritoriality decision tree.

[2] This list is not exhaustive. More examples of environmental measures with an extraterritorial element can for instance be found in the sustainability criteria for biofuels (see e.g. Emily Barrett Lydgate, 'Biofuels, Sustainability, and Trade-related Regulatory Chill' Journal of International Economic Law

protection requirements must be integrated into the definition and implementation of the Union policies and activities, in particular with a view to promoting sustainable development'. Due to this integration requirement, environmental protection forms an important element in the EU's trade policy and vice versa.[3] The examples discussed in this chapter aim to further detect the challenges posed by the interplay between trade and environment, and develop possible amendments to the extraterritoriality model. The purpose of the chapter is not to offer a comprehensive analysis or a normative view of the environmental policies at issue, but rather to focus on how trade law interacts with environmental policy, and how extraterritorial effects of measures addressing transboundary environmental concerns could be assessed in practice.

(2012) 15:1, 157; Mairon G Bastos Lima and Joyeeta Gupta, 'The Extraterritorial Dimensions of Biofuels Policies and the Politics of Scale: Live and Let Die?' Third World Quarterly (2014) 35:3, 391; Allan Swinbank and Carsten Daugbjerg, 'Improving EU Biofuels Policy? Greenhouse Gas Emissions, Policy Efficiency, and WTO Compatibility' Journal of World Trade (2013) 47:4, 813), animal welfare standards (Robert Howse and Joanna Langille, 'Permitting Pluralism: The *Seal Products* Dispute and Why the WTO Should Accept Trade Restrictions Justified by Noninstrumental Moral Values' Yale Journal of International Law (2012) 37:2, 367; WTO AB Report, *European Communities – Measures Prohibiting the Importation and Marketing of Seal Products* WT/DS401/AB/R (2014); CJEU Fifth Chamber, *Zuchtvieh-Export GmbH v Stadt Kempten* C-424/13 (23 April 2015)), or border carbon adjustments (see e.g. Reinhard Quick, 'The Debate Continues: Are Border Adjustments of Emission Trading Schemes a Means to Protect the Climate or Are They "Naked" Protectionism?' in I Govaere, R Quick and M C E J Bronckers (eds.), *Trade and Competition Law in the EU and Beyond* (Edward Elgar Publishing 2011); Javier de Cendra, 'Can Emissions Trading Schemes be Coupled with Border Tax Adjustments? An Analysis Vis-a-vis WTO Law' Review of European Community and International Environmental Law (2006) 15:2, 131; Sarah Davidson Ladly, 'Border Carbon Adjustments, WTO-Law and the Principle of Common but Differentiated Responsibilities' International Environmental Agreements (2012) 12, 63). For an interesting overview of policy with a 'territorial extension', see Joanne Scott, 'Extraterritoriality and Territorial Extension in EU Law' American Journal of Comparative Law (2014) 62, 87.

[3] See also Article 207 TFEU, reiterating the need for the EU's common commercial policy to be conducted 'in the context of the principles and objectives of the Union's external action' and requiring that trade agreements be 'compatible with the internal Union policies and rules'. See also for an interesting overview of policy coherence between EU environmental policy and other policy areas, Marisa Cremona, 'Coherence and EU Environmental Policy' in Elisa Morgera (ed.), *The External Environmental Policy of the European Union* (Cambridge University Press 2012) 25; Gracia Marin Duran and Elisa Morgera, *Environmental Integration in the EU's External Relations: Beyond Multilateral Dimensions* (Hart Publishing 2012).

6.2 *US – SHRIMP* REVISITED

6.2.1 Measure and Context

The *US – Shrimp* case has been extensively discussed throughout this book, mainly focusing on the AB's reasoning of a sufficient nexus between the regulating state and the concern addressed by a trade measure. Revisiting the case, this section will take a closer look at the specific measure and its context before applying the extraterritoriality decision tree. This exercise purports to determine whether the decision tree, if it had been available to the AB at the time, would have been of any use in substantiating the AB's decision. Where relevant, the decision tree will be applied to the state of affairs of 1996 (i.e. the existing legal framework at the time of the dispute).

Sea turtles are vulnerable animals, whose existence is being threatened by a number of human causes, such as the destruction of nesting and feeding habitats through coastal development, ocean pollution, entanglement in marine debris, or incidental capture in commercial fisheries, also called bycatch.[4] Shrimp fishers often use a process called bottom trawling, whereby a large net is dragged across the ocean floor.[5] Many sea turtles are accidentally caught in these shrimp trawl nets, and as sea turtles need to reach the surface to breathe, they often drown once caught in the nets.[6] Sea turtles are a fundamental link in marine ecosystems. They help maintain the health of sea grass beds and coral reefs that benefit commercially valuable species such as shrimp, lobster and tuna,[7] and facilitate nutrient cycling from water to land.[8] In addition to their intrinsic value

---

[4] See among others Rebecca L Lewison et al., 'Understanding Impacts of Fisheries Bycatch on Marine Megafauna' Trends in Ecology and Evolution (2004) 19:11, 598 (identifying fisheries bycatch as a primary driver of population declines); Bryan P Wallace et al., 'Impacts of Fisheries Bycatch on Marine Turtle Populations Worldwide: Toward Conservation and Research Priorities' Ecosphere (2013) 4:3, 40; Bryan P. Wallace et al., 'Global Patterns of Marine Turtle Bycatch' Conservation Letters (2010) 3, 131 (providing a comprehensive overview of reported data on sea turtle bycatch in fisheries worldwide from 1990 to 2008. The total reported turtle bycatch was approximately 85,000 turtles, with less than 1 % of total fishing fleets observed and reported, so the true total is very likely to be much higher).

[5] The Humane Society, Fact sheet on sea turtle excluder devices, at www.humanesociety.org/issues/fisheries/facts/turtle_excluder_device_ted.html.

[6] World Wildlife Fund (WWF) on sea turtles, at www.worldwildlife.org/species/sea-turtle.

[7] Ibid.

[8] See e.g. E G Wilson et al., *Why Healthy Oceans Need Sea Turtles: The Importance of Sea Turtles to Marine Ecosystems* (2010), Oceana, 5, at http://

as contributors to biodiversity, sea turtles thus play an important role in marine and terrestrial ecosystems.[9] There are seven recognized sea turtle species, all of which are included in Appendix I of the CITES Convention, and listed on the International Union for Conservation of Nature (IUCN) Red List as vulnerable, endangered or critically endangered.[10] Sea turtles are migratory species and can be found throughout the world; five species have been known to nest on US coasts or traverse through US waters.[11] The fact that turtle species are found throughout the world does not mean that all turtles actually migrate worldwide. While some species can travel from Japan to Mexico or from Asia to the US West Coast, other species migrate rather regionally.[12]

The US Endangered Species Act of 1973 (ESA) lists the sea turtle species that occur in US waters as endangered or threatened species, thereby prohibiting their taking within the US, within US territorial waters and the high seas.[13] Research subsequently conducted by the United States National Oceanic and Atmospheric Administration (NOAA) National Marine Fisheries Service (NMFS) during the 1970s and 1980s led to the conclusion that drowning of sea turtles in mechanical shrimp trawls was a major factor in the decline of sea turtle populations worldwide[14] and shrimp trawling operations had been shown to have the greatest impact on sea turtle populations in the Gulf of Mexico.[15] Driven by these findings,

---

oceana.org/sites/default/files/reports/Why_Healthy_Oceans_Need_Sea_Turtles.pdf.

[9] US Department of State on sea turtles, at www.state.gov/e/oes/ocns/fish/bycatch/turtles/.

[10] International Union for Conservation of Nature and Natural Resources, at www.IUCNredlist.org. Looking at regional subpopulations of particular species, a more accurate picture of threats and conservation priorities can be formed, see WWF and Zoological Society of London, *Living Blue Planet Report: Species, Habitats and Human Well-Being* (2015) 11.

[11] Sea Turtle Conservancy, at www.conserveturtles.org/seaturtleinformation.php?page=species_world.

[12] SEE Turtles Org., at www.seeturtles.org/sea-turtle-migration/. For an example of a sea turtle tracking program, see www.conserveturtles.org/satellitetracking.php.

[13] ESA 1973 Section 4 (the listed species to be found at www.nmfs.noaa.gov/pr/species/esa/listed.htm#turtles); WTO Panel Report, *United States – Import Prohibitions of Certain Shrimp and Shrimp Products* WT/DS58/R (1998), para. 14.

[14] US Department of State on sea turtles, at www.state.gov/e/oes/ocns/fish/bycatch/turtles/.

[15] Southeast Fisheries Science Centre of the US National Marine Fisheries Service (National Oceanic and Athmospheric Administration – US Department of Commerce), at www.sefsc.noaa.gov/labs/mississippi/ted/history.htm.

NOAA developed fishing gear technology called turtle excluded devices (TEDs) aimed at reducing the catch of sea turtles. TEDs both allow turtles to escape shrimp trawls, and shrimpers to retain their catch.[16] The TED is a metal grid of bars that attaches to a shrimp trawling net. It has an opening at either the top or the bottom, which creates a hatch to allow larger animals such as sea turtles, sharks, and larger fish to escape while keeping shrimp inside. When a heavy object hits the device, the hatch opens, providing an escape route.[17] In 1983, a formal NOAA programme was introduced to encourage shrimp fishermen to use TEDs voluntarily. However, the programme was not successful on a voluntary basis, resulting in the 1987 ESA regulations, requiring all shrimp trawlers to use TEDs in specified areas with high sea turtle mortality.[18]

In 1989, Section 609 of Public Law 101-162 was enacted, providing that shrimp harvested with fishing technology that may adversely affect sea turtles could not be imported into the US.[19] The import ban did not apply if the US president certified on an annual basis that the harvesting nation had a regulatory programme and an incidental take rate comparable to that of the US.[20] In order for a foreign regulatory programme to be considered comparable to the US programme, it needed to be required for foreign shrimp trawlers to use TEDs at all times.[21] The import ban thus did not apply to shrimp harvested by fishermen using TEDs, nor did the ban apply to shrimp harvested in countries that by policy or law required the use of TEDs. The US Court of International Trade ruled in October 1996 that the US had to apply the import ban as long as the country concerned had not been certified, even when the shrimp had been harvested by TED-equipped trawlers.[22] In other words, according to the ruling, the US had

[16] US Department of State, Under Secretary for Economic Growth, Energy and the Environment, at www.state.gov/e/oes/ocns/fish/bycatch/turtles/; WTO Panel Report, *US – Shrimp*, para. 15.

[17] NGO Humane Society, at www.humanesociety.org/issues/fisheries/facts/turtle_excluder_device_ted.html.

[18] 52 Fed Reg 24244 (29 June 1987).

[19] Fish and Fishing, Maritime Affairs, 16USC 1537, Public Law 101-162 Section 609(b)(1).

[20] Section 609 (b)(2).

[21] 1991 Guidelines, 56 Federal Register 1051 (10 January 1991), and subsequently 1993 Guidelines, 58 Federal Register 9015 (18 February 1993). The scope of Section 609 was originally limited by the 1991 and 1993 Guidelines to specific countries in the wider Caribbean/western Atlantic region; however, in 1995 the US Court of International Trade found this limitation of geographical scope illegal. The 1996 Guidelines extended the scope of Section 609 to shrimp harvested in all countries.

[22] The court later clarified that shrimp harvested by manual methods which do not harm sea turtles, by aquaculture and in cold water, could continue to be

to ban the import of shrimp from any country not meeting US-determined policy conditions. This state of affairs was challenged by India, Malaysia, Pakistan and Thailand before a WTO panel.

6.2.2 Extraterritorial Effect

The US measure aims to protect five sea turtle species that are known to occur in US waters. However, these species equally live beyond US waters, and might never even cross them. The US measure is equally targeting those turtles that are not found in US waters, by prohibiting the import of shrimp that were not harvested using TEDs in shrimp trawls. By not only looking at the fishing method of the individual fisherman, but also requiring policy changes by the exporting countries, the US measure has an impact on third countries.

6.2.3 The Decision Tree Applied

6.2.3.1 Inconsistency with substantive obligations under GATT

In *US – Shrimp*, a violation of Article XI GATT was not disputed by the US,[23] and the case thus focused on the analysis of Article XX GATT. Article XI GATT provides for the general elimination of quantitative restrictions on import and export restrictions. Quotas or restrictions through import licences are prohibited and as Section 609 prohibits the import of shrimp and shrimp products from countries that are not certified, the US did not contest that the import ban was inconsistent with Article XI GATT. The required certification of countries could be considered a type of import licence. Once a measure infringes upon Article XI, the analysis will turn to the general exceptions under Article XX GATT.

While not argued by the parties, the US measure could also be inconsistent with Article III GATT. It has been discussed previously that the idea that npr-PPMs fall outside the scope of Article III GATT stems from the first non-adopted *Tuna – Dolphin* GATT Panel Report.[24] Even if they could be considered under Article III, the second *Tuna – Dolphin* GATT Panel found that 'likeness' of products should be determined based on the physical characteristics of a product and not on the manner in which they

---

imported from non-certified countries (*Earth Island Institute v Warren Christopher*, 948 Fed. Supp. 1062 (CIT 1996)).

23 WTO Panel Report, *US – Shrimp*, para. 169.

24 See Chapter 2. See GATT Panel, *United States – Restrictions on Imports of Tuna (Mexico)* DS21/R (1991), para. 5.14.

are processed or produced.[25] The relationship between Article III GATT and Article XI GATT is partly addressed in the Interpretative Note Ad Article III. The Ad Note to Article III appears to exclude a simultaneous application of both provisions.[26] Different aspects of a measure may be scrutinized under both articles, however.[27] According to the Ad Note, two conditions must be met for a measure to fall under Article III: firstly, the measure must apply to imported and like domestic products; and secondly, the measure must be enforced at the time or point of importation of the imported product. Domestic measures, even if applicable at the border, remain covered by Article III.[28] If a measure is applied exclusively to imported products and is solely a border measure, then the relevant provision is Article XI.

In the case at hand, the US has domestic laws in place requiring the use of TEDs for shrimp trawlers,[29] and Section 609 extends the domestic rule to foreign fisheries. The import ban on shrimp harvested without the use of TEDs could thus also be considered under Article III GATT. In order to establish a violation under Article III GATT, the products at issue must be alike, and less favourable treatment must be accorded to imported products compared to domestic products. Treatment less favourable entails a modification of the conditions of competition to the detriment of the imported products. Determining likeness can be a crucial point for environmental measures: is shrimp harvested in a turtle-friendly manner like or unlike shrimp harvested in a turtle-unfriendly manner?[30] If likeness is determined through a competitive relationship, it may well be that physically identical products are nevertheless not considered 'like' when consumer preferences point to the contrary.[31] Are turtle-unfriendly shrimp an

---

25 GATT Panel, *United States – Restrictions on Imports of Tuna (EEC)* DS29/R (1994), para. 5.8.

26 See also WTO Panel Report, *European Communities – Measures Affecting Asbestos and Asbestos-containing Products* WT/DS135/R (2001), para. 8.91.

27 WTO Panel Report, *India – Measures Affecting the Automotive Sector* WT/DS146/R (2001), para. 7.224.

28 Peter C Mavroidis, *Trade in Goods: The GATT and the Other WTO Agreements Regulating Trade in Goods* (2nd edn., Oxford University Press 2012) 66.

29 16 USC 1531; 50 CFR 223.205.

30 See Chapter 2.

31 Reinhard Quick and Christian Lau, 'Environmentally Motivated Tax Distinctions and WTO Law: The European Commission's Green Paper on Integrated Product Policy in light of the "Like Product" and "PPM" Debates' Journal of International Economic Law (2003) 6:2, 419, 431; Marco C E J Bronckers and Natalie McNelis, 'Rethinking the "Like Product" Definition in

alternative for turtle-friendly shrimp? This seems very difficult to prove, as identical products are usually in a competitive relationship because they, at least potentially, compete with each other as substitutable products.[32] If turtle-friendly and turtle-unfriendly shrimp are considered like products, treatment no less favourable requires effective equality of opportunities for imported products to compete with like domestic products.[33] Such distinction in treatment can be formal or factual. Arguably, a *de facto* distortion exists due to the more developed US regulations on TEDs, including the voluntary programme on TEDs and the familiarity of US fishermen with the device; in contrast to fishermen in other countries that have no experience with TEDs, nor the financial capacities to develop them.[34] Such distortion would be sufficient to find an inconsistency with Article III, requiring justification under Article XX GATT.

6.2.3.2 Environmental objective and location of the concern

If a violation of substantive GATT obligations is established, justification can be sought under Article XX GATT. The analysis of the paragraphs of Article XX GATT consists of a two-tier test: firstly, the objective must be listed; and secondly, with regard to the relationship between the measure at issue and the societal value pursued, a degree of necessity – depending on the wording of the particular paragraph – must be shown. As explained in Chapter 5, the proposed extraterritoriality decision tree finds its legal basis in these criteria. Firstly, when looking at the environmental objective, the question is whether the environmental exception grounds under paragraphs (b) and (g) of Article XX GATT are limited to concerns within the territory of the imposing Member, or whether Members can also rely on the exceptions to address environmental concerns outside their territory. As there is no explicit jurisdictional restriction in Article XX GATT, it has been submitted that it should first be determined whether a measure is inward-looking (environmental harm fully within the territory of the regulating state), outward-looking (environmental harm fully outside the territory of the regulating state) or a combination of both.[35] Purely inward-looking measures will have a strong territorial connection and there is

---

GATT 1994: Anti-Dumping and Environmental Protection' in Marco C E J Bronckers (ed.), *A Cross-Section of WTO Law* (Cameron May 2000).

[32] Quick and Lau, 2003, 432. See also Chapter 5.3.3 on consumer behaviour.

[33] WTO Panel Report, *United States – Standards for Reformulated and Conventional Gasoline* WT/DS2/R (1996), para. 6.10.

[34] WTO Panel Report, *US – Shrimp,* para. 107. See also expert opinions at paras. 5.142–5.168.

[35] See Chapter 5.

little doubt that states can take action to address environmental harm within their territory.[36] Measures addressing a concern outside their territory could still be based on a territorial connection when the environment of the regulating state is substantially affected (inward/outward-looking or environmental effects both within and outside the territory). Without environmental effects on the territory, measures exclusively addressing outward-looking concerns will not pass the threshold for accepted extraterritoriality.

Sea turtles are migratory species. Five (out of seven recognized) species of sea turtles are considered as possibly living in US waters and fall under the US regulation. However, even though those species are known to traverse US waters, not all sea turtles traverse the world, and migration is often regional.[37] While some of the sea turtles in foreign waters as protected by the US measure might traverse US waters, the measure equally covers sea turtles that might not ever do so.[38] The US measure can thus be classified as a partly inward/partly outward-looking measure. The AB found a 'sufficient nexus' between the US and the sea turtles – 'some of the turtles swim in US waters some of the time' – but it failed to further define that requirement (when is a nexus 'sufficient' and why would turtles sometimes swimming in US waters be sufficient). The AB did not require an explicit or strong territorial link as per general international law principles, but applied a less stringent test – without expounding its reasoning. With regard to a required nexus it is submitted that considering the environmental effects of a decreased sea turtle population on the US's territory and/or biodiversity allows for a more systematic and substantiated analysis – an approach particularly relevant when addressing environmental concerns

---

36 See Albert Lin, 'The Unifying Role of Harm in Environmental Law' Wisconsin Law Review (2006) 3; Henrik Horn and Peter C Mavroidis, 'The Permissible Reach of National Environmental Policies' Journal of World Trade (2008) 42:6, 1107, 1133; Bernhard Jansen, 'The Limits of Unilateralism from a European Perspective' European Journal of International Law (2000) 11:2, 309, 312. See also International Law Commission, Draft Articles on Responsibility of States for Internationally Wrongful Acts (2001). Environmental damage can lead to state responsibility. During the drafting of the ARSIWA, there was some discussion to include massive environmental pollution among the provisions that would call for universal jurisdiction as violations of *jus cogens*. Such reference was nevertheless not included in the final draft.

37 NGO SEE Turtles, at www.seeturtles.org/sea-turtle-migration/. For an example of a sea turtle tracking program, see www.conserveturtles.org/satellitetracking.php.

38 See for instance the examples given by the appellees of green turtles in Pakistani waters or olive ridley turtles in Thai waters: WTO Panel Report, *US – Shrimp*, para. 64. See also the expert opinions, paras. 5.255–5.276.

that are less tangible, such as climate change. Furthermore, in line with the AB's implicit acceptance of a weaker link than normally required under public international law,[39] it has been advanced that the requirements of environmental effects to justify environmental trade measures are less stringent than under public international law and competition law.[40]

When simply transposed from those areas of law, the effects doctrine would require environmental effects on the territory to be direct, substantial and foreseeable (in order for an importing country to appeal for a justification under Article XX GATT). However, these requirements can be more flexible, i.e. less present, in an environmental context due to the international support a concern may find through international environmental law.[41] In contrast to effects under competition law, where national rules are applied extraterritorially in the absence of relevant international rules, there is a body of international (largely soft) environmental law that can support a justification of extraterritoriality for npr-PPMs, in addition to environmental effects on the territory of the regulating state.[42] Thus, even when environmental effects are weaker or more indirect, the additional international recognition of a substantive environmental norm could still lead to a permissible extraterritoriality claim under WTO law. This international characterization is assessed in the second step of the decision tree.[43] Any justification of an extraterritorial npr-PPM needs a combination of both elements, which can be seen as communicating vessels: stronger effects need less international support, whereas strong international support can make up for weaker effects. In any event, no matter how strongly a state would feel about diversity in the marine ecosystem worldwide, these concerns could not justify restrictions on shrimp imports caught with turtle-unfriendly methods if that state's environment is not affected by a decrease in sea turtle populations. Npr-PPMs addressing environmental concerns located outside the territory of the regulating state without effects on its territory cannot be justified under Article XX GATT, irrespective of the existing international support.

To what extent would a decrease in population or even extinction of sea turtles species affect biodiversity within the US? Scientific expertise is required to answer that question. Sea turtles are said to play an important role in ocean ecosystems by maintaining healthy sea grass beds and

---

39 See Chapter 4.

40 See Chapter 5.2.2. See also Chapter 4 on public international law and competition law.

41 See Chapter 5.2.2.2.

42 Ibid.

43 See Section 6.2.3.3.

facilitating nutrient cycling from water to land.[44] Nevertheless, according to sea turtle experts, our understanding of the ecological functions and impacts of sea turtles is a long way from providing clear answers to the question of their precise effects on biodiversity. There are many differing opinions, but there is little actual evidence to measure the environmental effects of a decline in sea turtle population, both globally and in the US.[45] While it can be assumed that a threat to those sea turtle species that are known to traverse US waters (and might nest on US shores[46]) would lead to more direct and substantial effects to the US ecosystem than to the ecosystems of countries whose waters are not crossed, this cannot be said with certainty. The impact of a decline in sea turtle population can only be considered in the long term. Confirming possible findings on environmental effects by demonstrating a reversal of effects after an increase of sea turtle populations requires even more time: it has been estimated that with consistent use of TEDs, it would take approximately 70 years for threatened sea turtle populations in the southeastern US to increase with an order of magnitude.[47] Where it is unclear how exactly and to what extent ecological damage will materialize, states could rely on a precautionary approach as recognized in international environmental law to act even in cases of uncertainty.[48] Environmental risks can be very difficult to predict and can often not be specified by a few precisely determined variables, but may instead be driven by the interaction of changes taking place

---

[44] See e.g. Wilson et al., *Why Healthy Oceans Need Sea Turtles: The Importance of Sea Turtles to Marine Ecosystems* (2010) 5, at http://oceana.org/sites/default/files/reports/Why_Healthy_Oceans_Need_Sea_Turtles.pdf.

[45] Interview with Dr Jack Frazier, Smithsonian Institute, National Zoological Park, Conservation and Research Center, October 2015. For an interesting study on the environmental effects of a decline in sea animals on the earth's nutrient cycle, see Christopher E Doughty et al., 'Global Nutrient Transport in a World of Giants' Proceedings of the National Academy of Sciences of the United States (PNAS) (2015) 112.

[46] See for an overview of nesting sites, www.conserveturtles.org/seaturtleinformation.php?page=nestingmap.

[47] Larry B Crowder et al., 'Predicting the Impact of Turtle Excluder Devices on Loggerhead Sea Turtle Populations' Ecological Applications (1994) 4:3, 437.

[48] See Chapter 5.2.3.2. The precautionary principle has not yet been recognized by panels or AB as customary international law. Due to the differing views on the matter by scholars, the AB has left the matter unsettled. The AB did recognize the principle as a principle of international environmental law. See WTO AB Report, *European Communities – Measures Affecting Asbestos and Asbestos-containing Products* WT/DS135/AB/R (2001), para. 123; WTO Panel Report, *European Communities – Measures Affecting the Approval and Marketing of Biotech Products* WT/DS291/R (2006), para. 7.87.

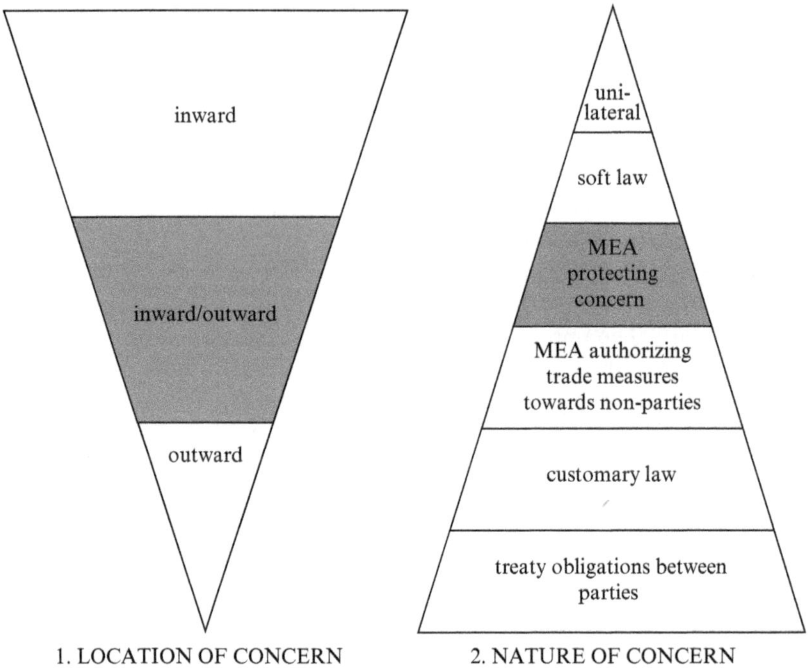

Figure 6.1 Decision tree US – Shrimp

at very different temporal and/or spatial scales.[49] Even though the precise magnitude of the impact of sea turtle extinction is yet unknown, it is clear that sea turtles do play an important role in the marine ecosystem, and not protecting these species will disrupt that natural system. It is likely that a decreased sea turtle population indeed affects the US marine (and possible terrestrial) ecosystem; however, uncertainty remains on how direct or substantial such effects are.[50]

In conclusion, the US TED measure is an inward/outward-looking measure, as illustrated in the first pyramid of Figure 6.1. Sea turtles are migratory species, playing an important role in ocean ecosystems. Whereas there is insufficient evidence today to determine the actual effects of

---

[49] Rosie Cooney and Andrew T F Lang, 'Taking Uncertainty Seriously: Adaptive Governance and International Trade' European Journal of International Law (2007) 18:3, 523.

[50] Interview with Dr Jack Frazier, Smithsonian Institute, National Zoological Park, Conservation and Research Center, October 2015.

declines in sea turtle populations on the US ocean or terrestrial ecosystem, it is plausible that the US is affected by declines of those turtle species that are known to occur in US waters and may nest on US shores. In case of weaker – i.e. less present – effects, a npr-PPM may find further support in international environmental law in order to be justified under Article XX GATT, as will be discussed in the following section. Should doubts remain about the requisite level of effects, in light of the complexity and long-term materialization of environmental effects, an additional appeal to the precautionary principle could reinforce the justification of the contested measure under Article XX.

6.2.3.3 Necessity and recognition of the concern

The second element that needs to be assessed under the subparagraphs of Article XX GATT is the degree of necessity.[51] This necessity test involves a three-stage analysis: first, the measure must be suitable to achieve the objective; second, the measure must be necessary to attain the objective; and third, determining the degree of necessity involves a process of weighing and balancing a series of factors, which results in an ad hoc, contextual assessment of each measure.[52] This includes, among others, a consideration of the trade-restrictiveness of the measure. Necessity takes different forms in the different paragraphs of Article XX GATT. Article XX(b) demands that measures are *necessary* to protect the environment, whereas Article XX(g) requires a measure to be *related to* the protection of an exhaustible resource. As argued in Chapter 5, international support can be considered as part of the necessity test.[53] Assessing the nature of the concern, or in other words, the level of recognition of a particular concern and/or substantive norm, is helpful to determine the acceptability of the measure at issue. The more common and important the interest, the more easily a measure will be deemed necessary.[54] The more international support for an environmental concern, the easier a measure will 'relate' to that policy objective.[55] As noted by the AB, the WTO agreements are not to be read

---

[51] See Chapter 5.2.3.

[52] See WTO AB Report, *Korea – Measures Affecting Imports of Fresh, Chilled and Frozen Beef* WT/DS161/AB/R (2000), para. 164; WTO AB Report, *EC – Asbestos*; WTO AB Report, *Brazil – Measures Affecting Import of Retreaded Tyres* WT/DS332/AB/R (2007), para. 182; WTO AB Report, *EC – Seal Products*, para. 5.169.

[53] See Chapter 5.2.3.

[54] WTO AB Report, *Korea – Various Measures on Beef*, para. 162.

[55] WTO AB Report, *United States – Import Prohibition of Certain Shrimp and Shrimp Products* WT/DS58/AB/R (1998), para. 135.

'in clinical isolation' from public international law,[56] and the exceptions of Article XX GATT should be interpreted in light of contemporary concerns, which can be evidenced by international instruments of environmental law.[57] The international support found in international environmental legal instruments is considered in combination with the environmental effects on the territory of the regulating state: stronger effects can be justified even with weaker international support, such as soft law instruments; whereas weaker environmental effects require more international support in order to pass the extraterritoriality threshold. States cannot adopt npr-PPMs with extraterritorial effects when the concern at issue is not yet recognized by any international instrument (i.e. unilateral norms).[58]

In the case at hand, the US measure aimed to protect sea turtles from bycatch of commercial fisheries by requiring the use of TEDs. Thus, firstly, can international support be found for the protection of sea turtles; and secondly, for the use of TEDs? The AB noted when assessing necessity under Article XX(g) (whether the measure related to the conservation of exhaustible natural resources) that the policy of protecting sea turtles is 'shared by all participants and third participants in this appeal, indeed, by the vast majority of nations in the world', referring to the, at the time, 144 parties to CITES, which included the complainants.[59] While CITES recognizes sea turtles as an endangered species, it does not oblige the adoption of specific conservation or protection measures.[60] CITES supports the concern addressed by turtle protection measures, but does not offer support for the specific method of using TEDs. The Convention on the Conservation of Migratory Species and Wild Animals (CMS) recognizes the need to protect sea turtles but emphasizes the importance of cooperation and concerted action with all respective states.[61] The CMS equally does not address specific protection measures.

---

[56] WTO AB Report, *United States – Standards for Reformulated and Conventional Gasoline* WT/DS2/AB/R (1996), p. 17. See also a recent example where the AB interpreted external treaty provisions in order to interpret WTO law: WTO, *Peru – Additional Duty on Imports of Certain Agricultural Products* AB Report 2015, WT/DS457/AB/R; James Mathis, 'WTO Appellate Body, *Peru-Additional Duty on Imports of Certain Agricultural Products,* WT/DS457/AB/R, 20 July 2015' Legal Issues of Economic Integration (2016) 43:1, 97, 105.

[57] WTO AB Report, *US – Shrimp*, para. 129.

[58] See Chapter 5.2.3.6.

[59] WTO AB Report, *US – Shrimp*, para. 135.

[60] Convention on International Trade in Endangered Species of Wild Fauna and Flora (1973) Appendix I.

[61] Convention on the Conservation of Migratory Species of Wild Animals (1979). In 2001 the Indian Ocean–South-east Asian Marine Turtle Memorandum

The use of TEDs is required by the Inter-American Convention for the Protection and Conservation of Sea Turtles (IAC), a Caribbean/Western Atlantic regional agreement with 12 signatories at the time, including the US; but to which none of the complainants were signatory.[62] Next to the IAC parties, a few other countries have opted to require the use of TEDs on shrimp trawl vessels subject to their jurisdictions.[63] Even though the US identified 19 countries in total using TEDs, the fact that the complainants and third parties to the dispute objected to the use of TEDs led the Panel to find that the mandatory use of TEDs could not be considered as a customarily accepted multilateral environmental standard.[64] Despite the emphasis of the CMS on concerted action and the provisions of Section 609 calling for the initiation of negotiations to conclude bilateral and multilateral agreements for the protection of sea turtles, the US failed to undertake such negotiations for an agreement on sea turtle conservation techniques with countries outside the Caribbean/Western Atlantic region before the imposition of the import ban.[65]

Applying the decision tree to this case, the international support at the time was limited to MEAs recognizing the need to protect sea turtles as threatened species (CITES, CMS). The US could not rely on the IAC with regard to the complainants, even though the IAC can be taken into account to demonstrate a wider use of TEDs beyond the US. However, in the absence of binding agreements between the US and the complainants on the matter, the question is why such agreement did not exist. Failure to

of Understanding came into effect, as a non-binding intergovernmental agreement to protect sea turtles in the Indian Ocean and the South-east Asia region. The MoU falls under the auspices of the Convention on the Conservation of Migratory Species of Wild Animals (Article IV, para. 4).

[62] Inter-American Convention (IAC) for the Protection and Conservation of Sea Turtles (1996) Annex III para. 3 The signatories at the time were Mexico, Venezuela, The Netherlands (Antilles), Peru, Brazil, Belize, Costa Rica, Ecuador, Honduras, Nicaragua and Uruguay. Later Argentina, Chile and Panama have joined. The treaty entered into force upon the ratification of the eighth state in 2001. The Convention is open for accession by any state in the Americas and the Caribbean.

[63] WTO Panel Report, *US – Shrimp*, para. 123; para. 7.57. Next to the signatories of the Inter-American Convention the US identified Colombia, El Salvador, Guatemala, Guyana, Indonesia, Nigeria, China, Thailand, Trinidad and Tobago as countries requiring the use of TEDs, and 'other nations in Asia and Africa had informed the US of their intention or desire to establish TEDs programmes'.

[64] Ibid. para. 7.59. The use of TEDs was also supported by the NGO WorldWildLife (WWF), at www.worldwildlife.org/species/sea-turtle.

[65] Ibid. para. 7.56; WTO AB Report, *US – Shrimp*, para. 166. The AB considered the negotiation efforts under the *chapeau*, see ibid para. 172.

conclude an agreement can be due to a number of reasons, and as the AB later held, it cannot be required that an agreement be *concluded*, rather, the emphasis must be on the efforts being made in negotiations.[66] Requiring that a multilateral agreement be *concluded* rather than displaying one's good faith in terms of efforts, would give any country party to the negotiations in effect a veto over the other country's actions, which would be unreasonable.[67] However, in the original proceedings no evidence was presented of any US attempts to negotiate such an agreement with the complainants. The fact that the US did not undertake any such efforts weakens a finding of necessity, as the PPM in question could be seen as a circumvention of the multilateral decision-making process. Nonetheless, the existing MEAs offer support for the US to undertake measures with regard to sea turtle protection.

Later, when the Panel considered the Article 21.5 DSU claim by Malaysia, the Panel found that the US had engaged in negotiations with the complainants and other countries in the Indian Ocean.[68] The US reached agreements with a number of countries, including three out of the four complainants (not Malaysia). In 2000, 24 countries, including the US, adopted the text of the South-East Asian Memorandum of Understanding as a non-binding instrument.[69] The Panel noted that the US was in favour of a legally binding agreement, but that it could not be held liable for the fact that other parties favoured a non-binding text.[70] Even though the US measure was found justifiable under Article XX GATT in the compliance proceedings, the US still had the continuing obligation to make serious efforts towards arriving at a binding agreement, to promote further international cooperation and agreement on the protection and conservation of sea turtles.

---

66 As argued in Chapter 5.2.3.6, in *US – Shrimp* the AB addressed this point under the *chapeau* as an aspect of the good faith test implied in the *chapeau* prohibition on arbitrary and unjustifiable discrimination. However, I submit it is more appropriate to consider at this stage of the decision tree whether attempts to international negotiations have been made.

67 WTO AB Report, *United States – Import Prohibition of Certain Shrimp and Shrimp Products, Recourse to Article 21.5 of the DSU by Malaysia* WT/DS58/AB/RW (2001), para. 123.

68 WTO Panel Report, *United States – Import Prohibition of Certain Shrimp and Shrimp Products, Recourse to Article 21.5 of the DSU by Malaysia* WT/DS58/RW (2001).

69 Under the auspices of the CMS. See Indian Ocean–South-east Asian Memorandum of Understanding, at www.ioseaturtles.org/.

70 WTO Panel Report, *US – Shrimp, Recourse to Article 21.5 of the DSU by Malaysia*, para. 5.83.

In conclusion, in light of the existing MEAs recognizing the threat to sea turtles combined with the likelihood of environmental effects on the US ecosystem, the US could indeed undertake action to protect migratory sea turtles that are at least partly located outside US territory. This outcome does not differ from the AB's outcome, which confirms that the AB's analysis was intuitively correct by not requiring a strong territorial link as per general international law principles. However, by considering scientifically determinable effects in combination with the international environmental legal framework, the decision tree has systematized and substantiated the AB's nexus test, providing for a rigorous assessment of environmental npr-PPMs. This two-tier test of effects and legal support warrants a wider scope for states to address extraterritorial concerns under Article XX GATT, as it stands, than would be permitted under public international law or competition law.[71]

The finding that the US could adopt measures with regard to sea turtle protection does not necessarily mean that the US could adopt a requirement for the use of TEDs. While the general threat to sea turtles is recognized in international instruments, there is less international support for the binding requirement to use TEDs, which makes it more challenging to accept that part of the measure as necessary. However, the question of the prescribed protection method must be considered separately from the question whether the US can protect sea turtles, even when located outside its territory (i.e. the extraterritorial element): both are subject to a necessity test. Having passed the extraterritoriality threshold, a Member still needs to comply with the other requirements of Article XX, including demonstrating why (the design of) the chosen measure is the least trade restrictive. The US would thus still need to demonstrate that the import ban on shrimp not harvested with TEDs was the least trade restrictive measure to reach the objective of turtle protection. With regard to the contribution of a measure to achieving its stated goal, the AB stated in *Brazil – Tyres* that even where the contribution of a law to protecting an environmental concern such as climate change is not immediately obvious because it is part of a broader programme, of which the impact can only be evaluated over time, that should not prevent a finding that such measure is necessary.[72] In the case at hand, the contribution can indeed only be evaluated over time. Assessing the contribution of TEDs to the protection and conservation of sea turtles remains very challenging: not only due to

---

[71] See Chapter 4 for a study on extraterritoriality under public international law and competition law.

[72] WTO AB Report, *Brazil – Retreaded Tyres*, para. 151.

the lack of systematic data collected,[73] but also due to other factors such as discrepancies between certification and the actual use of TEDs, and the political implications of trade embargoes, making it very difficult to attribute observations such as an increase in sea turtle populations to specific factors.[74]

6.2.3.4 *Chapeau*

Following the extraterritoriality analysis, a npr-PPM, like any other trade measure seeking justification, still needs to comply with the good faith requirements of the *chapeau* of Article XX. The analysis of the *chapeau* is thus not specific to npr-PPMs with an extraterritorial objective, but can offer additional safeguards against a possible overreach or abuse. The analysis of the *chapeau* does not form part of the decision tree, but is included in this assessment for the sake of completeness.

In its analysis under the *chapeau*, the AB in *US – Shrimp* focused on the inflexible nature of the measure,[75] the coercive effect of a country-based measure,[76] as well as the failure to engage in serious negotiations with countries other than the IAC parties.[77] Because of these elements, the US measure could not be justified under Article XX GATT. In the compliance proceedings, both the Panel and the AB held that due to the good faith efforts by the US to reach multilateral agreement and the increased flexibility of the measure, the measure was compliant with the *chapeau* and thus could be justified under Article XX.[78]

With regard to the coercive effect on other states, the import ban was first phrased as a combination of a country-based and a process-based measure: either shrimp was harvested by commercial shrimp trawl vessels using TEDs or in countries that were certified by the US government.[79]

---

[73] There are a few exceptions, such as a study in northern Australia by David Brewer et al., 'The Impact of Turtle Excluder Devices and Bycatch Reduction Devices on Diverse Tropical Marine Communities in Australia's Northern Prawn Trawl Fishery' Fisheries Research (2006) 81:2–3, 176.

[74] Interview with Dr Jack Frazier, Smithsonian Institute, National Zoological Park, Conservation and Research Center, October 2015.

[75] WTO AB Report, *US – Shrimp*, para. 177.

[76] Ibid. para. 162.

[77] Ibid. para. 166. The parties to the Inter-American Convention were at the time apart from the US: Brazil, Costa Rica, Mexico, Nicaragua and Venezuela.

[78] WTO Panel Report, *US – Shrimp, Recourse to Article 21.5 of the DSU by Malaysia*, paras. 5.42, 5.84, 5.104; WTO AB Report, *US – Shrimp, Recourse to Article 21.5 of the DSU by Malaysia*, para. 144. Revised Guidelines for the Implementation of Section 609 of Public Law 101-162.

[79] See Chapter 5.4.2.

Such certification could be granted where countries had adopted a regulatory programme for the protection of sea turtles that was comparable to that of the US and where the average take rate of bycatch was comparable to the US rate.[80] The US Court of International Trade ruled in October 1996 that the US had to apply the import ban to all shrimp imports as long as the country of origin had not been certified, thus including TED-caught shrimp. In other words, the US had to ban the import of shrimp from any country not meeting certain policy conditions.[81] The US measure thus became a purely country-based or government-policy measure.[82] The Panel reasoned that country-based measures cannot be accepted under the *chapeau* of Article XX, because 'if one WTO Member were allowed to adopt such measures, then other Members would also have the right to adopt similar measures on the same subject but with differing, or even conflicting, requirements', which would be a serious threat to the multilateral trading system.[83] For that reason the Panel found the country-based measure to fall outside the scope of Article XX.[84] The AB did not fully agree with the Panel's reasoning and emphasized that government-policy standards could in principle be justified under Article XX; however, the measure must be sensitive to the conditions in each country and the administrative process must meet minimum standards of transparency and procedural fairness. In complying with the AB decision, the US measure was revised to permit shrimp imports so long as the shrimp are harvested under conditions that do not adversely affect sea turtles, and to provide more flexibility in the recognition of foreign programmes eligible for US certification.[85] Under the revised guidelines, it became possible to acquire shrimp from countries that had not received a countrywide certification under the government-policy standard, when harvested using TEDs, allowing for a process-based standard in combination with the

---

[80] 1996 Guidelines, 61 Federal Register 17342 (19 April 1996), Pub L 101-162 para. 609(b)(1), (b)(2), 103 Stat 1038.

[81] WTO Panel Report, *US – Shrimp*, paras. 7.6, 7.16.

[82] Steve Charnovitz, 'The Law of Environmental "PPMs" in the WTO: Debunking the Myth of Illegality' Yale Journal of International Law (2002) 27:1, 59, 95.

[83] WTO Panel Report, *US – Shrimp*, para. 7.45.

[84] Ibid. para. 7.51.

[85] Revised Guidelines for the Implementation of Section 609 of Public Law 101-162, 64 Federal Register 3086 (8 July 1999). The US Court of Appeals for the Federal Circuit issued a ruling in June 1998 that vacated the CIT decision of 1996 that would not allow the import of TED-harvested shrimp in countries that were not certified under Section 609.

country-based standard.[86] Since every fisherman could in principle choose to use TEDs and export, the US measure should mainly be considered as a process-based measure.

With regard to the flexibility of a measure, the AB noted that conditioning market access on the adoption of a programme *comparable in effectiveness* (rather than *essentially the same)* can be allowed under Article XX as it allows the exporting Member to adopt a regulatory programme that is suitable to the specific conditions prevailing in its territory.[87] Discrimination results 'when the application of the measure at issue does not allow for any inquiry into the appropriateness of the regulatory program for the conditions prevailing in exporting countries'.[88]

6.2.4 Challenges

The main challenge for the extraterritoriality decision tree emerging from the analysis of the US sea turtle measure is the difficulty to determine environmental effects in light of insufficient scientific evidence. The number of factors and complex interaction to be considered in marine ecosystems, the challenge of systematic data collection, and the time span required for this type of research (long-term observations) make it an extremely difficult and enormous task to collect and present conclusive evidence. If there is a lack of scientific evidence demonstrating or rebutting the existence of environmental effects on the territory, and states were to adopt a precautionary approach to the concerns at issue, they must act with caution when the adopted measures affect other states. The wide international support for the conservation of sea turtles shows that even with the limited available knowledge, the international community is concerned about protecting the species. Even without knowing the exact magnitude of environmental effects, in light of what is known about the role of sea turtles in marine ecosystems, it is plausible that marine (and possibly also terrestrial) ecosystems will suffer. As already noted above, due to the fact that the targeted sea turtle species are known to occur in US waters, it is similarly plausible that the US ecosystem will be affected. US action with regard to sea turtles, even those located outside

---

[86] WTO Panel Report, *US – Shrimp, Recourse to Article 21.5 of the DSU by Malaysia*, para. 5.107; Charnovitz, 2002, 98.

[87] WTO AB Report, *US – Shrimp, Recourse to Article 21.5 of the DSU by Malaysia*, para. 144.

[88] WTO AB Report, *US – Shrimp*, para. 165. See for the expert opinions on the socio-economic factors that need to be taken into account when requiring the use of TEDs, WTO Panel Report, *US – Shrimp*, para. 5.142.

its territory, can thus be permitted under the decision tree. However, in light of the lack of evidence and uncertainty about the environmental effects of different protection methods, it is crucial to put strong emphasis on international cooperation and deliberation, as well as consideration of alternative measures. In the absence of strong international support and agreement, the flexibility of a measure, and accepting alternative protective initiatives, is key. Environmental protection measures should be adaptable to the environmental, social and economic conditions prevailing in the countries or areas where they are to be applied.[89] The safeguards of the subparagraphs of Article XX with regard to the design of the measure as well as the *chapeau* of Article XX play an important role in protecting against overreach by WTO Members, even where the extraterritoriality threshold is passed.

The outcome from the application of the decision tree to *US – Shrimp* does not differ from the AB's findings. However, where the AB relied on the 'sufficient nexus' between the US and the turtles, an approach that has been criticized for its ad hoc approach that might not hold in disputes dealing with less tangible environmental concerns, the decision tree allows for a more systematic and robust assessment of trade measures with extraterritorial effects. Where environmental effects on the territory of the regulating state are weaker, additional support for action can be found in international instruments of hard and/or soft law. A precautionary approach could furthermore be adopted where effects are still uncertain in light of the complexity and long-term materialization of environmental effects. *US – Shrimp* was already considered good precedent from an environmental perspective; but the current analysis has demonstrated that the AB's position was – despite its shortcomings – commendable from a legal perspective as well. The AB was correct in accepting weaker territorial effects within the regulating state under WTO law than would be required under public international law (and competition law), but should have expressed that more clearly and why it did so. The application of the decision tree to *US – Shrimp* has not only confirmed the AB's position but has strengthened and systematized it by considering environmental effects on the territory in combination with support for the concern at issue in international environmental law.

---

[89] Rio Declaration of Environment and Development (1992) Principle 2. See also WTO Panel Report, *US – Shrimp*, para. 7.52.

6.3 IUU FISHING

6.3.1 Measure and Context

The international community has increasingly realized the damaging economic, social and environmental impacts of illegal, unreported and unregulated (IUU) fishing.[90] Illegal fishing activities include fishing activities by vessels that have no permission from the state in whose waters they are fishing; or, fishing vessels flying the flag of states that are party to a relevant regional fisheries management organization, but operating in contravention of the measures adopted by that organization; or, fishing vessels acting in violation of national laws applicable in maritime waters or international obligations held by the flag state.[91] Unregulated fishing means fishing activities in the area of application of a relevant regional fisheries management organization by fishing vessels flying the flag of a state not party to that organization, contravening the measures of that organization; or in areas where there are no applicable measures in force, but where vessels are acting in a manner not consistent with responsibilities of the flag state for the conservation of living marine resources under international law.[92]

IUU fishing constitutes a threat to the sustainable exploitation of living aquatic resources and to marine biodiversity, jeopardizing international efforts to promote better ocean governance.[93] Destructive fishing methods cause damage to fisheries habitats and result in high levels of bycatch of non-target species, such as marine mammals, turtles and seabirds.[94] Furthermore, IUU fishing also has an impact on the socio-economic situation of those fishermen who do abide by the rules on conservation and

---

[90] IUU fishing encompasses a wide range of fishing activities which can be considered in violation of or without regard to applicable international, regional or national fisheries regulations and standards. For a comprehensive definition and scope of illegal, unreported and unregulated fishing, see Mary Ann Palma, Martin Tsamenyi and William Edeson, *Promoting Sustainable Fisheries: The International Legal and Policy Framework to Combat Illegal, Unreported and Unregulated Fishing* (Brill/Nijhoff 2010) Chapter 2; Jens Theilen, 'What's in a Name? The Illegality of Illegal, Unreported and Unregulated Fishing' Journal of Marine and Coastal Law (2013) 28, 533.

[91] Council Regulation (EC) No 1005/2008 of 29 September 2008 Establishing a Community System to Prevent, Deter and Eliminate Illegal, Unreported and Unregulated Fishing (IUU Regulation) (2008) Article 2(2).

[92] Ibid. Article 2(4).

[93] Ibid. recital (3).

[94] Palma, Tsamenyi and Edeson, 2010, 11.

management of fisheries resources.[95] High demand for specific seafood products (e.g. shark fin), the global character of fisheries production chains allowing for money laundering, and the anonymity and transactional speed that exists within global markets for vessel flags, crews and vessels allow in particular for IUU fishing. IUU fishing can even overlap with other forms of maritime crime such as piracy and drug smuggling.[96] IUU fishing can have negative consequences for food security as it can lead to the collapse of fisheries resources.[97] In light of these concerns, the FAO adopted an international plan of action in 2002 to prevent, deter and eliminate IUU fishing.[98] This voluntary Action Plan provides for a toolbox with measures with regard to e.g. monitoring, enforcement and economic incentives that can be used by flag states, coastal states and market states to combat IUU fishing within their jurisdiction.[99] Overall, governance of the global fisheries economy is a decentralized, but relatively coherently coordinated, system of treaties and non-binding international and regional fisheries instruments and private initiatives by NGOs such as the World Wide Fund for Nature (WWF) and Greenpeace.[100]

Traditionally, flag states have held a prominent position with respect to fisheries regulation and enforcement.[101] However, fishing vessels can circumvent IUU fishing obligations by flying the flag of state that is not party to any regional agreement (this can be a flag of convenience, without any genuine link to the flag state). Flag states that are unwilling or unable to regulate vessels flying its flag considerably complicate fisheries management.[102] Indeed, if all flag states would adopt and implement

---

[95] Council Regulation (EC) No 1005/2008 of 29 September 2008 Establishing a Community System to Prevent, Deter and Eliminate Illegal, Unreported and Unregulated Fishing (IUU Regulation) recital (6).

[96] Martin Tsamenyi et al., *Fairer Fishing: The Impact on Developing Countries of the European Community Regulation on Illegal, Unreported and Unregulated Fisheries* (Commonwealth Secretariat 2009) 7.

[97] Palma, Tsamenyi and Edeson, 2010, 4.

[98] FAO, International Plan of Action to Prevent, Deter and Eliminate Illegal, Unreported and Unregulated Fishing (2001). The Action Plan was adopted within the framework of the 1995 FAO Code of Conduct for Responsible Fisheries.

[99] FAO International Plan of Action, Title IV.

[100] See e.g. the setting up of a vessel black-list by Greenpeace, at www.greenpeace.org/international/en/campaigns/oceans/pirate-fishing/Blacklist1/, or the development of tracking technology for vessels on onboard surveillance by WWF, at www.worldwildlife.org/threats/illegal-fishing.

[101] Olav Schram Stokke, 'Trade Measures and the Combat of IUU Fishing: Institutional Interplay and Effective Governance in the Northeast Atlantic' Marine Policy (2009) 33, 339, 340.

[102] Ibid. 341.

principles contained in the United Nations Convention on the Law of the Sea (UNCLOS), the UN Fish Stocks Agreement,[103] the FAO Compliance Agreement and the FAO Code of Conduct, IUU fishing would not be as problematic as it is today. Trade measures can be effective tools in finding a solution to this problem.[104] Rather than focusing on flag states, trade measures will focus primarily on port states, particularly on port control where access to the market can be limited or prohibited. While fishing vessels may avoid the authorities of flag states and coastal states, they must come into port to bring their fish to market, so port state measures may be more effective in deterring IUU fishing because of their commercial importance.[105] The port is the market entry point, so it is a crucial economic choke point in the IUU fishing supply chain. Whereas vessels could easily fly under a convenient flag to circumvent national or international regulation, the market choice is of great economic importance.

The EU is the world's largest importer of fish and fish products.[106] In an effort to improve global fisheries' sustainability and address IUU fishing, the EU adopted the IUU Fishing Regulation 1005/2008, which stated explicitly that, as the world's largest market for fishery products, the 'Community has a specific responsibility in making sure that fishery products imported into its territory do not originate from IUU fishing'.[107]

---

[103] This agreement strengthens the duty to cooperate with other states on high seas fisheries by providing that only states that are members of a regional fisheries regime, or that agree to apply the conservation and management measures taken under such a regime, shall have access to the fishery. Enforcement mainly lies with flag-state responsibilities, such as preventing its vessels from engaging in high-seas fishing without a permit. Under the agreement, port states can conduct inspections of vessels and port states can prohibit landings or transhipment when it has been established that the catch has been taken in a manner contrary to the conservation and management measures on the high seas.

[104] Linda Chaves, *Illegal, Unreported and Unregulated Fishing: WTO-Consistent Trade Related Measures to Address IUU Fishing* (FAO 2000), para. 14.

[105] Blaise Kuemlangan and Michael Press, 'Preventing, Deterring and Eliminating IUU Fishing: Port State Measures' Environmental Policy and Law (2010) 40:6, 262, 264.

[106] Developed states absorb more than 80 % of total world fisheries imports in value terms, of which the EU accounts for approximately 40 %, and Japan and the US for around 35 %. Developing states are the largest exporters, at around 60 % in quantity of total fish exports. Cumulative net exports of fisheries products from developing states far exceed export earnings from major commodities such as coffee, bananas, and rubber. See UN, FAO, Fact Sheet, the International Fish Trade and World Fisheries, June 2008, at www.fao.org.

[107] Council Regulation (EC) No 1005/2008 of 29 September 2008 Establishing a Community System to Prevent, Deter and Eliminate Illegal, Unreported and Unregulated Fishing (IUU Fishing Regulation) recital (9). The regulation was

The IUU Fishing Regulation provides for a range of control and enforcement measures primarily aimed at keeping illegally caught fish off the EU market and has been designed to ensure proper control of the supply chain for imported fishery products. The regulation applies to all IUU fishing 'within the territory of the EU Member States, within Community waters, within maritime waters under the jurisdiction or sovereignty of third countries and on the high seas'.[108] In other words, all fishing activities at sea fall within the scope of the regulation, but fishing activities in internal waters of third states seem to be excluded.

Key elements of the IUU Fishing Regulation with trade implications are port control over third country fishing vessels, catch certification requirements, the establishment of a Community IUU vessel list, and the establishment of a list of non-cooperating third countries. The port control of third country vessels entails that landings or transhipments will only take place in designated ports and upon presentation of a catch certificate.[109] Such catch certificate must be validated by the flag state of the fishing vessel, certifying that catches have been made in accordance with the applicable laws, regulations and international conservation and management measures[110] – as any flag state has a duty under international law that fishing vessels flying its flag comply with international rules on conservation and management of fisheries resources. Flag states that want to grant certificates must notify the European Commission on their applicable law and the necessary checks their public authorities can carry out.[111] The Commission shall cooperate with third countries to facilitate this process. Without a valid catch certificate, fishery products cannot be imported into the EU.

The Commission can furthermore put vessels suspected of IUU fishing on a 'black list', including both vessels flying the flag of third countries and EU Member States. This blacklist results among others in a prohibition to

---

adopted in the framework of the Common Fisheries Policy and the Community Plan of Action for the Eradication of IUU Fishing, COM(2002)180 final. The Regulation entered into force in 2010.

108 IUU Fishing Regulation, Article 1(3).

109 Such certificate must contain the name of the fishing vessel, home port and registration number, call sign, licence number, information about the fishery product (type of species, catch areas, dates, weight, applicable conservation and management measures) and a declaration on export and import of the fishery product (if applicable). Catch documents and related documents validated in conformity with catch documentation schemes adopted by an RFMO will be accepted by the EU as catch certificates. IUU Fishing Regulation, Article 13.

110 Ibid. Article 12.

111 Ibid. Article 20.

fish in Community waters and no authorization will be granted to enter into a port of a Member State, except in case of *force majeure* (EU flagged vessels may only access their home port). EU Member States shall also refuse the granting of their flag to IUU fishing vessels.[112]

Next to the IUU vessel list, the European Commission can establish a list of non-cooperating third countries. A country may be identified as such if it 'fails to discharge the duties incumbent upon it under international law as flag, port, coastal or market State and to take action to prevent, deter and eliminate IUU fishing'.[113] This duty includes ratification of the international IUU fishing instruments, as well as membership to regional fisheries management organizations.[114] The importation into the EU of any fishery products caught by fishing vessels flying the flag of such countries shall be prohibited and catch certificates by that flag state will not be accepted.[115] It may be that the import ban only applies to a particular species or stock. The Commission can grant cautionary 'yellow cards', after which it engages in dialogue and cooperation, before handing out the actual 'red card' that puts a third country on the list of non-cooperating third countries (thereby banning all imports from fishing vessels flying their flag). Countries such as Fiji, South Korea and Philippines have been yellow-carded, but were delisted after adopting new legislation and improving their monitoring and control systems. Belize was red-carded but also saw the threat of sanctions lifted after making the required changes. Sri Lanka, Cambodia and Guinea, among others, were red-carded in 2014, and their fisheries products are still banned from import.[116]

---

112 Vessels can ask to review their status and to be removed from the list if evidence can demonstrate that the vessel did not engage in IUU fishing. Otherwise, a vessel can only be removed from the list if at least two years have lapsed since its listing during which time no further reports of alleged IUU fishing have been received (IUU Fishing Regulation, Article 28).

113 IUU Fishing Regulation, Article 31(3). Specific constraints of developing countries, the capacity of the competent authorities, the circumstances, the gravity of the IUU fishing manifestation etc. are taken into account by the Commission (Article 31(4)).

114 Ibid. Article 31(5).

115 Ibid. Article 38(1).

116 Fiji, Panama, Togo, and Vanuatu were yellow carded in 2012, South Korea in 2013, Philippines in 2014. Belize was red carded in 2014. All were delisted and had the threat of sanctions lifted (October 2013; South Korea and Philippines in April 2015). Sri Lanka, Cambodia and Guinea were also red carded in 2014, and their fisheries products are still banned from import. Ghana and Curacao received a yellow card in November 2013, and are developing new legislation and improving their monitoring, control and inspection systems. As a result, the process of dialogue and

6.3.2 Extraterritorial Effect

The extraterritorial effect of the EU IUU Fishing Regulation is apparent from the fact that EU port and market access is made dependent on fishing activities occurring in the high seas or in the maritime waters of other states.[117] The EU thereby extends her prescriptive jurisdiction beyond the vessels flying an EU flag and vessels fishing in EU waters and Exclusive Economic Zones (EEZ). Surely, the measure is only activated once port or market access is sought. So are all npr-PPMs with an extraterritorial effect, which makes that element of little help in determining whether this extension of European jurisdiction is justified.

6.3.3 The Decision Tree Applied

6.3.3.1 Inconsistency with substantive obligations under GATT

The IUU Fishing Regulation raises several questions under GATT. The prohibition of the importation or exportation on the basis of non-compliance with the catch certification requirement could be seen as a quantitative restriction under Article XI GATT, leading to an inconsistency and requiring the need for justification under Article XX. The catch certificate, containing information on, for example, vessel, catch area and date, authorizations, etc.,[118] must be validated by the flag state. This certificate could be considered as a (non-automatic) import licensing requirement under Articles 1(1) and 3 of the WTO Import Licensing Agreement, as the submission of documentation is required as a prior condition for importation.[119] The competent authorities of the importing Member States (mostly fisheries agencies or services[120] rather than customs) must check the certificate.[121] Import licences are considered quantitative restrictions, incompatible with Article XI GATT.[122]

---

cooperation with these three countries is still ongoing. Papua New Guinea received a formal warning by the Commission in June 2014, whereas Solomon Islands, Tuvalu, Saint Kitts and Nevis and Saint Vincent and the Grenadines were formally warned in December 2014. Thailand was yellow carded in April 2015.

117 Theilen, 2013, 548.

118 IUU Fishing Regulation, Annex II.

119 Despite this finding, the catch certificate requirement has not been notified by the EU to the Committee on Import Licensing.

120 List of Member States and their competent authorities concerning Articles 15(2), 17(8) and 21(3) of Council Regulation (EC) No 1005/2008 (OJ 2015/C 93/07).

121 IUU Fishing Regulation, Article 17.

122 The exemptions for fisheries under Article XI:2(c) GATT do not apply to the catch certificates at hand. See also WTO Panel Report, *India – Quantitative*

Likewise will the import ban pursuant to the flag state black list result in a violation of Article XI GATT.

However, even if enforced at the border, the IUU Fishing Regulation could also be considered an internal measure under Article III GATT, if the Regulation were applicable to both imported and domestic products.[123] The Regulation applies to fishing within and outside the EU, and to EU and third country fishing vessels.[124] In order to determine whether it violates Article III:4 GATT, likeness of the products and less favourable treatment of the imported products must be established. With regard to likeness, IUU fish products and non-IUU fish products (i.e. legally harvested fish) can be considered directly competitive or substitutable. It could perhaps be argued that based on consumer preferences (depending on evidence and market research) these products are not like,[125] or an argument could be made based on compliance with international obligations: illegally harvested products cannot be like legally harvested products.[126] In the absence of any conclusive guidance on those points, based on the other criteria such as physical characteristics, tariff classification and end-use, illegal and legal fish can be considered directly competitive. The group of imported products (products that seek importation) is like the group of domestic products (products that seek market access domestically) as both include in principle illegally and legally harvested fish products. Imports of IUU fish products are prohibited, as is bringing domestically caught IUU fish products on the market. The question is whether the IUU Fishing Regulation then accords less favourable treatment to the group of imported products, so as to protect domestic products. Treatment no less favourable requires an effective equality of competitive opportunities, or in other words, a determination whether the conditions of competition are modified to the detriment

---

Restrictions on Imports of Agricultural, Textile and Industrial Products WT/DS90/R (1999), para. V.75.

123 Ad Note to Article III GATT.

124 IUU Fishing Regulation, Article 1.

125 See Chapter 2.

126 See for an argumentation on likeness of legal and illegal products in the context of Timber, Duncan Brack, Alexander Chandra and Herjuno Kinasih, *The Australian Government's Illegal Logging Prohibition Bill: WTO Implications* (International Institute for Sustainable Development 2012), 9; Dylan Geraets and Bregt Natens, 'The WTO Consistency of the European Union Timber Regulation' Journal of World Trade (2014) 48:2, 433, 443; Andrew Mitchell and Glyn Ayres, 'Out of Crooked Timber: The Consistency of Australia's Illegal Logging Prohibition Bill with the WTO Agreement' Environmental and Planning Law Journal (2012) 29:6, 462, 468.

of the group of imported products.[127] As the regulation applies both to imported and domestic fish products, there is no *de jure* violation. As the catch certification requirement applies both to vessels flying EU and third country flags, and all vessels can be blacklisted, there is no *de facto* violation either. All certificates must be validated by the flag state, and refer back to, among others, international and regional conservation and management measures.[128] While there might be differences in the particular procedures in the flag state, the EU measure does not accord protection to domestic products. With regard to inspections and port measures for EU vessels that are not included in the regulation, differentiation between EU vessels and third country vessels does not lead to less favourable treatment of the third country vessels either, as the member countries are already subject to at least equally strict rules for inspection and reporting.[129] Accordingly, the IUU Fishing Regulation is unlikely to violate Article III GATT.

An argument could be made that the EU rules violate Article V GATT on freedom of transit. The EU itself brought that argument in a dispute with Chile over swordfish. Chile prohibited the transhipment of swordfish catches (taken from the high seas bordering Chile's EEZ) from foreign and Chilean vessels in Chile's ports when the catches were made in contravention of Chile's swordfish conservation rules.[130] The prohibition to unload the fish in Chile's ports was seen as a significant obstacle to further export. The EU is now imposing a similar measure: fish cannot be unloaded or transhipped in EU ports without a valid catch certificate in order to deter and prevent IUU fishing. Because of the reference to international obligations in the catch certificates, the EU could argue that the regulations imposed are nevertheless 'reasonable' under Article V:4 GATT. If that is not the case, the denial of port access for transhipment without a valid certificate could be considered a violation of Article V GATT.

---

[127] See Chapter 2.

[128] IUU Fishing Regulation, Article 15.

[129] For all EU fisheries legislation, see http://ec.europa.eu/fisheries/cfp/index_en.htm.

[130] Chile – Measures Affecting the Transit and Importing of Swordfish, WT/DS193, (WTO), withdrawn. The case was withdrawn in 2010 after mutual agreement between the parties was reached after a decade of negotiations. See e.g. Peter-Tobias Stoll and Silja Vöneky, 'The Swordfish Case: Law of the Sea v Trade' Zeitschrift für Ausländisches Öffentliches Recht und Völkerrecht (2002) 65, 21.

6.3.3.2 Environmental objective and location of the concern

Assuming that a violation of substantive WTO rules is established, the extraterritoriality question arises when seeking justification under Article XX GATT. Measures aiming to protect fish stocks could fall within both Article XX(b) and XX(g), as necessary for the protection of animal life and health and relating to the conservation of exhaustible resources.[131] The question is whether there is a jurisdictional limitation to these environmental objectives. Are paragraphs (b) and (g) limited to environmental concerns within the territory of the regulating state, or can members also rely on these exceptions to address concerns outside their jurisdiction?

The extraterritoriality decision tree first considers the location of the concern. As illustrated in Figure 6.2, the IUU Fishing Regulation has an inward- and an outward-looking purpose, as it addresses both the depletion of fish within EU waters and outside EU waters. Following the AB's reasoning in *US – Shrimp*, finding a 'sufficient nexus' due to some of the sea turtles traversing US waters, all migratory fish stock and species which may at one time or another traverse EU waters would lead to the establishment of a sufficient nexus. In response to the unconvincing sufficient nexus requirement, I propose to look at the environmental effects on the territory of the imposing country. In this case, evidence would need to demonstrate that the depletion of certain fish stocks has an impact on biodiversity, marine ecosystems or has, for instance, affected EU food supply, thus leading to direct, substantial and foreseeable effects on the EU environment. If fishing resources are shared and clearly present in EU waters, evidencing an impact on biodiversity should not be a big hurdle.[132] If no direct and substantial environmental effects on EU territory could be demonstrated (for instance, when a certain species is concerned that is not migratory and has little impact on global biodiversity), the measure will be considered outward-looking and will not pass the extraterritoriality threshold. In such case, states must seek

---

[131] FAO, *The State of World Fisheries and Aquaculture: Opportunities and Challenges* (2014). According to the report fish stocks are exhaustible. See also WTO AB Report, *US – Shrimp*; GATT Panel, *US – Tuna (Mexico)*; GATT Panel, *US – Tuna (EEC)*.

[132] See for instance FAO, *The State of World Fisheries and Aquaculture: Opportunities and Challenges* (2014); FAO/UNEP, Report of the Expert Meeting on Impacts of Destructive Fishing Practices, Unsustainable Fishing, and Illegal, Unreported and Unregulated (IUU) Fishing on Marine Biodiversity and Habitats, September 2009, FAO Report No 932, FIRF/R932; Africa Progress Panel, 'Protect our Fisheries' at www.africaprogresspanel.org/fishing; WWF on overfishing, at www.worldwildlife.org/threats/overfishing.

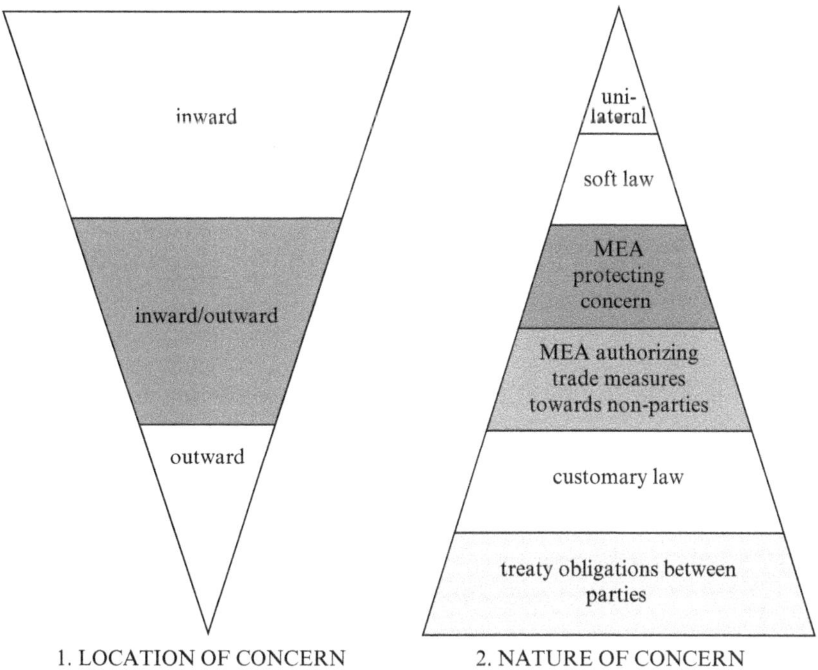

Figure 6.2 Decision tree IUU Fishing Regulation

other means to incentivize other states as well as producers to take action against IUU fishing.

6.3.3.3 Necessity and recognition of the concern

With regard to requirement of 'related to' or necessity, determining the degree of necessity involves a process of weighing and balancing a series of factors, which results in an ad hoc, contextual assessment of each measure.[133] In *Korea – Beef*, the AB stated that the more vital or important the concerns are that a measure is intended to protect, the easier it would be to accept that measure as necessary.[134] In that light, the necessity requirement is linked to the international support for an international concern.[135]

---

[133] WTO AB Report, *Korea – Various Measures on Beef*; WTO AB Report, *EC– Asbestos*; WTO AB Report, *Brazil – Retreaded Tyres.*

[134] WTO AB Report, *Korea – Various Measures on Beef*, para. 162.

[135] See Chapter 5.

The more common the interest, the more easily a measure will be considered necessary. Necessity refers to the question whether less trade restrictive measures can reach the same objective. A measure adopted by a WTO Member based upon or suggested by international instruments would find additional support for deeming a measure necessary. If a measure goes beyond what is proposed by international instruments, the imposing Member would need to demonstrate why it opted for this specific measure in order to demonstrate necessity.[136]

The general concern about sustainable fish resources management and IUU fishing is widely recognized through international and regional instruments, some of which are binding while others are non-binding. UNCLOS provides for the principles of sustainable and shared use of the high seas.[137] The FAO Compliance Agreement[138] and the UN Fish Stocks Agreement[139] are both binding instruments in a broader fisheries framework. Soft law instruments include the FAO Code of Conduct for Responsible Fisheries[140] and different UN resolutions on sustainable fisheries.[141] Whereas these instruments do not deal directly with IUU fishing, many issues dealt with in these instruments are related to IUU fishing, providing the catalyst for the development of more specific instruments to address IUU fishing, starting with the 2001 FAO Plan of Action (IPOA-IUU).[142] There are also environment-related

---

[136] The burden of proof to come up with less trade restrictive alternatives is on the complaining party. See WTO AB Report, *Brazil – Retreaded Tyres*, para. 156. WTO AB Report, *United States – Measures Affecting the Cross-border Supply of Gambling and Betting Services* WT/DS285/AB/R (2005), para. 309; WTO AB Report, *European Communities – Conditions for the Granting of Tariff Preferences to Developing Countries* WTO/DS246/AB/R (2004), para. 88; WTO AB Report, *Thailand – Customs and Fiscal Measures on Cigarettes from the Philippines* WT/DS371/AB/R (2011), para. 180.

[137] United Nations Convention on the Law of the Sea (1982) Part VII.

[138] FAO, Agreement to Promote Compliance with International Conservation and Management Measures by Fishing Vessels on the High Seas (1993). This agreement focuses among others on the issue of reflagging.

[139] UN, Agreement for the Implementation of the Provisions of the United Nations Convention on the Law of the Sea relating to the Conservation and Management of Straddling Fish Stocks and Highly Migratory Fish Stocks (1995).

[140] FAO, Code of Conduct for Responsible Fisheries, Adopted at the 28th Session of the FAO Conference, Rome, 31 October 1995.

[141] See e.g. Resolution 46/215 on a global moratorium on large-scale pelagic drift-net fishing; Resolution 49/116 on unauthorized fishing in zones of national jurisdiction and its impact on the living marine resources; Resolution 49/118 on fisheries bycatch and discards and their impact on the sustainable use of living marine resources.

[142] FAO, International Plan of Action to Prevent, Deter and Eliminate Illegal,

instruments of relevance to combating IUU fishing, such as CITES,[143] CMS,[144] the Convention of Biological Diversity (CBD)[145] and the Agenda 21.[146]

The FAO IPOA-IUU is the most specific international instrument to IUU fishing. It is a voluntary, non-binding agreement, but many of its provisions have been given binding legal effect through their incorporation in national, regional and international legal instruments. Furthermore, even if the instrument was initially non-binding, some norms could develop into customary international law. International instruments forming part of the broader framework to implement the IPOA-IUU include the FAO 2005 Rome Declaration on IUU fishing,[147] the FAO Model Scheme of Port State Measures[148] and the binding Agreement on Port State Measures to Combat IUU fishing.[149]

Next to the international instruments, a number of regional instruments also regulate IUU fishing through regional fisheries management organizations (RFMOs). States can either become a member of RFMOs or agree to apply their conservation and management measures. Non-members or non-participants in RFMOs are still under the international obligation to cooperate in the conservation of straddling and migratory fish stock, as laid down by other agreements.[150]

Unreported and Unregulated Fishing, 2001. See also Palma, Tsamenyi and Edeson, 2010, 57.

143 Convention on International Trade in Endangered Species of Wild Fauna and Flora (1973).

144 Convention on the Conservation of Migratory Species of Wild Animals (1979).

145 Convention on Biological Diversity (1992).

146 United Nations Conference on Environment and Development, Agenda 21 (1992) chapter 17 (protection of the oceans).

147 The 2005 Rome Declaration on Illegal, Unreported and Unregulated Fishing, Adopted by the FAO Ministerial Meeting on Fisheries, Rome, 12 March 2005. The Declaration was adopted to enlist the commitment of states to fully implement international fisheries instruments.

148 FAO, Model Scheme on Port State Measures to Combat Illegal, Unreported and Unregulated Fishing (2007).

149 FAO, Agreement on Port State Measures to Prevent, Deter and Eliminate Illegal, Unreported and Unregulated Fishing (2009). The Agreement will enter into force thirty days after the twenty-fifth instrument of ratification, acceptance, approval or accession.

150 UN, Agreement for the Implementation of the Provisions of the United Nations Convention on the Law of the Sea relating to the Conservation and Management of Straddling Fish Stocks and Highly Migratory Fish Stocks Article 17; FAO, Agreement to Promote Compliance with International

Relevant RFMOs[151] include the Commission for the Conservation of Southern Bluefin Tuna (CCSBT), the Northwest Atlantic Fisheries Organization (NAFO), the Northeast Atlantic Fisheries Commission (NEAFC),[152] the Commission for the Conservation of Antarctic Marine Living Resources (CCAMLR), the Indian Ocean Tuna Commission (IOTC), the Inter-American Tropical Tuna Commission (IATTC), the Western and Central Pacific Fisheries Commission (WCPFC) and the International Commission for the Conservation of Atlantic Tunas (ICCAT). The measures adopted by these RFMOs include the establishment of IUU vessel lists (for vessels flying the flag of non-contracting parties, as well as contracting and cooperating non-contracting parties), monitoring systems, port inspection schemes and trade-related measures such as prohibition of fish landings from IUU vessels.

The specific measures adopted by the EU IUU Fishing Regulation are mostly based on the mentioned international and regional instruments. For instance, the port state measures find support in the binding FAO Agreement on Port State Measures, as well as a number of RFMOs.[153] These port state measures include specific designation of ports, advance notice of port entry, vessel inspections and prohibition of landing and transhipment of vessels engaged in IUU fishing.[154] Furthermore, similar measures have been adopted by a range of developed and developing countries in their national legislation,[155] as well as in Plans of Action of regional cooperation.[156]

Conservation and Management Measures by Fishing Vessels on the High Seas preamble; Development, Agenda 21 para. 17.60; FAO Code of Conduct, Article 7.1.5.

151 There are over forty regional fisheries organizations, of which ten have been established under the FAO and the others created under international agreements between three or more contracting parties. These organizations can be divided into scientific research organizations, advisory and regional coordination organizations and management organizations (RFMOs).

152 For discussion of the NEAFC regime, see Stokke, 2009.

153 See among others ICCAT, NAFO, NEAFC, CCAMLR and IOTC.

154 When the EU challenged Chile's port access restrictions for swordfish imports (DS193, withdrawn after mutual agreement was reached), one of the claims of the EU was precisely the lack of international agreement supporting the Chilean measure.

155 See for an overview of national legislation on port state measures, FAO Database on Port State Measures (Portlex), at www.fao.org/legal/databases/portlex/en/. See for instance US Magnuson-Stevens Fishery Conservation and Management Reauthorisation Act prohibits import of fishery products from offending countries (16 USC 1826(a), (b)(3) and (b)(4)); New Zealand Fisheries Act 1996, Amendment Act No 2 1999, Article 113A; Australia, Fisheries Management Act 1991, Division 5A, Subdivision AA; Norway, Legal Order 6 August 1993.

156 For instance, the Lake Victoria Fisheries Organization adopted a Plan of

Catch certifications or other documentation that is required to accompany fish in order to identify its origin is commonly used in RFMOs. ICCAT, IATTC, IOTC and CCSBT have trade documentation schemes in order; CCAMLR requires catch documentation; NAFO and NEAFC have requirements for product labelling similar to a catch certification.[157] The vessel black list is a common and effective measure adopted by RFMOs to combat IUU fishing.[158] Members and cooperating non-members of the RFMOs shall take the necessary measures to ensure that no business is conducted with these black listed vessels and that proper actions are taken. ICCAT, NEAFC, CCAMLR, IATTC and IOTC require their members and cooperating non-members to prohibit the imports of fish from vessels on the IUU list.[159]

The non-cooperating states black list could be seen as more trade restrictive, as such a measure discriminates against vessels that operate consistently with international regulations but fly a 'wrong' flag.[160] However, similar measures have been adopted by, for instance, the

---

Action in 2004; the Southern African Development Community has made a statement of Commitment in 2008; the Southeast Asian Region adopted a Regional Plan of Action to Promote Responsible Fishing in 2007.

157 See also FAO, International Plan of Action to Prevent, Deter and Eliminate Illegal, Unreported and Unregulated Fishing para. 69.

158 For instance, ICCAT, IATTC, IOTC, WCPFC, SEAFO, NEAFC, NAFO and CCAMLR have established IUU vessel lists. See also International Plan of Action to Prevent, Deter and Eliminate Illegal, Unreported and Unregulated Fishing para. 81.4. Several regional regimes for tuna management (ICCAT, IOTC) have even introduced white lists (as opposed to black lists), whereby only explicitly named vessels are allowed to land or transship their catches in Member State ports.

159 ICCAT, Recommendation by ICCAT to establish a list of vessels presumed to have carried out IUU Fishing activities in the ICCAT Convention Area, 02-23 GEN, 2003, para. 9(e); NEAFC, Scheme of Control and Enforcement, Article 45(2)(e); CCAMLR, Conservation Measure 10-07 (2006), Article 11(f); CCAMLR, Conservation Measure 10-06 (2008), Article 18(vii); IATTC, Resolution C-05-07, Article 9(e); IOTC, Resolution 09/03, para. 12(e).

160 Stokke, 2009, 346. While this is true, in practice states can very easily reflag, and those vessels who are sincere in their intentions and indeed comply with IUU obligations could reflag to another state that is not blacklisted. Surely, there might be other considerations taken into account by vessels when deciding under which flag to fly; however, flags of convenience with suboptimal environmental standards should not be actively supported. Such a blacklist can thus act as an incentive, either for the vessels to pressure the flag state to adapt its legislation if they want to fly that flag, or for the flag state to take action if they do not want to lose vessels flying their flag. It could also be argued that controlling each vessel is more resource-intensive than blocking all vessels flying a certain flag, and thus less effective. The sole measure of checking vessels would thus not reach the same objective to effectively combat IUU fishing.

ICCAT, and thus find at least some international support. According to the IPOA-IUU, 'trade-related measures should only be used in exceptional circumstances, where other measures have proven unsuccessful to prevent, deter and eliminate IUU fishing, and only after prior consultation with interested States'.[161] The EU clearly refers to international obligations before blacklisting a non-cooperating country. In light of the multiple negotiations and available instruments, the EU could argue that other measures have proven unsuccessful when a country fails to respect its international obligations with regard to IUU fishing. A country is only blacklisted after at least six months of formal dialogue and consultation between the European Commission and the affected state after being yellow-carded. Nevertheless, due to the limited international support, this part of the measure will be under closer scrutiny under the extraterritoriality decision tree, even if inward environmental effects of IUU activities outside the EU can be shown within the EU.[162]

Applying the extraterritoriality decision tree to this analysis, the broad international support can be classified within the categories of treaty obligations between parties, MEAs authorizing trade measures towards non-parties, MEAs protecting the concern at issue as well as soft law. As the key elements and trade-related measures of the IUU Regulation find their support in binding treaty obligations, as well as MEAs recognizing trade measures, it can be concluded that the international support for and recognition of the concern would further justify the extraterritorial effects of the measure, and the extraterritoriality threshold would be passed for the IUU Fishing Regulation. This conclusion carries most weight for measures taken against imports of fish species explicitly covered under a treaty or RFMO, but similar measures taken on the basis of MEAs, recognizing the concern of species not covered by RFMOs, would also seem to have sufficiently widespread support through the more general agreements on IUU fishing.

Specific elements in the design of the IUU Fishing Regulation, unrelated to the extraterritorial nature of the regulation, that could furthermore come up in a necessity assessment,[163] can, for instance, relate to port control requirements for vessels, whereby one could wonder whether the

---

[161] FAO, International Plan of Action to Prevent, Deter and Eliminate Illegal, Unreported and Unregulated Fishing para. 66.

[162] See Section 6.3.4. See also Tsamenyi et al., 2009, xiv.

[163] See Chapter 5. The extraterritoriality threshold finds its legal basis in the subparagraphs of Article XX, but passing the threshold does not invalidate the rest of the analysis of Article XX, whereby the measure as a whole must not be

IUU Fishing Regulation foresees sufficient safeguards to protect third country vessels against delays in the procedures. A requirement that inspections 'cause minimum disturbance to the vessel's activities and cause no deterioration in fish quality' was proposed by the Commission but not included in the final IUU Fishing Regulation. Clear and transparent procedures must be developed, in order to avoid inconsistencies and discrimination in the implementation of port state measures.[164] The FAO Agreement on Port State Measures also recognizes that a balance must be sought between combating IUU fishing and appropriate safeguards against abuse of port state powers. Furthermore, with regard to the blacklisting of IUU vessels, whereas this listing is in line with international fisheries agreements, the application of interim measures may be necessary to ensure procedural fairness.[165]

6.3.3.4 *Chapeau*

Even if a measure passes the extraterritoriality threshold, and the extraterritorial aspect of the measure is no impediment for justification of a measure, a trade measure seeking justification still needs to comply with the conditions of the *chapeau* of Article XX GATT. The *chapeau* consists of three elements, which can be interpreted both together and apart: a measure shall not discriminate arbitrarily nor unjustifiably between countries where the same conditions prevail, nor shall the measure be a disguised restriction on international trade. These conditions can be seen as an expression of the principle of good faith,[166] which in this context can be reflected in a duty to cooperate and show respect for multilateral and international interests. In *US – Shrimp*, the AB emphasized the need for flexibility in a measure, as rigid and coercive measures are considered inconsistent with the *chapeau*.[167]

With regard to international interests and respect for multilateralism, the IUU Fishing Regulation follows up on multiple attempts at the regional and international level to come to agreement to combat IUU fishing, whereby trade restrictive measures have only been adopted after less restrictive measures have failed (such as control and inspection measures by the flag state). As has been outlined above, a range of binding and non-binding instruments prescribe actions against IUU fishing. The

more trade-restrictive than necessary, as well as the conditions of the *chapeau* of Article XX.

164 Tsamenyi et al., 2009, 46.

165 Ibid. 50.

166 WTO AB Report, *US – Shrimp*, para. 158.

167 See Chapters 1, 5.

EU in its Regulation has mainly implemented these obligations. Trade restrictions embedded in a multilateral framework make it more difficult to tailor provisions for protectionist reasons.

The measure can be considered coercive in the sense that it refers to the international obligations, and expects third country flag states and fishing vessels to comply with these obligations. These obligations are thus not unilaterally imposed – rather the EU acts as an enforcer of these international norms through its IUU Fishing Regulation. The flag state blacklist in particular is coercive in the sense that it requires countries to adapt their policies (rather than only target fishing vessels), and bring them in line with their international obligations. Non-cooperating states whose imports will be banned are identified based on transparent, clear and objective criteria relying on international standards,[168] whereby specific circumstances related to the resources and development level of the country can be taken into account. Depending on the transparent and objective application of these criteria, this would not lead to discrimination between countries where the same conditions prevail. However, for reasons of effectiveness and the fact that these countries are 'coerced' into 'adopting' their own international obligations rather than unilaterally imposed requirements, it can be argued that a country-based measure could be accepted in this case. Any blacklisting is furthermore combined with assistance and cooperation between the EU and the affected states and a state will first be warned by a yellow card before an import ban (red card) is made effective. The IUU Fishing Regulation has been mentioned in the WTO's Trade Policy Review, but no aspect has been indicated as potentially problematic.[169]

The vessel black list, leading to port measures against vessels, is not arbitrary, as objective and well-defined criteria can be determined in order to place vessels on the list. However, at this point the EU vessel list is solely based on vessel lists of RFMOs. In that regard it should be noted that each RFMO has its own procedures and criteria in placing vessels on a list, which at times can be politically motivated.[170] It is important that objective criteria are applied and provisions for transparency are respected.

---

168 IUU Fishing Regulation, recital (31).

169 See e.g. Trade Policy Review European Union, WT/TPR/S/284, 28 May 2013, p. 129; Trade Policy Review European Communities, WT/TPR/S/214, 6 April 2009, p. 114.

170 Isabella Lövin, *European Parliament Report on Combating Illegal Fishing at the Global Level – The Role of the EU* (European Parliament 2011) 14. However, regional schemes are open to regime outsiders (cooperating states) and a trend can be discerned that provisions for transparency are more respected; Stokke, 2009, 347.

Where the Regulation is more specific in its requirements, the Regulation allows for sufficient flexibility. For instance, with regard to the required catch certificates, the EU will also accept similar catch documentations and related documents that are in conformity with catch documentation schemes by RFMOs.[171]

6.3.4 Challenges

The main challenge for the extraterritoriality discussion in the IUU fishing case study is to what extent states can, through trade measures, enforce international obligations held by other states. The flag state blacklist as established by IUU Fishing Regulation goes beyond what is required by international law and is only rarely applied by RFMOs. As has been explained above, all imports from states on this blacklist are banned by not accepting any catch certificate issued by that state. As no fish or fish products can be imported without such a catch certificate, all imports from those states are effectively banned. In order to be delisted, the EU requires states to implement their international obligations related to sustainable and IUU fishing and adopt the necessary legislation. By targeting states rather than fishing vessels, the purpose of the measure is to create an effective incentive for the state to adapt its legislation. The EU is not just demanding that fish are being harvested with respect to certain standards, but is demanding real legislative change. As the EU only requires the implementation of existing international obligations of the targeted states,[172] and does not force them to implement new and/or EU-imposed (higher) norms (norm creation), the EU is acting with the objective of international norm enforcement and regime support.[173]

While this blacklisting is indeed proving to be rather effective, in light of the number of states that have been yellow- or red-carded in recent

---

[171] IUU Fishing Regulation, Article 13.

[172] As outlined in e.g. the FAO Compliance Agreement, the UN Fish Stocks Agreement, the relevant RFMOs etc. See Section 6.3.3.3.

[173] Unilateral trade measures as critical elements of a solution to the global fisheries problem, such as the EU's IUU Fishing Regulation, are suggested by Rashid Sumaila, *Trade Policy Options for Sustainable Oceans and Fisheries* (The E15 Initiative: Strengthening the Global Trade and Investment System for Sustainable Development, ICTSD and World Economic Forum 2016) 17; Margaret A Young, *Trade-Related Measures to Address Illegal, Unreported and Unregulated Fishing* (The E15 Initiative: Strengthening the Global Trade and Investment System for Sustainable Development, ICTSD and World Economic Forum 2015).

years and have effectively adapted their legislation,[174] such actions remain controversial. Can the EU act as an enforcer of international obligations? Is it a duty of powerful markets to use their commercial weight to the benefit of the global environment?[175] If it can be accepted that states have the right not to use their market for detrimental effects on health or the environment, can it then also be accepted that states will use their market as an incentive for other states to take positive action? If powerful states act upon such duty or responsibility, they should also have the responsibility to ensure that the targeted states are able to comply with the requirements, by offering assistance and the necessary management tools. In the case at hand, that is indeed what the EU has been doing: countries can ask for assistance at any stage, but after receiving a formal warning (yellow card), the Commission will engage in formal assistance and cooperation to help the targeted countries, in order to avoid a red card. Also, after a country has received a red card the EU will assist that country in taking the necessary measures so that the ban can be lifted.

Applying the decision tree to cases of norm enforcement, I would propose the following. Firstly, how strict is the requirement of norm enforcement? Does a measure require that products are produced in line with international standards? If so, the regular steps of the decision tree can be followed: if a measure is inward-looking or there are environmental effects on the territory of the regulating state, and the required standards find support for the concern in international instruments, the measure would pass the extraterritoriality threshold. However, if the measure requires a legislative change, in other words coerces another country into changing its laws (country-based measure), then I would argue that such a measure could be accepted only to the extent that what is required is already a binding obligation on the targeted country. The country black list as regulated by the EU IUU Fishing Regulation could thus be accepted to the extent that

---

[174] Fiji, Panama, Togo, and Vanuatu were yellow carded in 2012, South Korea in 2013, Philippines in 2014. Belize was red carded in 2014. All were delisted and had the threat of sanctions lifted (October 2013; South Korea and Philippines in April 2015). Sri Lanka, Cambodia and Guinea were also red carded in 2014, and their fisheries products are still banned from import. Ghana and Curacao received a yellow card in November 2013, and are developing new legislation and improving their monitoring, control and inspection systems. As a result, the process of dialogue and cooperation with these three countries is still ongoing. Papua New Guinea received a formal warning by the Commission in June 2014, whereas Solomon Islands, Tuvalu, Saint Kitts and Nevis and Saint Vincent and the Grenadines were formally warned in December 2014. Thailand was yellow carded in April 2015.

[175] See Chapter 5.5.1.

the required legislative changes are based solely upon binding international obligations under international and regional fisheries agreements.

6.4 AVIATION IN THE EU EMISSIONS TRADING SYSTEM

6.4.1 Measure and Context

One example of EU environmental regulation that has received a lot of attention since its adoption is the inclusion of aviation emissions into the EU ETS.[176] The EU's rule that requires emissions of all flights departing from or arriving at a European airport to be included in the EU ETS has led to strong international protests,[177] which eventually urged the Commission to put a hold on the full application of the Directive, limiting its scope to intra-European Economic Area (EEA) flights.[178] To allow time for negotiations on a global-market-based measure applying to aviation emissions under the ambit of ICAO, the EU ETS requirements are currently suspended for flights to and from non-European countries.[179]

The inclusion of aviation into the EU ETS will be studied as the main example of the extraterritorial reach of measures taken in light of climate change action. In April 2015, a Regulation was adopted to monitor and report emissions from shipping, in order to contribute to designing an international system to reduce emissions in the maritime sector.[180] From

---

[176] Directive 2008/101/EC of the European Parliament and of the Council of 19 November 2008 amending Directive 2003/87/EC so as to Include Aviation Activities in the Scheme for Greenhouse Gas Emission Allowance Trading within the Community (2008).

[177] See Grand Chamber CJEU, *Air Transport Association of America et al. v Secretary of State for Energy and Climate Change* C-366/10 (21 December 2011), See note [211] below: New Delhi Declaration; China's threat to cancel Airbus order; The US adopted the 'European Union Emissions Trading Scheme Prohibition Act' in 2011.

[178] Decision No 377/2013/EU of the European Parliament and of the Council of 24 April 2013 derogating temporarily from Directive 2003/87/EC establishing a scheme for greenhouse gas emission allowance trading within the Community (2013).

[179] The Commission is to report back on the issue after the 2016 ICAO Assembly. Ibid. Article 5.

[180] Regulation (EU) 2015/757 on the monitoring, reporting and verification of carbon dioxide emissions from maritime transport, and amending Directive 2009/16/EC (2015), See Article 1, 'This Regulation lays down rules for the accurate monitoring, reporting and verification of carbon dioxide (CO_2)

1 January 2018, companies will have to monitor CO_2 emissions for each ship[181] and from 2019 they will have to submit an emissions report concerning the CO_2 emissions for each ship.[182] Market-based mechanisms to reduce emissions would then only be foreseen in the medium to long term, with a strong preference for finding a multilateral solution.[183] As the monitoring obligations extend to all distances covered, including those outside waters under EU jurisdiction, a similar extraterritorial element as under the Aviation Directive is present. However, the nature of the obligations differs; ships are only subject to a monitoring requirement at this time, whereas aviation submissions were already to be included in EU ETS. I will refer back to the shipping example where relevant. The scope of the EU ETS might be broadened in the future, an example of which may be found in the Commission proposal to require emission allowances for importers of goods that would take emissions of the production process into account, so as to address carbon leakage.[184] No legislative proposal has yet been drafted in this respect.

---

emissions and of other relevant information from ships arriving at, within or departing from ports under the jurisdiction of a Member State, in order to promote the reduction of CO_2 emissions from maritime transport in a cost effective manner.'

[181] Ibid. Article 8. Companies are free to determine the monitoring method, as long as the method is consistent and accurate.

[182] Ibid. Article 14. Member States shall set up a system of penalties for failure to comply with the monitoring and reporting obligations (ibid. Article 20.).

[183] European Commission, Communication from the Commission to the European Parliament, the Council, the European Economic and Social Committee and the Committee of the Regions: Integrating Maritime Transport Emissions in the EU's Greenhouse Gas Reduction Policies (2013) 8. There is currently no international agreement on shipping emissions, but the International Maritime Organization (IMO) adopted in 2011 the Energy Efficiency Design Index (EEDI), which sets compulsory energy efficiency standards for new ships aiming to prevent air pollution from ships, and the Ship Energy Efficiency Management Plan (SEEMP), a management tool for shipowners. There is no agreement yet on any market-based measure to limit or reduce emissions. The Commission's 2011 White Paper on transport puts forward that the EU's emissions from maritime transport should be cut by at least 40 % of 2005 levels by 2050. International shipping is not yet covered by the EU's emission reduction target.

[184] Directive 2009/29/EC of the European Parliament and of the Council of 23 April 2009 amending Directive 2003/87/EC so as to improve and extend the greenhouse gas emission allowance trading scheme of the Community (2009) recital (25); European Commission, *Analysis of Options to Move Beyond 20% Greenhouse Gas Emission Reductions and Assessing the Risk of Carbon Leakage* (2010), 11; Kati Kulovesi, Elisa Morgera and Miquel Munoz, 'Environmental Integration and Multi-Faceted International Dimensions of EU Law: Unpacking the EU's 2009 Climate and Energy Package' Common Market Law Review (2011) 48, 829,

The issue of climate change needs little introduction. While scientists differ on the exact scope of the consequences of climate change and on the required contributions, there is no doubt that too little is being done today, while emissions continue to increase globally.[185] Climate change is an outstanding example of a global concern, affecting us all, but some countries and people considerably more than others. The most affected victims are not necessarily the largest emitters (rather the opposite) and those who are less affected cannot be allowed to ignore the effects of their actions. Every state has the responsibility to take action in accordance with its capabilities, as recognized in a number of international agreements, starting with the United Nations Framework Convention on Climate Change of 1992 (UNFCCC).[186]

International negotiations to mitigate the effects of climate change have been developed under the multilateral framework established by the UNFCCC.[187] Under this agreement, the Kyoto Protocol was adopted in 1997 (entered into force in 2005), by which a number of industrialized countries[188] agreed to reduce their greenhouse gas emissions by an average of 5.2 per cent below 1990 levels in the period 2008–2012.[189] The Kyoto

---

860; Nicole Ahner, 'Final Instance: World Trade Organization – Unilateral Trade Measures in EU Climate Change Legislation' EUI Working Papers 2009/58, 2009; R Quick, 'The Debate Continues: Are Border Adjustments of Emission Trading Schemes a Means to Protect the Climate or Are They "Naked" Protectionism?' in I Govaere, R Quick and M C E J Bronckers (eds.), *Trade and Competition Law in the EU and Beyond* (Cheltenham, UK, and Northampton, MA, USA: Edward Elgar Publishing 2011); Yassen Spassov, 'EU ETS: Upholding the Carbon Price Without Incidence of Carbon Leakage' Journal of Environmental Law (2012) 24:2, 311.

185 Intergovernmental Panel on Climate Change, *IPCC Fifth Assessment Report* (2013–2014), The IPCC reports can be found at www.ipcc.ch/. See also James Bacchus, *Global Rules for Mutually Supportive and Reinforcing Trade and Climate Regimes – E15 Expert Group on Measures to Address Climate Change and the Trade System* (ICTSD and World Economic Forum 2016), 10.

186 UNFCCC (1992). The notion that a state is responsible for pollution originating within its borders but traversing into another jurisdiction is also one of the most developed principles of international environmental law. See Jeremy Remy Nash, 'The Curious Legal Landscape of the Extra-Territoriality of US Environmental Laws' in G Handl, J Zekoll and P Zumbansen (eds.), *Beyond Territoriality: Transnational Legal Authority in an Age of Globalization* (Martinus Nijhoff 2012) 167.

187 UNFCCC (1992).

188 Thirty-seven industrialized countries and the EU committed to these reductions in the first commitment period (for the list of countries, see Annex I to the UNFCCC). Significantly, the US has never ratified the Kyoto Protocol.

189 Kyoto Protocol to the United Nations Framework Convention on Climate Change (1997). The Kyoto Protocol was adopted in Kyoto, Japan, on 11

Protocol distinguishes between developed countries carrying a heavier burden (Annex I countries) and non-Annex I countries, because the former are considered principally responsible for the high level of historical greenhouse gas emissions, and because they have greater capacity to take actions to reduce emissions. This distinction is an expression of the principle of 'common but differentiated responsibilities and respective capabilities' (CBDRRC).[190]

In December 2012, the Doha Amendment to the Kyoto Protocol was adopted, introducing commitments for a second commitment period running from 2013 to 2020. The parties[191] agreed to reduce emissions by at least 18 per cent below 1990 levels.[192] In December 2015, a new binding (albeit obligations of conduct rather than strictly of result so it will be very hard to enforce)[193] agreement on climate change was adopted at the COP21 in Paris and entered into force in November 2016.[194] Rather than

---

December 1997 and entered into force on 16 February 2005. The detailed rules for the implementation of the Protocol were adopted at COP 7 in Marrakesh, Morocco, in 2001, and are referred to as the 'Marrakesh Accords.' Its first commitment period started in 2008 and ended in 2012.

190 UNFCCC preamble; Article 4. The principle of CBDR-RC is one of the biggest challenges of environmental law, because it is debated how to best interpret and apply this principle of differentiation. The distinction between Annex 1 and non-Annex 1 countries can said to be no longer a reflection of the actual situation today, especially in light of emission contributions by countries such as China or India. See Section 6.4.3.3 for further discussion.

191 All 192 Parties to the Kyoto Protocol have agreed to the Doha Amendment establishing the second commitment period. However, only developed country Parties listed in the Kyoto Protocol's Annex B take on emission commitments under the Protocol. Thirty-eight developed country Parties, including the EU, its Member States and Iceland, have taken on legally binding emission commitments for the second period. Japan, New Zealand and the Russian Federation, which did have commitments for the first period, have not taken on commitments for the second period. This means that the second commitment period covers a much smaller share of global emissions – around 14–15 % – than the first. Thirty-eight countries have ratified the Amendment by July 2015. The EU has not yet ratified the Amendment, but the necessary legislation was adopted by the Council on 13 July 2015. The EU Member States will need to ratify the Amendment nationally in parallel. For an overview see http://unfccc.int/kyoto_protocol/doha_amendment/items/7362.php.

192 The EU and Iceland committed to a reduction of 20 %.

193 For a discussion of the legal form of the Agreement, see Joost Pauwelyn and Lilliana Andonova at www.ejiltalk.org/a-legally-binding-treaty-or-not-the-wrong-question-for-paris-climate-summit/; Jorge Vinuales at www.ejiltalk.org/the-paris-climate-agreement-an-initial-examination-part-iii-of-iii/; and Annalesi Savaresi at www.ejiltalk.org/the-paris-agreement-a-rejoinder/.

194 The agreement was prepared by the Ad Hoc Working Group on the Durban Platform for Enhanced Action (ADP). For updates, see http://unfccc.int/

a top-down agreement, prescribing national measures, the Paris deal is based on bottom-up contributions by individual countries. Before Paris, countries have agreed to publicly outline what post-2020 climate actions they intend to take, known as their 'Intended Nationally Determined Contributions' (INDCs).[195] These national contributions now carry the name of NDC's under the Agreement.[196] The Paris Agreement has set out that the parties will pursue efforts to limit the increase in the global average temperature to 1.5°C of pre-industrial levels.[197] However, the irony of this ambitious target is that two of the most polluting sectors, aviation and shipping, have been excluded from the Agreement – which may seriously jeopardize the fulfilment of the objective to limit the temperature increase to 1.5°C or keep it well below 2°C.

In light of the commitments made under Kyoto, the EU launched its ETS in 2005, as the first and biggest emissions trading scheme in the world.[198] The EU ETS is a cap-and-trade system aimed at reducing greenhouse gas emissions cost-effectively. The total amount of greenhouse gases that can be emitted by factories, power plants and other installations in the system is 'capped' or limited.[199] Participants receive a number of emission allowances based on historical emissions (benchmarks of sectoral best performing installations)[200] that they can trade on the emissions market: to sell, if they have a surplus, or to buy additional allowances when needed (either from participants in the

---

bodies/body/6645.php. The Agreement can be found at http://unfccc.int/resource/docs/2015/cop21/eng/l09r01.pdf. For an analysis of the engagements, see http://paristext2015.com/.

[195] For an overview of all INDCs, see www4.unfccc.int/submissions/indc/Submission%20Pages/submissions.aspx. The US for instance aims at reducing its emissions by 26–28 % below 2005 levels by 2025. China wants to lower carbon dioxide emissions per unit of GDP by 60 % to 65 % from 2005 levels by 2030.

[196] UNFCCC COP 21, Paris Agreement (2015) Articles 3, 4.

[197] Ibid. Article 2(1)(a).

[198] European Commission, *Forest Law Enforcement, Governance and Trade (FLEGT) – Proposal for an EU Action Plan* (2003) (EU ETS Directive).

[199] From the start, a number of energy-intensive industrial sectors were covered by the scheme, such as power stations, combustion plants, oil refineries, steel works, as well as factories making cement, glass, bricks, etc. Altogether the EU ETS covers around 45 % of total greenhouse gas emissions from the 28 EU countries. The EU ETS now covers more than 11,000 power stations and industrial plants in 31 countries, as well as emission from aviation. See http://ec.europa.eu/clima/policies/ets/index_en.htm.

[200] Commission Decision of 27 April 2001 determining transitional Union-wide rules for harmonized free allocation of emission allowances pursuant to Article 10a of Directive 2003/87/EC (2011/278/EU).

EU ETS or other international credits created by the Kyoto Protocol). In the first years of the EU ETS the majority of emission allowances was given for free to the participants, but auctioning is becoming the main method of allocating allowances.[201] Businesses now have to buy an increasing proportion of their allowances at auction. The limit on the total number of allowances available ensures that the allowances have a value. Installations must measure and report their emissions and surrender one allowance for every tonne of CO_2 emitted during annual compliance periods. They will be heavily fined upon failure to do so. The total number of allowances is gradually reduced so that total emissions will drop: in 2020 emissions should be 21 per cent lower than in 2005. The proportion of free allowances also decreases over time (so the proportion of needed allowances to be purchased will increase), thereby providing the financial incentive to participants to cut emissions. The goal is that the EU ETS, as the largest cap-and-trade scheme worldwide, can serve as a model and that over time similar national or regional schemes can be linked to the EU scheme.[202]

The aviation (and shipping) sectors are major contributor emitters of greenhouse gases.[203] Even though aviation emissions only account

---

[201] See http://ec.europa.eu/clima/publications/docs/factsheet_ets_en.pdf.

[202] The EU ETS is a complex scheme that is at the time of writing in phase 3, after a three-year pilot period (phase 1 – 2005–2007), and phase 2 coinciding with the first commitment period of the Kyoto Protocol (2008–2012). The European Commission is revising the system for phase 4 (2021–2030), see http://ec.europa.eu/clima/policies/ets/revision/index_en.htm. For an overview of its flaws and successes, see e.g. A D Ellerman and Paul L Joskow, *The European Union's Emissions Trading System in Perspective* (Massachusetts Institute of Technogoloy and Pew Center on Global Climate 2008); Martijn Verdonk et al., *Evaluation of Policy Options to Reform the EU Emissions Trading System: Effects on Carbon Price, Emissions and the Economy* (PBL Netherlands Environmental Assessment Agency 2013); Tim Laing et al., *Assessing the Effectiveness of the EU Emissions Trading System* (2013), Centre for Climate Change Economics and Policy; Friends of the Earth Europe, *The EU Emissions Trading System: Failing to Deliver* (2010); Stefan Weishaar, *Emissions Trading Design: A Critical Overview* (Edward Elgar Publishing 2014).

[203] Someone flying from London to New York and back generates roughly the same level of emissions as the average person in the EU does by heating their home for a whole year. Direct emissions from aviation account for about 3 % of the EU's total greenhouse gas emissions. The large majority of these emissions come from international flights. By 2020, global international aviation emissions are projected to be around 70 % higher than in 2005 even if fuel efficiency improves by 2 % per year. ICAO forecasts that by 2050 they could grow by a further 300–700 %. Shipping accounts for around 4 % of EU emissions. (European Commission at http://ec.europa.eu/clima/policies/transport/aviation/index_en.htm).

for 3 per cent of EU emissions, and 2 per cent of global emissions, air transport remains the least environmental-friendly transport method, and the ICAO estimates that these numbers can increase to 15–20 per cent of global emissions by 2050.[204] By including global aviation emissions in the EU ETS, the EU has the potential to cover almost 60 per cent of international aviation emissions.[205] No binding commitments were made for either aviation or shipping under the Kyoto Protocol, even though domestic aviation emissions were taken into account under the binding emission reduction targets. However, states failed to agree on how to tackle international aviation emissions mainly because they disagreed on how to allocate responsibility for these emissions. Annex I countries did agree to pursue the 'limitation or reduction of emissions of greenhouse gases from aviation through the International Civil Aviation Organization' but have been unable to do so.[206] The ICAO is a specialized UN Agency that serves as a forum for cooperation on civil aviation matters for its 191 members. Even though there has been discussion on environmental protection measures and emission reduction schemes ever since the 1990s, in 2004 the ICAO still had not come any closer to agreement on how to limit or reduce emissions from aviation. It adopted a resolution, endorsing the development of a global emissions trading scheme for aviation, as well as the idea of including aviation in existing emission trading schemes, but also urging states to refrain from unilateral action awaiting further discussions.[207]

The EU acted upon this ICAO 'proposition' by including aviation in its emission trading scheme: in 2009, Directive 2008/101 was adopted on aviation into the EU ETS. From 1 January 2012 onwards, emissions from all domestic and international (commercial) flights arriving at or departing from European airports (EU + the European Free Trade Association (EFTA)) were to be covered by the EU ETS. Not only emissions from within EU airspace, but from the entire flight, including over the high seas and airspace of third countries, would be covered.[208] The entire flight refers to an uninterrupted flight, thus for flights that transit only the last

---

[204] The UK Committee on Climate Change, 'International Aviation' at www.theccc.org.uk.

[205] Joanne Scott and Lavanya Rajamani, 'EU Climate Change Unilateralism' The European Journal of International Law (2012) 23:2, 469, 474.

[206] Kyoto Protocol to the United Nations Framework Convention on Climate Change Article 2

[207] ICAO Assembly Resolution A35-5 (2004), Appendix I, paragraph 2(c).

[208] There is a *de minimis* exception for commercial air transport operators operating two flights a day or less, or emitting less than 10,000 tonnes of CO_2/year.

leg of the journey counts.[209] Under the system, operators would only be allowed to fly as many tonne-kilometres as are covered by the allowances allocated to them, or acquired on the market. Airlines' allowances would be allocated based on the historical emissions from the period 2004–2006 and calculated through a formula taking account of fuel consumption. A percentage of allowances would be auctioned. Free allocations were to be given to new entrants and to existing airlines that are experiencing considerable growth. If a third state were to have measures in place for reducing emissions from aviation, the Commission would be obliged to seek to achieve an 'optimal interplay' between the EU and the foreign measures, in close consultation with the third state. This could then, for instance, lead to an exemption from the Directive.[210]

Despite the ICAO's 2004 endorsement of the idea to include emissions from aviation in emission trading systems, this unilateral EU action raised great controversy among states or airline operators.[211] In 2009, the US Air Transport Association of America together with American, Continental and United Airlines (ATA and others) challenged the validity of (the implementing measures of) Directive 2008/101 and their inclusion

[209] Under this system 75 states have no operator with flights to the EU, and 23 have commercial operators that qualify under the *de minimis* exception. (See presentation by A. Runge-Metzger, Aviation and Emission Trading, ICAO Council Briefing (29 September 2011), 24, at http://ec.europa.eu/clima/policies/transport/aviation/docs/presentation_icao_en.pdf.)

[210] Directive 2008/101/EC of the European Parliament and of the Council of 19 November 2008 amending Directive 2003/87/EC so as to Include Aviation Activities in the Scheme for Greenhouse Gas Emission Allowance Trading within the Community Article 25a.

[211] In September 2007 (after the Commission's proposal) a resolution was passed at the ICAO Assembly urging its members 'not to implement an emissions trading system on other contracting states' aircraft operators except on the basis of mutual agreement between those states'. See ICAO Assembly, A36-22: Consolidated Statement of Continuing ICAO Policies and Practices Related to Environmental Protection. A coalition of 26 countries opposing the EU ETS signed the New Delhi Agreement, including India, the US, China, the Russian Federation, Japan, Brazil and Saudi Arabia. ('coalition of the unwilling'); The US adopted the 'European Union Emissions Trading Scheme Prohibition Act' in 2011, making it illegal for US airlines to comply with the EU ETS requirements; China as well has forbidden its airlines to comply with EU ETS obligations, after blocking a billion-dollar order of Airbus aircrafts by Hong Kong Airlines, citing that as a retaliatory measure against the EU ETS. See also Lorenzo Schiano di Pepe, 'European Union Climate Law and Practice at the End of the Kyoto Era: Unilateralism, Extraterritoriality and the Future of Global Climate Law Governance' in Robert Percival, Jolene Lin and William Piermattei (eds.), *Global Environmental Law at a Crossroads* (Edward Elgar Publishing 2014) 292.

in the EU ETS through a British Court,[212] which turned to the CJEU for a preliminary ruling.[213] They claimed the Directive was unlawful as it was in breach of international treaties (the 1944 Chicago Convention on International Civil Aviation, the Kyoto Protocol and the EU–US Open Skies Agreement) because the EU ETS imposed a form of tax on fuel consumption; as well as principles of customary international law because the EU was seeking to apply the EU ETS beyond the EU's territorial jurisdiction.[214] The CJEU, in a controversial and much criticized judgment, rejected all claims and found the Directive to be valid and compatible with international law.[215] Nevertheless, in 2012 the EU decided to 'stop the clock' on including international aviation[216] in the EU ETS for one year to allow for a constructive dialogue within the ICAO, showing that the EU would not be the one to stand in the way of an international agreement.[217] The ICAO set up a high-level policy group tasked with proposing options for a market-based emission reduction measure. The Commission's decision to postpone the application of the

---

212 High Court of Justice of England and Wales, Queen's Bench Division, preliminary reference to CJEU on 8 July 2010.

213 Grand Chamber CJEU, C-366/10, *Air Transport Association of America et al. v Secretary of State for Energy and Climate Change.*

214 In particular, the Chicago Convention is claimed to forbid states to impose taxes, duties and charges on airline operators; the Kyoto Protocol requires aviation emissions to be addressed through the UN's International Civil Aviation Authority (ICAO); the Open Skies Agreement states that aircraft that enter, depart from or are within the territory of a party, are governed by the laws and regulations of that party (Article 7); that fuel load is exempted from taxes, duties or charges (Article 11); and that there shall be no discrimination between EU and US airlines when it comes to the adoption of environmental measures, as to ensure fair competition (Article 15(3)). The principles of customary international law referred to by the claimants are the sovereignty of states over their airspace, the illegitimacy of claims to sovereignty over the high seas, the freedom to fly over the high seas and that aircraft flying over the high seas should be governed by the laws of the country in which they are registered, save as expressly provided for by international treaty.

215 Grand Chamber CJEU, C-366/10, *Air Transport Association of America et al. v Secretary of State for Energy and Climate Change*, paras.124–129. Much has been written about the judgment, see among others Christina Voigt, 'Up in the Air: Aviation, the EU Emissions Trading Scheme and the Question of Jurisdiction' Cambridge Yearbook of European Legal Studies (2011–2012) 14, 475; Sanja Bogojevic, 'Legalising Environmental Leadership: A Comment on the CJEU's Ruling in C-366/10 on the Inclusion of Aviation in the EU Emissions Trading Scheme' Journal of Environmental Law (2012) 24:2, 345.

216 EU ETS obligations for intra-EU flights were not suspended, also with regard to non-EU based airlines.

217 European Commission Memo, 12 November 2012, 'Stopping the clock of ETS and aviation emissions following last week's ICAO Council'.

EU ETS to aviation was conditional upon results coming out of the ICAO negotiations by the end of 2013. Reactions to the decisions were mixed: while European airline carriers feared a two-tier system, other airline associations reacted more positively.[218] Others still opposed the inclusion of intra-EU flights.[219] For the period 2013–2016 the legislation has been amended so that only emissions from flights within the EEA fall under the EU ETS.[220] In October 2013, the ICAO Assembly reached agreement to develop a global market-based mechanism by fall of 2016. In October 2016 agreement was reached to set up a global carbon offsetting scheme (the so-called Carbon Offsetting and Reduction Scheme for International Aviation or CORSIA) that will start with a voluntary phase as from 2021.[221] The Commission needs to report to the European Parliament and the Council on the temporary modification to the inclusion of aviation into the EU ETS, in light of this outcome of the ICAO 39th Assembly in order to revise the scope of the EU ETS.[222]

6.4.2 Extraterritorial Effect

The extraterritorial effect of the original Aviation Directive (which is currently 'on hold' for those flights to and from non-European countries) lies in the fact that airlines have to participate in the EU ETS whereby emissions from the entire flight are covered, thus including those emissions of the part of the flight that falls outside EU jurisdiction (EU airspace). Airline operators that fail to comply with the ETS requirements will be

---

[218] Holman Fenwick Willan LLP, Aerospace EU and Regulatory, 'EU ETS Update: Stopping the Clock – Where Do We Go From Here?' February 2013, p. 2.

[219] The US for instance passed into law its anti-ETS bill (approved by the House of Representatives the day after the Commission announced the suspension).

[220] Decision No 377/2013/EU of the European Parliament and of the Council of 24 April 2013 derogating temporarily from Directive 2003/87/EC establishing a scheme for greenhouse gas emission allowance trading within the Community.

[221] ICAO Resolution A39-3: 'Consolidated statement of continuing ICAO policies and practices related to environmental protection – Global Market-based Measure (MBM) scheme', 6 October 2016.

[222] Regulation 421/2014 of the European Parliament and the Council of 16 April 2014 amending Directive 2003/87/EC establishing a scheme for greenhouse gas emission allowance trading within the Community, in view of the implementation by 2020 of an international agreement applying a single global market-based measure to international aviation emissions, Article 1. In light of the uncertainty with regard to the technical implementation of CORSIA, a substantive revision of the Aviation Directive will most likely be postponed until implementing measures have been adopted at ICAO level.

fined. The CJEU's main argument to reject any extraterritoriality claims was that the measure is only activated through physical presence in the EU, i.e. by landing at or departing from a EU airport. As the aircraft are at that point physically in the territory of the EU, they are subject to the unlimited jurisdiction of the EU.[223] While that is true, it has been indicated on multiple occasions in this book that that trigger does not negate the extraterritorial effect of the measure. The decision tree will be applied to see whether this extension of European jurisdiction is justified.

What is peculiar in the example of climate change is that despite the (almost) general recognition of the seriousness of the climate threat, it has proven to be very difficult to agree upon stringent and binding commitments, and there are plenty of 'excuses' (and undoubtedly, plenty of pressure from powerful actors) to avoid responsibility.[224] In that regard, states can feel compelled to complement the insufficient actions taken at the international level with domestic measures. However, numerous studies show that isolated action will not only lead to negative economic consequences domestically, but can also have a negative impact on the climate globally through carbon leakage.[225] In that regard, in order to reach the most effective outcome through unilateral action from an environmental perspective, all states *need* to get involved. By doing so, the effect of any environmental action will be more significant, creating an incentive for other countries to commit to environmental commitments themselves (domestically, bilaterally and/or multilaterally), if only to have a say in the decisions made. The unilateral actions taken by the EU in the Aviation Directive (as in the Shipping Regulation) encourage such action, and are even contingent upon it. The extension of the EU ETS, or in other

---

223 Grand Chamber CJEU, C-366/10, *Air Transport Association of America et al. v Secretary of State for Energy and Climate Change*, para. 124. A G Kokott argued that the EU merely induced or influences behaviour abroad, but does not compel certain behaviour and the Aviation Directive is therefore compatible with international law (para. 50).

224 Despite the difficulties that need to be overcome regarding scientific measuring methods etc., states' political preferences play an important role as well. This is of course inherent to the international legal system. However, the example of climate change shows particularly well the conflict between different approaches. The EU for instance advocates a top-down, multilateral and internationally driven model with binding targets, while the US for instance favours a bottom-up approach, whereby parties can define their own commitments and actions unilaterally. See Kati Kulovesi, 'Climate Change in EU External Relations: Please Follow My Example (or I Might Force You)' in Elisa Morgera (ed.), *The External Environmental Policy of the European Union* (Cambridge University Press 2012) 121.

225 Joshua Meltzer, 'Climate Change and Trade – The EU Aviation Directive and the WTO' Journal of International Economic Law (2012) 15:1, 111.

words the extraterritorial effect, can be avoided if other states take action, and if the goods or services are subject to adequate climate change regulation in those states or through an international system.[226]

6.4.3 The Decision Tree Applied

6.4.3.1 Inconsistency with substantive obligations under GATT and GATS

The first question that arises with regard to aviation is whether the EU measure illegally restricts airline services, or in other words: is there an inconsistency with GATS? Airline services provide a Mode 1 supply of a service, which is the supply of a service from the territory of one Member into the territory of another Member.[227] The GATS Annex on Air Transport Services exempts any measures affecting 'traffic rights' or 'services directly related to the exercise of traffic rights' from the application of the GATS.[228] Traffic rights are defined as the right to 'operate and/or to carry passengers, cargo and mail for remuneration . . . within or over the territory of a Member, including points to be served, routes to be operated, types of traffic to be carried . . . tariffs to be charged'.[229] The Aviation Directive does not directly affect traffic rights, it imposes an additional condition that airline operators need to comply with when landing or departing from EU airports. While arguably related to the terms of authorization to operate air services in a WTO Member's territory,[230] it is unclear to what extent this really affects or directly relates to traffic rights. Furthermore, the Directive does not impose a tariff, as was held by the CJEU,[231] because the costs (or possibly the gains for well-performing operators) depend on the airline's performance, as well as whether the home state has an

---

[226] Aviation Directive, Article 25a; Scott and Rajamani, 2012, 472.

[227] GATS, Article I:2(a).

[228] GATS, Annex on Air Transport Services, para. 2.

[229] GATS, Annex on Air Transport Services, para. 6(d). These have been laid down in the 1944 Chicago Convention on International Civil Aviation, as well as the multilateral Transit Agreement and Transport Agreement, and over 2,500 bilateral agreements. See WTO, Air Transport and the GATS, Documentation for the First Air Transport Review under the GATS, 2006, pp. 192–216. See also Meltzer, 2012, 125.

[230] Article 6 of the Chicago Convention lays down the right to fly into or transit third states' territories, or to land for technical reasons, but any air services over the territory must be authorized by that state, and must be operated 'in accordance with the terms of such authorization'.

[231] Grand Chamber CJEU, C-366/10, *Air Transport Association of America et al. v Secretary of State for Energy and Climate Change*.

emission reduction scheme in place.[232] Thus, GATS might still apply to the Directive, despite the Annex on Air Transport Services.

The Annex also stipulates that the GATS does not reduce or affect obligations under bilateral and multilateral agreements[233] and that the DSB may only be invoked when dispute settlement proceedings in bilateral and other multilateral agreements have been exhausted.[234] The point is to ensure the primacy of the ICAO system over WTO rules, where there is overlap.[235] However, that requires that the relevant dispute settlement bodies have competence over the matter, and that a dispute must arise with regard to their respective agreements. The only ruling on this matter by the CJEU did not find any violations of ICAO obligations.[236]

If the GATS were to apply and dispute settlement were available, it could be argued that the EU measure violates the MFN obligation under Article II:1 GATS. The measure can have a disproportionate effect on services and service suppliers in certain countries: the longer the distance covered, the higher the costs. The advantage granted would thus be directly linked to origin.[237] Furthermore, the exemption for airline operators whose home state has equivalent measures in place could violate the requirement to grant any advantage immediately and unconditionally to all WTO Members. Most of the other obligations under the GATS only apply to the extent that a Member has made specific commitments. Bartels has argued that the EU's commitments in Mode 2 (consumption abroad) in tourism services could be relevant, which could lead to a possible inconsistency with the national treatment obligation under Article XVII GATS, as flight ticket prices might become more expensive for flights originating outside the EU, compared to intra-EU flights.[238] If an inconsistency is

---

232 Directive 2008/101/EC of the European Parliament and of the Council of 19 November 2008 amending Directive 2003/87/EC so as to Include Aviation Activities in the Scheme for Greenhouse Gas Emission Allowance Trading within the Community Article 25a.

233 Annex on Air Transport Services, para. 1.

234 Annex on Air Transport Services, para. 4.

235 Lorand Bartels, 'The Inclusion of Aviation in the EU ETS: WTO Law Considerations' ICTSD Programme on Trade and Environment, April 2012, 23; Lorand Bartels, 'The WTO Legality of the Application of the EU's Emissions Trading System to Aviation' in C Lim and B Mercurio (eds.), *International Economic Law After the Global Crisis: A Tale of Fragmented Disciplines* (Cambridge University Press 2015).

236 Grand Chamber CJEU, C-366/10, *Air Transport Association of America et al. v Secretary of State for Energy and Climate Change.*

237 Bartels, 2012, 24.

238 Ibid. 25.

established, justification can be sought under the environmental exception of Article XIV(b) GATS.[239]

The EU aviation scheme also has implications for goods transported by airplanes and could thus be governed by GATT as well.[240] The CJEU determined that the EU's aviation scheme is not a tax measure[241] or any type of fiscal measure. The measure is not a charge either, as it will depend on the performances of the airline operators whether they will be charged, or be able to sell surplus allowances. In order to fall within the scope of Article III:2 GATT, the measure must be an internal charge: as airline operators are only charged upon entry or departure from EU airports, the charge incurs only within the EU. The imported and domestic goods must furthermore be like or directly competitive, which will depend on the facts of the case and the specific goods in question, but there is little reason that the use of airfreight will make them unlike. Furthermore, the charge applied to imported goods must be in excess of that applied to like domestic goods, for which the smallest amount of excess is too much.[242] Non-EU flights might cover longer distances, and depending on their performance, are thus likely to emit more CO_2, an excess cost that the airline operator may pass through to cargo rates. However, the distance from North-Africa to Southern Italy might be much shorter than from the North of Sweden to Greece. Airline operators may also decide to make a stop-over at an airport close to Europe, thereby limiting the application of the aviation scheme to only the last distance covered. Nevertheless, overall, it is likely that the costs for non-EU flights will be higher than for intra-EU flights, and that when they are passed through on cargo rates, non-EU goods will indirectly be charged higher.

---

[239] For the purpose of the analysis, justification will only be dealt with under Article XX GATT. However, the extraterritoriality decision tree can be transposed to Article XIV(b) GATS.

[240] The same regulatory scheme can be affect trade in goods and services; see WTO AB, *European Communities – Regime for the Importation, Sale and Distribution of Bananas III* WT/DS27/AB/R (1997), para. 211.

[241] Grand Chamber CJEU, C-366/10, *Air Transport Association of America et al. v Secretary of State for Energy and Climate Change*. The Court found that the scheme was not a tax or a charge because it was 'not intended to generate revenue for the public authorities, does not in any way enable the establishment, applying a basis of assessment and a rate defined in advance, of an amount that must be payable for tonne of fuel consumed for all the flights carried out in a calendar year'. Furthermore, the EU ETS requires airlines to purchase emission allowances through which the airlines gain a tradable property right. That is rather different from imposing a fiscal charge. See also Bartels, 2012, 9.

[242] WTO AB, *Japan – Taxes on Alcoholic Beverages II* WT/DS8/AB/R (1996), para. 23.

If the aviation scheme were considered a non-fiscal measure, the measure might be considered a quantitative restriction under Article XI GATT as a border measure, or under Article III GATT as an internal measure.[243] Under Article III:4 GATT, it could be argued that increased cargo rates would affect the internal sale of imported goods. If the imported and domestic products are like, treatment less favourable of the imported products must be established. As imported goods might be subject to additional costs due to the distance covered, the scheme might have a *de facto* detrimental impact on imported products, even though that is not necessarily the case for all imported products: if the country of origin of the airline operator has a comparable emissions system in place, those flights would not be covered, hence no additional costs would be borne under the EU ETS. In that regard, a finding that the scheme protects domestic products to the detriment of imported products is not obvious.

With regard to Article XI GATT, measures that have the effect of restricting imports and exports of products are prohibited. In *Colombia – Ports of Entry*, the Panel found that a measure that restricted the ports of entry could be seen as a quantitative restriction if the measure affected the cost of shipping products from the port of origin to the place of sale.[244] The question is whether the measure can have a restrictive *effect* on the importation of any given product, and not whether it concerns a right of importation.[245] This reasoning could be applied with regard to goods being imported through air transport,[246] as transport costs will likely increase through participation in the scheme, the costs of which are furthermore unpredictable depending on the price of allowances.[247] In that regard, it could be said that the Aviation Directive has a restrictive effect on imports within the meaning of Article XI:1.

Questions can also arise with regard to the freedom of transit under Article V GATT. Bartels has argued that the EU measure is not an 'unnecessary restriction' (Article V:3) or 'unreasonable regulation' (Article V:4) as it is unclear what the benchmarks are for necessary and

---

243 Bartels, 'The WTO Legality of the Application of the EU's Emissions Trading System to Aviation' 2015; Meltzer, 2012, 135.

244 WTO Panel Report, *Colombia – Ports of Entry* WT/DS366/R (2009), para. 7.258.

245 Bartels, 2012, 9.

246 Thirty-five per cent of global cargo by value occurs through air transport (IATA Data). While air cargo can be transported using dedicated freighter flights, approximately 50 % of air cargo is carried on passenger flights.

247 Bartels, 2012, 10.

reasonable. The scheme could be considered necessary or reasonable to implement the polluter pays principle in light of the climate change threat.[248] However, Article V:6 prohibits discrimination against products because they have transited via the territory of another WTO Member. If products from the same origin would be subject to different charges depending on whether they transited through a non-EU airport or not, a possible discrimination could be established. However, as it is likely that those products which transited would be subject to lower costs, and Article V:6 requires 'treatment no less favourable' for goods in transit, it is unlikely that the Aviation Directive would amount to a violation of Article V:6 GATT.[249]

6.4.3.2 Environmental objective and location of the concern

The environmental objective of the Aviation Directive and the EU ETS is clear: combating climate change and preventing the environmental damage that could arise as a consequence. Both Article XX(g) (the atmosphere is an exhaustible natural resource,[250] as is air or are the oceans, deserts, forests and the other living and non-living resources that would be affected by climate change) and Article XX(b) (e.g. the threat to biodiversity and extinction of plant species)[251] are very likely to qualify as valid grounds for environmental protection under Article XX GATT. The fact that the Aviation Directive might also address competitiveness concerns and serve to level the playing field is not necessarily an impediment: these objectives are not conflicting,[252] and it is inherent to complex regulation that multiple objectives can be addressed.[253] However, the regulating country needs to

---

248 Ibid. 14.

249 Meltzer, 2012, 140.

250 Ahner, 2009, 13.

251 See for examples of research on the effects of climate change on plant species: Botanic Gardens Conservation International, at https://www.bgci.org/policy/climate-change-and-plants/; Northern Arizona University, at news.nau.edu/plant-production-decline-climate-change-affects-soil-nutrients/.

252 There has been more debate about multiple conflicting objectives, a possibility that the AB seemed to reject in the *EC – Seal Products* case. For some commentaries on this position, see Donald Regan, 'Measures with Multiple Purposes: Puzzles from EC-Seal Products' Symposium on the WTO EC-Seal Products Case, AJIL Unbound (2015); Julia Qin, 'Accomodating Divergent Policy Objectives under WTO Law: Reflections on EC-Seal Products' Symposium on the WTO EC-Seal Products Case, AJIL Unbound (2015); Lorand Bartels, 'The Chapeau of the General Exceptions in the WTO GATT and GATS Agreements: A Reconstruction' American Journal of International Law (2015) 109:1, 95.

253 WTO Panel Report, *European Communities – Measures Prohibiting the Importation and Marketing of Seal Products* WT/DS401/R (2013), para. 7.399;

demonstrate that the main objective of the measure is indeed protection of the environment.[254] Even though these environmental concerns could fall within the material scope of Article XX, the question is whether there is a jurisdictional limitation to these environmental objectives: are paragraphs (b) and (g) limited to environmental concerns within the territory of the regulating state, or can members also rely on these exceptions to address concerns outside their jurisdiction?

The main challenge with climate change issues is exactly that all are affected, regardless of where the greenhouse gases are emitted. As Dannenmaier described it:

> concerns about climate change focus on the risk to human and non-human species as well as to habitat and natural landscapes; they also focus on the impact that measures to mitigate anthropogenic climate forcings might have on human economies and social prosperity.[255]

Air and the climate are the perfect examples of common resources, whereby every state automatically has an interest because all states are affected. Some will suffer the more direct consequences on their territory through droughts or floods, others might only feel the more indirect consequences such as rising sea levels, but there is sufficient evidence[256] pointing to the global consequences of climate change on the seas, on the climate, on biodiversity, even on migration, as they are all closely related and dependent on one another. Any state could thus in principle claim environmental effects on its territory. However, in order to pass the first step of the decision tree, the effects must be direct, substantial and foreseeable.

On the one hand, based on the present state of scientific knowledge,[257]

WTO AB Report, *United States – Measures Affecting the Production and Sale of Clove Cigarettes* WT/DS406/AB/R (2012), para. 113.

[254] This can be done through an assessment of the text, legislative history, structure and design of the measure. WTO Panel Report, *EC – Seal Products*, para. 7.401; Robert Howse and Donald Regan, 'The Product/Process Distinction – An Illusory Basis for Disciplining "Unilateralism" in Trade Policy' European Journal of International Law (2000) 11:2, 249, 280.

[255] Eric Dannenmaier, 'Constructing Transnational Climate Regimes' in Günther Handl, Joachim Zekoll and Peer Zumbansen (eds.), *Beyond Territoriality: Transnational Legal Authority in an Age of Globalization* (Martinus Nijhoff 2012) 521.

[256] See the Fifth IPCC Assessment Report (released in four volumes between September 2013 and November 2014) and previous IPCC Reports.

[257] See IPCC Reports; Eckard Rehbinder, 'Extra-Territoriality of Pollution Control Laws From a European Perspective' in G Handl, J Zekoll and

the mere fact that all states are affected can suffice to establish direct, substantial and foreseeable effects. On the other hand, the effects from such emissions cannot be considered 'direct'. As Voigt argues:

> due to the accumulation of GHG emissions from multiple sources and a plurality of emitters as well as due to the inertia of the climate system it is extremely difficult, if not impossible, to establish a direct link between the emitting activity and the local impact.[258]

I would argue nevertheless that as indeed all states are affected by climate change, npr-PPMs addressing emissions would qualify as measures with an inward- and an outward-looking effect. Nevertheless, because of the partly outward-looking effect, international support for the concern at issue is required to further justify the extraterritorial effects, as illustrated by Figure 6.3.

6.4.3.3 Necessity and recognition of the concern

As argued in Chapter 5, the necessity test of the paragraphs of Article XX can be interpreted to give added value to international support.[259] Several elements can be taken into account. The AB stated in *Korea – Beef* that the more vital or important the concerns are that a measure is intended to protect, the easier it would be accept that measure as necessary[260] so international support for an international concern can be a supporting factor in that regard.[261] Any assessment of international support and recognition would need to take into account, among others, the complexity of the issue, the negotiation history of agreements, the efforts for multilateral alternatives made by the country taking the unilateral measures, and the nature of the failure to reach full agreement (division about the concern itself or the appropriate action).

Necessity refers to an assessment whether less trade restrictive measures can reach the same objective. Where less international support exists for an objective or method to reach that objective, the threshold for proving there are no less trade restrictive alternatives will become higher. Equally, if a PPM is enforcing a treaty obligation, then that measure will most likely be considered appropriate and not more trade restrictive than necessary.

P Zumbansen (eds.), *Beyond Territoriality: Transnational Legal Authority in an Age of Globalization* (Martinus Nijhoff 2012) 158.

258 Voigt, 2011–2012, 501.

259 See Chapter 5.2.3.

260 WTO AB Report, *Korea – Various Measures on Beef*, para. 162.

261 See Chapter 5.2.3.

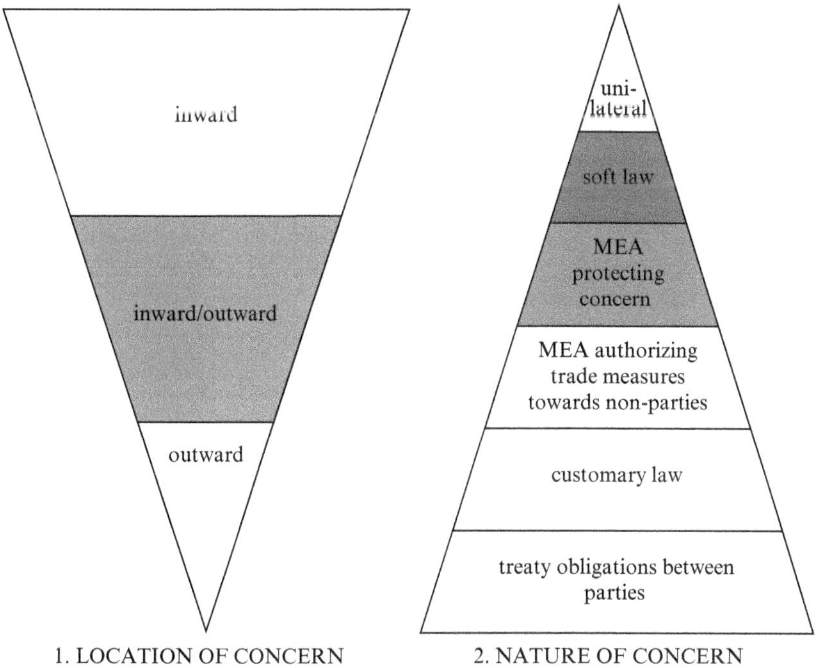

Figure 6.3 Decision tree aviation in the EU ETS

The material contribution to the achievement of the policy objective can also be considered.[262] The AB has stated in *Brazil – Retreaded Tyres*, a dispute *not* concerning climate change, that even where the contribution of a law to protecting an environmental concern such as climate change is not immediately obvious because it is part of a broader programme, of which the impact can only be evaluated over time, that should not prevent a finding that this measure is necessary.[263] Howse interpreted this unexpected reference to climate change as a message by the AB that 'it would not be inclined to second guess lightly the choices of WTO members on how to regulate in the area of climate change, given the complexity of policy design, the evolving nature of the problem and our understanding of it, and the multiple interactions of any particular policy with other policies'.[264] For instance, the objective of the EU ETS and the Aviation

[262] WTO AB Report, *Brazil – Retreaded Tyres*, para. 210.
[263] Ibid. para. 151.
[264] Robert Howse, 'Commentary: The Political and Legal Underpinnings

Directive is the reduction of emissions by a certain percentage by a certain date. Apart from the evaluation over time, it is also difficult to give a prognosis as the ETS has also been struggling with low carbon prices and a growing surplus of allowances due to the financial crisis, growing pains as the first and largest emissions trading system being set up, carbon leakage, etc.[265]

The general concern for climate change is recognized in the UNFCCC, ratified by 195 countries including all EU Member States, with its objective to stabilize greenhouse gas concentrations in the atmosphere at a level that would prevent dangerous anthropogenic interference with the climate system[266] and whereby states should protect the climate system and take precautionary measures to anticipate, prevent or minimize the causes of climate change and mitigate its adverse effects.[267] The Kyoto Protocol to the UNFCCC sets out binding emission reduction targets. The reports by the IPCC present a scientific view on the current state of knowledge in climate change and its potential environmental and socio-economic impacts.[268] The 2015 Paris Agreement emphasizes again the urgency of the threat of climate change and the need to hold the increase in the global average temperature well below 2°C above pre-industrial levels.[269] Climate change considerations are also reflected in EU bilateral and inter-regional cooperation, and the EU has included cooperation clauses on climate change in its association, partnership and trade agreements with developing countries.[270] It can thus be concluded that the general concern for climate change finds wide support through existing binding international agreements. However, much disagreement exists on the required efforts, the responsibility of historic emitters as opposed to new emitters, contradictory interests, financing etc., which led to the failure of the 2009 climate summit in Copenhagen.[271] The 2015 Paris climate summit was of major

---

of Including Aviation in the EU ETS' ICTSD Programme on Trade and Environment, April 2012, 30.

265 Laing et al., 2013. See in that regard also the Commission's efforts for a structural reform of the European carbon market, an update of which can be found at http://ec.europa.eu/clima/policies/ets/reform/index_en.htm.

266 UNFCCC Article 2.

267 Ibid Article 3.

268 The IPCC has been formed in 1988 by the World Meteorological Organization and the United Nations Environmental Programme. The fifth IPCC Assessment Report was released in four volumes between September 2013 and November 2014.

269 2015 Paris Agreement, Article 2.

270 Kulovesi, 2012, 138. See e.g. Cotonou Agreement, Article 32bis.

271 See http://unfccc.int/meetings/copenhagen_dec_2009/meeting/6295.php.

importance for the discussion of further stringent cooperation, and setting ambitious but necessary global reduction targets.[272]

With regard to emissions from international aviation, it is set out under Article 2(2) of the Kyoto Protocol[273] that the ICAO is to tackle the problem, but the ICAO has so far been unable to do so.[274] The EU's aviation scheme came as a unilateral response to failed efforts to reach international agreement on the issue within the ICAO.[275] In its 2004 Resolution A35-5, the ICAO explicitly endorsed the development of an emission trading system to reduce international aviation emissions. However, the Group on International Aviation and Climate Change, tasked with developing proposals for such a system, was only set up in 2007. In the 2010 Resolution A37-19, the ICAO Assembly recognized that 'some states may take more ambitious actions prior to 2020, which may offset an increase in emissions from the growth of air transport in developing states'. It also implicitly endorsed unilateral measures, 'urging states to respect the guiding principles listed in the Annex, when designing new and implementing existing market-based measures for international aviation', even when it also urged them to 'engage in constructive bilateral and/or multilateral consultations and negotiations with other states to reach an agreement'.[276] Whereas the EU lodged a

---

[272] Elizabeth Kolbert, *The Weight of the World* (24 August 2015) at www.newyorker.com/magazine/2015/08/24/the-weight-of-the-world.

[273] 'Parties included in Annex I shall pursue *limitation* or *reduction* of emissions of greenhouse gases . . . from aviation and marine bunker fuels, working through the International Civil Aviation Organization and the International Maritime Organization, respectively.' Unlike other sectors, responsibility for cutting international aviation emissions was not given to individual countries (parties). Instead reductions should be achieved by Annex 1 Parties working through international bodies that regulate these modes of transport – ICAO for aviation and IMO for maritime transport.

[274] In October 2016 an agreement was reached to set up a global carbon offsetting scheme (the so-called Carbon Offsetting and Reduction Scheme for International Aviation or CORSIA) that will start with a voluntary phase as from 2021. See note 221.

[275] For an overview of the failed proposals and negotiations, see Transport and Environment, 'Grounded: How ICAO failed to tackle aviation and climate change and what should happen now' 2010, at www.transportenvironment.org/sites/te/files/media/2010_09_icao_grounded.pdf, 4; Steven Truxal, 'The ICAO Assembly Resolutions on International Aviation and Climate Change: An Historic Agreement, a Breakthrough Deal and the Cancun Effect' Air and Space Law (2011) 36:3, 217, 217.

[276] Consolidated statement of continuing ICAO policies and practices related to environmental protection, IAO Assembly Res A37-19, 8 Oct 2010, paras. 6(c), 10.

reservation setting out that the Chicago Convention did not require contracting parties to obtain the consent of other parties before applying market-based measures to operators of other states,[277] a number of other states lodged reservations expressly denying that unilateral measures were permitted.[278] Thus, one could say that there is definitely recognition at an international level that action with regard to aviation emissions is required, but the support for unilateral action is doubtful. However, the EU did engage in consultations and negotiations, though these did not lead to any results at the time of adoption of the Aviation Directive. One could say that the 'stop the clock' action did induce a sense of urgency to come to an international agreement before the EU 'starts the clock' again, as international agreement was reached in October 2016, the technical implementation of which needs to be developed over the next years. It remains to be seen whether other states are as committed to developing a robust agreement as they were fierce in protesting against EU action. In any case, Article 4(1)(b) and (f) of the UNFCCC establishes a common responsibility for all states to reduce greenhouse gas emissions. Continued opposition by ICAO members to ambitious international action is not consistent with the obligations and responsibilities of states under the UNFCCC.

With regard to the inclusion of both departing and arriving flights in the system, there is no agreement under the UNFCCC or the IPCC guidelines as to how responsibility for greenhouse gas emissions from international aviation (nor international shipping) should be apportioned between them. While Article 3(5) of the UNFCCC acknowledges the right of parties to adopt unilateral acts to combat climate change, without specifying how these international emissions should be allocated, the question of when, if ever, it may be lawful for states to enact unilateral measures that include extraterritorial greenhouse gas emissions is left open.[279] According to the IPCC guidelines, countries are responsible for the emissions that arise in the territories under their jurisdiction (a territorial or production-based

---

[277] Bartels, 'The WTO Legality of the Application of the EU's Emissions Trading System to Aviation' 2015, 436.

[278] As was noted above, in 2011 the ICAO Council endorsed a working paper presented by 26 ICAO Members, containing a New Delhi declaration, which 'urged the EU and its MS to refrain from including flights by non-EU carriers to/from an airport in the territory of an EU Member State in its emissions trading system'. See ICAO working paper, 'Inclusion of international civil aviation in the EU ETS' C-WP/13790, 17 October 2011.

[279] Joanne Scott, 'The Geographical Scope of the EU's First-Order and Second-Order Climate Responsibilities: An Exploration' Cambridge Yearbook of European Legal Studies (2015) 17, 92, 8.

consumption system);[280] however, emissions that arise in international airspace are not allocated to individual countries. Thus, the guidelines do not specify which consumed fuel or which ship/flight movements are to be attributed to which state.[281] The EU has opted for a framework that allocates responsibility for aviation emissions to the departure state: if arriving flights are subject to adequate climate change regulation in the state of departure, they can be exempted from the EU ETS.[282] Where a departure state fails to take responsibility for aviation emissions by adopting the necessary measures, the EU as the arrival state asserts a right to 'step in'.[283] This unilateral determination by the EU is one of the controversial aspects of the measure, as it has now opted for a criterion of market access, currently unsupported by international agreement – but note that there is no agreement in support of any other solution either.

The Aviation Directive does not make a distinction between developed and developing countries, and might in that regard not be in line with international recognition for the principle of CBDRRC.[284] The principle

---

[280] A production-based system boundary allocates responsibility for GHG emissions in the state where these emissions are generated or produced. A consumption-based system on the other hand allocates GHG emissions according to the country of the consumer, usually based on final consumption. The total GHG emissions of a state then equal the emissions of consumption added with the emissions of production of imports reduced by the emissions of production of exports. According to a territorial or production-based system boundary, the GHG emissions of developed countries (so called Annex I countries) appear to have levelled off in recent years, while from the perspective of a consumption-based system boundary they have continued to rise at an annual rate of approximately 10 %. See Scott, 2015, 7, referring to Alice Bows and John Barrett, "Cumulative Emission Scenarios Using a Consumption-Based Approach: A Glimmer of Hope?' Carbon Management (2010) 1:1, 161, 168.

[281] Scott, 2015, 17. See IPCC Guidelines Vol. 1 and chapter 3.5 (water borne transportation) and 3.6 (civil aviation) of Vol. 2.

[282] Directive 2008/101/EC of the European Parliament and of the Council of 19 November 2008 amending Directive 2003/87/EC so as to Include Aviation Activities in the Scheme for Greenhouse Gas Emission Allowance Trading within the Community Article 25a.

[283] Joanne Scott and Lavanya Rajamani, 'Contingent Unilateralism: International Aviation in the European Emissions Trading Scheme' in Bart Van Vooren, Steven Blockmans and Jan Wouters (eds.), *The EU's Role in Global Governance: The Legal Dimension* (Oxford University Press 2013) 213.

[284] The CBDRRC principle is articulated in Article 3 of the UNFCCC and lies at the heart of the international compact on climate change. The Impact Assessment to the Commission's proposal for the Aviation Directive argued that the directive would be in conformity with the principle, but the Commission argued later that the principle does not apply as the Aviation Directive applies to businesses and the CBDRRC principle applies to states

implies differentiation based on the level of economic development and capabilities of a country, as well as on the contribution to global environmental harm.[285] CBDRRC is one of the biggest challenges of environmental law, because it is debated how best to interpret and apply this principle of differentiation. The problem is that a distinction is often made between Annex I and non-Annex I countries to the Kyoto Protocol, a distinction that can no longer be said to be a reflection of the actual situation today, as some of the richest countries in the world are excluded from Annex I.[286] Also it is questionable whether the Annex I/non-Annex I distinction is the right approach for climate change,[287] in light of, for instance, the massive and increasing emission contributions by countries such as China or India. It is disputed whether the CBDRRC principle is a legal obligation or merely a consideration that should be taken into account. Yet, as a fundamental part of the climate change regime,[288] it can be argued that there is at least a duty of good faith to take the principle into account when drafting policy, including unilateral instruments.[289]

The CBDRRC principle can manifest itself through differential

(see Runge-Metzger, 40, at http://ec.europa.eu/clima/policies/transport/aviation/docs/presentation_icao_en.pdf).

285 See Principle 7 of the Rio Declaration, defining CBDRRC and stating that '[t]he developed countries acknowledge the responsibility that they bear in the international pursuit to sustainable development in view of the pressures their societies place on the global environment and of the technologies and financial resources they command.'

286 Such as Kuwait, United Arab Emirates, Brunei, Singapore, and Qatar, which are among the top 20 richest countries in the world. Also OECD members such as Chile and South Korea are excluded.

287 Pieter Pauw et al., 'Different Perspectives on Differentiated Responsibilities: A State-of-the-Art Review of the Notion of Common but Differentiated Responsibilities in International Negotiations' Deutsches Institut für Entwicklungspolitik Discussion Paper, 6/2014 (2014), 2.

288 The principle of CBDRRC can also be read into the preamble to the WTO Agreement, stating 'seeking both to protect and preserve the environment and to enhance the means for doing so in a manner consistent with their respective needs and concerns at different levels of economic development'. For other possible manifestations of the principle in WTO law, see Fabio Morosini, 'Trade and Climate Change: Unveiling the Principle of Common but Differentiated Responsibilities from the WTO Agreements' George Washington International Law Review (2010) 42, 714, 723.

289 Pananya Larbprasertporn, 'The Interaction between WTO Law and the Principle of Common but Differentiated Responsibilities in the Case of Climate-Related Border Tax Adjustments' Goettingen Journal of International Law (2014) 6:1, 145, 149; Scott and Rajamani, 2012, 478; Pauw et al., 2014.

treatment with regard to implementation, with regard to assistance, and more disputed, with regard to key obligations.[290] That duty of good faith could also be read in the *chapeau* of Article XX GATT, which would leave an opening for the EU to implement CBDRRC in a climate change related trade measure.[291] Differentiation between developed and developing countries based on objective criteria should not pose a problem at WTO level, as it could be interpreted as special and differential treatment in light of the 1979 Enabling Clause.[292] In *EC – Tariff Preferences*, the AB emphasized the importance of elaborating objective criteria for differentiating between developing countries and ensuring that such criteria would be applied transparently and consistently, and allow for the necessary flexibility.[293]

---

[290] Scott and Rajamani, 2012, 478.

[291] Michael Hertel, 'Climate-Change-Related Trade Measures and Article XX: Defining Discrimination in Light of the Principle of Common but Differentiated Responsibilities' Journal of World Trade (2011) 45:3, 653, 676.

[292] GATT Contracting Parties, Decision of 28 November 1979 (L/4903) on Differential and more favourable treatment reciprocity and fuller participation of developing countries. The Enabling Clause has been applied with regard to tariff preferences, but also allows for special and differential treatment with regard to non-tariff measures (paragraph 2(b)). See also Alexander Keck and Patrick Low, 'Special and Differential Treatment in the WTO: Why, When and How?', ERSD-2004-03, WTO Staff Working Paper (2004). Special and differential treatment allows for differentiated treatment for developing countries by justifying a deviation from the MFN obligation. What could in theory lead to some discussion is when a non-Annex I country under the Kyoto protocol would not have listed itself as a developing country under the WTO. In that regard differential treatment that is made according to Annex I – non-Annex I countries could conflict with the countries qualifying for special and differential treatment. A further distinction could then be made between countries based on their economic capabilities, which would justify differentiation under the Enabling Clause; and between countries based on their historic and current share in emissions (responsibility), which would not lead to discrimination between countries where the same conditions prevail, as these conditions would be linked to the objective of the measure, emission reductions. The E15 Expert Group on Trade and Climate Regimes proposes common action by the UNFCCC and the WTO to clarify the differences, if any, between the concept of common but differentiated treatment in the climate regime and the concept of special and differential treatment in the WTO. See Bacchus, *Global Rules for Mutually Supportive and Reinforcing Trade and Climate Regimes – E15 Expert Group on Measures to Address Climate Change and the Trade System* (ICTSD and World Economic Forum 2016) 14.

[293] WTO AB Report, *European Communities – Conditions for the Granting of Tariff Preferences to Developing Countries* WT/DS246/AB/R (2004), para. 182. Scott and Rajamani propose two options for the EU to implement CBDRRC into the Aviation Directive. First, the EU could differentiate between countries in terms of the conditions required for an exemption of the system. Developing countries should be required to adopt measures to reduce the climate impact of

In conclusion, there is wide international agreement about climate change in the form of the UNFCCC, as well as the recognition within the ICAO that aviation emissions need to be reduced. The Kyoto Protocol is a binding agreement prescribing specific commitments – though with notable exceptions, such as the US and China, and withdrawals, such as Canada. The 2015 Paris Climate Agreement is a binding agreement setting out an ambitious limit to the increase of the average global temperature – but excludes the aviation sector. Thus, if the Aviation Directive constitutes a violation of WTO law, and the measure would need to be justified under Article XX GATT, the extraterritoriality threshold is passed with regard to product-based measures that target emissions from airline operators, as, firstly, environmental effects on the territory can be demonstrated, and secondly, there is wide international support for the general concern of reducing emissions in the fight against climate change.

However, there is no agreement yet on the methods for reduction of aviation emissions: a global emission trading system is still under development and it remains unclear which system boundary will be applied. In order to determine support for the methods prescribed, scientific research and/or state practice should be considered. If there is no state practice, and no consensus on the appropriate methods (e.g. the Aviation Directive opts for a primary responsibility for the country of departure), a deferential approach should be adopted with respect to the scientific validity of the prescribed rules. If alternative, less trade restrictive methods would exist, it is up to the imposing Member to demonstrate why it opted for this specific measure and justify why the objective cannot be reached through reasonably available less trade restrictive measures.[294] For lack of alternatives that are reasonably available at this moment, the EU ETS could be accepted as long as the choices made are substantiated by evidence demonstrating to the extent possible the effectiveness of the system.

6.4.3.4 *Chapeau*

The *chapeau* prohibits arbitrary and unjustifiable discrimination between countries where the same conditions apply. In terms of aviation emissions and the effect of those emissions, the same conditions apply for all

---

their flights commensurate with their respective (historic) responsibilities and capabilities. Surely, as any choice to be made, this will be a subjective exercise, but such criteria ensure a fair differentiation. Second, the revenues raised as a result of developing country flights in the ETS could be committed to a global climate fund, used for the financing of climate mitigation and adaptation activities in developing countries. See Scott and Rajamani, 2012, 487.

[294] WTO AB Report, *EC – Seal Products*, para. 5.215.

countries. The fact that some countries produce greater emissions than others does not matter for this finding.[295] The Directive applies to all airline operators irrespective of their country of origin. While this might result in higher emissions costs for longer distances, it cannot be said that this amounts to discrimination that is arbitrary or unjustifiable. In principle, all airlines can opt to make transit stops, and all operators can be exempt from the Directive for inbound flights if their home country has appropriate climate regulation in place.[296] In view of this latter condition, countries with equivalent climate regulation could be found to differ from countries without such regulation. As different conditions apply in these countries, differentiation does not amount to unjustifiable or arbitrary discrimination. By exempting operators when third country schemes are in place, as well as through multiple references to the ICAO and international emission trading schemes,[297] the EU Directive is open for and contingent on international developments.

In determining which countries are considered for an exemption, it is important to have clear, objective and transparent criteria in place to determine the adequacy of third country programmes.[298] In its original proposal, the Commission suggested that an exemption for a non-EU country should be made conditional upon the adoption of measures that are at least equivalent to the requirements of the Aviation Directive.[299] That reference for equivalence was later dropped in the decision-making process, but is still included in the preamble of the adopted Directive.[300] Equivalence can be interpreted in several ways; for instance, effort-based or outcome-based. It is in any case important that sufficient flexibility is allowed for the third country to determine how to reach the objectives. In 2013 the Commission had proposed as an amendment to the Aviation Directive an exemption for flights to and from developing countries

---

[295] In *US – Shrimp* for instance, the AB also did not quantify the number of turtles: it was sufficient that they existed in the affected countries.

[296] Directive 2008/101/EC of the European Parliament and of the Council of 19 November 2008 amending Directive 2003/87/EC so as to Include Aviation Activities in the Scheme for Greenhouse Gas Emission Allowance Trading within the Community Article 25a(1).

[297] Ibid. recital (9).

[298] See in that regard also WTO AB Report, *EC– Tariff Preferences*, para. 183.

[299] See Commission proposal for a EU ETS Directive, COM(2006)818, 20 Dec 2006, 21.

[300] Directive 2008/101/EC of the European Parliament and of the Council of 19 November 2008 amending Directive 2003/87/EC so as to Include Aviation Activities in the Scheme for Greenhouse Gas Emission Allowance Trading within the Community recital (17).

accounting for less than 1 per cent of total revenue tonne-kilometres, as specified in the ICAO resolution, but only if they are also beneficiaries of the EU's GSP.[301] Such a criterion would most likely not have complied with the *chapeau*, as from an environmental perspective this exemption is entirely arbitrary. There is no environmental rationale behind GSP beneficiaries.[302] Furthermore, the reason why flights departing from countries with adequate climate regulation could be exempted from the system is to avoid a double burden for flight operators. The Aviation Directive provides an exemption for arriving flights, based on the regulation of departure. As this is not yet an internationally accepted system boundary (even though referring to the country of departure is most closely linked to the established production-based emission allocation system), if a third country system would adopt a different standard, the EU may have to consider different exemptions as well.[303]

6.4.4 Challenges

Apart from the particular challenges related to aviation emissions and climate change regulation (for instance, the operationalization of CBDRRC or the system boundary determination: production-based or consumption-based),[304] the example of the Aviation Directive allows for

---

301 Proposal for a Directive of the European Parliament and of the Council amending Directive 2003/87/EC establishing a scheme for greenhouse gas emission allowance trading within the Community, in view of the implementation by 2020 of an international agreement applying a single global market-based measure to international aviation emissions, COM/2013/0722 final, recital 10. This proposal was not adopted in the amending regulation, which only refers to an exemption for non-commercial aircraft operators emitting less than 1,000 tonnes CO_2 per annum, without any reference to developing or developed countries. (Regulation (EU) 421/2014 of the European Parliament and of the Council of 16 April 2014 amending Directive 2003/87/EC establishing a scheme for greenhouse gas emission allowance trading within the Community, in view of the implementation by 2020 of an international agreement applying a single global market-based measure to international aviation emissions, recital 9.).

302 Bartels, 'The WTO Legality of the Application of the EU's Emissions Trading System to Aviation' 2015, 480.

303 See also WTO AB Report, *US – Shrimp*, 161.

304 The Directive prescribes not to include EU-arriving flights when an equal or similarly adequate system is in place in the country of departure (*Directive 2008/101/EC of the European Parliament and of the Council of 19 November 2008 amending Directive 2003/87/EC so as to Include Aviation Activities in the Scheme for Greenhouse Gas Emission Allowance Trading within the Community* Article 25a(1)). Article 3(5) of the UNFCCC acknowledges the right of parties to adopt unilateral acts to combat climate change, but it does not specify the system boundary to be

the identification of challenges that are of broader relevance for the extraterritoriality discussion as well.

Firstly, as has already been indicated above,[305] climate change affects all states and any measure that a state would adopt to fight climate change would thus be considered as both inward- and outward-looking. If substantial and direct environmental effects can be demonstrated, a first important hurdle to establish jurisdiction for measures with an extraterritorial effect is passed. The second step of the decision tree is then of crucial importance: the international support for the environmental concern in question is very relevant to determine the acceptable scope of extraterritorial measures. If international law prescribes binding obligations, as in the IUU fishing example, then a state could adopt country-based measures, with the aim to 'force' other states to change their legislation and act in accordance with their obligations under international law.[306] However, if international law does not lay down binding obligations, or is not specific enough, then one could argue that states are only allowed to adopt product-based measures. The regulatory space to impose product-based measures is larger, because such a measure targets the product or service that will actually enter the market, and does not *impose* anything on a sovereign third country (even though surely depending on the export flows there might be an incentivizing effect to adapt legislation in the country of origin as well). The use of country-based measures would only be accepted as leverage, when binding obligations already exist and countries refuse to comply with these obligations. A country that consciously chooses not to take part in an international system, without taking adequate measures itself, cannot be forced to comply with such a system. Nevertheless, process-based measures targeting producers (or in this case operators) can be imposed and can indirectly create an incentive for governments to take action. For instance, if the US finds the Kyoto Protocol and its mechanisms fundamentally flawed, then it should install alternatives with methods that it deems more appropriate, but the US cannot refuse to undertake action so as to do its fair share, when the global impact of its actions is undeniable. While the EU cannot force the US to commit to obligations under, for example, the Kyoto Protocol, it can condition market access for US operators, which may lead to increased pressure

relied upon by states in operationalizing measures of this kind (e.g. consumption-based or production-based). It therefore does not settle the question of when, if ever, it may be lawful for states to enact unilateral measures that include extraterritorial GHG emissions within their scope.

305 See Section 6.4.3.2 for the assessment of inward- and outward-looking.

306 See Section 6.3.4.

on the US government to act. The Aviation Directive is a process-based measure (compliance is at the level of individual flights, targeting the emissions from the specific flights arriving and departing from the EU). The option for an exemption if the country of departure has climate regulation in place should be seen as a 'contingency-clause', through which the EU wants to avoid double counting. While such a clause also holds an incentive for third countries to adopt legislation and participate in creating a global system, the formal objective of the exemption is not to target other governments and force them to adopt legislation. The EU exemption can be seen as a reward for third countries' efforts.[307]

Secondly, the existence of binding obligations points to, as in the IUU fishing example, a case of norm enforcement. However, the example of aviation emissions could rather be classified as norm furtherance: there is wide support for the concern, there are some commitments, but international negotiations are stalled. Through its measure the EU has created an incentive to boost negotiations at the ICAO level, and hopefully to set up other national or regional emissions trading systems. In a case of norm furtherance, there can be agreement on the importance of the concern, but not on the appropriate way to act. Thus, such measures are not necessarily based on existing international standards, but they nevertheless address global concerns in relation to which there is international agreement on their importance.[308] Norm enforcement and norm furtherance can be complemented with a third category, norm creation. Norm creation would occur in case of unknown or little-known concerns, upon which states would like to act and create incentives for others to act. However, in line with norm enforcement and norm creation, unless a measure is only inward-looking and does not affect other states, states should first focus on raising international awareness and seeking international cooperation. If that would not work, then depending on the origin of the failure (no recognition of the specific concern, or as in the case of climate change, no agreement on the appropriate method to tackle the concern), that failure could possibly support further action, and be considered as an action of norm furtherance.

Thirdly, unilateral actions in the absence of international action raise the question of responsibility. Do states have an additional responsibility, or even a duty, to act beyond their own 'fair share' when other states, or

[307] Joanne Scott, 'The New EU "Extraterritoriality"', Common Market Law Review (2014) 51, 1, 110.

[308] Joanne Scott, 'Extraterritoriality and Territorial Extension in EU Law', The American Journal of Comparative Law (2014) 62, 87, 124.

even the international community as a whole, neglect to act and honour their responsibilities?[309] Caney distinguishes between two ways of climate justice: firstly, burden-sharing justice, focusing on how the problem should be shared fairly among the duty-bearers;[310] secondly, harm-avoiding justice, taking as a starting point the imperative to prevent climate change. Under the latter, the burden of someone who is failing or neglecting its own burden will (need to) be taken over someone else. Caney therefore identifies two types of responsibilities: first-order responsibilities, the obligation for an agent to do its fair share; and second-order responsibilities; responsibilities that seek to induce agents that fail to comply with their first-order responsibilities to step into line.[311] Second-order responsibilities would operate on the principle that 'with power comes responsibility', whereby power can be defined as 'A has power over B to the extent that he can get B to do something that B would not otherwise do'.[312] A strong market can thus become a powerful tool to incentivize conduct through market access, because of a moral responsibility to exploit that power. Applied to the example of GHG emissions, states would have a first-order responsibility over emissions generated within their territory (based on the territorial-based system constructed by the IPCC guidelines), and extraterritorial emissions (generated outside their territory) would then be considered second-order responsibilities. However, as aviation and shipping emissions are excluded from the IPCC guidelines, these responsibilities could be applied differently. Scott has argued that states enjoy the autonomy to 'plug this system gap' as long as the sovereign equality of other states is respected.[313] The difficulty with the first- and second-order

---

309 Anne Schwenkenbecher, 'Bridging the Emissions Gap: A Plea for Taking Up the Slack', Philosophy and Public Issues (2013) 3:2, 271.

310 He identifies several principles of burden-sharing justice, such as the principle that those who have caused the problem should bear the burden; the principle that those who have the ability to pay should bear the burden; and the principle that those who have benefited from the activities that cause climate change should bear the burden: Simon Caney, 'Two Kinds of Climate Justice: Avoiding Harm and Sharing Burdens', Journal of Political Philosophy (2014) 22:2, 125, 126.

311 Ibid. 134. See also Scott, 2015.

312 Caney, 2014, 141.

313 Thus, any gap-filling system that is endorsed by a state must be susceptible to replication by all other states without this resulting in the double counting of the GHG emissions. The exemption given to flights departing in third countries with climate regulation in place should be seen in that light: if only the country of departure regulates emissions, double-counting will be avoided. The inclusion of emissions of flights departing from countries without climate regulation could then be seen as an exercise of second-order responsibility by the EU. See Scott, 2015, 18.

responsibilities is to determine when a state has not done its share. Who will determine how to share the burden, if the international community cannot reach agreement on this? Arguably, the refusal or delays in reaching such agreement can already be a failure to comply with first-order responsibilities. In that regard the 'most common position' could be used as a benchmark to determine what can be expected from states – even if this would not be a legal obligation without agreement on that issue. For instance, the standard set by the 37 states that committed to new reductions under the Kyoto-amendment could be seen as a benchmark. When that benchmark is not reached, second-order responsibilities could come into play.[314] Scott has proposed certain safeguards against their abuse: the overall efforts of countries should be taken into account, and not just in a specific sector; objective criteria must be given when exercising second-order responsibilities in a specific sector to guarantee that the measures are not adopted to rebut competitive disadvantages; and, the CBDRRC principle should be taken into account when assessing the 'fair share'.[315] Overall, it is submitted that states cannot 'unilaterally' set the benchmarks for second-order responsibilities: state action must rely on soft law instruments at least, supported by as many states as possible. However, precisely in light of the continued lack of international agreement, 'sovereign equality of states' should not be used as an excuse to oppose international action and escape one's moral responsibilities.

6.5 TIMBER AND FOREST LAW ENFORCEMENT, GOVERNANCE AND TRADE

6.5.1 Measure and Context

In 2003 the European Commission developed the Forest Law Enforcement, Governance and Trade (FLEGT) Action Plan. Illegal logging, or logging in violation of national laws (as well as the non-existence or weakness of local laws), is a global problem that can lead to substantial negative

[314] It is highly debatable whether the commitments under Kyoto can even be seen as a 'fair share' to tackle climate change. Numerous studies also show that the EU emission reduction targets are far beyond what would be required. Ibid. 24.

[315] Ibid. 26. CBDRRC should not necessarily follow the Kyoto division between Annex I and non-Annex I countries, but can be calculated by other parameters. See for instance the Climate Equity Reference Calculator, developed by EcoEquity and the Stockholm Environment Institute, at www.gdrights.org/calculator/.

economic, environmental and social consequences.[316] From an environmental perspective, illegal logging can cause serious damage through deforestation and has a negative impact on climate change and biodiversity, for instance through the logging of national parks.[317] Deforestation is a serious threat: at the current rate of loss, tropical rainforests could disappear within 100 years.[318] Although the supply-side of the problem lies in timber-producing countries, the EU as a major source of demand can play an important role by not exploiting illegal logging operations and only allowing legally harvested timber on the market.

The FLEGT Action Plan has led to the adoption of two key pieces of legislation: the 2005 FLEGT Regulation, allowing for the control of the entry of timber to the EU from countries entering into bilateral FLEGT voluntary partnership agreements (VPA) with the EU,[319] and the 2010 Timber Regulation as an overarching measure to prohibit placing illegal timber and timber products on the EU market, laying down obligations on operators who place timber on the market.[320] Next to these regulations, the Action Plan has further encouraged private and public initiatives to support the fight against illegal logging, such as commitments by timber trade federations and companies through Codes of Conduct to eliminate illegally harvested timber from their supply chains. The EU furthermore commits to increased dialogue through existing

---

[316] Economically, illegal logging leads to lost revenues in timber-producing countries and undermines the competitiveness of legitimate forest industry operators; socially, it can lead to among others conflicts over land and resources, corruption, organized crime and armed conflicts. In that light see also the so-called conflict timber, timber traded by armed groups, the proceeds of which are used to fund armed conflicts.

[317] European Commission, *Forest Law Enforcement, Governance and Trade (FLEGT) – Proposal for an EU Action Plan* 4. One should be aware that legal logging does not necessarily mean sustainable logging: this is why attention needs to be paid to the development (and enforcement) of laws supporting sustainable management of the environmental resources as well.

[318] Non-legally Binding Instruments on All Types of Forests (UNGA Resolution A/RES/62/98, 17 December 2007).

[319] Council Regulation (EC) No 2173/2005 of 20 December 2005 on the establishment of a FLEGT licensing scheme for imports of timber into the European Community (2005) (FLEGT Regulation). See also the implementing regulation 1024/2008, laying down detailed provisions relating to the conditions for acceptance of the FLEGT licence, and for the application of the system of imports of timber products.

[320] Regulation (EU) No 995/2010 of the European Parliament and of the Council of 20 October 2010 Laying Down the Obligations of Operators Who Place Timber and Timber Products on the Market (2010) (Timber Regulation). The Regulation entered into force in 2013.

institutional structures with importing and exporting countries (notably including the US and Japan), integration of FLEGT in development cooperation programming at the stage of country strategy papers, and use of external funding.[321]

The 2005 FLEGT Regulation establishes a licensing scheme system for imports of timber.[322] The EU is to conclude VPAs with third countries, under which 'legally produced or acquired' timber can be imported into the EU with a corresponding licence, verifying the legality of imported timber. Without such licence timber cannot be imported from those countries.[323] Legality of timber harvests is to be checked against compliance with the national law of the harvesting/exporting country as set out in the VPA.[324] One of the elements that can be given attention in defining 'legality' is compliance with environmental legislation of the country of harvest. In this regard, the EU is working with willing third countries on the legality of timber as a neutral concept, rather than the politically charged sustainable forest management that has resisted international definition thus far.[325] The main incentive for third countries to participate in the FLEGT VPA process – apart from access to the EU market – is receiving priority assistance for the upgrading of their legal and administrative framework related to forest management.[326] This is supported by the FAO, which is managing a global project funded by the EU to help African, Caribbean

---

321 Marin Duran and Morgera, 2012, 273.

322 FLEGT Regulation. For an assessment of FLEGT, see the report by the Court of Auditors, 'EU support to timber-producing countries under the FLEGT action plan', Luxembourg: Publications Office of the European Union, 2015, at www.eca.europa.eu/Lists/ECADocuments/SR15_13/SR_FLEGT_EN.pdf.

323 The first VPA to be signed was with Ghana, followed by the Republic of Congo, Cameroon, Indonesia, Central African Republic and Liberia. Negotiations are ongoing with Cote d'Ivoire, Democratic Republic of the Congo, Gabon, Guyana, Honduras, Laos, Malaysia, Thailand and Vietnam (last update January 2017).

324 The different VPAs determine legality on the basis of the legislation in the exporting country, with input of national stakeholders in that country. Six countries have signed a VPA and are currently developing the systems needed to control, verify and licence legal timber (Cameroon, Central African Republic, Ghana, Indonesia, Liberia, Republic of the Congo); while nine others are currently negotiating (Cote d'Ivoire, Democratic Republic of the Congo, Gabon, Guyana, Honduras, Laos, Malaysia, Thailand, Vietnam).

325 Marin Duran and Morgera, 2012, 273. Relying on the legislation of the third country arguably aims to ensure the third country's ownership of the initiative, as well as demonstrate respect for its national sovereignty over its forest resources.

326 E.g. Article 15 VPA EU-Ghana.

and Pacific (ACP) countries in the review of their legislation and upgrading of their forest governance and law enforcement capacities. By participating in the FLEGT VPA system, exporting countries undertaking efforts to tackle illegal logging ensure that only legally harvested timber will be accepted into the EU market, while importers purchasing timber will have a guarantee on the origin and legality of the timber, increasing market confidence for timber from the participating countries.[327] In principle, every timber-producing country can participate, but the EU identified priority countries to be approached for participation, including Cameroon, Gabon, Congo, Ghana, Russia, Brazil, Papua New Guinea, Indonesia and Malaysia.[328] Timber originating from countries that have not concluded a VPA with the EU, is subject to the Timber Regulation.[329]

The 2010 Timber Regulation prohibits the placing on the EU market of illegally harvested timber and timber products, and requires EU operators who place timber products on the market to exercise 'due diligence'.[330] In the absence of an internationally agreed definition, legal timber is defined as timber that is in compliance with the laws of the countries where it is harvested.[331] Due diligence entails that the operator must minimize the risk of illegal timber in the supply chain, by providing information on the trader and the supply, and by assessing the risks to illegal timber in the supply chain.[332] Monitoring organizations shall regularly evaluate due diligence systems and the competent authorities shall carry out checks on operators.[333] Traders are furthermore under the obligation throughout the supply chain to ensure they can identify the operators or traders who have supplied the timber and, where applicable, the traders to whom they supplied the timber.[334] Penalties include fines proportionate to the

---

327 European Commission, *Forest Law Enforcement, Governance and Trade (FLEGT) – Proposal for an EU Action Plan* 12.

328 Minutes from an ad hoc meeting on the FLEGT donor coordination of 26 February 2004.

329 The Timber Regulation also applies to FLEGT partner countries, but imports of timber from those countries should be considered to have been legally harvested provided those timber products have FLEGT licences. Operators thus only have to verify the validity of documentation for FLEGT-licensed timber and for timber with a CITES permit. In that way, an additional incentive is created for third countries to engage in VPA negotiations. See, Timber Regulation, recital (9).

330 Timber Regulation, Article 4.

331 Ibid. recital (14); Article 2(f) and (g).

332 Ibid. Article 6. Monitoring organizations shall regularly evaluate due diligence systems and the competent authorities shall carry out checks on operators.

333 Ibid. Articles 8, 10.

334 Ibid. Article 5.

environmental damage and economic detriment, seizure of the timber and timber products concerned, and suspension of the authorization to trade.[335]

6.5.2 Extraterritorial Effect

The 2005 FLEGT Regulation might be considered as having an extraterritorial effect because imports will depend on the harvesting process in the country of origin. However, the conditions of import have been agreed upon in bilateral agreements (VPAs), and any 'extraterritorial effect' thus has the consent of the third country. The norm to be protected is determined by national law, supported by international law; and the sanction for a violation of that norm is clearly agreed upon in the VPAs.[336] The 2010 Timber Regulation is more relevant to our discussion of unilaterally imposed measures with an extraterritorial effect and the following sections will thus focus on that regulation only.

The extraterritorial effect of the Timber Regulation lies in the fact that EU market access is made dependent on the logging process occurring in third countries (non-VPA-countries). If timber has been logged illegally, thus in violation of the national laws of the harvesting country, then that timber is not allowed to be placed on the EU market.[337] Even though the EU does not prescribe what legality entails, but rather enforces the norms of the third country, access to the EU market is linked to an activity occurring outside the EU's borders as regulating 'country'. The following assessment of the decision tree will be applied to determine whether jurisdiction can be established for this type of enforcement, and whether it matters that the enforced norms are the norms of the harvesting country, rather than externally imposed norms.

6.5.3 The Decision Tree Applied

6.5.3.1 Inconsistency with substantive obligations under GATT

The Timber Regulation could be considered as a quantitative import restriction imposed at the border under Article XI GATT, or as an internal measure under Article III GATT. Even though the Timber

335 Ibid. Article 19.

336 E.g. VPA between the EU and the Republic of Cameroon on FLEGT, Article 4.

337 Both illegally logged timber from outside the EU and from within the EU are not allowed on the market.

Regulation does not explicitly prohibit the importation of illegally harvested timber, it prohibits the 'placing on the market' of illegally logged timber, foreseeing penalties upon infringements of the Regulation.[338] This creates a *de facto* restriction on the importation of timber,[339] leading to an inconsistency with Article XI.[340] However, even if enforced at the border, the Timber Regulation could also be considered an internal measure under Article III GATT, applicable both to imported and domestic products.[341] The national treatment obligation requires WTO Members not to treat foreign products less favourably than like domestic products. The Timber Regulation does not make a distinction between domestic and imported products but refers to 'placing on the market' of products, which can be through import, but equally through the placing on the market of domestically grown timber.[342] The Regulation is thus rather an internal measure that can be enforced at the border.

In considering likeness under Article III:4 GATT, the groups of products to be compared must be determined. Both groups of domestic and imported products can contain legal timber and illegal timber. If legal and illegal timber are identical, except for the fact that the former was logged in compliance with local laws and the latter not, then the group of imported timber products as a whole must be considered and compared to the group of domestic timber products as a whole. If legal and illegal timber products are not considered to be like, because of a strong preference by consumers for legal timber products, for instance, then the group of imported legal timber must be compared to the group of domestic legal timber. Imported timber is then like domestic timber, where the characteristics, end use of and consumer preferences for the wood type(s) put the products in a competitive relationship. Even though the legality of imported timber is determined by the national laws of the country of origin, and the legality of domestic timber is subject to domestic laws – and what is legal under one national system is not necessarily legal under

338 Timber Regulation, Article 19.

339 WTO Panel Report, *Argentina – Measures Affecting the Export of Bovine Hides and the Import of Finished Leather* WT/DS155/R (2000), para. 11.20.

340 Geraets and Natens, 2014, 440. In *Brazil – Tyres* the Panel held that a system of fines could have a restrictive effect on importation, see WTO Panel Report, *Brazil – Measures Affecting Import of Retreaded Tyres* WT/DS332/R (2007), para. 7.372.

341 Ad Note to Article III GATT.

342 See for an example of felling licences for UK grown timber, www.forestry.gov.uk/pdf/ON033EUTimberRegulationsv2.pdf/$FILE/ON033EUTimberRegulationsv2.pdf.

another system – all types of legal timber would still be in a competitive relationship on the importing market, and be considered 'like' for the purpose of this analysis. With regard to illegal timber, it can be questioned whether WTO rules apply to 'illicit' goods.[343] Can trade in illegal goods (as determined by the laws of the country of origin) be regulated by public measures (not allowing those goods equals a product ban), and if so, can those measures be subject to rules of non-discrimination etc.? This seems unlikely.

If the products are like, it needs to be determined whether the imported products are treated less favourably so as to afford protection to domestic products; in other words, whether the conditions of competition are modified to the detriment of the group of imported products. As the regulation applies both to imported and domestically produced timber, there is no *de jure* violation. Could there be a *de facto* violation because the national laws of country of origin and country of import may differ? If timber is considered illegal in the country of origin, but would have been considered legal under the rules of the importing country due to lower standards, would this amount to treatment less favourable? Unless the regulatory requirements for legality in the importing country would be such as to clearly protect domestic production, these different regulatory requirements by themselves cannot amount to less favourable treatment. From a EU perspective, it seems unlikely that in light of the EU's efforts with respect to forestry management, EU local requirements would be less stringent than the requirements in third countries. Furthermore, national timber regulation is likely to be based on international private and public standards and norms.

The remaining question, then, is whether imported products bear a heavier burden than domestic products. The Timber Regulation is applied even-handedly: even though the proportion of affected imports might be higher than the proportion of domestic production, mainly because of the higher proportion of imported timber on the market,[344] the Regulation does not modify the conditions of competition in that market to the detriment of the imported products.[345] It could possibly be argued that the due diligence requirements for operators that place timber on the market are harder to fulfil with regard to imported products than for domestic products, because of uncertainty about the foreign origin, and

---

[343] Geraets and Natens, 2014, 440; Mitchell and Ayres, 2012, 468; Brack, Chandra and Kinasih, 2012, 9.

[344] Forest Trends, *European Trade Flows and Risks* (2013), Forest Trends, at http://forest-trends.org/documents/files/doc_4085.pdf.

[345] WTO AB Report, *Korea – Various Measures on Beef*, para. 135.

the distance making it more difficult to evaluate and examine the correctness of information. The imported products might then be at a competitive disadvantage. Nevertheless, this is not to protect domestic products, and the mere different impact does not lead to treatment less favourable.[346] It is thus unlikely that the Timber Regulation is inconsistent with Article III:4 GATT.

The Timber Regulation could arguably be inconsistent with Article I:1 GATT, because of the discrimination between identical products based on the country of origin. Rather than referring to general environmental-friendly criteria, the Timber Regulation refers to the national laws of the harvesting country. Legality, and thus the right to be placed on the market, is determined based on the national laws of the harvesting country. Timber products that are physically identical, and logged in a similar way, could be legal according to the laws of country A but illegal according to the laws of country B. In this way, the Regulation could confer indirect 'advantages' on products from some countries (those with less stringent national laws), without according them to all like products originating in other WTO Members.

It is unlikely that the Timber Regulation would fall within the scope of the TBT Agreement because, firstly, the Timber Regulation is a non-product-related PPM, whereas the TBT Agreement may only apply to 'related' PPMs.[347] Whether 'related' can also include non-physical characteristics of a product has not yet been clarified in the case law. Secondly, even if the TBT Agreement could apply to npr-PPMs, it is not clear whether the Timber Regulation prescribes a technical regulation, as it does not lay down any rules itself, but refers to the national laws of the harvesting country. It is possible, however, that implementing measures could qualify as technical regulations under the TBT Agreement, for instance when EU Member States require the marking of imported products to indicate origin or verification.[348] However, the Timber Regulation itself does not prescribe such rules.

6.5.3.2 Environmental objective and location of the concern

Assuming it can nevertheless be established that the Timber Regulation violates WTO law, a justification needs to be found in Article XX GATT, where the question of extraterritoriality arises. Sustainable forest

---

346 WTO AB Report, *EC – Seal Products*, para. 5.108.

347 See Chapter 2.

348 Akiva Fishman and Krystof Obidzinski, 'European Union Timber Regulation: Is It Legal?' Review of European Community and International Environmental Law (2014) 23:2, 258., 273.

management can be an environmental objective both under Article XX(b) (protection of flora and fauna), and Article XX(g). Forests are definitely exhaustible, and avoiding trade in illegal timber can contribute to preventing deforestation. Also the objectives of climate change and biodiversity have widely been recognized as important environmental objectives. Again, the question is whether there is a jurisdictional limitation to these environmental objectives: are paragraphs (b) and (g) limited to environmental concerns within the territory of the regulating state, or can members also rely on these exceptions to address concerns outside their jurisdiction?

With regard to forests within the EU, there is no doubt that the EU can take the necessary measures. With regard to forests outside the EU, however, it is again a question of whether the deforestation of those forests and illegal harvesting of timber can have sufficient environmental effects on EU territory in order for the measure to be considered both inward- and outward-looking. In order to justify an exercise of jurisdiction, the environmental effects must be direct, substantial and foreseeable. Several elements can be taken into account to determine these effects. Firstly, forests are the green lungs of our planet and can be considered a common resource. Secondly, decreased forests have an impact on global biodiversity and climate change.[349] As those are global concerns that affect the planet as a whole, every state is affected and this could in principle substantiate a claim of environmental effects on EU territory.[350] Measures taken to protect forests would thus qualify as measures having an inward- and outward-looking effect, as there are environmental effects both within and outside the territory of the regulating country. Because of the partly outward-looking effect, further support for the concern at issue is still required to strengthen the exercise jurisdiction, as illustrated by Figure 6.4.

6.5.3.3 Necessity and recognition of the concern

The necessity test of the subparagraphs of Article XX GATT can be interpreted to give added value to international support. Determining the degree of necessity involves a process of weighing and balancing a series of factors, which results in an ad hoc, contextual assessment of each

---

[349] See IPCC, Climate Change and Biodiversity (Habiba Gitay et al. eds., 2002), Climate Change and Biodiversity, (Thomas E Lovejoy and Lee Hannah eds., 2005); see also Harro Van Asselt, 'Managing the Fragmentation of International Environmental Law: Forests at the Intersection of the Climate and Biodiversity Regime', NYU Journal of International Law (2012) 44, 1205, 1213.

[350] See Section 6.3.3.2 when discussing effects of climate change.

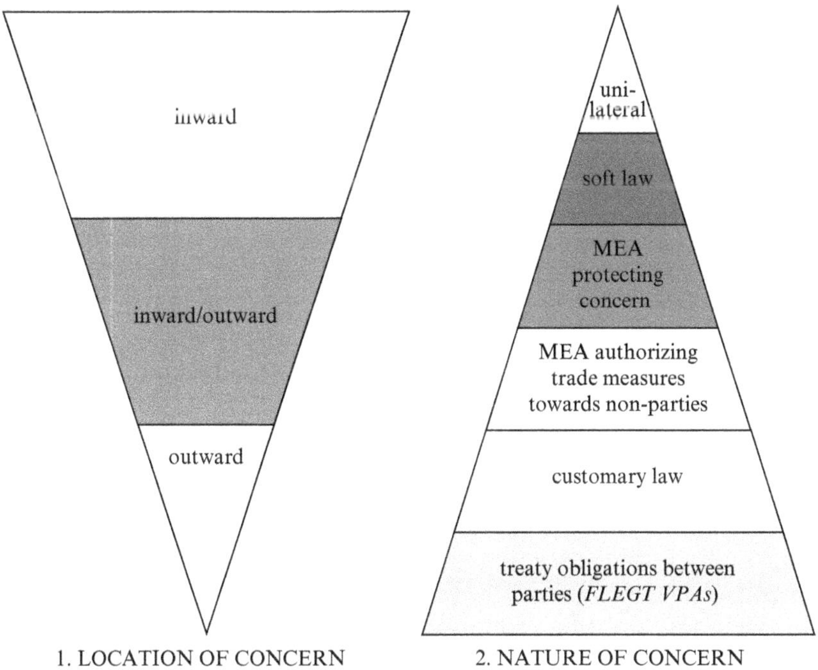

Figure 6.4 Decision tree Timber Regulation

measure.[351] The more common a concern – as recognized by international support for that particular concern – the more easily a measure addressing it will be considered necessary.[352] Necessity also assesses whether less trade restrictive measures can reach the same objective. If a measure finds support in or is even prescribed by international agreements, it is less likely that a measure will have a protectionist objective and that the measure would be considered too trade restrictive.[353]

At the Earth Summit in Rio 1992, the international community failed to reach agreement on a global forest convention. Two soft law instruments were adopted: the Forest Principles[354] and Chapter 11 on deforestation

---

[351] WTO AB Report, *Korea – Various Measures on Beef*; WTO AB Report, *EC – Asbestos*; WTO AB Report, *Brazil – Retreaded Tyres*.

[352] WTO AB Report, *Korea – Various Measures on Beef*, para. 162.

[353] See Chapter 5.

[354] UNCED, *Statement of Principles for a Global Consensus on the Management, Conservation and Sustainable Development of All Types of Forest* (1992).

of Agenda 21.[355] Since 1992, in the absence of a hard law international instrument on forests, sustainable forest matters are addressed in a fragmented and uncoordinated manner by a large number of private and public, international and regional soft law instruments.[356] At the UN level, the Intergovernmental Panel on Forests was established in 1995 in order to share knowledge between states, and was replaced by the United Nations Forum on Forests in 2001.[357] In 2008 the UN General Assembly adopted a resolution on 'Non-legally Binding Instrument on All Types of Forests' (NLBI), strengthening commitment to sustainable forest management through, among others, national forest programmes.[358] The NLBI also promotes bilateral, regional and international cooperation aimed at curbing trade in illegal timber, without any binding obligations or commitments, however. In 1994, the United Nations Conference on Tropical Timber adopted International Tropical Timber Agreement (ITTA), succeeding an earlier 1983 ITTA, seeking to promote trade in timber from sustainable sources.[359] Its successor agreement, the ITTA of 2006, further emphasizes the need to improve the distribution and trade of legally harvested timber.[360] There have been a series of regional initiatives addressing forest law enforcement and governance, starting with the Asia Forest Law Enforcement and Governance process, raising awareness, and bringing together governments of timber-producing and

---

355 UN Conference on Environment and Development, Agenda 21 chapter 11.

356 For a comprehensive overview, see Jeremy Rayner, Alexander Buck and Pia Katila, *Embracing Complexity in International Forest Governance: A Way Forward* (International Union of Forest Research Organizations, 2010); Bows and Barrett, 2010; Lars Gulbrandsen, 'Overlapping Public and Private Governance: Can Forest Certification Fill the Gaps in the Global Forest Regime?', Global Environmental Policy (2004) 4; European Commission, *Forest Law Enforcement, Governance and Trade (FLEGT) – Proposal for an EU Action Plan* 24. A well-known example of a private initiative is the Forest Stewardship Council Certification Scheme. This organization has promoted responsible management of the world's forests since 1993. Its main tools are standard setting, certification and labelling. Use of the FSC logo is intended to signify that the product comes from responsible sources – environmentally appropriate, socially beneficial and economically viable. The FSC label is used on a wide range of timber and non-timber products from paper and furniture to medicine and jewellery. See http://us.fsc.org.

357 See www.un.org/esa/forests/forum/.

358 GA Res 62/98, UN Doc, A/RES/62/98 (31 January, 2008).

359 International Tropical Timber Agreement, Geneva, 26 January 1994. Forty-five parties ratified the Agreement.

360 International Tropical Timber Agreement, Geneva, 27 January 2006. Seventy-two parties have ratified the Agreement.

consuming countries, civil society and the private sector.[361] A similar process is ongoing in Africa.[362] Both focus mainly on the legality of logging.

Using trade measures as a tool to promote sustainable forest management and legal logging has furthermore been recognized in CITES, with regard to the timber species listed, and its implementation in the EU Wildlife Regulation.[363] The International Tropical Timber Organization (ITTO) and CITES collaborate on a programme to ensure that international trade in CITES-listed timber species is consistent with sustainable management.[364] Furthermore, initiatives such as the 1998 G8 Action Programme on Forests have made the elimination of trade in illegally logged timber a priority.[365] The UN Security Council has been active against 'conflict timber' through imposing trade bans on all timber traded by armed groups coming from war zones that might be illegally exploited and used to fuel armed conflicts.[366] The EU is not alone in using trade measures in the fight against illegal logging: Australia and the US have adopted similar legislation.[367]

Forest management is furthermore linked to biodiversity and the fight against climate change. Under the UNFCCC, countries have committed to undertake action with regard to forests as 'sinks and reservoirs of greenhouse gases'. The linkages between climate change and biodiversity loss

---

[361] For an overview of the Forest Law Enforcement and Governance East Asia, see Morosini, 2010.

[362] African Law Enforcement and Governance, Ministerial Declaration 2003, at http://siteresources.worldbank.org/INTFORESTS/Resources/AFLEGMinisterialDeclaration_English.pdf.

[363] A listing under the Appendices of CITES means that timber products from these species can only be imported into the EU when accompanied by an export permit from the country of origin and an EU import permit. Export permits are valid only if the timber was harvested legally within the country of origin, and an import permit can only be granted when it is established that the granting of such a permit would not have a detrimental effect on the survival of the species or the extent of the territory occupied by it.

[364] See www.cites.org/eng/prog/itto.php.

[365] G8 Action Programme on Forests, initiated in 1998. See e.g. www.g8.utoronto.ca/foreign/forests.html; www.mofa.go.jp/policy/economy/summit/2002/g8forest2.html.

[366] E.g. Security Council Resolution 1521 (2003) and Resolution 1579 (2004) against Liberia. The EU FLEGT Action Plan points to the need to advance work on conflict timber, with a view to set up an international process similar to the Kimberly Process to diamonds (European Commission, *Forest Law Enforcement, Governance and Trade (FLEGT) – Proposal for an EU Action Plan* 21).

[367] US Lacey Act (16USC §§3371–3378) as amended in 2008; Australia Illegal Logging Prohibition Act 2012, No 166, 2012.

are manifold and complex.[368] Since 2007, REDD (reducing emissions from deforestation and forest degradation) has become an important part of the negotiations for long-term cooperative actions under the UNFCCC[369] and deforestation issues are increasingly addressed in the context as a REDD-plus item. Through a REDD mechanism, countries with tropical forests could be compensated for their efforts to reduce the rate of deforestation and enhance sustainable forest management.[370]

The Convention on Biological Diversity (CBD) is the first MEA (with almost universal membership, albeit excluding the US)[371] approaching the protection of biological diversity, including forests, in a comprehensive manner. Under its ecosystem approach, particular attention is paid to the management and protection of biological resources, and forests form an important part of these resources, even though no explicit reference is made to forests. As forests are important for, among others, flora and fauna and natural heritage, the parties have acknowledged that forest issues are covered by the CBD mandate.[372] In 2002, the parties adopted an expanded work programme on forests, which provided an extensive set of goals, objectives and activities for the conservation of forest biodiversity and the fair and equitable sharing of benefits arising from the utilization of forest genetic resources.[373] The programme does not include quantified, time-bound targets, but lists a wide range of possible activities that can be undertaken at the national level.

Thus, the EU has been an active proponent of a global forest convention, but in light of the failure of reaching binding agreement at an international level, the EU has focused on a unilateral and bilateral approach to ensure the legality of timber brought within its borders.[374] The

---

[368] See IPCC, Climate Change and Biodiversity (Habiba Gitay et al. eds., 2002), Climate Change and Biodiversity, (Thomas E. Lovejoy and Lee Hannah eds., 2005), see also Van Asselt, 2012, 1213.

[369] It will most likely take some time before fully fledged rules for REDD are set up. In the mean time, several multilateral actions have been undertaken to support the development of and readiness for REDD, such as the Forest Carbon Partnership Facility (supported by the World Bank), and the UN-REDD Programme (established by FAO).

[370] Van Asselt, 2012, 1222.

[371] 1992 Convention on Biological Diversity. The Convention has 196 parties. The US is the only nation that is not a party: while it has signed, it has not ratified the CBD. See www.cbd.int/information/parties.shtml.

[372] Philippe Le Prestre, 'The CBD at Ten: The Long Road to Effectiveness', Journal of International Wildlife Law and Policy (2002) 5, 269, 276.

[373] CBD Decision VI/22 'Forest Biological Diversity', UN Doc UNEP/CBD/COP/6/20 Annex I (2002).

[374] Annalisa Savaresi, 'EU External Action on forests: FLEGT and the

EU has a clear bottom-up strategy for building international consensus on sustainable forest management.[375] The concern of sustainable forest management has definitely been recognized at an international level, but the international community has so far been unable to agree on a binding regime. Both in its FLEGT and Timber Regulations, the EU is not creating new norms, but relying on definitions of legality based on the national law of the exporting country, which are often also based on international standards.[376] Making use of trade measures as a tool for sustainable forest management has been recognized in instruments such as CITES or the G8 Action Programme on Forests. In that regard, one could say that there is clear international support from different fora for the concern at issue (tackling illegal harvesting of timber), as well as for making use of trade measures. In light of the foregoing, it can be concluded that the extraterritoriality threshold would be passed.

6.5.3.4 *Chapeau*

Any measure that has complied with the extraterritoriality decision tree and has thus passed the extraterritoriality threshold, still needs to comply with the conditions of the *chapeau* of Article XX in order to be justified under the general exceptions. The *chapeau* is an expression of the principle of good faith, and several elements have been presented that play a role in the analysis of the *chapeau*, such as a duty to cooperate, respect for multilateralism, a responsiveness to international developments and a need for flexibility in how to attain the environmental objectives. It has been questioned whether one could read a duty to assist in the *chapeau*, meaning that when a country imposes a measure, it should also provide for the necessary management elements for success, such as transfer of technology or knowledge.[377]

The Timber Regulation is a product-based measure, whereby the finding of legality of timber products depends on the legislation in the harvesting country. The VPAs concluded pursuant to the FLEGT Regulation are bilateral agreements, under which the partner countries agree with the EU on the conditions of import. The EU is clearly aiming for a consensual and cooperative approach to address deforestation by exporter and importer countries. Reliance on the legislation of the third country arguably aims

---

Development of International Law' in Elisa Morgera (ed.), *External Environmental Policy of the European Union: EU and International Law Perspectives* (Cambridge University Press 2012) 149.

[375] Marin Duran and Morgera, 2012, 273.

[376] E.g. explicit reference to international standards in the VPA EU-Cameroon.

[377] See Chapter 5.4.

to ensure the third country's ownership of the initiative, as well as demonstrate respect for its national sovereignty over its forest resources.[378] Relying on the national law of the harvesting country to determine legality could lead to different standards applying depending on where the timber was harvested. However, as the Timber Regulation itself is neutral, this possible differential treatment cannot be seen as arbitrary or unjustifiable discrimination. The rationale of such differential treatment clearly bears a relationship to the objective of the measure, which is preventing the illegal harvesting of timber and its trade. The purpose of cooperation is also to serve as an incentive to come to international agreement, including a common definition and legal framework for the legal harvesting of timber.

With regard to assistance, a measure should be assessed in a broader regulatory context. For instance, the FLEGT Regulation is closely linked to the Timber Regulation, and all countries producing timber can enter into negotiations with the EU to become a FLEGT partner, so they would then be able to issue FLEGT licences with a presumption of legality for timber products. As a FLEGT partner, the EU will grant assistance to the partner country for the upgrading of its legal and administrative framework related to forest management. VPAs can provide for financing and technical contributions from the EU,[379] as well as market incentives, such as encouragement of public and private procurement policies and market promotion.[380]

6.5.4 Challenges

FLEGT is a cooperative effort for the enforcement of forest law, and more particularly the enforcement of national laws of the harvesting country. If country A is incapable of sufficiently enforcing its norms, to what extent can country B 'assist' with that enforcement? If country A believes that milder enforcement is appropriate than what country B adheres to, could country B then opt for stricter enforcement for imports coming from A? With the FLEGT Regulation and the VPAs, the EU has clearly opted for a consensual approach, whereby both parties agree on the concern to be protected and the norm (the legality definition under national law); as well as the applicable sanction, being no market access. In the absence of VPAs, the EU stills seeks to prohibit market access through the Timber Regulation. Under the Timber Regulation, the definition of 'legal timber'

---

378 Marin Duran and Morgera, 2012, 274.

379 E.g. Article 15(4) VPA between the EU and Ghana.

380 E.g. Article 18 VPA between the EU and Ghana.

is still based on the national law of the harvesting country, but the measure is unilateral in the sense that there is no cooperation or assistance between country of export and country of import. Operators importing timber into the EU have an obligation of due diligence, to minimize the risk of bringing illegal timber to the market, which can be penalized, among others, with the seizure of the products.[381] The EU is not imposing a definition of legal timber, and it could thus very well be that legality definitions differ from country to country. However, as the definition of illegality implies that illegal products cannot legally be placed on the market, the EU's measure to prohibit the market entry of illegally logged timber is in line with the national laws of the country of origin. The sanctions that can be imposed upon violation of the law should be considered separately from the legal norm of legality: those sanctions are to be prescribed under national law (e.g. pecuniary penalty in country A, while seizure of the illegal goods if they are placed on the market in country B).[382]

What if country A exempts exports from more stringent domestic regulation? Can the country of import then still 'enforce' the more stringent domestic regulation on imports? It seems only reasonable that the importing country can solely refer to the national laws as they apply to the product at issue: if not considered illegal in the country of origin, then it cannot be considered illegal by the country of import based on that national legislation. Thus, enforcement of third country norms allows the importing state to impose measures with an extraterritorial effect, as long as that measure fully relies on the applicable law of the country of origin. Where the country of import imposes additional obligations to a particular product, the measure is no longer only 'enforcing' third country norms. Those additional obligations would then need to be examined under the decision tree to assess whether they are acceptable as well. This example of third country norm enforcement shows that an additional type of measure needs to be added to the second pyramid of the decision tree determining international support: enforcement of norms of the country of origin, i.e. enforcement of third country norms.

In the FLEGT and timber example, the EU is not imposing a standard for legality, and not imposing new norms. Nor is the EU explicitly enforcing or furthering existing international norms. Rather, the EU is enforcing third country norms, shared by a common concern for sustainable forest

---

381 Timber Regulation, Article 6.

382 Ibid. Article 19. The sanctions for the EUTR are furthermore set by the EU Member States, leading to a variation of sanctions across the Member States as well. See Commission Report to the Parliament and the Council, 18 February 2016 (COM(2016)74 final), p. 4.

management. The EU is supporting the further development of international law through a clear bottom-up approach, and is thereby acting as a regime generator. That regime cannot work without the cooperation of both exporting and importing states, and the EU is acting upon its responsibility to involve the necessary actors in the most sustainable way. The cooperation with FLEGT partners as well as the market access incentives will hopefully lead to the development of a multilateral/international regime.[383]

One could wonder whether the Timber Regulation with its reference to national law could not have a counterproductive effect and lead to a race to the bottom, whereby countries will consciously impose weak legislation with regard to the harvesting of timber, in order to ensure 'legal' supply. However, political pressure by other countries in similar conditions, as well as regional and international organizations can hopefully convince the harvesting countries of the importance of sustainable forest management.[384] Precisely because these environmental concerns have a global impact, it is important that all states are involved and have ownership. Furthermore, even though countries can formally adopt legislation, the legal culture of the country in question will affect compliance and enforcement, which is difficult to control. Even though under the Timber Regulation operators need to exercise due diligence when placing timber products on the EU market, their actions are limited by the available information from the country of origin. Distinguishing between countries based on their legal culture is likely to be a too sensitive and arbitrary exercise in order to pass a non-discrimination test under, for instance, the *chapeau* of Article XX GATT. If it were found that certain laws are structurally not complied with, importing states would need to engage in talks and assistance to work towards respecting the rule of law. Extraterritorial trade measures relying on third country legislation, such as the EU Timber Regulation, thus need to be coupled with other assisting measures where necessary to optimize an effective outcome.

---

[383] For a review of the functioning and effectiveness of the Timber Regulation, see the Commission Report to the Parliament and the Council, 18 February 2016 (COM(2016)74 final) and the Staff Working Document on the evaluation of the Regulation of the Timber Regulation, 18 February 2016 (SWD(2016)34 final), at http://ec.europa.eu/environment/forests/eutr_report.htm.

[384] So far, no race to the bottom has been identified, and the multitude of forestry initiatives seem rather to lead to upward harmonization. See Christine Overdevest and Jonathan Zeitlin, 'Assembling an Experimentalist Regime: Transnational Governance Interactions in the Forest Sector Revisited' in Laszlo Bruszt and Gerald A McDermott (eds.), *Leveling the Playing Field: Transnational Regulatory Integration and Development* (Oxford University Press 2014) 245.

6.6 REGIME GENERATORS: AN *EX-ANTE* APPROACH TO THE DECISION TREE

The case studies have demonstrated that npr-PPMs have different degrees of international 'back-up', which lead to different degrees of 'regime-generating potential'.[385] That back-up refers both to support for the environmental concern (e.g. climate change) and support for the method of action and protection (e.g. a cap-and-trade-system). While there might, for instance, be international support (through hard or soft law) for a particular environmental *concern*, there might not yet be agreement on a common *method* to address that concern. As a matter relevant to determine the necessity of a measure, the assessment of international support must consider both. With regard to appropriate methods of environmental protection, scientific reports and/or state practice in the absence of international agreement can be considered.

Four categories of regime generators can be distinguished: international norm enforcement, third country norm enforcement, norm furtherance and norm creation. While the latter three can only be permitted in the form of process-based npr-PPMs (targeting the specific production process), international norm enforcement may also be permitted in the form of country-based measures, under which npr-PPMs do not only target the specific production process, but make market access conditional on the country of origin. Country-based measures are more restrictive because products that are produced in accordance with the PPM will not be accepted on the market as long as the country of origin does not comply with the prescribed measure (e.g. adopt measures to protect sea turtles comparable to the US TED requirement). Country-based measures are furthermore more intrusive on the sovereignty of the country of production, as they coerce that state into adopting a policy that it otherwise might not have. The following models demonstrate the acceptable scope of action for each type of regime generator. Whereas the decision tree as proposed in Chapter 5 is conceptualized as an *ex-post* tool for adjudicators, this further subdivision is equally useful for legislators *ex-ante* by outlining the available scope of action.

---

385 See Chapter 5.5.2.

6.6.1 International Norm Enforcement

6.6.1.1 International norm enforcement: country-based measure

International norm enforcement through country-based measures, targeting the country of origin rather than only the specific production process, can only be permitted when binding international obligations exist (either through treaties that bind the affected parties or customary law) for the country of production. In case of direct and substantial environmental effects within the regulating state, the highest level of support through international obligations leads to acceptance of the extraterritorial effect. The coercive effect on other countries can be accepted because those countries are already bound by their international obligations and the targeted state is thus not coerced into adopting rules it does not deem appropriate. Rather, what is required is compliance with its international obligations. If the treaty in question does not foresee hard enforcement options, a trade measure by a treaty party can create an incentive for compliance – as long as the npr-PPM does not contravene the treaty in question. When the

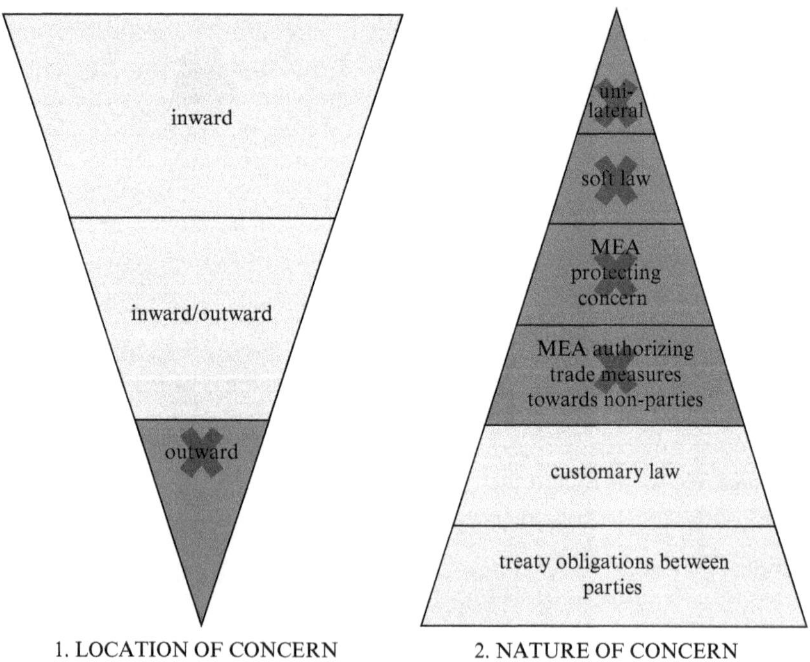

Figure 6.5 Decision tree international norm enforcement: country-based measure

extraterritoriality threshold is passed, a trade measure will still need to comply with the conditions of the *chapeau* of Article XX GATT, which can be interpreted as a good faith obligation. For instance, country-based measures combined with technical assistance in order to help the country reach the prescribed requirements can increase acceptance by the targeted states.

6.6.1.2 International norm enforcement: process-based measure

Measures of international norm enforcement targeting the specific production process rather than the country are less intrusive than country-based measures and could be accepted even in case of widespread support of the norm through soft law (rather than only through hard law). International norm enforcement implies that a more binding obligation exists that can be enforced; however, if it could be demonstrated through an assessment of the international framework on the concern at issue that the soft law framework is widely supported and is recognized by a large number of states as an 'unwritten rule', such a soft law norm could in principle also be

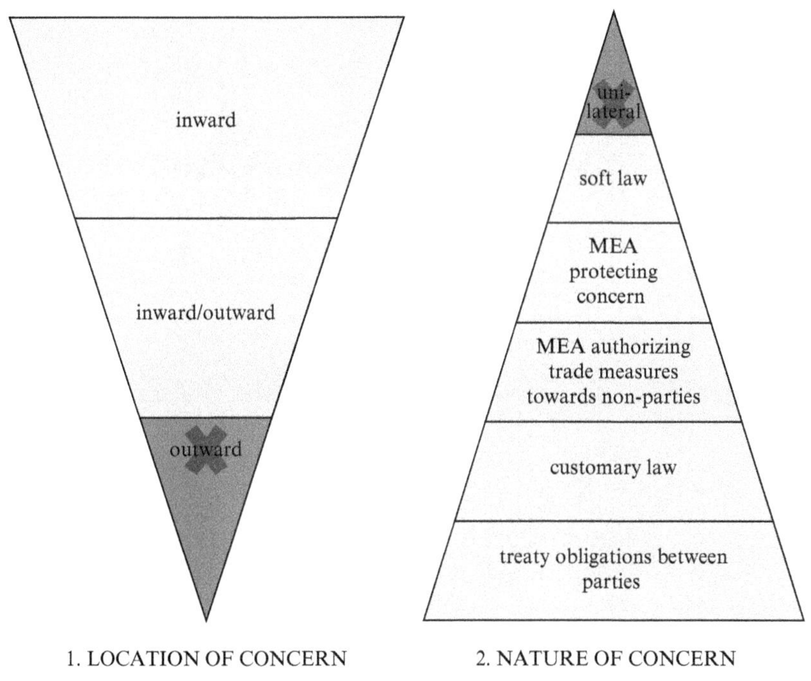

Figure 6.6 Decision tree international norm enforcement: process-based measure

'enforced'. An assessment of the soft law norm should consider the membership, reasons for failure to conclude a binding agreement and ongoing negotiations. International norm enforcement of soft law is only acceptable when states can demonstrate direct and substantial effects within their territory (inward or inward/outward-looking measures). If there are no or only weak or indirect effects (outward-looking measure), and there are no binding international obligations, then less trade restrictive measures need to be applied, such as for instance labelling (market incentives rather than market bans).

6.6.2 Third Country Norm Enforcement

Third country norm enforcement through process-based measures can be accepted when the importing state conditions market access on compliance with the legislation of the country of export, and can thus be seen as 'enforcing' the legislation of the country of export. When the requirements of the importing country do not conflict with the requirements of the exporting country, no further international support is needed

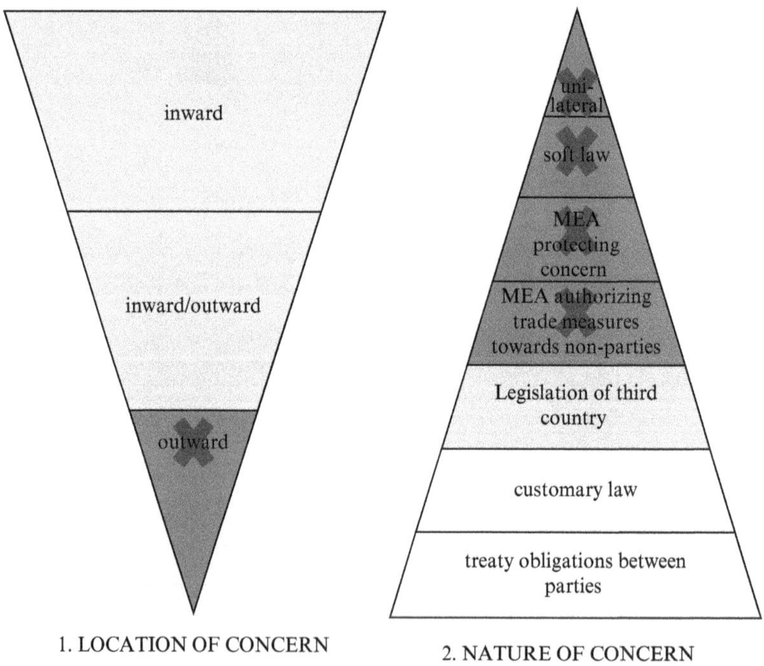

Figure 6.7 Decision tree third country norm enforcement

to impose such measure (e.g. prohibition to be placed on the market in both countries). However, if the enforcement measure in the importing country goes beyond what is required in the country of export, additional international support is needed for that part of the measure. That part of the measure will then either be seen as norm furtherance, or possibly even norm creation.

6.6.3 Norm Furtherance

Process-based trade measures with the purpose of international norm furtherance can be accepted if the measure is either inward-looking or direct, substantial and foreseeable environmental effects on the territory can be discerned; and if there is sufficient international support for a concern. As international obligations do not yet exist, support needs to be assessed through soft law means. An assessment of that support, taking into account the membership, reasons for failure to conclude a binding agreement, and ongoing negotiations, needs to be conducted. There can be (dis)agreement on the concern itself, or on the appropriate

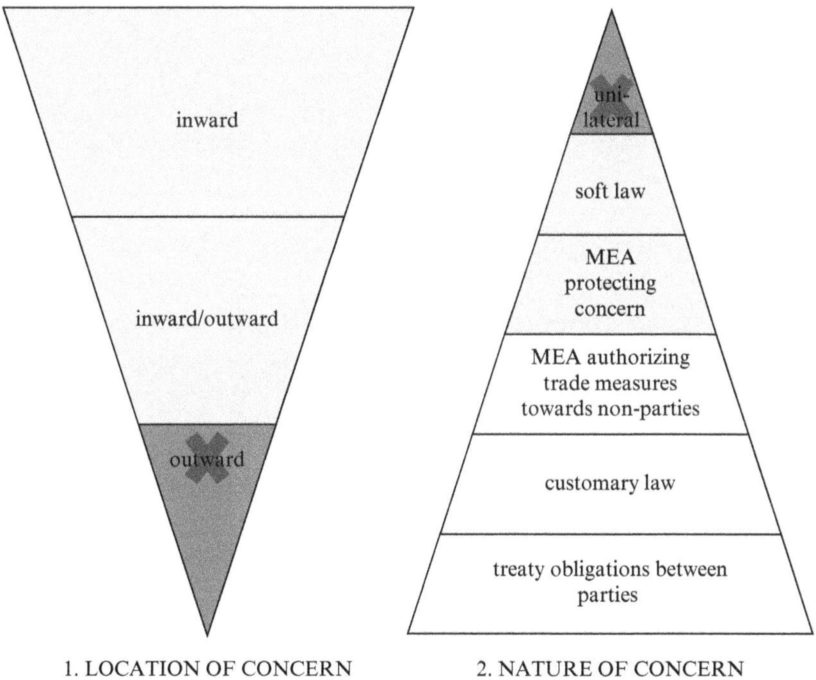

Figure 6.8 Decision tree norm furtherance

method to protect that concern. If states agree that an environmental concern needs to be protected, but there is no scientific consensus on how to reach that goal, it is proposed that as long as there is plausible/acceptable scientific support to act in a certain way, measures protecting that goal could be accepted. This can be read into the necessity test, whereby states need to show that the measures they are taking are indeed necessary and proportionate. The burden of proof is on the complaining party to suggest less trade restrictive alternatives, and thus also alternatives that might rebut the credibility and appropriateness of the scientific method.

6.6.4 Norm Creation

Norm creation would occur in case of unknown or little-known concerns, upon which states would like to act and create incentives for others to act. Unless a measure is strictly inward-looking, states cannot impose trade measures with an extraterritorial effect in the absence of international agreement. Even if there are direct environmental effects

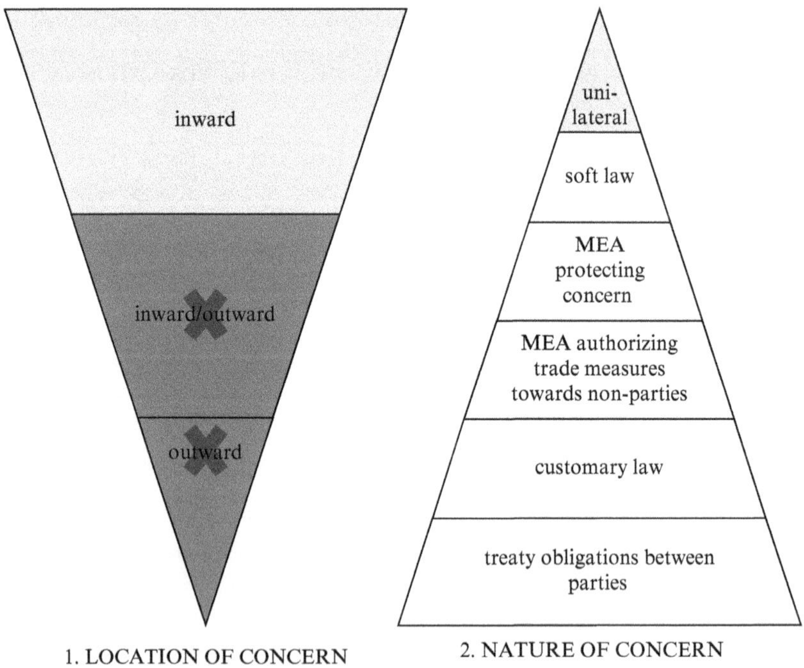

Figure 6.9 Decision tree norm creation

within the territory, when the measure is also outward-looking and affecting other states, states should have recourse to multilateral action, rather than unilateral action, by raising international awareness and focusing on international negotiations. If such negotiations would not work, then depending on the reason for failure (no recognition of the specific concern, or no agreement on the appropriate method to tackle the concern), measures of norm creation could become measures of norm furtherance, for which the (newly found) support at that stage needs to be assessed. Even though arguably this is the situation where PPMs might be needed the most, these unilateral measures both in form and in substance should be avoided within the multilateral trading system. States should commit to multilateralism, and at least attempt to involve other states before imposing trade measures that will affect countries and their producers. Furthermore, if states and/or their consumers are genuinely concerned about a (partly) outward-looking concern, an alternative path of action could be to seek justification under the exception for moral concern, Article XX(a) GATT.[386]

6.7 CONCLUSION

The examples discussed above have illustrated the application of the decision tree. All four measures are npr-PPMs with an environmental objective taken in the absence of a well-functioning international regime governing the concern in question – substantive norms are either lacking, not binding, incomplete, or unenforceable. While they are all regime generators, they can be distinguished based on the degree of available international support for, and recognition of, the norm imposed by the npr-PPM. The IUU Fishing Directive is an example of 'international norm enforcement', the Timber Regulation is an example of 'third country norm enforcement', and both the US TED measure and the Aviation Directive are examples of 'norm furtherance'. A fourth category, of which no example has been discussed, would be 'norm creation', whereby no international support for a certain concern yet exists, and for which further support is required before npr-PPMs with an extraterritorial effect can be accepted. Whereas the latter category requires the most stringent application of the decision tree, the former category of 'international norm enforcement' allows for the most leeway for unilateral action.

386 See Chapter 5.3 on moral concerns.

The following observations on the extraterritoriality decision tree can be made. First of all, before the analysis – including the extraterritoriality question – turns to Article XX GATT, a trade measure needs to violate substantive WTO obligations. As long as a measure is designed in a manner consistent with WTO obligations, that measure is allowed under WTO law irrespective of its extraterritorial effects. Any controversy about possible extraterritorial effects would then need to be dealt with outside the ambits of WTO. The Timber Regulation and the Aviation Directive have, for instance, demonstrated that a violation is anything but obvious. The question under Article XX is then whether a measure can be justified when a state is addressing an environmental concern that is at least partly located outside its territory.

Secondly, states adopting npr-PPMs must be affected by the environmental concern, and must seek international support for the concern at issue through international environmental legal instruments. Due to this combination of environmental effects and international recognition of a particular concern, WTO Members are granted a wider scope for extraterritorial action than would normally be permitted under public international law or competition law: even where effects are weaker or more indirect, npr-PPMs with an extraterritorial effect could still be justified under Article XX GATT. The considerations of effects and international support can be seen as communicating vessels: stronger effects require less international support in order to be justified, weaker effects need more international support and vice versa. States cannot impose extraterritorial npr-PPMs when they are either not affected by the environmental concern, or when there is no international support yet recognizing the concern at issue. Where effects are uncertain in light of long-term effects and the available knowledge of environmental risks, reliance on the precautionary principle should not be opposed.

Thirdly, the decision tree systematizes and substantiates the AB's sufficient nexus test as developed in *US – Shrimp:* while intuitively correct, the AB did not expound why it implicitly accepted a weaker territorial link than normally required under public international law, neither did it elaborate on the impact of the migrating sea turtles on the US by the mere act of swimming through US waters. Through a rigorous assessment of a npr-PPM and its context, the decision tree confirms the AB's (implied) position that WTO law, as it stands, leaves a wide scope for environmental trade measures.

Lastly, the extraterritoriality framework is embedded in Article XX GATT, which includes checks to balance the right of members to regulate with the right of other members to free trade, through, for example, the necessity test with respect to the design of the measure[387] and the *chapeau*. There is no one-size-fits-all solution for environmental trade measures and contextual assessment is key, both in the assessment of the extraterritoriality decision tree and as the further justification of a measure.

[387] See for instance the incentivizing measures taken regarding biofuels: all biofuels are accepted on the market, but if not produced according to EU sustainability standards, those fuels cannot count towards Member States' renewable energy targets.

7. Conclusion: outlook and final remarks

7.1 A WIDE SCOPE TO ADDRESS GLOBAL ENVIRONMENTAL CONCERNS THROUGH TRADE MEASURES

This book has sought to answer whether states, in the absence of international environmental action, can unilaterally impose trade measures targeting foreign production processes (PPMs) in order to protect transboundary environmental resources. Does WTO law allow for 'extraterritorial' trade measures addressing these concerns? Or does it act as a stumbling block for alternative solutions to global environmental challenges? There has been a long-standing perception that PPMs that do not leave a final trace in the imported product (npr-PPMs) cannot be accepted under the existing trade rules because of their extraterritorial character. However, that perception does not correspond to reality. Whereas current WTO law does not include an explicit jurisdictional limitation, it is submitted that the rules can be interpreted rigorously to allow a wide scope for environmental npr-PPMs, while still safeguarding against overreach. In that light, environmentalists should not fear that trade rules will impede environmental protection, and trade advocates should not fear that allowing environmental protection through npr-PPMs will undermine the global trading system. Trade measures can contribute to progress on global environmental priorities, rather than complicate or impede it. Unilateral trade measures can be a much-needed alternative when multilateral or concerted environmental solutions are missing.

The book has demonstrated that WTO law, as it stands, leaves considerable scope for states to impose npr-PPMs addressing transboundary environmental concerns. By looking at WTO law from the perspective of other fields of law where an extraterritorial application of laws is accepted practice, an extraterritoriality decision tree has been proposed to assess extraterritoriality claims under WTO law, and more particularly under Article XX GATT. In trade law, extraterritoriality is not as much a question of *jurisdiction*, but of *justification*. Trade measures only apply to products that access the market of the regulating country: due to this territorial trigger, npr-PPMs can better be defined as measures with an *extraterritorial effect*, rather than as 'full' extraterritorial measures. Can that effect be justified when a measure is targeting an environmental concern (partly) located outside the territory of the regulating state? It is submitted that states can impose environmental npr-PPMs when, firstly, the regulating state is affected by the concern at issue, and, secondly, where that concern is recognized as such in international environmental law. In the landmark case *US – Shrimp* the AB found a 'sufficient nexus' between the US and the threatened sea turtles to justify the extraterritorial reach of the US measure. The AB did not require an explicit or strong territorial link as per general international law principles, but applied a less stringent test. While intuitively correct, the AB's nexus test was unsatisfactory in its wording and implementation. The extraterritoriality decision tree as proposed in this book systematizes and substantiates the assessment of trade measures addressing transboundary environmental concerns under Article XX GATT. Considering environmental effects on the territory of the regulating state in combination with support for the concern in international environmental law enables a robust review of trade measures with an extraterritorial effect. This two-tier test warrants a wider scope for states to address extraterritorial concerns under Article XX GATT than would be permitted under public international law or competition law.

As the text of Article XX GATT (as well as its context) is silent on its scope, any interpretation such as the one proposed in this book could be disputed. In order to settle all discussion on persistent uncertainties, such as the acceptability of npr-PPMs and the scope of the WTO agreements, WTO Members must opt to clarify or change the law. Amendments to Article XX GATT, adopting an interpretative understanding to clarify the meaning of existing obligations, adopting a plurilateral agreement on the interpretation of WTO rules, or even a moratorium on dispute settlement in the area of clean energy were some of the policy options proposed by experts in the recent International Centre for Trade and Sustainable Development (ICTSD) and World Economic Forum E15 Initiative on Trade and Sustainable Development.[1] However, this study contends that, before going down the long and challenging road of treaty amendments,

[1] Ricardo Melendez-Ortiz, *Enabling the Energy Transition and Scale-Up of Clean Energy Technologies: Options for the Global Trade System* (E15 Expert Group on Clean Energy Technologies and the Trade System 2016) 17; James Bacchus, *Global Rules for Mutually Supportive and Reinforcing Trade and Climate Regimes – E15 Expert Group on Measures to Address Climate Change and the Trade System* (ICTSD and World Economic Forum 2016) 17; Ricardo Melendez-Ortiz and Richard Samans, *Strenghtening the Global Trade and Investment System in*

much can be done *de lege lata*. It has been demonstrated that the WTO legal framework that states can and must work with today is not as limited or controversial as often assumed. Rather, WTO law leaves quite some scope to the Members to make use of trade measures to further global environmental protection.

7.2 CHALLENGES AND DILEMMAS

The decision tree proposes a systematic approach to assess the extraterritorial effect of environmental measures under Article XX GATT. While the appeal of the model lies in its simplicity, relevant challenges and dilemmas have been identified, both of a conceptual and practical nature, to which there is no conclusive answer yet within WTO law. These points are worth noting, because of their importance for the drafting and effective functioning of environmental legislation and environmental trade measures. They show in particular the interplay between law, politics and science: the international community of state and non-state actors will need to engage to build a comprehensive framework for environmental protection, where the needs and capabilities of all involved are respected.

7.2.1 The Principle of Common but Differentiated Responsibilities and Respective Capabilities

Even though not explicitly mentioned in the decision tree, it is important to implement the principle of CBDRRC into environmental policy. At the international level, when drafting international agreements, the principle should be taken into account in the division of states' environmental action burden. At a national level and through unilateral trade measures, it is more difficult to operationalize the principle when there is no international agreement on how that burden should be divided. A unilaterally determined division of burden can hardly be reconciled with international decision-making. Rather, the principle of CBDRRC can manifest itself in unilateral npr-PPMs through, for instance, the implementation of structural assistance for countries with limited capacities, lower standards or longer transition periods. In other words, developed countries have to take the needs of developing countries into account to the extent possible when designing their policy. Such an application of the principle of CBDRRC

the 21st Century: Synthesis Report (The E15 Initiative: Strengthening the Global Trade and Investment System for Sustainable Development, 2016) 91.

could also be read in a duty of good faith as expressed in the *chapeau* of Article XX GATT.

7.2.2 The Inherent Uncertainty of Environmental Science

Scientific evidence is needed not only to determine the existence and degree of environmental effects, but also to determine the appropriateness and effectiveness of the environmental method and the substance of environmental policy. A number of challenges have been identified in relation to the reliance on science. Firstly, one can only work with the information and data available. The incredibly complex interaction of different factors and actors, through time and space, complicate any scientific analysis. Environmental scientists have to contend with relatively limited knowledge, with environmental harm or effects or causal links that can take decades or centuries to manifest themselves, with inherent uncertainty about the what, how and when.

Secondly, due to this complexity, diverging opinions will likely each find supporting evidence. Who is then to determine the 'truth'? Who is to determine the most appropriate approach? One of the most significant accomplishments of the climate regime is the development of the IPCC, a cooperation engaging thousands of experts.[2] Where possible, that approach should be extrapolated elsewhere, albeit on a smaller scale. Any assessment of environmental effects should be as objective as possible, outlining different views, and indicating what is known, what is not known, and what is assumed and suspected.

Thirdly, decision-makers must act upon the available scientific evidence, an assessment involving both facts and value.[3] For instance, the UNFCCC has as its objective the stabilization of atmospheric concentrations of greenhouse gases at levels that would prevent 'dangerous' anthropogenic interference with the climate system. However, when do these levels become dangerous? Assessing risk is a scientific task, but determining the acceptable level is as much a value judgment and such decisions require inferences, choices, and assumptions that themselves reflect policy preferences.[4] Whether states rely on precautionary measures or undertake a cost-benefit approach to risk is equally a matter of political judgment. Environmental decision-making often raises questions that involve science

---

[2] See for more information and reports, www.ipcc.ch.

[3] Daniel Bodansky, 'The Legitimacy of International Governance: A Coming Challenge for International Environmental Law?' American Journal of International Law (1999) 93:3, 596, 621.

[4] Ibid.

but cannot be answered in purely scientific terms.[5] With regard to these political judgments, WTO panels and the AB should, where possible, adopt a deferential approach: where WTO Members are consistent in their approach (e.g. either adoption of the precautionary principle or not; non-discriminatory baseline data for domestic and imported producers; etc.) the environmental policy goals of members should be accepted as such.

7.2.3 The Catch-22 of Unknown Concerns

A state wants to act upon an unknown or little-known concern that finds no support yet internationally can only do so within its own territory. These concerns are defined as unilateral concerns under the decision tree, and cannot be the object of an extraterritorial PPM due to the lack of international support and recognition. Efforts must first be made to raise international awareness and instigate international negotiations. This can be criticized, as arguably these unknown concerns are most in need of PPMs. However, while those concerns that are not yet supported internationally but may nonetheless have a global impact are indeed in dire need of alternative action, it is nevertheless important to respect the sovereignty of states and the nature of the international community as it stands today. States should commit to multilateralism, and at least attempt to involve other states before imposing trade measures that will affect other countries and their producers. If international negotiations do not result in a multilateral agreement, the reason(s) for failure (e.g. no recognition of the specific concern, or no agreement on the appropriate method to tackle the concern) would need to be assessed to see whether there might be more informal support on the specific concern; for instance, including NGO reports and civil society initiatives. If states and/or their consumers are genuinely concerned about an unknown concern, an argument for justification of a npr-PPM could possibly be brought under the exception for moral concerns, Article XX(a) GATT.

7.2.4 Towards a Duty of Market Power

Powerful markets are in a stronger position to make use of extraterritorial PPMs and it has been demonstrated that they have no legal excuse not to do so. The power of exclusion will be stronger when exporters have no real choice of targeting another market, and subscribing to the imposed rules is the price of trading with that market. However, does the

---

[5] Bodansky, 1999, 622.

legal possibility to make use of PPMs to protect environmental concerns also entail a legal or moral responsibility or *duty* of indeed making use of PPMs? In other words, do states have a duty not to allow the market to be used for environmental harm? No legal duty can be read in WTO rules or any environmental instrument today. However, states have a moral duty to act in order to protect the environment and ensure sustainable development, as recognized in a number of instruments,[6] including the preamble of the Marrakesh Agreement. The protection of the commons may require leadership and creating an incentive to comply with higher environmental norms can be a tool for such leadership. When an international, multilaterally agreed solution is lacking, when the international system is deadlocked, when progress in environmental protection of the commons fails to materialize, alternatives are required. Those states that are in the position to make effective use of those alternatives should create the much-needed incentives to put a spurt on international progress. A similar duty is suggested with regard to human rights protection through the Maastricht Principles on Extraterritorial Obligations of States in the Area of Economic, Social and Cultural Rights, as has been discussed in Chapter 4.

Furthermore, while protection of common environmental concerns must be founded on a practice of burden-sharing justice, where others are not respecting or complying with their burden, it must be complemented with a practice of harm-avoiding justice. Such practice implies that those who can will take an additional burden from those who are not doing their part. This type of responsibility has been described by Caney as second-order responsibilities.[7] Environmental measures with an extraterritorial effect could be described as second-order responsibilities: the imposing state attempts to involve other actors and create incentives for other countries to act. With power comes responsibility, and it could be argued that where a state is capable of using its market power to create incentives to stimulate and encourage environmental protection, it should do so. A duty of good faith as expressed in the *chapeau* of Article XX GATT could guide such responsibility in order to avoid abuse: PPMs could be complemented with the necessary management and assistance tools to guarantee that other countries, and in particular developing countries, are in a position to comply with the imposed laws.

---

[6] See for instance UN, 2030 Agenda on Sustainable Development, UN Resolution A/RES/70/1 of 25 September 2015; UNFCCC COP 21, Paris Agreement, FCCC/CP/2015/L9, 2015.

[7] Simon Caney, 'Two Kinds of Climate Justice: Avoiding Harm and Sharing Burdens' Journal of Political Philosophy (2014) 22:2, 125.

7.3 FINAL REMARKS

This book has answered in the affirmative the question whether states *could* apply trade measures to address global environmental concerns. However, *should* they do so? The objective answer to that question requires a political effectiveness and economic efficiency analysis, which is beyond the scope of this book. Subjectively, the following can be noted. Global environmental threats are a reality, and international action is required in order to slow down further degradation. The international system is lagging and while important – albeit symbolic at times – steps are taken such as the 2015 Paris Agreement on Climate Change, the international community of states is failing to set out concrete and ambitious action. States seek alternatives that can exceed the suboptimal level of environmental protection that is limited to state's boundaries and trade measures offer opportunities. Indeed, there are pitfalls, and indeed there is a risk to abuse and disguised protectionism. As also pointed out by the E15 Expert Group on Trade and Climate Change, the interplay between trade and the climate regime is ideally determined in concert by both WTO Members and UNFCCC parties. In the absence of such accord, WTO experts in WTO dispute settlement will draw the line of permissible climate measures.[8] While entrusting WTO experts with that task will not necessarily lead to wrong results, they might not be sufficiently equipped to make decisions with potentially far-reaching implications. Nonetheless, this book has shown that WTO law provides for protection mechanisms against abusive trade measures and sufficient safeguards against jurisdictional overreach and abuse of power as laid out in the decision tree. The multilateral nature of the trading system and the sovereignty of other states are respected to the extent possible in light of global concerns. Unilateral environmental action can incentivize further international cooperation; hence under the current circumstances the way forward is through such action and there is no good reason to accept the multilateral paralysis.

Sustainable development is one of the core objectives of the WTO. It has often been questioned whether the current WTO treaty obligations do not form an obstacle to achieving this objective. This study's main contention is that this concern is unwarranted. First, there is no reason to think that the WTO legal regime constitutes an impediment to global environmental action. Second, in the absence of global environmental agreements, unilateral trade measures remain a powerful tool to stimulate better environmental protection. It has been demonstrated that current

[8] Bacchus, 2016, 14.

WTO law leaves more room for environmental npr-PPMs with an extraterritorial reach than is often thought. At the same time, WTO law includes disciplines with which abusive measures can be weeded out. In conclusion, governments cannot hide behind the pretext that WTO law prevents them from using their markets, through trade-related measures, for environmental progress: WTO law is no excuse for environmental inaction.

Bibliography

Ahner, N, 'Final Instance: World Trade Organization – Unilateral Trade Measures in EU Climate Change Legislation' EUI Working Papers 2009/58, 2009.

Akehurst, M, 'Jurisdiction in International Law' British Yearbook of International Law (1972–1973) 46, 145.

Ali Khan, L, *The Extinction of Nation-States: A World Without Borders* (Kluwer Law International 1996).

Amnesty International, *Universal Jurisdiction: A Preliminary Survey of Legislation Around the World* (2011).

Anderson, K, 'Environmental and Labor Standards: What Role for WTO?' in K Anderson and B Hoekman (eds.), *The Global Trading System,* Vol. 4: New Issues for the WTO (IB Tauris 2002).

Ankersmit, L and J Lawrence, 'The Future of Environmental Labelling: *US – Tuna II* and the Scope of the TBT' Legal Issues of Economic Integration (2012) 39:1, 127.

Ankersmit, L, J Lawrence and G Davies, 'Diverging EU and WTO Perspectives on Extraterritorial Process Regulation' Minnesota Journal of International Law (2012) 21:1, 14.

Baade, H, 'The Eichmann Trial: Some Legal Aspects' Duke Law Journal (1961) 10:3, 400.

Bacchus, J, *Global Rules for Mutually Supportive and Reinforcing Trade and Climate Regimes – E15 Expert Group on Measures to Address Climate Change and the Trade System* (ICTSD and World Economic Forum 2016).

Baker, D I, 'Extraterritoriality and the Rule of Law: Why Friendly Foreign Democracies Oppose Novel, Expansive US Jurisdiction Claims by Non-Resident Aliens Under the Alien Tort Statute' Maryland Journal of International Law (2013) 28:1, 42.

Bal, S, 'International Free Trade Agreements and Human Rights: Reinterpreting Article XX of the GATT' Minnesota Journal of International Law (2001) 10:1, 62.

Bartels, L, 'Article XX of GATT and the Problem of Extraterritorial Jurisdiction: The Case of Trade Measures for the Protection of Human Rights' Journal of World Trade (2002) 36:2, 353.

Bartels, L, 'The Inclusion of Aviation in the EU ETS: WTO Law Considerations' ICTSD Programme on Trade and Environment, April 2012.

Bartels, L, 'The Chapeau of the General Exceptions in the WTO GATT and GATS Agreements: A Reconstruction' American Journal of International Law (2015) 109:1, 95.

Bartels, L, 'The WTO Legality of the Application of the EU's Emissions Trading System to Aviation' in C Lim and B Mercurio B (eds.), *International Economic Law After the Global Crisis: A Tale of Fragmented Disciplines* (Cambridge University Press 2015).

Basedow, J, 'International Antitrust: From Extraterritorial Application to Harmonization' Louisiana Law Review (2000) 60:4, 1037.

Bastos Lima, M G and J Gupta, 'The Extraterritorial Dimensions of Biofuels Policies and the Politics of Scale: Live and Let Die?' Third World Quarterly (2014) 35:3, 391.

Berkowitz, D, K Pistor and J-F Richard, 'The Transplant Effect' The American Journal of Comparative Law (2003) 51:1, 163.

Bernie P, A Boyle and C Redgwell, *International Law and the Environment* (3rd edn., Oxford University Press 2009).

Besson, S, 'The Extraterritoriality of the European Convention on Human Rights: Why Human Rights Depend on Jurisdiction and What Jurisdiction Amounts To' Leiden Journal of International Law (2012) 25, 857.

Betlehem, D, 'The End of Geography: The Changing Nature of the International System and the Challenge to International Law' European Journal of International Law (2014) 25:1, 9.

Bhagwati, J and P C Mavroidis, 'Is Action against US Exports for Failure to Sign Kyoto Protocol WTO-legal?' World Trade Review (2007) 6:2, 299.

Bianchi, A, 'Comment on Harold G. Maier – Jurisdictional Rules in Customary International Law' in K M Meessen (ed.), *Extraterritorial Jurisdiction in Theory and Practice* (Kluwer Law International 1996).

Bilder, R B, 'The Role of Unilateral State Action in Preventing International Environmental Injury' Vanderbilt Journal of Transnational Law (1981) 14:1, 51.

Bodansky, D, 'The Legitimacy of International Governance: A Coming Challenge for International Environmental Law?' American Journal of International Law (1999) 93:3, 596.

Bodansky, D, 'What's So Bad about Unilateral Action to Protect the Environment?' European Journal of International Law (2000) 11:2, 339.

Bogojevic, S, 'Legalising Environmental Leadership: A Comment on the CJEU's Ruling in C-366/10 on the Inclusion of Aviation in the EU

Emissions Trading Scheme' Journal of Environmental Law (2012) 24:2, 345.

Boisson de Chazournes, L, 'Unilateralism and Environmental Protection: Issues of Perception and Reality of Issues' European Journal of International Law (2000) 11:2, 315.

Bossuyt, M, 'The Direct Applicability of International Instruments on Human Rights' Revue belge de droit international (1980) 15, 317.

Botteman, Y and A Patsa, 'The Jurisdictional Reach of EU Anti-Cartel Rules: Unmuddling the Limits' European Competition Journal (2012) 8:2, 365.

Bows, A and J Barrett, 'Cumulative Emission Scenarios Using a Consumption-Based Approach: A Glimmer of Hope?' Carbon Management (2010) 1:1, 161.

Brack, D, A Chandra and H Kinasih, *The Australian Government's Illegal Logging Prohibition Bill: WTO Implications* (International Institute for Sustainable Development 2012).

Brack, D and K Gray, *Multilateral Environmental Agreements and the WTO* (Royal Institute of International Affairs and International Institute for Sustainable Development 2003).

Bradford, A, 'The Brussels Effect' Northwestern University Law Review (2012) 107:1, 1.

Brewer, D, D Heales, D Milton, Q Dell, G Fry, B Venables, and P Jones, 'The Impact of Turtle Excluder Devices and Bycatch Reduction Devices on Diverse Tropical Marine Communities in Australia's Northern Prawn Trawl Fishery' Fisheries Research (2006) 81:2–3, 176.

Brill, C A and B A Carlson, 'US and Japanese Antimonopoly Policy and the Extraterritorial Enforcement of Competition Laws' The International Lawyer (1999) 33:1, 75–118.

Bronckers, M C E J and N McNelis, 'Rethinking the "Like Product" Definition in GATT 1994: Anti-Dumping and Environmental Protection' in M C E J Bronckers (ed.), *A Cross-Section of WTO Law* (Cameron May 2000).

Broude, T and P I Levy, 'Do You Mind If I Don't Smoke? Products, Purpose and Indeterminacy in *US – Measures Affecting the Production and Sale of Clove Cigarettes*' World Trade Review (2014) 13:2, 357.

Brown Weiss, E, 'Environment and Trade as Partners in Sustainable Development: A Commentary' American Journal of International Law (1992) 86, 728.

Bulto, T S, 'Patching the "Legal Black Hole": The Extraterritorial Reach of States' Human Rights Duties in the African Human Rights System' South African Journal on Human Rights (2011) 27:2, 249.

Buxbaum, H L, 'Territory, Territoriality, and the Resolution of

Jurisdictional Conflict' American Journal of Comparative Law (2009) 57, 631.

Cameron, H, 'The Evolution of the Trade and Environment Debate at the WTO' in A Najam, M Halle and R Melendez-Ortiz (eds.), *Trade and Environment: A Resource Book* (International Institute for Sustainable Development, International Centre for Trade and Sustainable Development, The Regional and International Networking Group 2007).

Cameron, J, P Demaret and D Geradin (eds.), *Trade and the Environment: The Search for Balance* (Cameron May 1994).

Cameron, J and K Gray, 'Principles of International Law in the WTO Dispute Settlement Body', International and Comparative Law Quarterly (2001) 50:2, 248.

Caney, S, 'Two Kinds of Climate Justice: Avoiding Harm and Sharing Burdens' Journal of Political Philosophy (2014) 22:2, 125.

Cassel, D, 'Extraterritorial Application of Inter-American Human Rights Instruments' in F Coomans and M T Kamminga (eds.), *Extraterritorial Application of Human Rights Treaties* (Intersentia 2004).

Cerna, C M, 'Extraterritorial Application of the Human Rights Instruments of the Inter-American System' in F Coomans and M T Kamminga (eds.), *Extraterritorial Application of Human Rights Treaties* (Intersentia 2004).

Chang, H, 'An Economic Analysis of Trade Measures to Protect the Global Environment' Georgetown Law Journal (1995) 83:6, 2131.

Charney, J, 'The Persistent Objector Rule and the Development of Customary International Law' British Yearbook of International Law (1985) 56:1, 1.

Charnovitz, S, 'GATT and the Environment: Examining the Issues' International Environmental Affairs (1992) 4:3, 203.

Charnovitz, S, 'A Taxonomy of Environmental Trade Measures' Georgetown International Environmental Law Review (1993) 6:1, 1.

Charnovitz, S, 'The Moral Exception in Trade Policy' Virginia Journal of International Law (1998) 38, 689.

Charnovitz, S, 'The Law of Environmental "PPMs" in the WTO: Debunking the Myth of Illegality' Yale Journal of International Law (2002) 27:1, 59.

Charnovitz, S, '*Belgian Family Allowances* and the Challenge of Origin-based Discrimination' World Trade Review (2005) 4:1, 7.

Chaves, L, *Illegal, Unreported and Unregulated Fishing: WTO-Consistent Trade Related Measures to Address IUU Fishing* (FAO 2000).

Cheyne, I, 'Environmental Unilateralism and the WTO/GATT System' Georgia Journal of International and Comparative Law (1995) 24:3, 433.

Cheyne, I, 'The Use of the Precautionary Principle in WTO Law and EC Law' (European Union Studies Association Biennial Conference 2005).

Choi, W-M, *'Like Products' in International Trade Law. Towards a Consistent GATT/WTO Jurisprudence* (Oxford University Press 2003).

Chuang S-C, D-T Kao, Y-H Cheng and C-A Chou, 'The Effect of Incomplete Information on the Compromise Effect' Judgment and Decision Making (2012) 7:2, 196.

Colangelo, A J, 'A Unified Approach to Extraterritoriality' Virginia Law Review (2011) 97:5, 1019.

Colangelo, A J, '*Kiobel*: Muddling the Distinction Between Prescriptive and Adjudicative Jurisdiction' Maryland Journal of International Law (2013) 28:1, 65.

Conconi, P and T Voon, '*EC-Seal Products*: The Tension Between Public Morals and International Trade Agreements' World Trade Review (2016) 15:2, 211.

Conrad, C R, *Processes and Production Methods (PPMs) in WTO Law: Interfacing Trade and Social Goals* (Cambridge University Press 2011).

Coomans, F, 'The Extraterritorial Scope of the International Covenant on Economic, Social and Cultural Rights in the Work of the United Nations Committee on Economic, Social and Cultural Rights' Human Rights Law Review (2011) 11:1, 1.

Coomans, F and R Künneman (eds.), *Cases and Concepts on Extraterritorial Obligations in the Area of Economic, Social and Cultural Rights* (Intersentia 2012).

Cooney, R and A T F Lang, 'Taking Uncertainty Seriously: Adaptive Governance and International Trade' European Journal of International Law (2007) 18:3, 523.

Cooreman, B, 'Addressing Environmental Concerns Through Trade: A Case For Extraterritoriality?' International and Comparative Law Quarterly (2016) 65:1, 229.

Cooreman, B, *Addressing Global Environmental Concerns Through Trade: Extraterritoriality Under WTO Law From a Comparative Perspective* (Leiden: Meijers Research Institute and Graduate School of the Leiden Law School 2016).

Cooreman, B, 'Extraterritorial Environmental Concerns and Public Morals: Testing the Limits of Article XX(a) GATT after *Seals*' Journal of International Trade and Arbitration Law (2016) 5, 519.

Coppel, J, 'A Hard Look at the Effects Doctrine of Jurisdiction in Public International Law' Leiden Journal of International Law (1993) 6:1, 73.

Cottier, T, *Renewable Energy and Process and Production Methods* (The E15 Initiative: Strengthening the Global Trade and Investment System for Sustainable Development 2015).

Cottier, T, P Delimatsis and N Diebold, 'Article XIV GATS: General Exceptions' in R Wolfrum, P-T Stoll and C Feinäugle (eds.), *WTO-Trade in Services* (Martinus Nijhoff Publishers 2008).
Crawford, J, *Brownlie's Principles of Public International Law* (8th edn., Oxford University Press 2012).
Cremona, M, 'Coherence and EU Environmental Policy' in E Morgera (ed.), *The External Environmental Policy of the European Union* (Cambridge University Press 2012).
Crowder, L B, D T Crouse, S S Heppell and T H Martin, 'Predicting the Impact of Turtle Excluder Devices on Loggerhead Sea Turtle Populations' Ecological Applications (1994) 4:3, 437.
Crowley, M A and R Howse, '*Tuna-Dolphin II*: A Legal and Economic Analysis of the Appellate Body Report' World Trade Review (2014) 13:2, 321.
Crutchfield-George, B, L V Dymally and K A Lacey, 'Increasing Extraterritorial Intrusion of European Union Authority into US Business Mergers and Competition Practices: US Multinational Businesses Underestimate the Strength of the European Commission From *GE-Honeywell* to *Microsoft*' Connecticut Journal of International Law (2004) 19:3, 571.
Cuyvers, L, 'The Sustainable Development Clauses in Free Trade Agreements: An EU Perspective for ASEAN?' UNU-CRIS Working Papers W-2013/10, 2013.
Da Costa, K, *The Extraterritorial Application of Selected Human Rights Treaties*, Vol. 11 (Martinus Nijhoff Publishers 2013).
Dabbah, M, 'Future Directions in Bilateral Cooperation: A Policy Perspective' in A T Guzman (ed.), *Cooperation, Comity and Competition Policy* (Oxford University Press 2011).
Dale, G, 'The European Union's Steel Leghold Trap Ban: Animal Cruelty Legislation in Conflict with International Trade' Colorado Journal of International Environmental Law and Policy (1996) 7, 441.
Dannenmaier, E, 'Constructing Transnational Climate Regimes' in G Handl, J Zekoll and P Zumbansen (eds.), *Beyond Territoriality: Transnational Legal Authority in an Age of Globalization* (Martinus Nijhoff 2012).
Davey, W J and K E Maskus, '*Thailand-Cigarettes (Philippines)*: A More Serious Role for the "Less Favourable Treatment" Standard of Article III:4' World Trade Review (2013) 12:2, 163.
Davidow, J, 'Extraterritorial Antitrust and the Concept of Comity' Journal of World Trade (1981) 15:6, 500.
Davidson Ladly, S, 'Border Carbon Adjustments, WTO-Law and the Principle of Common but Differentiated Responsibilities' International Environmental Agreements (2012) 12, 63.

De Boer, T M, 'Living Apart Together: The Relationship Between Public and Private International Law' Netherlands International Law Review (2010) 57:2, 183.

De Cendra, J, 'Can Emissions Trading Schemes be Coupled with Border Tax Adjustments? An Analysis Vis-a-vis WTO Law' Review of European Community and International Environmental Law (2006) 15:2, 131.

De Cruz, P, *A Modern Approach to Comparative Law* (Kluwer Law International 1993).

De Cruz, P, *Comparative Law in a Changing World* (3rd edn., Routledge-Cavendish 2007).

De Schutter, O, *Extraterritorial Jurisdiction as a Tool for Improving the Human Rights Accountability of Transnational Corporations* (Katholieke Universiteit Leuven in collaboration with the Office of the UN High Commissioner for Human Rights (Special Representative to the UN Secretary General on the issue of human rights and transnational corporations and other enterprises) 2006).

De Schutter, O, 'Globalization and Jurisdiction: Lessons from the European Convention on Human Rights' Baltic Yearbook on International Law (2006) 6, 185.

De Schutter, O, A Eide, A Khalfan, M Orellana, M Salomon and I Seiderman, 'Commentary to the Maastricht Principles on Extraterritorial Obligations of States in the Area of Economic, Social and Cultural Rights' Human Rights Quarterly (2012) 34, 1084.

Deane, F, 'The WTO, the National Security Exception and Climate Change' Carbon and Climate Law Review (2012) 2, 149.

Diamond, L S, '*Empagran*, The FTAIA and Extraterritorial Effects: Guidance to Courts Facing Questions of Antitrust Jurisdiction Still Lacking' Brooklyn Journal of International Law (2006) 31:3, 805.

DiClemente, D and D Hantula, 'Applied Behavorial Economics and Consumer Choice' Journal of Economic Psychology (2003) 24, 589.

Diebold, N, 'The Morals and Order Exceptions in WTO Law: Balancing the Toothless Tiger and the Undermining Mole' Journal of International Economic Law (2008) 11:1, 43.

Dodge, W S, 'Extraterritoriality and Conflict-of-Laws Theory: An Argument for Judicial Unilateralism' Harvard International Law Journal (1998) 39:1, 101.

Dodge, W S, '*Morrison*'s Effects Test' Southwestern Law Review (2011) 40, 687.

Donovan, D F and A Roberts, 'The Emerging Recognition of Universal Civil Jurisdiction' American Journal of International Law (2006) 100:1, 142.

Doughty, C E, J Roman, S Faurby, A Wolf, A Haque, E S Bakker, Y Malhi,

J B, Dunning and J-C Svenning, 'Global Nutrient Transport in a World of Giants' Proceedings of the National Academy of Sciences of the United States (PNAS) (2015) Vol. 112.

Doyle, C, 'Gimme Shelter: The "Necessary" Element of GATT Article XX in the Context of the *China-Audiovisual Products* Case' Boston University International Law Journal (2011) 29, 143.

Dupuy, P-M and J E Vinuales, *International Environmental Law* (Cambridge University Press 2015).

Duttwiler, M, 'Authority, Control and Jurisdiction in the Extraterritorial Application of the European Convention on Human Rights' Netherlands Quarterly of Human Rights (2012) 30:2, 137.

Eberle, E J, 'The Method and Role of Comparative Law' Washington University Global Studies Law Review (2009) 8:3, 451.

Ehring, L, '*De Facto* Discrimination in World Trade Law: National and Most-Favoured-Nation Treatment – or Equal Treatment?' Journal of World Trade (2002) 36:5, 921.

Ellerman, A D and P L Joskow, *The European Union's Emissions Trading System in Perspective* (Massachusetts Institute of Technology and Pew Center on Global Climate 2008).

English, R, 'Law of Armed Conflict Means That Anti-detention Provision in ECHR May be Disapplied by Iraqi Detainee' UK Human Rights Blog, 16 September 2014, available at https://ukhumanrightsblog.com/2014/09/16/law-of-armed-conflict-means-that-anti-detention-provision-in-echr-may-be-disapplied-re-iraqi-detainee/.

Esty, D C, *Greening the GATT: Trade, Environment and the Future* (Peterson Institute 1994).

Esty, D C, 'Bridging the Trade-Environment Divide' Journal of Economic Perspectives (2001) 15:3, 113.

Etsuko, K, *Competition Law and Policy in Japan and the EU* (Cheltenham, UK, and Northampton, MA, USA: Edward Elgar Publishing 2014).

Europe Economics, *An Analysis of the Issue of Consumer Detriment and The Most Appropriate Methodologies to Estimate It* (DG SANCO European Commission, 2007).

European Commission, *Analysis of Options to Move Beyond 20% Greenhouse Gas Emission Reductions and Assessing the Risk of Carbon Leakage* (European Commission 2010).

European Commission, Brief of the European Commission on Behalf of the EU as Amicus Curiae in Support of Neither Party in *Kiobel v Royal Dutch Petroleum* Co. Doc. No. 10-1491 (2012).

European Commission, Communication from the Commission to the European Parliament, the Council, the European Economic and Social Committee and the Committee of the Regions: Integrating Maritime

Transport Emissions in the EU's Greenhouse Gas Reduction Policies COM(2013) 479 final (2013).

FAO, *The State of World Fisheries and Aquaculture: Opportunities and Challenges* (2014).

Faure, M, and X Zhang, 'Towards an Extraterritorial Application of the Chinese Anti-Monopoly Law that Avoids Trade Conflicts' George Washington International Law Review (2013) 45, 101.

Fishman, A and K Obidzinski, 'European Union Timber Regulation: Is It Legal?' Review of European Community and International Environmental Law (2014) 23:2, 258.

Flett, J, 'WTO Space for National Regulation: Requiem for a Diagonal Vector Test' Journal of International Economic Law (2013) 16:1, 1.

Forest Trends, *European Trade Flows and Risks* (Forest Trends 2013) available at http://forest-trends.org/documents/files/doc_4085.pdf.

Foure, J, H Guimbard and S Monjon, 'Border Carbon Adjustment in Europe and Trade Retaliation: What would be the Cost for European Union?' CEPII Working Paper (2013) 34.

Fowler, M R and J M Bunck, *Law, Power and the Sovereign State: The Evolution and Application of the Concept of Sovereignty* (Pennsylvania State University Press 1995).

Fox, E M, 'Modernization of Effects Jurisdiction: From Hands-Off to Hands-Linked' International Law and Politics (2009) 42, 159.

Fox, E M, 'Antitrust Without Borders: From Roots to Codes to Networks' in A T Guzman (ed.), *Cooperation, Comity and Competition policy* (Oxford University Press 2011).

Francioni, F, 'Extraterritorial Application of Environmental Law' in K M Meessen (ed.), *Extraterritorial Jurisdiction in Theory and Practice* (Kluwer 1996).

Francioni, F, 'Environment, Human Rights and the Limits of Free Trade' in F Francioni (ed.), *Environment, Human Rights and International Trade* (Hart Publishing 2001).

Frank, T, 'The Emerging Right to Democratic Governance' American Journal of International Law (1992) 86:1, 46.

Friedberg, J J, 'The Convergence of Law in an Era of Political Integration: The Wood Pulp Case and the Alcoa Effects Doctrine' University of Pittsburgh Law Review (1991) 52:2, 289.

Friends of the Earth Europe, *The EU Emissions Trading System: Failing to Deliver* (2010).

Gaines, S E, 'Processes and Production Methods: How to Produce Sound Policy for Environmental PPM-Based Trade Measures?' Columbia Journal of Environmental Law (2002) 27:2, 383.

Gal, M, 'Extraterritorial Application of Antitrust – The Case of a

Small Economy (Israel)' NYU Center for Law, Economics and Organization, Law and Economics Research paper Series Working Paper 09-03.
Ganesh, A, 'Understanding the EU Missionary Principle' (2014), available at https://ssrn.com/abstract=2498539.
Gardbaum, S, 'Human Rights and International Constitutionalism' in J L Dunoff and J P Trachtman (eds.), *Ruling The World? Constitutionalism, International Law, and Global Governance* (Cambridge University Press 2009).
Gemkow, T, 'The International Law(s) of Regulatory Extraterritoriality: Causes and Consequences of Rule Variations' Paper at SGIR 7th Pan-European Conference on International Relations (2010).
Geradin, D, M Reysen and D Henry, 'Extraterritoriality, Comity and Cooperation in EU Competition Law' in A T Guzman (ed.), *Cooperation, Comity and Competition Policy* (Oxford University Press 2011).
Geraets, D and B Natens, 'The WTO Consistency of the European Union Timber Regulation' Journal of World Trade (2014) 48:2, 433.
Gerber, D J, 'Prescriptive Authority: Global Markets as a Challenge to National Regulatory Systems' Houston Journal of International Law (2014) 26:2, 288–308.
Glendon, M A, P G Carozza and C B Picker, *Comparative Legal Traditions* (3rd edn., Thomson West 2008).
Gordley, J, 'Extra-Territorial Legal Problems in a World Without Nations: What The Medieval Jurists Could Teach Us' in G Handl, J Zekoll and P Zumbansen (eds.), *Beyond Territoriality: Transnational Legal Authority in an Age of Globalization* (Martinus Nijhoff 2012).
Graves, C T, 'Extraterritoriality and its Limits: The Iran and Libya Sanctions Act of 1996' Hastings International and Comparative Law Review (1998) 21:3, 715.
Green, A, 'Climate Change, Regulatory Policy and the WTO: How Constraining are Trade Rules?' Journal of International Economic Law (2005) 8:1, 143.
Grewal, D S, 'Network Power and Globalization' Ethics and International Affairs (2006) 17:2, 89.
Grewal, D S, *Network Power: The Social Dynamics of Globalization* (Yale University Press 2008).
Griffin, J P, 'Extraterritoriality in US and EU Antitrust Enforcement' Antitrust Law Journal (1999) 67:1, 159.
Grote, R, 'Article XXIII GATS' in R Wolfrum, P-T Stoll and C Feinäugle (eds.), *WTO-Trade in Services* (Martinus Nijhoff Publishers 2008).
Guber, D, *The Grassroots of a Green Revolution: Polling America on the Environment* (Cambridge, MA: MIT Press 2002).

Gulbrandsen, L, 'Overlapping Public and Private Governance: Can Forest Certification Fill the Gaps in the Global Forest Regime?' Global Environmental Policy (2004) 4:2, 75–99.

Haas, M, *International Human Rights: A Comprehensive Introduction* (2nd edn., Routledge 2014).

Hakimi, M, 'Unfriendly Unilateralism' Harvard International Law Journal (2014) 55:1, 105.

Hamner, K J, 'The Globalization of Law: International Merger Control and Competition Law in the United States, the European Union, Latin America and China' Journal of Transnational Law and Policy (2002) 11:2, 385.

Hampson, F, 'The Scope of the Extraterritorial Applicability of International Human Rights Law' in G Gilbert, F Hampson and C Sandoval (eds.), *The Delivery of Human Rights: Essays in Honour of Professor Sir Nigel Rodley* (Routledge 2011).

'Harvard Research on International Law: Jurisdiction with Respect to Crime' 29: supplement 1, American Journal of International Law (1935), 435, 445.

Hertel, M, 'Climate-Change-Related Trade Measures and Article XX: Defining Discrimination in Light of the Principle of Common but Differentiated Responsibilities' Journal of World Trade (2011) 45:3, 653.

Hill-Cawthorne, L, 'The Grand Chamber Judgment in Hassan v UK' EJIL Talk, 16 September 2014.

Hixson, K, 'Extraterritorial Jurisdiction Under the Third Restatement of Foreign Relations Law of the United States' Fordham International Law Journal (1988) 12:1, 127.

Hock, B, 'Intimations of Global Anti-Bribery Regime and the Effectiveness of Extraterritorial Enforcement: From Free-Riders to Protectionism' TILEC Discussion Paper 2014-009, 2014.

Horn, H and P C Mavroidis, 'The Permissible Reach of National Environmental Policies' Journal of World Trade (2008) 42:6, 1107.

Horn, H and P C Mavroidis, 'To B(TA) or not to B(TA)? On the Legality and Desirability of Border Tax Adjustments From a Trade Perspective' The World Economy (2011) 34:11, 1911.

Howse, R, 'From Politics to Technocracy – and Back Again: The Fate of the Multilateral Trading Regime' American Journal of International Law (2002) 96, 94.

Howse, R, 'Commentary: The Political and Legal Underpinnings of Including Aviation in the EU ETS' ICTSD Programme on Trade and Environment, April 2012.

Howse, R and J Langille, 'Permitting Pluralism: The *Seal Products* Dispute and Why the WTO Should Accept Trade Restrictions Justified by Noninstrumental Moral Values' Yale Journal of International Law (2012) 37:2, 367.

Howse, R, J Langille and K Sykes, 'Pluralism in Practice: Moral Legislation and the Law of the WTO after *Seal Products*' New York University Public Law and Legal Theory Working Papers (2015).

Howse, R and D Regan, 'The Product/Process Distinction – An Illusory Basis for Disciplining "Unilateralism" in Trade Policy' European Journal of International Law (2000) 11:2, 249.

Huck, S, J Zhou and C Duke, *Consumer Behavioural Biases in Competition: A Survey* (UK Office of Fair Trading 2011).

Hudec, R E, 'GATT Legal Restraints on the Use of Trade Measures Against Foreign Environmental Practices' in J Bhagwati and R E Hudec (eds.), *Fair Trade and Harmonization: Prerequisites for Free Trade?*, Vol. 2 (The MIT Press 1996).

Hudec, R E, 'GATT/WTO Constraints on National Regulation: Requiem for an "Aim and Effects" Test' International Lawyer (1998) 32:3, 619.

Intergovernmental Panel on Climate Change, *IPCC Fifth Assessment Report* (United Nations Environment Programme and World Meteorological Association 2013–2014).

International Bar Association, *Report of the Task Force on Extraterritorial Jurisdiction* (2009).

International Commission of Jurists, *The Arab Court of Human Rights: A Flawed Statute for an Ineffective Court* (2015).

International Law Association, *Final Report on the Exercise of Universal Jurisdiction in Respect of Gross Human Rights Offences* (2000).

International Law Commission, *Report on the Work of the Fifty-eighth Session – Annex V: Extraterritorial Jurisdiction* (2006).

Ireland-Piper, D, 'Prosecutions of Extraterritorial Criminal Conduct and the Abuse of Rights Doctrine' Utrecht Law Review (2013) 9:4, 68.

Ismer, R and K Neuhoff, 'Border Tax Adjustment: A Feasible Way to Support Stringent Emission Trading' European Journal of Law and Economics (2007) 24:2, 137.

Jackson, J H, 'World Trade Rules and Environmental Policies: Congruence or Conflict?' Washington and Lee Law Review (1992) 49:4, 1227.

Jackson, J H, 'Sovereignty-Modern: A New Approach to an Outdated Concept' American Journal of International Law (2003) 97:4, 782.

Jackson, T, *Motivating Sustainable Consumption: A Review of Evidence on Consumer Behaviour and Behavioural Change* (Sustainable Development Research Network, 2005).

Jansen, B, 'The Limits of Unilateralism From a European Perspective' European Journal of International Law (2000) 11:2, 309.

Jansen, B and M Lugard, 'Some Considerations on Trade Barriers

Erected for Non-Economic Reasons and WTO Obligations' Journal of International Economic Law (1999) 2:3, 530.
Jennings, R Y, 'Extraterritorial Jurisdiction and the United States Antitrust Laws' British Yearbook of International Law (1957) 33, 146.
Jennings, R Y, 'Sovereignty and International Law' in G Kreijen et al. (eds.), *State, Sovereignty, and International Governance* (Oxford University Press 2002).
Kadelbach, S, 'The Territoriality and Migration of Fundamental Rights' in G Handl, J Zekoll and P Zumbansen (eds.), *Beyond Territoriality: Transnational Legal Authority in an Age of Globalization* (Martinus Nijhoff 2012).
Kahneman, D and A Tversky, 'Choices, Values, and Frames' American Psychologist (1984) 39:4, 341.
Kälin, W, 'Displacement and Climate Change: Towards Defining Categories of Affected Persons' Working Paper submitted by the Representative of the UN Secretary-General on the Human Rights of Internally Displaced Persons, 25 August 2008.
Kälin, W and J Künzli, *The Law of International Human Rights Protection* (Oxford University Press 2009).
Kälin, W and N Schrepfer, 'Protecting People Crossing Borders in the Context of Climate Change Normative Gaps and Possible Approaches' UNHCR, PPLA/2012/01, 2012.
Kamba, W J, 'Comparative Law: A Theoretical Framework' International and Comparative Law Quarterly (1974) 23:3, 485.
Kameoka, E, *Competition Law and Policy in Japan and the EU* (Edward Elgar Publishing 2014).
Kamminga, M T, 'Universal Civil Jurisdiction: Is It Legal? Is It Desirable?' American Society of International Law Proceedings (2005) 99, 123.
Keck, A and P Low, 'Special and Differential Treatment in the WTO: Why, When and How?' WTO Staff Working Paper ERSD-2004–03, 2004.
Keitner, C I, 'Rights Beyond Borders' Yale Journal of International Law (2011) 36:1, 55.
Keohane R, S Macedo and A Moravcsik, 'Democracy-Enhancing Multilateralism' International Organization (2009) 63:1, 1.
Khor, M, 'The Climate and Trade Relation: Some Issues' South Centre Research Paper (2009).
King, H, 'The Extraterritorial Human Rights Obligations of States' Human Rights Law Review (2009) 9:4, 521.
Kivetz, R and I Simonson, 'The Effects of Incomplete Information on Consumer Choice' Journal of Marketing Research (2000) 37:4, 427.
Knox, J H, 'The Judicial Resolution of Conflicts Between Trade and the Environment' Harvard Environmental Law Review (2004) 28, 1.

Knox, J H, 'A Presumption against Extraterritoriality' American Journal of International Law (2010) 104, 351.

Kokkini-Iatridou, D, 'Some Methodological Aspects of Comparative Law' Netherlands International Law Review (1986) 33:2, 143.

Kolbert, E, *The Weight of the World* (*The New Yorker* 24 August 2015) available at www.newyorker.com/magazine/2015/08/24/the-weight-of-the-world.

Kontorovich, E, 'Kiobel Surprise: Unexpected by Scholars but Consistent with International Trend' Notre Dame Law Review (2014) 89, 1671.

Krämer, L, 'Environmental Protection and Trade – The Contribution of the European Union' in R Wolfrum (ed.), *Enforcing Environmental Standards: Economic Mechanisms as Viable Means?* (Springer 1996).

Kreijen, G, M Brus, J Duursma, E De Vos, and J Dugard (eds.), *State, Sovereignty, and International Governance* (Oxford University Press 2002).

Kuemlangan, B and M Press, 'Preventing, Deterring and Eliminating IUU Fishing: Port State Measures' Environmental Policy and Law (2010) 40:6, 262.

Kulovesi, K, 'Climate Change in EU External Relations: Please Follow My Example (or I Might Force You)' in E Morgera (ed.), *The External Environmental Policy of the European Union* (Cambridge University Press 2012).

Kulovesi, K, 'Climate Change and Trade: At the Intersection of Two Interacting Legal Regimes' in E Hollo, K Kulovesi and M Mehling (eds.), *Climate Change and the Law* (Springer 2013).

Kulovesi, K, E Morgera and M Munoz, 'Environmental Integration and Multi-Faceted International Dimensions of EU Law: Unpacking the EU's 2009 Climate and Energy Package' Common Market Law Review (2011) 48, 829.

Kuner, C, 'Extraterritoriality and the Fundamental Right to Data Protection' EJIL Talk, 16 December 2013.

Kuner, C, 'Extraterritoriality and Regulation of International Data Transfers in EU Data Protection Law' International Data Privacy Law (2015) 5:4, 235.

Kysar, D A, 'Preferences for Processes: The Process/Product Distinction and the Regulation of Consumer Choice' Harvard Law Review (2004) 118:2, 526.

Laing T, M Sato, M Grubb, and C Comberti, *Assessing the Effectiveness of the EU Emissions Trading System* (Centre for Climate Change Economics and Policy, Working Paper 126, 2013).

Langer, M, 'The Diplomacy of Universal Jurisdiction: The Political Branches and the Transnational Prosecution of International Crimes' American Journal of International Law (2011) 105:1, 1.

Larbprasertporn, P, 'The Interaction between WTO Law and the Principle of Common but Differentiated Responsibilities in the Case of Climate-Related Border Tax Adjustments' Goettingen Journal of International Law (2014) 6:1, 145.

Lawson, R, 'The Concept of Jurisdiction and Extraterritorial Acts of State' in G Kreijen et al. (eds.), *State, Sovereignty, and International Governance* (Oxford University Press 2002).

Lawson, R, 'Life After Bankovic: On the Extraterritorial Application of the European Convention on Human Rights' in F Coomans and M T Kamminga (eds.), *Extraterritorial Application of Human Rights Treaties* (Intersentia 2004).

Layton, A and A M Parry, 'Extraterritorial Jurisdiction – European Responses' Houston Journal of International Law (2004) 26:2, 309.

Le Prestre, P, 'The CBD at Ten: The Long Road To Effectiveness' Journal of International Wildlife Law and Policy (2002) 5, 269.

Levenstein, M and V Suslow, 'The Changing International Status of Export Cartel Exemptions' American University International Law Review (2005) 20:4, 785.

Levy, P I and D Regan, '*EC-Seal Products*: Seals and Sensibilities (TBT Aspects of the Panel and Appellate Body Reports)' World Trade Review (2015) 14:2, 337.

Lewinsohn-Zamir, D, 'Consumer Preferences, Citizen Preferences, and the Provision of Public Goods' Yale Law Journal (1998) 108:2, 377.

Lewison R L, L B Crowder, A J Read, and S A Freeman, 'Understanding Impacts of Fisheries Bycatch on Marine Megafauna' Trends in Ecology and Evolution (2004) 19:11, 598.

Lin, A, 'The Unifying Role of Harm in Environmental Law' Wisconsin Law Review (2006) 3, 897–984.

Lipsky, A and K Wilmot, 'The Foreign Trade Antitrust Improvements Act: Did Arbaugh Erase Decades of Consensus Building?' The Antitrust Source (2013) 12:6, 10.

Lövin, I, *European Parliament Report on Combating Illegal Fishing at the Global Level – The Role of the EU* (European Parliament 2011).

Low, P, G Marceau and J Reinaud, 'The Interface between the Trade and Climate Change Regimes: Scoping the Issues' WTO Staff Working Paper ERSD-2011-1.

Lowe, V, 'Sovereignty and International Economic Law' in W Shan, P Simons and D Singh (eds.), *Redefining Sovereignty in International Economic Law* (Hart Publishing 2008).

Lowenfeld, A F, 'Conflict, Balancing of Interests and the Exercise of Jurisdiction to Prescribe: Reflections on the Insurance Antitrust Case' American Journal of International Law (1995) 89, 42.

Lowenfeld, A F, *International Litigation and the Quest for Reasonableness* (Clarendon Press 1996).

Lydgate, E B, 'Biofuels, Sustainability, and Trade-related Regulatory Chill' Journal of International Economic Law (2012) 15:1, 157.

Maheshwari, K and S Reis, 'Extraterritorial Application of the Competition Act and Its Impact' Competition Law Reports, January 2012, 144.

Maier, H G, 'Jurisdictional Rules in Customary International Law' in K M Meessen (ed.), *Extraterritorial Jurisdiction in Theory and Practice* (Kluwer Law International 1996).

Mann, F A P, 'The Doctrine of Jurisdiction in International Law' Recueil des Cours of The Hague Academy of International Law (1964) 111, 1–162.

Mann, F A P, 'The Doctrine of International Jurisdiction Revisited After Twenty Years' Recueil des Cours of The Hague Academy of International Law (1984) 186, 9.

Mann, H and Y Apea, 'Issues and Debates: Dispute Resolution' in A Najam, M Halle and R Melendez-Ortiz (eds.), *Trade and Environment: A Resource Book* (International Institute for Sustainable Development, International Centre for Trade and Sustainable Development, The Regional and International Networking Group 2007).

Manners, I, 'The Normative Ethics of the European Union' International Affairs (2008) 84:1, 45.

Marceau, G, 'A Call for Coherence in International Law: Praises for the Prohibition Against "Clinical Isolation" in WTO Dispute Settlement' Journal of World Trade (1999) 33:5, 87.

Marceau, G, 'A Comment on the Appellate Body Report in *EC-Seal Products* in the Context of the Trade and Environment Debate' RECIEL (2014) 23:3, 318.

Marceau, G and J P Trachtman, 'The Technical Barriers to Trade Agreement, the Sanitary and Phytosanitary Measures Agreement, and the General Agreement on Tariffs and Trade: A Map of the World Trade Organization Law of Domestic Regulation of Goods' Journal of World Trade (2002) 36:5, 811.

Marin Duran, G and E Morgera, 'Case Note: WTO India-EC GSP Dispute: The Future of Unilateral Trade Incentives Linked to Multilateral Environmental Agreements' Review of European Community and International Environmental Law (2005) 14:2, 173.

Marin Duran, G and E Morgera, *Environmental Integration in the EU's External Relations: Beyond Multilateral Dimensions* (Hart Publishing 2012).

Markesinis, B S, 'Richter, Rechtswissenschaftler und das Studium und die

Anwendung Ausländischen Rechts' in B S Markesinis (ed.), *Foreign Law and Comparative Methodology: A Subject and A Thesis* (Hart Publishing 1997).

Marwell, J, 'Trade and Morality: The WTO Public Morals Exception after *Gambling*' New York University Law Review (2006) 81, 802.

Mathis, J, 'WTO Appellate Body, *Peru-Additional Duty on Imports of Certain Agricultural Products,* WT/DS457/AB/R, 20 July 2015' Legal Issues of Economic Integration (2016) 43:1, 97.

Mavroidis, P C, 'Trade and Environment After the *Shrimps-Turtles* Litigation' Journal of World Trade (2000) 34:1, 73.

Mavroidis, P C, *Trade in Goods: The GATT and the Other WTO Agreements Regulating Trade in Goods* (2nd edn., Oxford University Press 2012).

Mavroidis, P C, 'Driftin' Too Far From Shore – Why the Test for Compliance with the TBT Agreement Developed by the WTO Appellate Body is Wrong, and What Should the AB Have Done Instead' World Trade Review (2013) 12:3, 509.

Mavroidis, P C, 'Reaching Out For Green Policies: National Environmen tal Policies in the WTO Legal Order' EUI Working Papers RSCAS 2014/21, 2014.

Mavroidis, P C and K Saggi, 'What Is Not So Cool About *US-Cool* Regulations? A Critical Analysis of the Appellate Body's Rulings on *US-Cool*' World Trade Review (2014) 13:2, 299.

McLachlan, C, 'The Principle of Systemic Integration and Article 31(3)(c) of the Vienna Convention' International and Comparative Law Quarterly (2005) 54:2, 279.

Melendez-Ortiz, R, *Enabling the Energy Transition and Scale-Up of Clean Energy Technologies: Options for the Global Trade System* (E15 Expert Group on Clean Energy Technologies and the Trade System 2016).

Melendez-Ortiz, R and R Samans, *Strengthening the Global Trade and Investment System in the 21st Century: Synthesis Report* (The E15 Initiative: Strengthening the Global Trade and Investment System for Sustainable Development 2016).

Meltzer, J, 'Climate Change and Trade – The EU Aviation Directive and the WTO' Journal of International Economic Law (2012) 15:1, 111.

Meng, W, *Extraterritoriale Jurisdiktion im öffentlichen Wirtschaftsrecht* (Springer 1994).

Meng, W, 'Extraterritorial Effects of Legislative, Judicial and Administrative Acts' in R Bernhardt (ed.), *Encyclopedia of Public International Law*, Vol. 2 (Elsevier 1995).

Meunier, S and K Nicolaidis, 'The European Union as a Conflicted Trade Power' Journal of European Public Policy (2006) 13:6, 906.

Michaels, R, 'The Functional Method of Comparative Law' in M Reimann and R Zimmermann (eds.), *The Oxford Handbook of Comparative Law* (Oxford University Press 2006).
Milanovic, M, *Extraterritorial Application of Human Rights Treaties: Law, Principles and Policy* (Oxford University Press 2011).
Milanovic, M, 'Al-Skeini and Al-Jedda in Strasbourg' European Journal of International Law (2012) 23:1, 121.
Miller, D J and J Davidow, 'Antitrust at the United Nations: A Tale of Two Codes' Stanford Journal of International Law (1982) 18, 347.
Miller, S, 'Revisiting Extraterritorial Jurisdiction: A Territorial Justification for Extraterritorial Jurisdiction under the European Convention' European Journal of International Law (2009) 20:4, 1223.
Miltner, B, 'Revisiting Extraterritoriality After *Al-Skeini*: The ECHR and Its Lessons' Michigan Journal of International Law (2012) 33:4, 693.
Ming Du, M, 'The Rise of National Regulatory Autonomy in the GATT/WTO Regime' Journal of International Economic Law (2011) 14:3, 639.
Ming Du, M, '"Treatment No Less Favourable" and the Future of National Treatment Obligation in GATT Article III:4 after *EC-Seal Products*' World Trade Review (2016) 15:1, 139.
Mitchell, A and G Ayres, 'Out of Crooked Timber: The Consistency of Australia's Illegal Logging Prohibition Bill with the WTO Agreement' Environmental and Planning Law Journal (2012) 29:6, 462.
Morgera, E, 'Ambition, Complexity and Legitimacy of Pursuing Mutual Supportiveness through the EU's External Environmental Action' Edinburgh School of Law Research Papers 2012/02, 2012.
Morgera, E (ed.), *The External Environmental Policy of the European Union: EU and International Law Perspectives* (Cambridge University Press 2012).
Morgera, E, 'The EU and Environmental Multilateralism: The Case of Access and Benefit-Sharing and the Need for a Good-Faith Test' Cambridge Yearbook of European Legal Studies (2013) 16, 109.
Morosini, F, 'Trade and Climate Change: Unveiling the Principle of Common But Differentiated Responsibilities from the WTO Agreements' George Washington International Law Review (2010) 42, 714.
Najam, A, M Halle and R Melendez-Ortiz (eds.), *Trade and Environment: A Resource Book* (International Institute for Sustainable Development, International Centre for Trade and Sustainable Development, The Regional and International Networking Group 2007).
Nash, J R, 'The Curious Legal Landscape of the Extra-Territoriality of US Environmental Laws' in G Handl, J Zekoll and P Zumbansen

(eds.), *Beyond Territoriality: Transnational Legal Authority in an Age of Globalization* (Martinus Nijhoff 2012).
Neumayer, E, *Greening Trade and Investment: Environmental Protection Without Protectionism* (Earthscan 2001).
Neumayer, E, 'WTO Rules and Multilateral Environmental Agreements' in K P Gallagher and J Werksman (eds.), *The Earthscan Reader on International Trade and Sustainable Development* (Earthscan Publications Ltd 2002).
Nicolaidis, K and R Howse, '"This Is My EUtopia…': Narrative as Power' Journal of Common Market Studies (2002) 40:4, 767.
Nicolaidis, K and G Shaffer, 'Transnational Mutual Recognition Regimes: Governance Without Global Government' Law and Contemporary Problems (2005) 68, 263.
Nollkaemper, A, 'The Legality of Moral Crusades Disguised in Trade Laws: An Analysis of the EC "Ban" on Furs From Animals Taken by Leghold Traps' Journal of Environmental Law (1996) 8:2, 237.
Norpoth, J, 'Mysteries of the TBT Agreement Resolved? Lessons to Learn for Climate Policies and Developing Country Exporters from Recent TBT Disputes' Journal of World Trade (2013) 47:3, 575.
Notes, 'Constructing the State Extraterritorially: Jurisdictional Discourse, the National Interest and Transnational Norms' Harvard Law Review (1990), 103:6, 1273–1305.
Notes, 'Predictability and Comity: Toward Common Principles of Extraterritorial Jurisdiction' Harvard Law Review (1985) 98, 1310.
Nyst, C, 'Interference-based Jurisdiction over Violations of the Right to Privacy' EJIL Talk, 21 November 2013.
O'Riordan, T, J Cameron and A Jordan (eds.), *Reinterpreting the Precautionary Principle* (Cameron May 2001).
Oderkerk, M, 'The Importance of Context: Selecting Legal Systems in Comparative Legal Research' Netherlands International Law Review (2001) 48:3, 293.
OECD, *Report on Trade and Environment to the OECD Council at Ministerial level* (1995).
OECD, *Processes and Production Methods (PPMs): Conceptual Framework and Considerations on Use of PPM-based Trade Measures* (1997).
OECD, *International Enforcement Cooperation: Secretariat Report on the OECD/ICN Survey on International Enforcement Cooperation* (2013).
OECD, *Challenges of International Cooperation in Competition Law Enforcement* (2014).
Oreskes, N and E M Conway, *Merchants of Doubt* (Bloomsbury Press 2010).
Ortino, F, 'From "Non-Discrimination" to "Reasonableness": A Paradigm

Shift in International Economic Law?' Jean Monnet Working Paper, NYU School of Law 01/05 (2004).

Overdevest, C and J Zeitlin, 'Assembling an Experimentalist Regime: Transnational Governance Interactions in the Forest Sector Revisited' in L Bruszt and G A McDermott (eds.), *Leveling the Playing Field: Transnational Regulatory Integration and Development* (Oxford University Press 2014).

Palma, M A, M Tsamenyi and W Edeson, *Promoting Sustainable Fisheries: The International Legal and Policy Framework to Combat Illegal, Unreported and Unregulated Fishing* (Brill/Nijhoff 2010).

Palmeter, D and P C Mavroidis, *Dispute Settlement in the World Trade Organization Practice and Procedure* (2nd edn., Cambridge University Press 2004).

Parker, R W, 'The Use and Abuse of Trade Leverage to Protect the Global Commons: What We Can Learn From the Tuna-Dolphin Conflict' Georgetown International Environmental Law Review (1999) 12:1, 1.

Parrish, L A, 'The Effects Test: Extraterritoriality's Fifth Business' Vanderbilt Law Review (2008) 61:5, 1455.

Parrish, L A, 'Evading Legislative Jurisdiction' Notre Dame Law Review (2012) 87:4, 1673.

Parrish, L A, '*Kiobel,* Unilateralism, and the Retreat from Extraterritoriality' Maryland Journal of International Law (2013) 28:1, 208.

Partiti, E, 'The Appellate Body Report in *US – Tuna II* and Its Impact on Eco-Labelling and Standardization' Legal Issues of Economic Integration (2013) 40:1, 73.

Paul, J R, 'The Transformation of International Comity' Law and Contemporary Problems (2008) 71:3,19.

Paust, J J, 'The Bush-Cheney Legacy: Serial Torture and Forced Disappearance in Manifest Violation of Global Human Rights Law.' Barry Law Review (2012) 18:1, 61.

Pauw, P, S Bauer, C Richerzhagen, C Brandi, and H Schmole, 'Different Perspectives on Differentiated Responsibilities: A State-of-the-Art Review of the Notion of Common but Differentiated Responsibilities in International Negotiations' Deutsches Institut für Entwicklungspolitik Discussion Paper 6/2014 (2014).

Pauwelyn, J, 'The Role of Public International Law in the WTO: How Far Can We Go?' American Journal of International Law (2001) 95:3, 535.

Pauwelyn, J, 'Recent Books on Trade and Environment: GATT Phantoms Still Haunt the WTO' European Journal of International Law (2004) 15:3, 575.

Pauwelyn, J, 'Comment: The Unbearable Lightness of Likeness' in

M Panizzon, N Pohl and P Sauvé (eds.), *GATS and the Regulation of International Trade in Services* (Cambridge University Press 2008).

Pauwelyn J, *Conflict of Norms in Public International Law: How WTO Law Relates to Other Rules of International Law* (Cambridge University Press 2009).

Pelkmans, J and A Correia de Brito, *Transatlantic MRAs: Lessons for TTIP?* (CEPS Special Report 2015).

Perisin, T, 'Is the EU Seal Products Regulation a Sealed Deal? EU and WTO Challenges' International and Comparative Law Quarterly (2013) 62:2, 373.

Peters, A, 'Surveillance Without Borders? The Unlawfulness of the NSA-Panopticon, Part I' EJIL Talk, 1 November 2013.

Picker, C B, 'Comparative Legal Cultural Analyses of International Economic Law: A New Methodological Approach' Chinese Journal of Comparative Law (2013) 1:1, 1.

Pieth, M, L Low and P Cullen, *The OECD Convention on Bribery: A Commentary* (Cambridge University Press 2007).

Prakhar, P, N Ghandi, P Chatterjee, S Reis, M S Ananth, and P Jain, *Competition Law in India: A Report on Jurisprudential Trends* (Nishith Desai Associations, June 2015) available at www.nishithdesai.com/fileadmin/user_upload/pdfs/Research%20Papers/Competition_Law_in_India.pdf.

Puth, S, *WTO und Umwelt: Die Produkt-Prozess-Doktrin* (Duncker and Humblot 2003).

Qin, J, 'Defining Nondiscrimination under the Law of the World Trade Organization' Boston University International Law Journal (2005) 23, 215.

Qin, J, 'Accommodating Divergent Policy Objectives under WTO Law: Reflections on EC-Seal Products' Symposium on the WTO EC-Seal Products Case, AJIL Unbound (2015).

Quick, R, 'The Debate Continues: Are Border Adjustments of Emission Trading Schemes a Means to Protect the Climate or Are They "Naked" Protectionism?' in I Govaere, R Quick and M C E J Bronckers (eds.), *Trade and Competition Law in the EU and Beyond* (Edward Elgar Publishing 2011).

Quick, R and C Lau, 'Environmentally Motivated Tax Distinctions and WTO Law: The European Commission's Green Paper on Integrated Product Policy in Light of the "Like Product-" and "PPM-" Debates' Journal of International Economic Law (2003) 6:2, 419.

Raustiala, K, 'Rethinking the Sovereignty Debate in International Economic law' Journal of International Economic Law (2003) 6:4, 841.

Raustiala, K, 'Form and Substance in International Agreements' American Journal of International Law (2005) 99:3, 581.
Raustiala, K, *Does the Constitution Follow the Flag* (Oxford University Press 2009).
Raustiala, K, 'NGOs in International Treatymaking' in D B Hollis (ed.), *The Oxford Guide to Treaties* (Oxford University Press 2012).
Rayner, J, A Buck and P Katila, *Embracing Complexity in International Forest Governance: A Way Forward* (International Union of Forest Research Organizations 2010).
Read, R, 'Process and Production Methods and the Regulation of International Trade' in R Read and N Perdikis (eds.), *The WTO and the Regulation of International Trade: Recent Trade Disputes Between the European Union and the United States* (Edward Elgar Publishing 2005).
Regan, D, 'Regulatory Purpose and "Like Products" in Article III:4 of the GATT (With Additional Remarks on Article III:2)' Journal of World Trade (2002) 36:3, 443.
Regan, D H, 'Further Thoughts on the Role of Regulatory Purpose under Article III of the General Agreement on Tariffs and Trade' Journal of World Trade (2003) 37:4, 737.
Regan, D, 'Measures with Multiple Purposes: Puzzles from EC-Seal Products' Symposium on the WTO EC-Seal Products Case, AJIL Unbound (2015).
Rehbinder, E, 'Extra-Territoriality of Pollution Control Laws from a European Perspective' in G Handl, J Zekoll and P Zumbansen (eds.), *Beyond Territoriality: Transnational Legal Authority in an Age of Globalization* (Martinus Nijhoff 2012).
Reid, E, *Balancing Human Rights, Environmental Protection and International Trade* (Hart Publishing 2015).
Reisman, M, 'Unilateral Action and the Transformation of the World Constitutive Process: The Special Problem of Humanitarian Intervention' European Journal of International Law (2000) 11, 3–18.
Reuven, A-Y, 'National Regulation of Multinational Enterprises: An Essay on Comity, Extraterritoriality and Harmonization' Columbia Journal of Transnational Law (2003) 42:1, 5.
Rotherham, T, 'Issues and Debates: Standards and Labelling' in A Najam, M Halle and R Melendez-Ortiz (eds.), *Trade and Environment: A Resource Book* (International Institute for Sustainable Development, International Centre for Trade and Sustainable Development, The Regional and International Networking Group 2007).
Roxstrom, E, M Gibney and T Einarsen, 'The NATO Bombing Case (*Bankovic et al v Belgium et al*) and The Limits of Western Human

Rights Protection' Boston University International Law Journal (2005) 23, 55.
Ryngaert, C, 'Universal Tort Jurisdiction over Gross Human Rights Violations' Netherlands Yearbook of International Law (2007) 38:3, 3.
Ryngaert, C, *Jurisdiction in International Law* (edition by V Lowe, Oxford University Press 2008).
Ryngaert, C, *Jurisdiction in International Law* (2nd edn., Oxford University Press 2015).
Sands, P, 'Treaty, Custom and the Cross-Fertilization of International Law' Yale Human Rights and Development Law Journal (1998) 1:1, 85.
Sands, P, *Principles of International Environmental Law* (Cambridge University Press 2003).
Sari, A, 'Jaloud v Netherlands: New Directions in Extra-Territorial Military Operations' EJIL Talk, 24 November 2014.
Sato, C, 'Extraterritorial Application of EU Competition Law: Is It Possible for Japanese Companies to Steer Clear of EU Competition Laws?' Journal of Political Science and Sociology (2010) 11, 23.
Savaresi, A, 'EU External Action on Forests: FLEGT and the Development of International Law' in E Morgera (ed.), *External Environmental Policy of the European Union: EU and International Law Perspectives* (Cambridge University Press 2012).
Scassa, T and R J Currie, 'New First Principles? Assessing the Internet's Challenges to Jurisdiction' Georgetown Journal of International Law (2011) 42:4, 1017.
Schiano di Pepe, L, 'European Union Climate Law and Practice at the End of the Kyoto Era: Unilateralism, Extraterritoriality and the Future of Global Climate Law Governance' in R Percival, J Lin and W Piermattei (eds.), *Global Environmental Law at a Crossroads* (Edward Elgar Publishing 2014).
Schiff Berman, P, *Global Legal Pluralism: A Jurisprudence of Law Beyond Borders* (Cambridge University Press 2012).
Schoenbaum, T J, 'International Trade and Protection of the Environment: The Continuing Search for Reconciliation' American Journal of International Law (1997) 91:2, 268.
Schreuer, C, 'The Waning of the Sovereign State: Towards a New Paradigm for International Law?' European Journal of International Law (1993) 4, 447.
Schwarz-Liebermann von Wahlendorf, H A, *Droit Comparé: Théorie Générale et Principes* (LGDJ 1978).
Schwenkenbecher, A, 'Bridging the Emissions Gap: A Plea for Taking Up the Slack' Philosophy and Public Issues (2013) 3:2, 271.

Scott, J, 'Extraterritoriality and Territorial Extension in EU Law' American Journal of Comparative Law (2014) 62, 87.

Scott, J, 'The New EU "Extraterritoriality"' Common Market Law Review (2014) 51, 1.

Scott J, 'The Geographical Scope of the EU's First-Order and Second-Order Climate Responsibilities: An Exploration' Cambridge Yearbook of European Legal Studies (2015) 17, 92.

Scott, J and L Rajamani, 'EU Climate Change Unilateralism' The European Journal of International Law (2012) 23:2, 469.

Scott, J and L Rajamani, 'Contingent Unilateralism: International Aviation in the European Emissions Trading Scheme' in B Van Vooren, S Blockmans and J Wouters (eds.), *The EU's Role in Global Governance: The Legal Dimension* (Oxford University Press 2013).

Secretary-General of the UN, *The Scope and Application of the Principle of Universal Jurisdiction: Report of the Secretary-General* (Oxford University Press 2011).

Seibert-Fohr, A, 'United States Alien Tort Statute' in R Wolfrum (ed.), Max Planck Encyclopedia of Public International Law, Vol. 10 (Oxford University Press 2012).

Shaffer, G, 'WTO Blue-Green Blues: The Impact of US Domestic Politics on Trade-Labor, Trade-Environment Linkages for the WTO's Future' Fordham International Law Journal (2000) 24:1, 607.

Shaffer, G and D Bodansky, 'Transnationalism, Unilateralism and International Law' Legal Studies Research Paper Series Research Paper No 11-34 (2011).

Shaffer, G and J P Trachtman, 'Interpretation and Institutional Choice at the WTO' Virginia Journal of International Law (2011) 52:1, 103.

Shan, W, P Simons and D Singh (eds.), *Redefining Sovereignty in International Economic Law* (Hart Publishing 2008).

Shaw, M N, *International Law* (6th edn., Cambridge University Press 2008).

Skinner, J, 'A Green Road to Development: Environmental Regulations and Developing Countries in the WTO' Duke Environmental Law and Policy Forum (2010) 20:1, 245.

Sokol, D, 'International Antitrust Institutions' in A T Guzman (ed.), *Cooperation, Comity and Competition Policy* (Oxford University Press 2011).

Spar, D L, 'Developments in the Law: Extraterritoriality' Harvard Law Review (2011) 124:5, 1226.

Spassov, Y, 'EU ETS: Upholding the Carbon Price Without Incidence of Carbon Leakage' Journal of Environmental Law (2012) 24:2, 311.

Stephens, B, 'Extraterritoriality and Human Rights After Kiobel' Maryland Journal of International Law (2013) 28:1, 256.
Stern, B, 'Can the United States Set Rules for the World? A French View.' Journal of World Trade (1997) 31:4, 5.
Stevens, M, 'The Precautionary Principle in the International Arena' Sustainable Development Law and Policy (2002) 2:2, 13.
Stevens, S, 'The Increased Aggression of the EC Commission in Extraterritorial Enforcement of the Merger Regulation and Its Impact on Transatlantic Cooperation in Antitrust' Syracuse Journal of International Law and Commerce (2002) 29, 263.
Stigall, D E, 'International Law and Limitations on the Exercise of Extraterritorial Jurisdiction in US Domestic Law' Hastings International and Comparative Law Review (2012) 35:2, 323.
Stokke, O S, 'Trade Measures and the Combat of IUU Fishing: Institutional Interplay and Effective Governance in the Northeast Atlantic' Marine Policy (2009) 33, 339.
Stoll, P-T and S Vöneky, 'The Swordfish Case: Law of the Sea v Trade' Zeitschrift für Ausländisches Öffentliches Recht und Völkerrecht (2002) 65, 21.
Sumaila, R, *Trade Policy Options for Sustainable Oceans and Fisheries* (The E15 Initiative: Strengthening the Global Trade and Investment System for Sustainable Development, ICTSD and World Economic Forum 2016).
Sunstein, C, 'Endogenous Preferences, Environmental Law' Journal of Legal Studies (1993) 22:2, 217.
Svantesson, D, 'Extraterritoriality and Targeting in EU Data Privacy Law: The Weak Spot Undermining the Regulation' International Data Privacy Law (2015) 5:4, 226.
Swaine, E, 'Cooperation, Comity and Competition Policy: United States' in A T Guzman (ed.), *Cooperation, Comity and Competition Policy* (Oxford University Press 2011).
Swan, A C, 'The Hartford Insurance Company Case: Antitrust in the Global Economy – Welfare Effects and Sovereignty' in J S Bhandari and A O Sykes (eds.), *Economic Dimensions in International Law: Comparative and Empirical Perspectives* (Cambridge University Press 1997).
Sweeney, B, 'International Governance of Competition and the Problem of Extraterritorial Jurisdiction' in J Duns, A Duke and B Sweeney (eds.), *Comparative Competition Law* (Edward Elgar Publishing 2015).
Swinbank, A and C Daugbjerg, 'Improving EU Biofuels Policy? Greenhouse Gas Emissions, Policy Efficiency, and WTO Compatibility' Journal of World Trade (2013) 47:4, 813.
Sykes, A O, 'Domestic Regulation, Sovereignty and Scientific Evidence

Requirements: A Pessimistic View' Chicago Journal of International Law (2002) 3:2, 353.
Tams, C, *Enforcing Obligations Erga Omnes in International Law* (Cambridge University Press 2005).
Tapia, J and A Ditzel Faraco, 'Latin American Antitrust Law and Policy: An Overview of Three Jurisdictions – Brazil, Chile and Colombia' in J Duns, A Duke and B Sweeney (eds.), *Comparative Competition Law* (Edward Elgar Publishing 2015).
Theilen, J, 'What's in a Name? The Illegality of Illegal, Unreported and Unregulated Fishing' International Journal of Marine and Coastal Law (2013) 28, 533.
Thomas, C, 'Should the World Trade Organization Incorporate Labor and Environmental Standards?' Washington and Lee Law Review (2004) 61, 347.
Trachtman, J P, 'Regulatory Jurisdiction and the WTO' Journal of International Economic Law (2007) 10:3, 631.
Trachtman, J P, 'Persistent Objectors, Cooperation, and the Utility of Customary International Law' Duke Journal of Comparative and International Law (2010) 21, 221.
Trimble, P, 'The Supreme Court and International Law: The Demise of Restatement Section 403' American Journal of International Law (1995) 85, 53.
Truxal, S, 'The ICAO Assembly Resolutions on International Aviation and Climate Change: An Historic Agreement, a Breakthrough Deal and the Cancun Effect' Air and Space Law (2011) 36:3, 217.
Tsamenyi M, M A Palma, B Milligan, and K Mfodwo, *Fairer Fishing: The Impact on Developing Countries of the European Community Regulation on Illegal, Unreported and Unregulated Fisheries* (Commonwealth Secretariat 2009).
Tucker, K L, 'In the Wake of *Empagran* – Lights Out on Foreign Activity Falling Under Sherman Act Jurisdiction? Courts Carve Out a Prevailing Standard' Fordham Journal of Corporate and Financial Law (2010) 15, 807.
Uhkubo, N and Z Shishido, 'Cooperation, Comity and Competition Policy: Japan' in A T Guzman (ed.), *Cooperation, Comity and Competition Policy* (Oxford University Press 2011).
UNCTAD, *Trade and Environment Review* (2006).
UNCTAD, *The Green Economy: Trade and Sustainable Development Implications* (2011).
UNEP and WTO, *Trade and Climate Change: WTO-UNEP Report* (2009).
Van Alebeek, R and A Nollkaemper, 'The Legal Status of Decisions by Human Rights Treaty Bodies in National Law' in H Keller and

G Ulfstein (eds.), *Human Rights Treaty Bodies: Law and Legitimacy* (Cambridge University Press 2011).
Van Asselt, H, 'Managing the Fragmentation of International Environmental Law: Forests at the Intersection of the Climate and Biodiversity Regime' NYU Journal of International Law (2012) 44, 1205.
Van Calster, G, *International and EU Trade Law: The Environmental Challenge* (Cameron May 2000).
Van Damme, I, 'Inherent Powers of and for the WTO Appellate Body' Graduate Institute Geneve CTEI Working Paper 102 (2008).
Van Damme, I, 'Treaty Interpretation by the WTO Appellate Body', European Journal of International Law (2010) 21:3, 605.
Van den Bossche, P, N Schrijver and G Faber, *Unilateral Measures Addressing Non-Trade Concerns: A Study on WTO Consistency, Relevance of Other International Agreements, Economic Effectiveness and Impact on Developing Countries of Measures concerning Non-Product-Related Processes and Production Methods* (Ministry of Foreign Affairs, Netherlands 2007).
Van den Bossche, P and Z Werner, *The Law and Policy of the World Trade Organization: Text, Cases and Materials.* (3rd edn., Cambridge University Press 2008).
Van Gerven, Y and L Hoet, 'Gencor: Some notes on Transnational Competition Law Issues – *European Court of First Instance 25 March 1999, T-102/96, Gencor Ltd. v Commission*' Legal Issues of Economic Integration (2001) 28:2, 195.
Van Schaack, B, 'The United States' Position on the Extraterritorial Application of Human Rights Obligations: Now is the Time for Change' International Law Studies (2014) 90, 20.
Vandenhole, W, 'EU and Development: Extraterritorial Obligations under the International Covenant on Economic, Social and Cultural Rights' in M Salomon, A Tostensen and W Vandenhole (eds.), *Casting the Net Wider: Human Rights, Development and New Duty-Bearers* (Intersentia 2007).
Verdonk M, C Brink, H Vollebergh, and M Roelfsema, *Evaluation of Policy Options to Reform the EU Emissions Trading System: Effects on Carbon Price, Emissions and the Economy* (PBL Netherlands Environmental Assessment Agency 2013).
Vermulst, E and B Driessen, 'The Choice of a Switch: The European Reaction to the Helms-Burton Act' Leiden Journal of International Law (1998) 11:1, 81.
Vidigal, G, 'From Bilateral to Multilateral Law-Making: Legislation, Practice, Evolution and the Future of Inter Se Agreements in the WTO' European Journal of International Law (2013) 24:4, 1027.

Vogel, D, *Trading Up: Consumer and Environmental Regulation in a Global Economy* (Harvard University Press 1997).
Voigt, C, 'Up in the Air: Aviation, the EU Emissions Trading Scheme and the Question of Jurisdiction' Cambridge Yearbook of European Legal Studies (2011–2012) 14, 475.
Von Bernstorff, J, M Jacob and J Dingfelder Stone, 'The Alien Tort Statute Before the US Supreme Court in the *Kiobel* Case: Does International Law Prohibit US Courts to Exercise Extraterritorial Civil Jurisdiction over Human Rights Abuses Committed Outside of the US?' Zeitschrift für Ausländisches Öffentliches Recht und Völkerrecht (2012) 72:3, 579.
Voon, T, 'Sizing Up the WTO: Trade-Environment Conflict and the Kyoto Protocol' Journal of Transnational Law and Policy (2000) 10:1, 71.
Vranes, E, *Trade and the Environment: Fundamental Issues in International Law, WTO Law and Legal Theory* (Oxford University Press 2009).
Wagner-von Papp, F, 'Competition Law and Extraterritoriality' in A Ezrachi (ed.), *Research Handbook on International Competition Law* (Edward Elgar Publishing 2012).
Wallace, B P, C Y Kot, A D DiMatteo, T Lee, L B Crowder, and R L Lewison, 'Impacts of Fisheries Bycatch on Marine Turtle Populations Worldwide: Toward Conservation and Research Priorities' Ecosphere (2013) 4:3, 40.
Wallace, B P, R L Lewison, S L McDonald, R K McDonald, C Y Kot, S Kelez, R K Bjorkland, E M Finkbeiner, S Helmbrecht, and L B Crowder, 'Global Patterns of Marine Turtle Bycatch' Conservation Letters (2010) 3, 131.
Weishaar, S, *Emissions Trading Design: A Critical Overview* (Edward Elgar Publishing 2014).
Weiss, F, 'Extra-Territoriality in the Context of WTO Law' in G Handl, J Zekoll and P Zumbansen (eds.), *Beyond Territoriality: Transnational Legal Authority in an Age of Globalization* (Martinus Nijhoff 2012).
Wilde, R, 'The "Legal Space" or "Espace Juridique" of the European Convention on Human Rights: Is It Relevant for Extraterritorial State Action?' European Human Rights Law Review (2005) 10, 115.
Wilson, E G, K L Miller, D Allison, and M Magliocca, *Why Healthy Oceans Need Sea Turtles: The Importance of Sea Turtles to Marine Ecosystems* (Oceana 2010), available at http://oceana.org/sites/default/files/reports/Why_Healthy_Oceans_Need_Sea_Turtles.pdf.
WTO, *Harnessing Trade for Sustainable Development and a Green Economy* (2011).
Wu, M, 'Free Trade and the Protection of Public Morals: An Analysis of the Newly Emerging Public Morals Clause Doctrine' Yale Journal of International Law (2008) 33, 215.

WWF and Zoological Society of London, *Living Blue Planet Report: Species, Habitats and Human Well-Being* (2015).
Yearwood, R F, *The Interaction Between World Trade Organisation (WTO) Law and External International Law: The Constrained Openness of WTO Law (A Prologue to a Theory)* (Routledge 2012).
Young, M A, 'Trade Measures to Address Environmental Concerns in Faraway Places: Jurisdictional Issues' Review of European Community and International Environmental Law (2014) 23:3, 302.
Young, M A, *Trade-Related Measures to Address Illegal, Unreported and Unregulated Fishing* (The E15 Initiative: Strengthening the Global Trade and Investment System for Sustainable Development, ICTSD and World Economic Forum 2015).
Zagel, G M, 'WTO & Human Rights: Examining Linkages and Suggesting Convergence' IDLO Voices of Development Jurists Paper Series (2005) 2:2.
Zhou, W, '*US – Clove Cigarettes* and *US – Tuna II (Mexico)*: Implications for the Role of Regulatory Purpose under Article III:4 of the GATT' Journal of International Economic Law (2012) 15:4, 1075.
Ziemele, I, 'Human Rights Violations by Private Persons and Entities: The Case Law of International Human Rights Courts and Monitoring Bodies' EUI Working Papers 2009/8, 2009.
Zimmermann, A, 'Extraterritorial Application of Human Rights Treaties – The Case of Israel and the Palestinian Territories Revisited.' in I Buffard, J Crawford, A Pellet and S Wittich (eds.), *International Law Between Universalism and Fragmentation: Festschrift in Honour of Gerhard Hafner* (Martinus Nijhoff 2008).
Zleptnig, S, *Non-Economic Objectives in WTO Law: Justification Provisions of GATT, GATS, SPS and TBT Agreements*, Vol. 1 (Mads Andenas ed., Martinus Nijhoff Publishers 2010).
Zweigert, K and H Kötz, *Introduction to Comparative Law* (3rd edn., Oxford University Press 1998).

Index